PENGUIN BOOKS
LONDON: THE CIRCLE LINE GUIDE

David Wallace was born in 1956 and educated at the University of Oxford, where he obtained a degree in philosophy, politics and economics. Following a period as a reporter for Essex County Newspapers, he was a researcher on the science and technology series *The Real World* for Television South. He has continued to work for television as director of the BBC's *Animals Roadshow* and *Countryfile*. He is the author of *Unit 731 – Secret of Secrets*.

David Wallace

PENGUIN BOOKS

PENGUIN BOOKS

Published by the Penguin Group
27 Wrights Lane, London W8 5TZ, England
Viking Penguin Inc., 40 West 23rd Street, New York, New York 10010, USA
Penguin Books Australia Ltd, Ringwood, Victoria, Australia
Penguin Books Canada Ltd, 2801 John Street, Markham, Ontario, Canada L3R 1B4
Penguin Books (NZ) Ltd, 182–190 Wairau Road, Auckland 10, New Zealand

Penguin Books Ltd, Registered Offices: Harmondsworth, Middlesex, England

First published 1990
1 3 5 7 9 10 8 6 4 2

Maps drawn by Reginald and Marjorie Piggott

For permission to reproduce
copyright material grateful
acknowledgment is made
to the British Railways Board,
Geographer's A–Z Map Co. Ltd,
Her Majesty's Stationery Office
and London Regional Transport

Made and printed in Great Britain by
Cox and Wyman Ltd, Reading, Berks.

Filmset in 9/11 pt Linotron Times by
Rowland Phototypesetting Ltd, Bury St Edmunds, Suffolk

Contents

CENTRAL LINE

Introduction

London's Underground is used by some 80 per cent of its 9 million annual overseas visitors, without including a further 14 million domestic tourists to the capital. It is generally the cheapest, fastest and surest way of reaching most destinations in London. Few visitors, and not many of London's residents, ever manage to get to grips with the city's complex network of Red Bus routes and most cannot afford to travel everywhere by taxi. Thanks to Henry Beck's celebrated Underground map (see pages xii–xiii), a design classic in its own right, people can quickly grasp how to move round these subterranean highways. Above ground, the Underground's roundel symbol hails the traveller back to the system.

The Underground's roundel, a circle intersected by a horizontal line, forms the basis of this book. Within easy distance of stations on the Circle Line, and the portion of the Central Line that intersects it, are nearly all London's major tourist sights. Furthermore, each Circle Line station is situated in or near a separate *quartier* of London, each with its own distinctive character and feeling. The idea that Underground stations are gateways from which these different areas can easily be walked, and understood, is the guide's underlying logic.

The guide starts with St James's Park ⊖ on the Circle Line. Within easy walking distance is the royal centre of London – the Queen's residence at Buckingham Palace, and her court at St James's. The book continues anticlockwise along the Circle Line to Westminster ⊖, the political and administrative centre of Britain, to Embankment ⊖, the geographical heart of London, and finally reaches Victoria ⊖. The second section of the book deals with Underground stations on the Central Line, starting in the east in the heart of the Square Mile of the City with Bank ⊖ and finishing with Queensway ⊖ in the west. To avoid duplication, a number of chapters have joined two Tube stations together; in some cases the second station is on the Piccadilly Line.

The third section is about Outer London. From a terminus near Tower Hill ⊖, for example, the Docklands Light Railway travels east above and through London's Docklands to the southernmost tip of the Isle of Dogs. There a pedestrian tunnel leads under the Thames to historic Greenwich. Boats return upstream to the centre of the city. Sights in the Outer London section are ordered alphabetically in four quadrants – south-east, south-west, north and east. Each feature has its own travel details. Throughout the guide places of interest are in **bold** type and numbers correspond to those on the maps. Cross-references to information in other chapters are shown thus: (*St James's Park* ⊖).

The index contains information about addresses, opening hours and admission charges. Where there is more than one Underground station near any particular sightseeing feature, the index indicates which one is the nearest.

Tickets for the Underground must be bought *before* travelling, either from a ticket machine or the ticket counter at the station. Tickets must be kept during the journey, as they are collected at the destination. All Underground stations on the Circle Line and Central Line covered as chapters in this book lie within the Zone 1 charge bracket of the Underground system. Journeys further afield may cross into other of the system's five fare zones, for which there may be an additional charge. Under-5s travel free. Under-14s travel at a reduced fare, as do 14- and 15-year-olds with a child-rate photocard, available from Post Offices and London Regional Transport's Travel Information Centres. Senior citizens also travel free with a photocard, available from Post Offices. Books of tickets *cannot* be purchased, but specialist tickets *are* available from Travel Information Centres. These tickets will almost certainly save time and money. Underground trains generally run from 5.30 a.m. to midnight on Mondays to Saturdays, and from 7.30 a.m. to 11.30 p.m. on Sundays. Temple, Cannon Street and Chancery Lane ⊖s are closed on Sundays.

Acknowledgments

My special thanks are due to Martin Page, who researched this book. His meticulous accumulation and organization of information about the vast subject of London would not have been possible without months of careful study and footslogging.

I am also indebted to my wife Jo, who patiently read and typed much of the manuscript, and to my parents, who kindly walked many of the chapters. Thanks are owed as well to Paul Castle at London Regional Transport, and to Tim Binding and Barbara Horn. The British Tourist Authority library and the *London Encyclopaedia* were particularly useful sources of information.

UNDERGROUND

High Barnet
Totteridge & Whetstone
Woodside Park
West Finchley
Finchley Central
East Finchley
Highgate
Archway
Tufnell Park
Kentish Town
Cockfosters
Oakwood
Southgate
Arnos Grove
Bounds Green
Wood Green
Turnpike Lane
Manor House
Finsbury Park
Arsenal
Holloway Road
Caledonian Road
King's Cross St. Pancras
Euston
Euston Square
Russell Square
Goodge Street
Drayton Park
Highbury & Islington
Essex Road
Old Street
Angel
Farringdon
Barbican
Moorgate
Chancery Lane
Holborn
Bank
St. Paul's
Liverpool Street
Covent Garden
Leicester Square
Aldwych
Mansion House
Blackfriars
Temple
Cannon Street
Embankment
Charing Cross
London Bridge
Borough
Lambeth North
Elephant & Castle
Kennington
Brixton

Theydon Bois
Debden
Loughton
Buckhurst Hill
Roding Valley
Chigwell
Grange Hill
Woodford
South Woodford
Snaresbrook
Leytonstone
Leyton
Stratford
Epping
North Weald
† Ongar
Hainault
Fairlop
Barkingside
Newbury Park
Redbridge
Wanstead
Gants Hill
No service after 20 00

Tottenham Hale
Walthamstow Central
Blackhorse Road
Seven Sisters

Hornchurch
Upminster
Elm Park
Upminster Bridge
Dagenham East
Dagenham Heathway
Becontree
Upney
Barking
East Ham
Upton Park
Plaistow
West Ham
Bromley-by-Bow
Bow Road
Devons Road
All Saints
Bow Church

Bethnal Green
Shoreditch
Aldgate East
Aldgate
Stepney Green
Whitechapel
Limehouse
Shadwell
Westferry
Poplar
Wapping
West India Quay
Rotherhithe
Heron Quays
South Quay
Crossharbour
Mudchute
Island Gardens
Surrey Docks
New Cross Gate
New Cross
Greenwich

RIVER THAMES

Tower Hill
Tower Gateway

Key to lines

Bakerloo	**East London**	**Piccadilly**
Central	**Jubilee**	**Victoria**
Circle	**Metropolitan**	⇌ **British Rail**
District	**Northern**	**Docklands Light Railway**

O Interchange stations
⇌ Connections with British Rail
⇌ Connections within walking distance
★ Closed Sundays
★ Closed Saturdays and Sundays
▲ Served by Piccadilly line early mornings and late evenings Mondays to Saturdays and all day Sundays
† See poster maps at Underground stations for opening and closing times of these stations

CIRCLE LINE

St James's Park ⊖ & Green Park ⊖

St James's Park is the most royal of all the royal parks of London, surrounded by palaces, royal residences and former royal residences. In addition to Buckingham Palace and St James's Palace are the Queen Mother's residence at Clarence House; Marlborough House; the magnificent Carlton House Terrace, commemorating the Prince Regent's one-time palatial London residence; as well as the barracks of the Brigade of Guards, the monarch's personal bodyguard.

Queen Elizabeth II is the sixth monarch to have lived at Buckingham Palace. The palace's famous façade and balcony look east along The Mall, London's grand processional highway, and out over the pretty St James's Park. Throughout the year thousands of people gather outside the palace gates, like Christopher Robin and Alice, to watch the colourful ceremony of the Changing of the Guard.

Buckingham Palace is strictly closed to the public, but within its grounds the Queen's wonderful art collection can be visited in the Queen's Gallery. Also open to the public is the Royal Mews, which houses the Queen's ceremonial horses, the magnificent Gold State Coach, and the Glass Coach.

After the restoration of the monarchy in 1660, the St James's area began to flourish, drawn by the magnetism of Charles II's court at Whitehall Palace. Although it lapsed a little when William III moved to his palace at Kensington, the area blossomed after the Hanoverians returned the court here. British monarchs resided at St James's Palace from 1698 until Queen Victoria took up residence at Buckingham Palace in 1837.

Aristocratic London was inevitably attracted to such royal splendour. The area north of St James's Park is still famed for the great gentlemen's clubs that stand, proud yet anonymous, along Pall Mall and St James's Street. Originating in coffee houses once located here, these unique upper-class British institutions had their heyday in Regency times; to be elected to one today is to join some of Britain's most powerful circles. White's, Boodle's and Brooks's are to be found at the northern, and the Carlton Club at the southern end of St James's Street, while Pall Mall houses the United Oxford and Cambridge, the Reform, the Travellers' and the Athenaeum.

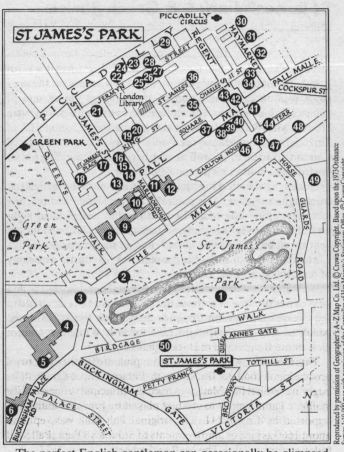

The perfect English gentleman can occasionally be glimpsed here, darkly tailored, cuffs showing half an inch of perfect linen and with a rosy bloom to his face after lunch at his club. And here in St James's this English gentleman can still purchase the finest bespoke hats, shoes, shirts and suits, as well as the best wines, cigars and silver.

⊖　　⊖　　⊖

North along Queen Anne's Gate from St James's Park ⊖ and across Birdcage Walk is St James's Park. A footpath leads over the park's charming lake to The Mall, the royal processional road from Admiralty Arch to Buckingham Palace.

St James's Park (1) is the oldest, and the most attractive, of London's royal parks. It was once used by Henry VIII as a nursery for his deer. For a century afterwards the park remained a place for military reviews and royal relaxation. James I built a menagerie here and had formal gardens laid out, but it was his grandson, Charles II, who, on return from exile, had the land properly landscaped and planted, modelled on the grounds of palaces he had seen on the Continent. He opened a long strip of water known as the Canal, which attracted numerous flocks of birds. He also opened the park to the public. For the aristocracy it became a place to see and be seen in – an all-consuming hobby for the rich. For a time in the 18th century, however, the park degenerated and became the scene of less civilized toings and froings, frequented by prostitutes and robbers. Today's picturesque park is essentially that designed by the architect John Nash (1752–1835) in 1828. Nash reshaped the lake and laid out winding paths, lawns, flower-beds and groups of trees.

The park has always been noted for its birds, especially waterfowl. In 1873 an ornithologist listed 18 different species; now there are nearly 100, including ducks, geese, pelicans and gulls. They are best seen from the bridge over the lake, and are fed every afternoon on the lawn near Duck Island. Note the beautiful view east across the lake towards Whitehall. Glance west to catch a glimpse of Buckingham Palace.

The Mall (2), with its distinctive pink surface, is the royal processional road to Buckingham Palace. The original thoroughfare, called Pall Mall, was once the principal venue of *paille maille*, a game similar to croquet played by French nobility and imported by Charles II. The original Pall Mall was replaced about 1660 as part of improvements to St James's Park. Pall Mall today runs parallel to The Mall to the north.

In the 18th century it became fashionable to promenade along The Mall. Between 1903 and 1904, as part of a national memorial to Queen Victoria, The Mall was widened to form a processional route running from Admiralty Arch in the east to the Queen Victoria Memorial and Buckingham Palace in the west. The old Mall, now the Horse Ride, runs near by to the north.

Set in front of Buckingham Palace in a spacious circus is the focus of Aston Webb's memorial scheme to Queen Victoria. The 82-ft/25-m tall white marble and bronze **Queen Victoria**

Memorial (3) was unveiled in 1911 by George V, who knighted its creator, Thomas Brock (1847–1922), on the spot. The memorial, which weighs 2,300 tons, is crowned by a gilded bronze figure of Victory, with Courage and Constancy at her feet. The enthroned figure of Queen Victoria faces east down The Mall, surrounded by a number of allegorical figures in dark bronze representing those virtues for which she was renowned: Justice, Truth and Motherhood.

Buckingham Palace (4) has been the London residence of British kings and queens since Queen Victoria ascended the throne in 1837. When the sovereign is in residence, the Royal Standard flies from the palace's flagstaff. The royal family's private apartments, relatively few in number, occupy the north range overlooking Green Park. The rest of the building comprises state apartments and rooms for palace staff and domestic purposes. Investitures and large state banquets take place in the largest apartment, the Ball Room. The thousands of guests for the Queen's garden parties pass through the Bow Room.

The palace's 300 rooms and extensive grounds occupy the former site of Buckingham House, built by the Duke of Buckingham in 1703. King George III bought the house in 1762 for Queen Charlotte and they occupied it as their private, rather than state, residence. It was King George IV who decided that Buckingham House should become his official residence, and in 1821 John Nash was commissioned to produce designs to turn it into a palace. The cost of Nash's extensive plans for work on the existing house and the addition of a three-sided court open on the east, in front of which was to stand the Marble Arch (*Marble Arch* ⊖) eventually mounted to a staggering £700,000, not including the triumphal arch. Nash's design also attracted much criticism and, following the death of George IV in 1830, he was dismissed for overspending. His successor, Edward Blore (1787–1879), enclosed the courtyard with an east front facing The Mall, providing the now familiar view of the palace and its famous balcony. Marble Arch was later removed to its present site at the north end of Park Lane. The palace was eventually ready for occupation in 1837. In 1913 Aston Webb refaced its east façade with Portland stone to harmonize with his Queen Victoria memorial scheme. Most of the rest of the palace is in Bath stone.

The forecourt of Buckingham Palace is patrolled by sentries from the five units of Foot Guards. Guardsmen wear full dress uniform, which comprise their distinctive bearskin headgear, scarlet tunic and dark blue trousers. The ceremony of the Changing of the Guard, an impressive display of marching, takes place at 11.30 a.m. daily (alternate days Sept.–Mar.) provided affairs of state and the weather permit. Half an hour earlier, the Queen's Colour is trooped from Friary Court, St James's Palace, along The Mall to Buckingham Palace. Meanwhile, the New Guard is led by a massed band from either the Chelsea or the Wellington Barracks to the palace forecourt, where it advances towards the Old Guard and touches hands, symbolizing the handing over of the keys. The Old Guard is then marched back to the barracks and the New Guard dismissed to take its position. A detachment of the New Guard also marches to St James's Palace to relieve the Old Guard there.

The Guards regiment on duty can be identified by their tunic buttons. Single buttons are worn by the Grenadiers and pairs by the Coldstreams, while the Scots' Guards' buttons are grouped in threes, the Irish Guards' in fours and those of the Welsh Guards in fives.

Buckingham Palace is never open to the public, but the Royal Mews and the Queen's Gallery can be visited. They are located on the south side of the palace.

The **Queen's Gallery (5)**, which occupies a former private chapel of Buckingham Palace, presents changing exhibitions of art from the Queen's collections. Although the gallery is small, some of the greatest works of art and furniture, gathered by such discerning royal connoisseurs as Charles I, Frederick, Prince of Wales, George III, George IV and Prince Albert, have been shown here since it was opened in 1962. The royal collection includes paintings by Holbein, Brueghel, Van Dyck (Charles I in three positions), Rembrandt, Vermeer, Rubens, Canaletto and Gainsborough as well as drawings by Leonardo, Raphael and Michelangelo, to list but a few. Furniture and clocks include Jensen's inlaid table bearing William III's cypher, Queen Charlotte's jewel cabinet by William Vile and a four-sided astronomical clock commissioned by George III. George IV's taste in French decorative arts is illustrated by a roll-top desk by Reisener and the Comtesse de Provence's jewel cabinet.

The **Royal Mews (6)** houses the Queen's horses, carriages and cars. Built in 1825 by Nash around a square courtyard and clock tower, the great stables are located on the north and west sides, the state coaches on the east. Here, presided over by the Crown Equerry, live the grooms, saddlers, carpenters and carriage-builders behind the world's most regal equestrian establishment.

The Gold State Coach, made in 1762 for George III, has been used at every coronation since that of George IV in 1821. Gilded all over, its decoration is exceptional. Cipriani's painted panels act as a perfect complement to Sir William Chambers's fairy-tale design. The framework of the body is formed of eight palm trees. It is slung by braces on to four gilt figures: the front pair proclaim the Monarch of the Ocean through conches used as horns; the rear figures hold imperial *fasces* topped with tridents. Three cherubs, representing England, Scotland and Ireland, stand at the centre of the roof holding the sceptre, the sword of state and the ensign of knighthood, respectively. Pulled by eight horses, the coach has, unusually, no coachman's seat. The horses are reined by postilions walking alongside the carriage.

The Irish State Coach is ranked as the No. 2 coach in the Royal Mews, and the Scottish State Coach, the lightest, brightest and most elegant of the coaches, is No. 3. It has large glass windows and transparent panels on the roof and was used by Queen Elizabeth, the Queen Mother, for the Silver Jubilee in London. Other coaches include: the 1902 State Landau, used by the Queen to meet foreign heads of state on visits to Buckingham Palace; Queen Alexandra's State Coach, used during the State Opening of Parliament to convey the Imperial State Crown ahead of the Queen's procession from Buckingham Palace to the Palace of Westminster; and the Glass Coach, used for nearly all royal weddings to convey the bride and bridegroom from the church. There are also state landaus, semi-state landaus, the Town Coach, Ascot landaus, barouches, sociables, phaetons, victorias, broughams, clarences, a curricle and a number of other light coaches.

Close to the State Carriage House is the stable where the Windsor Grey and Cleveland Bay carriage horses are kept. In the State Harness Room is possibly the finest display of harnesses in existence, consisting of many different sets, all decorated with gilt or brass ornamentation. In the Saddle Room a wonderful array of historic saddles and saddle clothes is displayed. The Old Carriage House contains a collection of carriages and sledges from Balmoral and Sandringham. In addition to wonderful examples of coachmen's livery, the Royal Mews also houses various state motor cars, including Rolls-Royce Phantoms IV, V and VI. The Queen's cars are a Daimler Jaguar saloon and a Ford brake. The Duke of Edinburgh has a Range Rover. The motor cars are not on display, as they are in constant use, but can often be seen being driven in or out.

The Royal Mews comes under the jurisdiction of the Master of the Horse and is administered by the Crown Equerry. The equerry is responsible for the upkeep and care of the Queen's 30 horses (10 greys and 20 bays), her 5 coachmen, 15 grooms (who act as postilions on ceremonial occasions) and her range of 70 carriages.

To the north of Buckingham Palace is **Green Park (7)**, the smallest of the royal parks, extending north to Piccadilly. Created by Charles II in 1667, it was once a favourite site for duels and has also witnessed the rise, and fall, of many early balloonists. From Queen's Walk, which runs along its eastern side, are seen some of the remaining great mansions of London, notably Bridgewater House and Ullswater House.

A short distance east from the Queen Victoria Memorial on the north side of The Mall is **Lancaster House (8)**, another of these great mansions. Queen Victoria, impressed by its beauty, is said to have remarked to the Duchess of Sutherland on a visit here, that she had come from her 'house', Buckingham Palace, to her host's 'palace'. Undoubtedly, Lancaster House is one of London's great mansions, spanning the end of the Georgian era and the beginning of the Victorian.

It was begun in 1825 by Benjamin Wyatt for the 'grand old' Duke of York, but the Duke died before work was complete and the house passed to the Marquess of Stafford, one of his many creditors. Named Stafford House, it was completed by Robert Smirke and Charles Barry. During the last century the house was the scene of many social and political gatherings. In 1912 the lease was obtained by Sir William Lever, who renamed the building after his native county, the Royal Duchy of Lancaster. As Lord Leverhulme, he eventually presented the lease to the nation to house the London Museum (*Barbican* ⊖). The museum moved out in 1946 and today the house functions as a centre for government receptions and conferences, and is closed to the general public.

Lancaster House is formed as a solid rectangle of Bath stone, three storeys high with a giant portico. Most of the interior decoration, influenced by the Louis XV style, is the work of Wyatt, although the great Staircase Hall, the most splendid of its kind and date in England, is by Barry. Among many fine rooms is the first floor State Drawing Room, with its striking coffered ceiling, and the Great Gallery, an enormous apartment nearly 120 ft/36.5 m long with a ceiling painting, *St Chrysogonus Borne to Heaven by Angels*, by Guercino.

Clarence House (9) has been the London home of HM Queen Elizabeth, the Queen Mother, since her daughter's coronation in 1953. When she is in residence, her personal flag, the Royal Standard impaled by the Bowes-Lyon coat of arms, flies from the flag-pole on the roof of the house. Clarence House derives its name from the Duke of Clarence, third son of George III, who came to the throne as William IV (reigned 1830–37). He occupied a previous house on this site. John Nash completed the present stuccoed building in 1828 and William continued to live here, as Buckingham Palace was as yet unfinished. Clarence House is not open to the public.

Henry VIII commissioned the blue-diapered red-brick **St James's Palace (10)** in 1532 as a manor house for his wife Anne Boleyn. Their intertwined initials can still be seen carved over the gatehouse arch leading into Colour Court. Originally built on the site of a lepers' hospital for women founded at the time of the Norman Conquest and dedicated to St James the Less, Bishop of Jerusalem, the palace derived its name from this dedication. The main gatehouse on Pall Mall, with its four octagonal turrets and octagonal clock, survives from the 16th century structure together with parts of the Chapel Royal, scene of many royal weddings, including Queen Victoria's in 1840. The palace was originally designed around four courts: Ambassadors' Court, Colour Court (both now private), Engine Court and Friary Court, which faces on to Marlborough Road.

After the destruction by fire of Whitehall Palace in 1698, St James's Palace became the monarch's official London residence until Queen Victoria moved to Buckingham Palace in 1837. Its great days were in Stuart, Orange and Hanoverian times. Charles II was born here, as were his brother James II, James II's children and the future queens Mary and Anne. St James's Palace remains the statutory seat of the court, and to it are accredited the ambassadors of foreign powers. The proclamation of new sovereigns traditionally takes place from a balcony in Friary Court. The Changing of the Guard also takes place here each day before the colour is lodged in the Palace Guard Room.

St James's Palace is now occupied by the grace-and-favour apartments of the Gentlemen- and Yeomen-at-Arms, and the Lord Chamberlain. It is not open to the general public.

The **Queen's Chapel (11)** (Inigo Jones, 1627), in Marlborough Gate, was the first classical style church in England. It was designed by Inigo Jones for Maria, the Spanish Infanta, intended bride of Charles I. Work stopped after their wedding plans were abandoned, but began again for his subsequent marriage to Henrietta Maria. Sir Christopher Wren began remodelling the chapel in 1661 for Charles II's wife, Catherine of Braganza.

Sir Christopher Wren created the simple, dignified design of **Marlborough House (12)** (1711) for the first Duke and Duchess of Marlborough, and succeeding Dukes of Marlborough occupied the house until the Crown acquired the property in 1817. Wren's original building was two storeys high. The upper storeys, porch, balustrade and north range were added by James Pennethorne in 1863 for the occupancy of the Prince of Wales, later Edward VII. Vast early-18th-century murals by Louis Laguerre celebrating Marlborough's victories decorate the interior. The ceilings of the Blenheim Saloon are adorned with beautiful allegorical paintings (c. 1636) by Orazio Gentileschi, originally created for the Queen's House, Greenwich. In 1959 the Queen placed the house at the disposal of the Commonwealth, and it now houses the Commonwealth Secretariat and Commonwealth Foundation. Members of the public are admitted by prior appointment only.

In the 17th century **St James's Street (13)** was the approach to St James's Palace from Piccadilly. Today it is renowned for a number of exclusive shops and, like Pall Mall, for its gentlemen's clubs. On the east side of the street, at No. 3, is **Berry Bros & Rudd (14)**. Behind this 18th-century bow-fronted façade George Berry developed his reputation for excellence as a wine merchant in the early 1800s. Above the shop window is the sign of a coffee mill, a relic from the days of his predecessor William Pickering, who once ran a flourishing business here selling the finest coffee, tea, chocolate and sugar. During Pickering's time it became fashionable for customers, rather than their groceries, to be weighed on the shop's Great Scales. The beams, together with nine leather-bound tomes recording weights, are still to be seen today. To date, the books have amassed 30,000 entries, including the weights of Napoleon III, Beau Brummell, Byron, Pitt, Peel, the Prince Regent (later George IV) and the Aga Khan. In 1923 Berry Bros furnished the wine cellar in Queen Mary's doll's house, each tiny bottle filled with the wine on its label. However, the shop, with its gleaming oak-panelling, uneven elm floors, engravings of its past illustrious customers and glass-fronted cabinets of ancient bottles, does not generally display its wares. Customers are expected to know their requirements. Otherwise, a member of the shop's staff will recommend a vintage from the firm's magnificent wine list.

Around 1840 **Lock & Co (15)** invented the bowler hat. The shop's staff still refer to the hat as a 'coke', after landowner William Coke, who entrusted Lock's to make suitable headgear for his gamekeepers. He stipulated that their hats should be hardened and close-fitting so as not to be easily blown off by the wind. A prototype, made by Thomas and William Bowler, was brought to the shop to be tested. Thereupon Coke ceremoniously jumped on it. The hat withstood the shock and so today we have the bowler hat. Lock's, in their distinguished history, have also had the distinction of making Lord Nelson's hats, complete with eye patch. The business first opened at No. 6, St James's Street in 1764 in a building that is thought to date from 1690. The shop front is from 1728.

The last duel in London is said to have been held in Pickering Place, a concealed enclave of four little 18th-century brick houses located between Berry Brothers and Rudd, and Lock and Co.

An atmosphere of genteel elegance greets the customer at England's foremost bespoke shoemakers, **Lobb's (16)**, at Nos. 7–9 St James's Street. Founded in the 18th century by John Lobb, the business is still run by the same family. Royal Warrants decorate the shop's walls and wooden models of the foot, or 'lasts', for Queen Victoria and King George V are proudly displayed in a huge showcase.

Opposite Lobb's is the **Carlton Club (17)**, founded by members of the Conservative Party in 1832. To this day club members are still required to adhere to the tenets of the Conservative Party. The club is not open to the general public.

West from St James's Street, at No. 27 St James's Place, is **Spencer House (18)**, a Palladian mansion built in 1766 by the first Earl Spencer, a direct ancestor of the Princess of Wales. The house is believed to be still owned by a family trust and now accommodates offices; it is not open to the general public.

Opposite St James's Place and leading east from St James's Street is King Street. A few paces to the east of its junction with Bury Street are two world-famous art businesses: **Christie's (19)**, at No. 8, and **Spink & Son (20)** next door. Christie's, the fine-art auctioneers, were established in 1766. In the late 18th century the founder, former midshipman James Christie, sold anything from chamber-pots to furniture, but by the early 1800s his auction rooms had become fashionable for art sales. Today Christie's annual turnover runs into hundreds of millions of pounds. The auction rooms are open to the public. Sales are generally held in the morning, so the best time to view is the afternoon.

Spink and Son began business as goldsmiths just over a century earlier. They moved into the art business and have become one of the largest dealers in the world. Spink and Son also specialize in jewellery and antique silver. Their Oriental and coin departments are much renowned. Spink's factory designs and makes decorations and medals for many countries.

Jermyn Street, at the northern end of Bury Street, is one of London's most select shopping streets and the centre of bespoke shirtmaking for gentlemen. Much more intimate and refined than Piccadilly, now a busy traffic-laden thoroughfare that runs parallel to the north, it retains an abundance of high-quality shops whose pedigrees often stretch back for centuries, although architecturally nothing remains of Henry Jermyn's original street of the early 1860s. Its exclusive atmosphere is matched by its high prices. Perhaps the most famous bespoke shirtmakers and tailors in Jermyn Street is **Turnbull & Asser (21)** at No. 71. A family firm founded in 1885, Turnbull & Asser is the most long established of the twenty or so firms of Jermyn Street shirtmakers, and their shirts are still hand-cut on the premises.

At the heart of Alfred Dunhill's shop, first established in 1907 on the Duke Street corner of Jermyn Street and internationally

known for its smokers' requisites and other fine goods, is the
Humidor Room, a cellar for keeping fine cigars. Customers'
cigars are housed in privacy at exactly the right temperature and
humidity in 300 lockers. Dunhill will not reveal who, apart from
its chairman, has cigars in its keep. Every Dunhill pipe is
hand-made and recognizable by the white spot at the top of the
mouthpiece. Dunhill's is also noted for its men's fashions,
watches and luggage.

True to the tradition of its founders, **Fortnum & Mason (22)**
seeks to provide the finest food in the world in an atmosphere of
elegance, recapturing the best from the past, yet keeping a
dignified pace with the present. Fortnum's Fountain Restaurant
and Soda Bar, entered via Jermyn Street, is *the* place for
afternoon tea. Fortnum & Mason has become a British institution. Its name is synonymous with the choicest of foods, and
the shop is justly famous for its luxury hampers full of delicacies.

In 1707 William Fortnum, one of Queen Anne's footmen,
opened a grocery shop near here with a friend, Hugh Mason.
Armed with a knowledge of the needs of the royal household,
and by importing exotic foods through the East India Company,
their business flourished. During the Peninsular War gentlemen
officers often required Fortnum & Mason's to send packed cases
of food to the site of their military campaigns. The company
opened a special department supplying the needs of the gentlemen's clubs in St James's. In 1854, in the thick of the Crimean
War, Queen Victoria herself ordered a dispatch of concentrated
beef tea from Fortnum's to Florence Nightingale. It was a
pattern for much of the store's trade, catering for the needs of
those requiring sustenance at all times and in all places. By the
mid-19th century Fortnum & Mason had achieved world-wide
fame, and Royal Warrants of Appointment were received from
throughout Europe.

In 1925, completely rebuilt, Fortnum & Mason's new premises were opened with additional departments selling clothes
and gifts. The food hall on the ground floor, however, remains
the epicure's delight. Today, on the hour, figures of Mr Fortnum
and Mr Mason appear from inside pavilions in a handsome
ornamental clock mounted on the store's Piccadilly frontage,
and bow to each other to the accompaniment of an 18th-century
air played on seventeen bells.

Lit by skylights and wrought-iron lamps, **Princes Arcade (23)**
evokes the elegant, bygone era of small-scale shops. Behind the

Regency-style bow windows of Bayly's Gallery, at No. 8, is the charm of a shop stuffed with a clutter of Victoriana and other collector's items. Bespoke shoemakers Wildsmith and Co. have been established for six generations, and this family firm proudly displays in its window outlines of the feet of Lord Palmerston and Prince Napoleon, Napoleon's half-brother, as well as those of other eminent customers. **Swaine, Adeney, Brigg & Sons (24)**, at the northern end of Princes Arcade in Piccadilly, sells umbrellas, canes and walking-sticks of every variety – hazel, ash, cherry, polished blackthorn and malacca – as well as whips and hunting horns. James Ross, who founded the business in 1750, was a whip-maker, and the shop can still supply anything from a polo whip to a cat-o'-nine-tails. For the toothless huntsman, the shop thoughfully provides a horn with a specially fitted reed.

Continuing east along Jermyn Street, Court perfumers **Floris (25)**, at No. 89, have remained a family firm for seven generations since Spaniard Juan Famenias Floris set up his barber's shop at this address in 1730. The shop's rare Spanish mahogany interior fittings came from the Great Exhibition of 1851. Its customers have included Princess Grace of Monaco and Mick Jagger.

Further east, and easily whiffed on a warm day, is an entirely different fragrance, the distinctly healthy odour of **Paxton & Whitfield (26)**, purveyors since 1797 of the finest English and European cheeses. Their expertise in selecting and storing cheeses is unrivalled, and for many people the sight of a 60-lb/ 27-kg cloth-bound drum of Cheddar is a novel experience. Epicures of the Paxton & Whitfield Cheese Club are delivered each month a special selection of five matured cheeses from the shop's stock of more than 300 different varieties. York and Bradenham hams hang invitingly from the ceiling.

Shirtmakers **Harvie & Hudson (27)**, at No. 97, have one of the finest mid-Victorian shop-fronts in London. Astleys, at No. 109, is a mecca for pipe smokers throughout the world, and Bates, the famous hatters, is opposite at No. 21.

Commissioned by Henry Jermyn, the Earl of St Albans, **St James's Piccadilly (28)** is the only church built by Sir Christopher Wren (1632–1723) on an entirely new site. The Earl's coat of arms, stars and a crescent moon, are to be found on the keystone of the arch by the tower. The forerunner of the 18th-century urban church, St James's had remarkable auditory qualities enabling the entire congregation to clearly distinguish the preacher's words. Wren considered it his ideal conception of a parish church.

The exterior is of plain brick with Portland stone dressings. A new replica spire was added as part of Sir Albert Richardson's post-war restorations. The church's spacious galleried interior reaches upward to a barrel vault richly decorated with plaster-work. Wren's master craftsman, Grinling Gibbons (1648–1721), is responsible for the marble font, formed into a tree of life supported by Adam and Eve, and Gibbons also made the handsome limewood reredos and the organ case. The Renatus Harris organ of 1685 was given to St James's by Queen Mary in 1691.

Through the centuries St James's has been renowned for its fashionable congregation and for society weddings. It is also home to a small arts and crafts market in the church forecourt on Fridays and Saturdays.

Further east along Jermyn Street is the rear entrance to **Simpson's of Piccadilly (29)**, whose tradition is based on fine clothes, particularly the Daks trademark. Housed in London's first welded steel building, erected in 1936 and now a listed building, Simpson's has achieved a reputation for up-to-date men's and women's fashions without the loss of a tradition of classic gentlemen's outfitting.

Continuing east along Jermyn Street across Lower Regent Street and south on to Haymarket, on the east side are the **Design Centre (30)**, **Burberry's (31)** and the **Theatre Royal (32)**. The national showcase for the best in contemporary British design, the Design Centre houses changing exhibitions as well as products for sale. These goods, which display the centre's label, are chosen using a stringent set of design criteria: that they are well made, easy to use and maintain, suited to their purpose, stylish and value for money. Vistors may also consult the Design Council's index, an illustrated catalogue of products whose design is considered above average.

Thomas Burberry began trading in 1856 in Basingstoke. Inspired by the qualities of local farmers' smocks, he developed a fabric that was both untearable and weatherproof, yet cool and comfortable to the wearer; he called it 'gabardine'. Burberry's 'trenchcoats' were worn in the First World War, and Nansen, Scott, Amundsen and Shackleton took them on their polar expeditions. The coats, with their distinctively patterned linings,

have been known simply as 'Burberrys' after Edward VII
continually used the name.

Haymarket has two theatres. On its east side is the vast
pedimented portico of the Theatre Royal, built by John Nash in
1821. **Her Majesty's Theatre (33)**, best known for musicals, is
opposite, on the corner of Charles II Street.

Behind Her Majesty's Theatre, off Charles II Street, is the
Royal Opera Arcade (34). This delightful covered passage of tiny
Regency shop-fronts nestling below a sequence of elegant lanterns was London's earliest shopping arcade. It was built by
John Nash and G. S. Repton in 1817 as part of their scheme to
improve the Haymarket Opera House, now Her Majesty's
Theatre. In the 1850s opera glasses and books on opera
could be hired, and greatcoats and bonnets left here during
performances.

St James's Square (35), with its towering plane trees, is the
oldest square in the West End, laid out in 1673 by Henry Jermyn
on land presented to him by Charles II. Today, however, houses
from the 18th century surround the square's central garden.
Only **No. 4 St James's Square (36)** has survived from the original
development, and it, too, has been remodelled, following a fire
in 1725. The London Library, the biggest private lending library
in the country, is at No. 14 (1896), and Chatham House, No. 10
(1736), has been home to three Prime Ministers: William Pitt,
Lord Derby and William Gladstone. At the centre of the garden
is the William III Monument by John Bacon the Younger
(1807). This equestrian statue shows the King as a Roman
general. Portrayed under the horse's hoof is the molehill that
caused the King's fatal riding accident.

The square's south-east corner leads on to Pall Mall.

Pall Mall (37), like its successor The Mall, was once the venue for
games of *pallo a maglio* (*paille maille*, pell mell or ball to mallet),
a game with some similarity to croquet. The game originated in
Italy and was popular with gentlemen in France during the 16th
century. It was a favourite sport of Charles II and nobility took
up the pastime here in the 17th century. The floor of the royal
alley was strewn with powdered cockleshells and 'The King's
Cockle Strewer' was employed to water the surface in order to
keep the boxwood balls moving fast. Dust created by busy local

coach traffic, however, affected play. To solve the problem, a new highway was laid out in 1661 and the street soon became known as Pall Mall.

Always a fashionable street, Pall Mall today houses many of London's best known and most prestigious gentlemen's clubs. These include the **Reform Club (38)**, at Nos. 104–5, which was established by leading Whigs around the time of the Reform Bill in 1832. This same Bill, a milestone on the road to universal suffrage, was also to cause the Whigs' opponents, the Conservatives, to form the Carlton Club, in nearby St James's Street, as a meeting place where they could discuss reversing their disastrous electoral fortunes of that year. It was in the Reform's smoking room that Jules Verne's character Phileas Fogg took the bet to travel around the world in eighty days. In 1981 club membership was opened to women. The club is not open to the general public.

The **Travellers' Club (39)**, at No. 106, was founded as a convivial haunt and point of reunion for gentlemen with adventure and experience abroad. Its members number many diplomats. The club is not open to the general public.

The **Athenaeum Club (40)**, at No. 107, was founded in 1824 for artists, writers and scientists. It is the intellectual élite of London's clubs, and many top academics are members. The majority of Prime Ministers, Cabinet ministers, archbishops and top civil servants and many major literary figures have also been included in its membership.

On the south-east side of the junction between Pall Mall and Waterloo Place is the **Institute of Directors (41)**, the world's largest body representing business leaders. The building, by Nash (1828), was formerly the United Services Club, founded in 1815 for British Officers from the Napoleonic Wars. It was the first building in London to be designed specifically as a club; it is not open to the general public.

At the centre of Waterloo Place is the **Guards' Crimea Memorial (42)**, made from Russian cannon by John Bell, commemorating the men from three regiments of Foot Guards who fell during the Crimean War. A figure of Florence Nightingale with her lamp stands in front. To the north-west is the **Crafts Council Gallery (43)**, a national centre for the promotion of contemporary craftsmanship through its exhibition programme and information centre.

The Duke of York Column bisects John Nash's majestic **Carlton House Terrace (44)**, a visual feast of white façades, each thirty-one bays wide, with central pediments and giant Corinthian columns and balconies. Nash was commissioned in 1827 to design terraces similar to those of his Regent's Park scheme (*Baker Street* ⊖). The round, pink granite **Duke of York Column (45)** commemorates Frederick, 'the Grand Old Duke of York' (d. 1827), second son of George III and Commander-in-Chief of the British Army, immortalized in the nursery rhyme as the indecisive leader who marched his men to top of the hill, then marched them down again. Benjamin Wyatt's column, 124 ft/37.8 m high, was suggested to be of such height as to enable the Duke to escape his creditors, to whom he owed £2 million at his death. The bronze statue of the Duke is by Sir Richard Westmacott (1834). The column and statue cost £26,000, paid for by public subscription, and every man in the Army was required to donate one day's pay.

At No. 6 Carlton House Terrace is the **Royal Society (46)**, formed in 1660 and the oldest scientific society in the world enjoying an unbroken existence. Its members constitute Britain's scientific élite, and the Society has organized many scientific expeditions, advised numerous governments on various subjects and continues to award medals for original research. Some of the world's greatest minds have been presidents of the Royal Society, including Wren (1680–81), Newton (1703–26), Lister (1895–9) and Rutherford (1925–30). The Royal Society may be visited by prior appointment only.

The Duke of York Steps lead down to the **Institute of Contemporary Arts (47)** Its founder, Herbert Read, declared at its first exhibition in 1948 that the ICA, as it is commonly known, was 'not another museum, another bleak exhibition gallery, another classical building in which insulated and classified specimens of a culture are displayed for instruction, but an adult play-centre, a workshop where work is joy, a source of vitality and daring experiment'. That exhibition brought together the work of Arp, Bacon, Brancusi, Braque, Calder, Chagall, De Chirico, Dali, Ernst, Giacometti, Hepworth, Kandinsky, Klee, Kokoschka, Magritte, Matisse, Miro, Modigliani, Moore, Nicholson, Paolozzi, Picasso, Man Ray, Roualt, Sutherland and others. Its history is studded with today's 'greats', once contemporary 'unknowns'. Its vision has been challenging, inevitably provocative, bringing an international perspective to contemporary art

and providing a model for similar centres across the world. The
ICA's three galleries, cinema, video library, theatre, seminar
room, bookshop, bar and café, open seven days a week in this
elegant Nash terrace, have been a meeting place for architects,
poets, philosophers, composers, painters and artists since 1968,
linking differing art forms and artists with the 500,000 members
of the public who visit each year. The ICA still jealously guards
its independence, receiving only a fraction of its income from
government subsidy.

Conservative by comparison with the ICA is the work of
various art societies, among them the Association of Illustrators
and the Royal Society of Portrait Painters, displayed at the **Mall
Galleries (48)**, a short distance east along The Mall.

Return along the eastern side of St James's Park. Beyond the
concrete citadel built during the Second World War to protect
Sir Winston Churchill and his advisers, and now covered with
grass and creepers, is **Horse Guards Parade (49)**. Each year on
the Saturday nearest 11 June the Trooping of the Colour takes
place on Horse Guards Parade to mark the sovereign's Official
Birthday. Performed regularly since 1805, it originated from the
ancient military custom to carry, or troop, flags and banners in
front of soldiers, thereby familiarizing them with the colours
around which they would rally on the battlefield. The colour
paraded on this major state occasion, held in the presence of Her
Majesty the Queen, has now lost its strictly operational association and has come to embody the spirit and traditions of the
unit in question. The Queen is Colonel-in-Chief of all seven
regiments of the Household Division. For many years the
Queen rode side-saddle on her horse Burmese during the event,
but since the recent retirement of Burmese, she has arrived by
carriage and presided over the event standing on a low platform.

The ceremony of Beating the Retreat is also performed each
year on Horse Guards Parade in late May or early June to the
stirring music of mounted bands, massed bands, trumpeters and
the pipes and drums. Its title does not refer to the defeat or
retreat from the field of battle, but the retreat of daylight. The
onset of night is signalled, or 'beaten'.

Near by, the Guards Memorial shows five First World War
guardsmen in front of a stone cenotaph. The five bronze figures
were cast from the metal of German guns captured by guardsmen. Two impressive guns stand at Horse Guards Parade: one, a

Turkish gun made in 1524, captured in 1801 by the British Army in Egypt, which is mounted on a carriage with a figure of Britannia reclining on a lion and threatened by a crocodile, the other, a mortar resting on the body of a griffon, commemorating the raising of the siege of Cadiz by the Duke of Wellington.

Return along Birdcage Walk to the **Guards Museum (50)** in the grounds of the Wellington Barracks. Marching day in, day out, to and from royal palaces is only the ceremonial part of the guardsman's duties. The active-service role of all five regiments of Foot Guards is even more distinguished. The Guards Museum, beneath the parade ground of Wellington Barracks, details the regiments' stories from the birth of the King's Guards at the Restoration through to the nuclear age. Beyond the museum's entrance, flanked by two tall dummy guardsmen resplendent in bearskins and full scarlet dress, is a life-size diorama of the three principal figures of Lady Butler's painting *Hold High the Colours!*, depicting the spirited defence by the colour party of the Royal Scots Fusilier Guards at the Battle of Alma in the Crimea in 1854. Two of the figures, Ensign Lindsay and Sergeant McKechnie, were among the first six recipients of the Victoria Cross. Other exhibits include: the tunic worn by the Queen in her role as Colonel-in-Chief of the Grenadier Guards; a special section about the Guards' considerable contribution to the victory at Waterloo in 1815; Field Marshal Earl Alexander's fur-lined flying jacket, a garment that this then debonair young Irish Guards captain wore throughout the North African and Italian campaigns of the Second World War; and an exhibit about the Long Range Desert Group, the forerunner of the Special Forces, formed by Colonel David Stirling, Scots Guards, based on volunteers from the Household Division.

Westminster ⊖

Westminster houses the centre of political and administrative power in Britain. Parliament is the country's supreme legislative authority, and in nearby Whitehall are the headquarters of many government ministries, the nation's corridors of executive power. Downing Street, a cul-de-sac off Whitehall, houses the official residences of the Prime Minister and the Chancellor of the Exchequer.

The origin of Westminster as the predominant location of political power in London and the City as its financial centre dates back to Edward the Confessor's decision, in the 11th century, to build Westminster Abbey and move his main royal residence upstream from the City to a riverside site nearby. This move separated the commercial capital from the source of royal power and justice, a distinction still evident today. Edward's Palace of Westminster was the principal residence of English kings until Henry VIII abandoned it for Whitehall Palace in 1512. The Houses of Parliament now occupy the site of this former palace and have retained its original title.

Westminster Abbey could perhaps be described as the nation's Valhalla and forms a unique pageant of British history. Most kings and queens are buried there. In the Abbey's Undercroft Museum one can come face to face with the famous dead through their royal death masks and wax effigies. The Abbey itself is an architectural masterpiece of the 13th and 14th centuries, and has been the setting of nearly every coronation since that of William the Conqueror in 1066.

From an underground bunker known as the Cabinet War Rooms, in the depths of Whitehall, Churchill and his Cabinet governed the country during the Second World War. This dark complex of offices and claustrophobic corridors is now open to the public.

The Changing of the Horse Guard, ceremonial Britain at its most colourful, can be seen each day at 11 a.m. (noon on Sundays) in Horse Guards, on the west side of Whitehall. Near by is the 'grandest room in England', the Banqueting Hall of Banqueting House. The only remaining part of the Royal Palace of Whitehall, the hall has magnificent proportions and breathtaking ceilings by Rubens.

WESTMINSTER

- WHITEHALL
- HORSEGUARDS AV.
- VICTORIA EMBANKMENT
- Thames
- WATERLOO
- YORK RD
- HORSE GUARDS RD
- 18
- 16 17
- Ministry of Defence
- 15
- DOWNING ST
- 14
- 13
- KING CHARLES ST
- 19
- DERBY GT.
- WESTMINSTER
- GT GEORGE ST
- PARLIAMENT ST
- BROAD SANCTUARY
- 2
- 1
- 3
- 4
- OLD PALACE YARD
- 5
- DEAN'S YARD
- 6
- WESTMINSTER BRIDGE
- WESTMINSTER BR.
- 12
- Houses of Parliament
- Riverside Walk
- St. Thomas's Hospital
- County Hall
- 11
- LAMBETH NORTH
- BRIDGE ST
- KENNINGTON RD
- LAMBETH PALACE ROAD
- River Thames
- GREAT PETER ST
- TUFTON ST
- MILLBANK
- SMITH SQ.
- 7
- HORSEFERRY RD
- LAMBETH BR.
- 10
- 9
- 8
- LAMBETH ROAD
- N

THE PALACE OF WESTMINSTER

- N
- 14 St Stephen's Entrance
- 19 Old Palace Yard
- 13 Westminster Hall
- 12 New Palace Yard
- 15
- Members' Entrance
- Norman Porch
- Peers' Entrance
- Cloister Court
- Star Chamber Court
- 10 Victoria Tower
- Chancellor's Court
- State Officers' Court
- Moses Room
- St. Stephen's Court
- Ministers' Room
- Clock Tower
- 11
- Robing Room
- Royal Gallery
- House of Lords
- 18 Peers' Lobby
- Central Lobby
- 16
- Commons Lobby
- 'Aye' House of Commons 17 'No'
- Speaker's Court
- 1.1
- Royal Court
- Peers' Court
- Peers' Inner Court
- Commons Inner Court
- Commons Court
- Speaker's Green
- Lower Waiting Hall
- Peers' Library
- Dining Room
- Commons Library
- Speaker's Residence
- Terraces
- River Thames

Reproduced by permission of Geographer's A–Z Map Co. Ltd. © Crown Copyright. Based upon the 1973 Ordnance Survey 1:10,000 map with permission of the Controller of Her Majesty's Stationery Office. © Crown Copyright.

Elsewhere in the Westminster ⊖ area, but at some distance, is the Imperial War Museum, a unique and varied collection of artefacts of wars in this century.

⊖   ⊖   ⊖

The **Houses of Parliament (Palace of Westminster) (1)** are immediately opposite the ⊖. Britain has never had a written constitution. Its system of parliamentary government has been the result of gradual evolution spanning many centuries. Parliament is the supreme legislative authority in Britain and has three elements: the Queen, the House of Lords and the House of Commons. There are 650 elected Members of Parliament (MPs) sitting in the House of Commons: 523 for England, 38 for Wales, 72 for Scotland and 17 for Northern Ireland. The Lords sit separately in the Palace of Westminster and are constituted on entirely different principles. The Lords consist of the Lords Spiritual, who are the Archbishops of Canterbury and York, the Bishops of London, Durham and Winchester and twenty-one other bishops of the Church of England; and the Lords Temporal, who are subdivided into hereditary peers and peeresses, life peers and peeresses and Lords of Appeal ('law lords'), who are appointed to assist the House in its judicial duties and who form the highest court in the land.

The majority of ministers in the British Government are members of the Commons, but the Government, to explain and expound its policy and legislation programme, is represented by ministers in the Lords as well.

Since the beginning of Parliament the balance of power has undergone a complete change. Until the 20th century the Lords' power of veto over measures proposed by the Commons was, theoretically, unlimited. The Parliament Act of 1911 curtailed the Lords' power over most bills passed by the Commons, and abolished the veto over bills dealing exclusively with expenditure and taxation. Today it is generally accepted that the Lords' function is the revision of legislation, not to rival the Commons.

The Houses of Parliament occupy the site of a former royal palace, the Palace of Westminster, an official title that it retains today. The palace was the principal residence of English kings from the reign of Edward the Confessor (1042–66) until Henry VIII abandoned it for Whitehall Palace in 1512. Little remains of the original buildings except Westminster Hall, begun in 1097 by William II. It was enlarged by Richard II at the end of the

14th century, by which time the court in all its aspects – administrative, judicial and parliamentary – had its headquarters in Westminster.

The Lords were accommodated in the Palace from their beginnings, but the Commons had no permanent meeting place until 1547, when they were given the Palace's Royal Chapel of St Stephen. The Commons assembled here until 1834, the year that the Palace was almost completely destroyed by fire. Only Westminster Hall and the crypt and cloisters of St Stephen's survived.

The present Houses of Parliament, completed in 1860, are the work of Charles Barry (1795–1860) and his assistant, Augustus Pugin (1812–52). Barry's acclaimed late-Gothic style building rises beside the Thames with two beautifully balanced, yet dissimilar, towers, and Gothic pinnacles and windows punctuating the extensive waterfront from end to end. Evidence of Pugin's picturesque ornamentation is everywhere, especially the rich interior detailing of panelled ceilings, stained-glass, wallpaper, fireplaces, even inkwells and umbrella stands. After incendiary bombs destroyed the Commons' chamber in 1941, Sir Giles Gilbert Scott restored and simplified Pugin's extreme Gothic decoration.

It is difficult to secure a place in the Strangers' Gallery to see the Commons at work. British residents must write in advance to their local MP. Foreign and Commonwealth visitors can apply to their Embassy or High Commission for a card of introduction. It is also possible to join the public queue outside the Palace's St Stephen's Entrance, but a wait of one or two hours is common in the afternoons. The Commons sits earlier on Friday and it is easier to gain admission to the Gallery then or on Mondays to Thursdays in the evenings. Admission to the Strangers' Gallery of the Lords by queueing is on Tuesdays, Wednesdays and some Mondays. The Houses of Parliament can be toured only by arrangement with an MP or Peer.

Towering 316 ft/96.3 m above Bridge Street, opposite Westminster ⊖, is **Clock Tower (1.1)**, usually referred to as **Big Ben**. This is, in fact, the name of the great hour bell rather than the tower or clock. Big Ben is the largest striking, most powerful and most accurate public clock in the world. Its peal is familiar across the globe and broadcast nightly on British television.

After the fire of 1834, it was decided that a Clock Tower would be built containing a very large striking clock – 'a noble clock, indeed a King of Clocks'. In 1846 Parliament held a design competition refereed by Sir George Airey, the Astronomer Royal. Its rules specified that the first stroke of each hour on the proposed clock was to be accurate to within one second, and its time to be telegraphed to Greenwich Observatory (*Outer London*) twice a day for checking. Many thought such accuracy impossible, and it was seven years before barrister and amateur horologist Edmund Beckett Denison's design was chosen. Leading clockmakers E. J. Dent were selected to construct the clock, which included Denison's famous Double Three-Legged Gravity Escapement, a refinement that ensured outside influences, such as wind force, on the clock hands were not transmitted to the pendulum. In 1859 the clock mechanism was hauled up eleven floors to the clock room. At the centre of the mechanism is the 13-ft/4-m-long pendulum, which beats every two seconds, controlling the timekeeping. It is so finely adjusted that the addition of the weight of a single pre-decimal penny results in a two-fifths of a second gain in twenty-four hours. It once took thirty man-hours a week to wind the clock.

Above this room are the famous faces of the clock, each 23 ft/ 7 m in diameter. The tip of each minute-hand travels 120 miles/ 193 km each year. Above the clock faces is the belfry, which houses the hour bell, Big Ben, and four quarter bells. The quarter bells ring out a tune called the Westminster Chimes, taken from music by Handel. The first Big Ben was cast near Stockton-on-Tees and, at 16 tons, was the largest bell ever cast in Britain. But in October 1857, after having been shipped to London and pulled across Westminster Bridge by sixteen white horses, it cracked during testing in New Palace Yard. A second bell, of 13 tons cast from its predecessor's metal, was produced at the Whitechapel Bell Foundry (*Aldgate & Liverpool Street* ⊖). It rang out for the first time on 11 July 1859. Big Ben's name is thought to derive either from Sir Benjamin Hall, a man of considerable girth, who supervised its installation, or from the nickname of popular boxing champion Benjamin Caunt.

Inside the lantern above the belfry is the Ayrton Light, which is lit whenever Parliament is at work after dark.

On the corner of Bridge Street and Parliament Square is **New Palace Yard (1.2)**. The 'new' derives from the new palace proposed by William II and started in 1097. Only Westminster Hall, on the south side of the yard, was completed. The entrance used by Members is here.

Westminster Hall (1.3) is the oldest surviving building of the ancient Palace of Westminster, built by William II ('Rufus') in 1097–9 as a northern extension of Edward the Confessor's original palace. Richard II's master mason, Henry Yevele (c. 1320–1400), transformed the hall. By 1399 he had heightened and buttressed the Norman walls to carry a great roof of oak created by master carpenter Hugh Herland. This roof is one of the greatest surviving achievements of English medieval carpentry. Its hammer-beam is one of the earliest and largest of its kind and covers the building in a single span without the need of supporting columns.

Westminster Hall became the centre of administration outside the City walls. Grand Councils and, later, some early parliaments were held here. Throughout the Middle Ages it was used for ceremonies and banquets. From the 13th century the Hall housed the Law Courts, and the Royal Courts of Justice met here until 1882. Sir William Wallace, Sir John Oldcastle (Shakespeare's Falstaff), Sir Thomas More, Anne Boleyn, Guy Fawkes and Charles I all stood trial in this building.

Since the 19th century, the bodies of monarchs and eminent statesmen have lain in state here, including Gladstone, Edward VII and Churchill.

Public access is through the north entrance in New Palace Yard. Visitors to the Strangers' Gallery can view its interior from a dais at the top of the stairs from St Stephen's entrance.

St Stephen's Entrance (1.4) is the public entrance to the Houses of Parliament. Queue here, when Parliament is sitting, for admission to watch a debate from the Strangers' Gallery of the House of Commons. Entry is from 4.15 p.m. on Mondays to Thursdays, and from 10 a.m. on Fridays. For the House of Lords, admission is from 2.30 p.m. on Tuesdays, Wednesdays and Thursdays and occasionally on Mondays and Fridays.

St Stephen's Entrance leads into **St Stephen's Hall (1.5)**. After the fire of 1834 architect Charles Barry constructed this long, narrow hall on the site of the 14th-century St Stephen's Chapel. During the Reformation, under the Chantries Act of 1547, which secularized all private chapels, this chapel was presented to the Commons. Members then sat in the choir stalls, facing each other during debates on opposite sides much as in the Commons' Chamber today. A brass plate marks the position of the Speaker's Chair, which replaced the altar, and it is probable that the tradition of bowing to his chair derives from genuflexion before the altar.

The Royal Chapel of St Stephen also had a lower chapel, which survived the fire and was rededicated as the Chapel of St Mary Undercroft. Members of Parliament may marry and have their children baptized here.

From the **Central Lobby (1.6)** corridors lead northward to the House of Commons Lobby and Chamber, and southward to the House of Lords. Here members of both houses meet for informal discussion and members of the public can meet their MP's.

During Sir Giles Gilbert Scott's restoration of the **House of Commons (1.7)** after Second World War damage much care was taken to preserve the essential features of Barry's building, although much of Pugin's Gothic decoration was simplified. The only surviving section from 1834 is the entrance to the chamber, known as the Churchill Arch and now flanked by statues of Churchill and Lloyd George. Above the doorway is the crest of Airey Neave, the MP killed in 1979 by a terrorist bomb in the Members' car park.

The House of Commons is supervised by the Speaker. His entrance is preceded by the Serjeant-at-arms bearing the mace, the symbol of royal authority. The Speaker's Chair stands before the Table of the House at the north end of the Chamber. The Clerk of the House sits at the Table, which bears the dispatch boxes and mace. Running the length of the Chamber on both sides are the traditional green hide benches, from which members face each other across the 'floor of the house'. Members speak from wherever they are sitting and must not step across the red lines drawn down both sides of the Chamber. The popular explanation is that from behind those marks two men with drawn swords are unable to reach each other.

Since 1642, when Charles I burst into St Stephen's Chapel demanding the arrest of five members, no monarch has been allowed into the Commons Chamber. When the monarch attends the State Opening of Parliament (see below), the Commons repair to the Chamber of the Lords. In 1950, however, George VI was allowed to visit the Commons Chamber to inspect the Second World War rebuilding.

The number of seats (437) falls short of the membership (650) of the Commons. During the war Churchill insisted that the number of seats remain the same to preserve the intimacy of the debating chamber. The drama was intensified on great occasions, he pointed out, when Members had to crowd into the space around the doors and the gangways between the seats.

When a vote is required, a division is called. Members voting *for* a motion go into the Division Lobbies to one side of the Speaker, those *against* passing to the other.

The gallery above the Speaker's Chair is used by reporters from *Hansard* (the daily verbatim report of debates), and representatives of the British and foreign media.

Each year, usually in November, in the **House of Lords (1.8)** the monarch performs the State Opening of Parliament, a ceremony little changed since the 16th century. Prior to the sovereign's arrival at the Palace of Westminster, the Yeomen of the Guard conduct a thorough search of the vaults below the House of Lords. This precaution dates from 1605, when Guy Fawkes and his fellow conspirators attempted to kill James I by blowing up Parliament during the ceremony. Their plan was foiled, however, after one of the conspirators, Francis Tresham, warned his brother-in-law, Lord Monteagle, not to attend the House that day, 5 November. The Government was alerted and Fawkes was discovered in the cellars. His Gunpowder Plot is celebrated annually on Guy Fawkes night, 5 November.

Riding in the Irish State Coach and accompanied by members of the royal family, the monarch is greeted by a salute on arrival at the palace. The sovereign then proceeds to the Lords via the Robing Room. Meanwhile the Commons are summoned by the Gentleman Usher of the Black Rod, the Royal Messenger, to hear the Queen's Speech in the Lords. As Black Rod crosses the Commons' Lobby, the door of the Chamber is shut in his face. Black Rod strikes the door three times with his rod and is admitted. He then leads the Commons to the Lords.

The Queen's Speech is, in fact, a statement of the Government's legislative intentions for the next session of Parliament and is read by the monarch from the throne at the south end of the Lords' Chamber. The throne stands on raised steps, which, when the House is in normal sitting, are used as seats by Privy Counsellors and the eldest sons of peers. Before the throne is a red ottoman, known as the Woolsack, on which the Lord Chancellor sits as Speaker of the House of Lords. In front are two similar woolsacks, used by judges at the opening of Parliament, and the Table of the House, at which the Clerks sit. The Woolsack is said to have been adopted during the reign of Edward III (1327–77) as a reminder of the importance of the wool trade to English prosperity.

Red leather benches are arranged on both sides of the House;

Government benches on one side and the Opposition's on the other. The first two benches on the Government side are reserved for the bishops. At the opposite end from the throne are the cross-benches, for Members who do not adhere to Britain's two main parties.

There are around 2,000 members of the Lords and in the course of a year about 800 attend, with a daily average of 290. The lobbies in which the Lords record their votes, 'Content' or 'Not Content', are on either side of the Chamber.

The State Opening of Parliament is broadcast on television, and the Lords' proceedings are frequently broadcast on radio.

Old Palace Yard (1.9) is the original courtyard of Edward the Confessor's palace and the scene of two notable executions: Guy Fawkes in 1606, and Sir Walter Raleigh in 1618. Richard I (Coeur de Lion), the adventurous Crusader of the 12th century, is commemorated with an equestrian statue by Carlo Marochetti (1861).

Victoria Tower (1.10), the taller of the palace's two towers at 336 ft/102.4 m, houses the archive of parliamentary documents. Master copies of every Act of Parliament since 1497 are kept here. The Union Jack is hoisted above this tower when Parliament is sitting and, if the sovereign is present, the Royal Standard is also flown.

The sovereign enters Parliament by Victoria Tower on State occasions. The tower leads to the **Robing Room**, where the sovereign assumes the Imperial State Crown and the crimson parliamentary robe used at the opening of Parliament. Adjacent to the Robing Room is the **Royal Gallery**. The walls of this processional way display two 45-ft-/13.7-m-long frescoes by Daniel Maclise: *The Death of Nelson* and *The Meeting of Wellington and Blücher*.

Parliament Square (2) was laid out by Sir Charles Barry in 1868 as an approach to the Palace of Westminster. The square has sculptures of Sir Winston Churchill (Robert Jones, 1973); Boer leader Field Marshal Jan Christian Smuts, who became pro-British (Jacob Epstein, 1958); Viscount Palmerston (Thomas Woolner, 1876); Sir Robert Peel (Matthew Noble, 1876) and Abraham Lincoln.

For nearly 400 years **St Margaret's Westminster (3)** has been the parish church of the House of Commons, although a church was founded here as far back as the 12th century. The present St Margaret's was built in 1523, but much of its fine Perpendicular-style architecture is the result of Sir George Gilbert Scott's mid-19th century remodelling.

As a piece of Renaissance stained glass, its Flemish east window is unparalleled in London. Made by order of Ferdinand and Isabella of Spain as part of the dowry of Catherine of Aragon, then engaged to Henry VII's eldest son, Prince Arthur, it depicts the prince and his wife in a crucifixion scene. Arthur died, however, and the work of art was tactfully dispatched to Waltham Abbey when his younger brother, Henry VIII, married Catherine after his accession. It was restored to St Margaret's in 1758.

In the early 20th century St Margaret's was *the* church for society weddings. Churchill and Lord Mountbatten made their marriage vows here. Many Americans living in London have also married here, having been granted a special licence by the Archbishop of Canterbury. In 1888 American citizens presented a portrayal of Sir Walter Raleigh landing in Virginia, which is set in the church's west window. Raleigh was beheaded outside the church in 1618 and is buried beneath the altar. Another gift from the United States is a window depicting the poet John Milton, who married his second wife here in 1656.

Consecrated over 900 years ago, **Westminster Abbey (4)** is a unique pageant of British history, both as a great religious centre and as an architectural masterpiece predominantly of the 13th and 16th centuries. The setting for nearly every coronation since that of William the Conqueror in 1066, most kings and queens of England are also buried here. Westminster Abbey is the scene of memorial services to national figures and of most royal weddings and funerals. Neither a cathedral nor a parish church, Westminster Abbey is termed 'royal peculiar', thereby under the jurisdiction of a Dean and Chapter and subject only to the sovereign. Its official title is the Collegiate Church of St Peter in Westminster.

The Abbey was founded by King Edward the Confessor in the 11th century on the site of an earlier church known as Westminster (or 'West Monastery'). In 1139 Edward was canonized and his remains were later transferred to a place of honour behind the Abbey's high altar.

Little of Edward's building survives, but Henry III's wish for

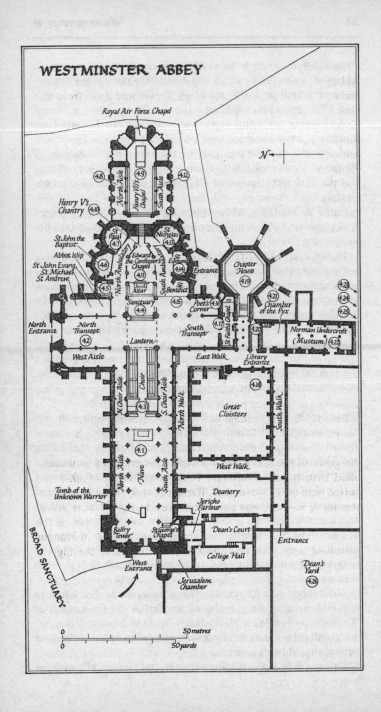

WESTMINSTER ABBEY

Royal Air Force Chapel

4.8 4.9 4.12

N

North Aisle

Henry VII's Chapel

South Aisle

Henry V's Chantry
4.10

St Paul
4.7

St Nicholas
4.13

St John the Baptist

North Ambulatory

Abbot Islip

Edward the Confessor's Chapel
4.11

St Edmund
4.14

Entrance

Chapter House
4.19

St John Evang,
St Michael
St Andrew
4.6

4.5

Altar

South Ambulatory

St Benedict

4.21

4.23

4.24

Sanctuary
4.4

Poet's Corner 4.16

Chamber of the Pyx

4.25

4.15

North Entrance

North Transept
4.2

Lantern

South Transept

St Faith's Chapel

4.17

4.20

Norman Undercroft (Museum) 4.22

West Aisle

East Walk

Library Entrance

N Choir Aisle

Choir

S Choir Aisle

North Walk

4.18

Great Cloisters

South Walk

4.3

Nave

North Aisle

South Aisle

West Walk

Tomb of the Unknown Warrior

4.1

Deanery

Jericho Parlour

Belfry Tower

St George's Chapel

Dean's Court

Entrance

BROAD SANCTUARY

College Hall

Dean's Yard
4.26

West Entrance

Jerusalem Chamber

0   50 metres

0   50 yards

a worthier setting for Edward's remains led to the present Abbey's construction, which began in 1245. Most of the eastern end of the church is in Early English style and dates from this time. The nave was rebuilt by the medieval architect Henry Yevele in the late 14th century to correspond with the rest of the church, but his work was not completed until the early 16th century. Two important later additions to the Abbey were Henry VII's Perpendicular-Gothic chapel, completed in 1519, and the twin west towers of Nicholas Hawksmoor in the 18th century.

Enter Westminster Abbey by the west door. Guided 'Super Tours' are available at the reception desk in the south aisle of the nave.

The Gothic **nave (4.1)**, at 102 ft/31 m, is the highest such nave in England. Purbeck marble piers, unchanged since medieval times, support the open galleries running above the aisles, which in turn bear the vaulted ceiling. Stylistically, the combined effect is highly consistent, rare in English church architecture of this scale and achieved despite a time span of nearly 250 years.

Immediately to the right is the Chapel of St George, the Warriors' Chapel. On its east side is a 15th-century stained-glass window believed to depict the Black Prince. On the pier at the corner of the chapel is a painting of Richard II (c. 1390), the first known contemporary painting of an English monarch.

Directly facing the main west door is a green marble tablet to the memory of Sir Winston Churchill (1875–1965). It is positioned close to perhaps the best known memorial in the Abbey, the grave of the Unknown Warrior. This grave, of an unidentified British soldier brought back from France in 1920 and buried here on 11 November, Remembrance Day, commemorates those soldiers who gave their lives during the First World War and who have no known place of burial. Displayed on the pier north of the grave is the Congressional Medal of Honour bestowed upon the Unknown Warrior in 1921, the highest military distinction conferred by the United States.

In the central aisle of the nave is the burial place of explorer David Livingstone (d. 1873). The monument on the left side of the choir screen commemorates scientist Sir Isaac Newton (d. 1727).

The brightly coloured windows lighting the nave north aisle were designed by Sir Ninian Comper (1864–1960). Each pair depicts the kings and their abbots responsible for the building

of Westminster Abbey. In the bottom left-hand corner of the
window showing Henry V (the seventh eastward) is Dick
Whittington, the famous Lord Mayor of London, and his cat.
Whittington administered the king's revenues for building work
at the Abbey.

At the eastern end of the north aisle visitors are charged an
admission fee to see the ambulatory, transepts and chapels. The
north choir aisle, 'Musicians' Aisle', celebrates notable composers and performers, among them Henry Purcell (d. 1695),
a former organist at the Abbey, and Benjamin Britten
(d. 1976).

The **north transept (4.2)** is often called 'Statesmen's Aisle'.
Gladstone and Palmerston are buried here and have statues
erected to them. There are also monuments to Disraeli, Peel
and Pitt the Elder. The rose window tracery is 19th-century
with 18th-century stained-glass by Sir James Thornhill
(1675–1734).

The Gothic-style **choir (4.3)** stalls and screen, positioned here
in 1848, were designed by Edward Blore (1787–1879). Until the
middle of the 16th century Westminster Abbey was a Benedictine monastery. The monks sang their daily services in the
enclosed choir, a tradition that has continued in the present
collegiate church. Today members of the choir wear scarlet
cassocks, like the clergy, which derives from the Abbey's status
as a 'royal peculiar'. Details of the daily services are displayed at
the west door.

Dominating the rear of the **sanctuary (4.4)** is a gilded high
altar screen made in 1867 to Sir George Gilbert Scott's scintillat-
ing design. The sedilia (priests' seats), right of the altar, were
erected about 1300. Their backboards show early 14th-century
paintings of two kings, probably Henry III and Edward I. On
the sedilia's left is the tomb of Anne of Cleves (d. 1557), the
fourth wife of Henry VIII and the only one of his six wives to
lie in the Abbey. Above the tomb is an 18th-century Madonna
and Child triptych by Bicci de Lorenzo (1375–1452), in front of a
16th-century tapestry thought to have once formed part of the
scenery for a Latin play at Westminster School. The Cosmati
paving on the sanctuary floor, now mostly obscured by carpet,
was constructed by craftsmen with materials from Rome in 1268.

On the north side of the sanctuary stand three medieval tomb
chests. Nearest the altar is that of Edmund ('Crouchback'), Earl
of Lancaster (d. 1296), the younger son of Henry III. The

westernmost tomb is occupied by his first wife, Aveline (d. 1274), and separating them is Aymer de Valence, Earl of Pembroke, a cousin of Edward I.

Coronations take place in the sanctuary. The Coronation Chair is brought here from the Chapel of St Edward the Confessor (*see* 4.11) and placed before the High Altar for the ceremony.

Abbot Islip was the penultimate Abbot at Westminster. The carving on the frieze above the lower windows of the **Chapel of Abbot Islip (4.5)** shows his rebus, an eye and the figure of a man slipping out of a tree, hence I - slip. The **Chapel of Our Lady of the Pew and St John the Baptist (4.6)** has a modern alabaster Virgin and Child. In the Chapel of St John there is an enormous monument to Hunsdon (d. 1596), a former Abbot of Westminster. The **Chapel of St Paul (4.7)** is said to have contained the cloth in which St Paul's head was wrapped after his execution, a relic reputedly donated by Edward the Confessor. The inventor of the uniform public Penny Post, Sir Rowland Hill (d. 1879), is buried here.

Queen Elizabeth's Chapel (4.8) forms the north aisle and is one of a number of chapels within the Chapel of Henry VII (*see* 4.9). Henry VII commissioned a chapel as a memorial to Henry VI, who was murdered while at prayer in the Tower of London. Work began in 1503, probably supervised by the master mason Robert Vertue. His vaulted ceilings are one of the architectural glories of the Tudor period. Henry VII died in 1509. The chapel was completed in 1519 and Henry VIII dedicated it to his father.

Queen Elizabeth's Chapel contains the splendid marble canopied tomb of Elizabeth I (1533–1603). Her sister, Mary I, who reigned from 1553 until 1558, is buried in the same tomb. Beyond them are the tombs of two infant daughters of James I. Set into the wall between them is a stone casket containing remains throught to be those of the Young Princes, Edward V (b. 1470) and his brother Richard, Duke of York (b. 1472), allegedly murdered in the Tower of London in 1483.

The **Chapel of Henry VII (4.9)**, used since 1725 as the Chapel of the Order of the Bath, is festooned with brightly coloured banners, crests and mantels of the Knights Grand Cross of the Order. These motifs are repeated on the wooden stalls (*c.* 1520). Beneath the seats are beautifully carved misericords on which monks once leaned to rest their legs. Crowded below the windows in the apsidal chapels are groups of 16th-century statues of saints. Ninety-five of the original 107 pieces survive, each a beautiful individual study.

Edward VI (d. 1553) is buried beneath the altar, which stands on the west side of the high, railed tomb of Henry VII and his consort, Elizabeth of York. This tomb was designed by Pietro Torrigiani in 1518. Thomas Ducheman's bronze grille, which surrounds the tomb, is decorated with Tudor emblems of greyhounds, dragons and roses. It is likely that Ducheman was also responsible for the gates to the chapel, mounted with royal emblems of Henry Tudor and his antecedents.

The northernmost apsidal chapel contains the tomb of George Villiers, first Duke of Buckingham, designed by Hubert le Sueur (1595–1650). In the next chapel is a monument to another, unrelated, Duke of Buckingham, John Sheffield (d. 1721), for whom Buckingham House, later Buckingham Palace (*St James's Park* ⊖), was built. The central apsidal chapel is now the Royal Air Force Memorial Chapel. The brightly coloured memorial window incorporates the crests of the sixty-eight Fighter Squadrons that took part in the Battle of Britain in 1940. Below the window, to the left, a perspex-covered hole marks the spot where a bomb fragment penetrated the wall in 1941. A floor slab marks the original burial place of Oliver Cromwell (d. 1658). Following the Restoration of the monarchy, Cromwell's remains were exhumed and symbolically displayed at Tyburn.

Over the modern bridge is **Henry V's Chantry Chapel (4.10)**. Built by his command so that masses could be said for his soul, this two-storey chapel was not completed until 1450, twenty-eight years after his death. His tomb is on the left, before the entrance to St Edward's shrine. Its gilt covering has long gone, like the former solid silver head now replaced with one of polyester resin. In the upper storey is the altar, which is still used on 31 August, the anniversary of Henry's death, and on 25 October, St Crispin's Day, when the Battle of Agincourt took place. Visitors are permitted to visit the upper storey only on these two days. Henry V's wife, Catherine de Valois, is buried in the altar.

The **Chapel of St Edward the Confessor (4.11)** commemorates the founder of Westminster Abbey, who died in 1066 and was canonized nearly 100 years later. Henry III was responsible for the construction of a shrine dedicated to St Edward, whose remains were brought here in 1269. Enter St Edward's Chapel through the gates, made in 1431, displaying the oldest tracery in England.

To the right is a beautiful early bronze effigy of Eleanor of Castile (d. 1290), cast by William Torel. Eleanor's husband, Edward I, erected twelve stone crosses marking the stages of her funeral procession from Harby in Nottinghamshire to Westminster Abbey. The last of the crosses was placed at Charing Cross (*Embankment* ⊖). Next to Eleanor is the tiny tomb of Princess Elizabeth Tudor, daughter of Henry VII, who died in 1495 at the age of three. The builder of much of the Abbey, Henry III (d. 1272) is celebrated in a gilded bronze effigy by Torel (1291). The large tomb is of Edward I (d. 1307). Known as 'Longshanks' on account of his height (6 ft 2 in/1.88 m), he was the first monarch to be crowned in the present church.

In the centre of the Chapel is Edward the Confessor's shrine. It is in two parts. The lower, prepared by Henry III, is of Purbeck marble and contains the saint's body. The upper is a stepped wooden construction, made after the original golden feretory had been looted during the dissolution of the monasteries in 1540. Despite the dissolution, most of the statuary in Westminster Abbey was saved, thanks to its royal associations, but part of the Abbey's revenues were transferred to St Paul's Cathedral (*St Paul's* ⊖), hence the expression 'robbing Peter to pay Paul' (the Collegiate Church of St Peter is the Abbey's official title).

Every English monarch except two since Edward II in 1308 has been crowned seated in the **Coronation Chair**. The oak chair, originally made for Edward I by Master Walter in 1300, stands against the screen that backs the High Altar and is painted decoratively and set with jewels. Edward I specified that the chair should incorporate the Stone of Scone, which he had captured from the Scots, for whom it had served as the throne since the ninth century, in 1296. The sword, 7 ft/2 m in length, and the ceremonial shield beside the chair once belonged to Edward III (1327–77).

The tombs on the south side of the chapel are those of Richard II (d. 1399) and his consort, Anne of Bohemia (d. 1394); Margaret of York (d. 1472), daughter of Edward IV, and Edward III (d. 1377). Also here is the tomb chest of Edward's wife, Queen Philippa of Hainault (d. 1369), who pleaded with her husband to spare the Burghers of Calais.

The south aisle of the Chapel of Henry VII is **Lady Mar-**

garet's Chapel (4.12) and contains the tomb of Mary, Queen of Scots, executed at Fotheringay in 1587 by order of Elizabeth I. She was originally buried at Peterborough Cathedral, but her son, James I, interred her remains in this tomb built by Cornelius Cure in 1612. Further east is the tomb of Lady Margaret Beaufort, Henry VII's mother. The tomb, by Pietro Torrigiani, is England's first Renaissance work. Buried beneath the altar are four late-Stuart monarchs; Anne, William III, Mary II and Charles II. The third tomb in this chapel is that of the Countess of Lennox (d. 1578), grandmother of James I.

In the south ambulatory, opposite the entrance to the **Chapel of St Nicholas (4.13)**, is a retable, believed to be English work of about 1270. It depicts St Peter, the patron saint of Westminster Abbey, and next to him Christ holding an orb.

The 13th-century heraldic stained-glass in **St Edmund's Chapel (4.14)** is the oldest in the church. A tomb chest on the right is that of William de Valence (d. 1296), half-brother of Henry III. It is remarkably well carved with clothes and accoutrements, and is the only tomb in England decorated with Limoges champlevé enamel work.

The tomb of Cardinal Simon de Langham (d. 1376), the Benedictine Abbot of Westminster (1349–62) and Archbishop of Canterbury from 1366, lies in the **Chapel of St Benedict (4.15)**. Opposite the Chapel of St Benedict, at the rear of the sedilia, is a tomb believed to be that of Serbert (d. 616). Legend has it that this East Saxon king founded the original Westminster Abbey and that the church was consecrated by St Peter.

The east aisle of the **south transept (4.16)** is famed for its monuments to writers. On the east wall in 'Poets' Corner' is an altar chest believed to be the burial place of Geoffrey Chaucer (d. 1400), author of *The Canterbury Tales* and the first great poet in the English language. On the floor in front of Chaucer's tomb are tablets to Byron, D. H. Lawrence and Dylan Thomas among others.

In the south transept William Shakespeare (1564–1616) is commemorated in a full-length statue (1731) by William Kent. Late 13th-century wall paintings of St Christopher and St Thomas, discovered in 1936, adorn the south wall.

Glance up at the rose, or wheel, window, the largest example of its kind. Although its painted glass dates from 1902, in the spandrels below are two superbly crafted angels dating from the 13th century.

The door in the south transept's south wall leads into the **Chapel of St Faith (4.17)** (*c*. 1249), with its 13th-century painting of St Faith over the altar. This chapel is intended for private prayer.

The 13th-century doorway in the south choir aisle is one of the best examples in the Abbey. It leads into the Abbey Precinct, where, in the **Great Cloister (4.18)** Benedictine monks once went about their daily business. To the right, the north cloister is used as a brass rubbing centre. At the far end note the circular indentations in the benches made in the 14th century by novice monks for the game 'Nine Men's Morris'.

On the east side of the Great Cloister is a range of buildings that formed part of the medieval Benedictine monastery: the Chapter House, Pyx Chamber and Undercroft.

The **Chapter House (4.19)**, a great octagonal building whose beautiful vaults spring from a slender central pillar, was completed in 1257 and belongs to Henry III's magnificent rebuilding of the Abbey. The monks' daily meeting here was called 'Chapter' because it included the reading of a chapter from the *Rule of St Benedict*. Soon after the building's completion, however, Henry III's Great Council met here and, from the middle to the end of the 14th century, it was the meeting place of the House of Commons. Used for many centuries after the Dissolution to store state documents, including the Domesday Book, it was restored by Sir George Gilbert Scott in 1868. His restoration revealed the original encaustic tiled floor, its surface consisting mainly of geometrical patterns and stylized foliage and animals, still in excellent condition. Visitors are required to put on covers for their shoes to protect this rare 13th-century floor.

Below the windows runs a continuous arcade of arches enclosing three distinct series of wall paintings. The first two, a Last Judgement in the courtly International Gothic style, and a series depicting the Apocalypse, were given by Brother John of Northampton, a monk of the Abbey in the late 14th century. The third, a series of birds and beasts, is perhaps as late as 1500. Above the inside of the entrance doorway is one of the most important groups of medieval sculpture to survive in England. Life-size standing figures depict the Annunciation, with Mary to the right and Gabriel on the left.

During the summer, on Wednesdays between midday and 3 p.m., the **Chapter Library (4.20)**, with its 15th-century hammer-

beam roof, is open to the public. Many of the library's furnishings were added nearly a century later.

The low groin-vaulted **Pyx Chamber and Treasury (4.21)** is
among the first monastic buildings added to Edward the Confessor's foundation, dating from shortly after the Norman
Conquest. It was originally part of the undercroft beneath the
monks' dormitories and was completed between 1065 and 1090.
Henry III used the chamber as a treasury as early as 1249 and it
has since remained under Crown jurisdiction.

Its name derives from the sample of coinage stored in wooden
boxes, called pyxes. In approximately 1281 the first 'trial of the
pyx' took place here, a public demonstration that the coinage
was pure. This annual ceremony, still carried out today, deter-
mines that the gold and silver content in newly minted coins
must not fall below a prescribed minimum. Since 1871 this
ceremony has taken place at the Goldsmiths' Hall (*Cannon
Street & Mansion House* ⊖).

On display in the Pyx Chamber is the greater part of the
church plate belonging to the Dean and Chapter of West-
minster. The collection dates from the 17th century. All earlier
Abbey plate was lost either at the Reformation or in the
Commonwealth. Chalices, flagons, patens and a large alms dish
from about 1660 are displayed together with a splendid silver
basin and ewer made in 1714. Plate from St Margaret's
Westminster recently added to the collection includes two
Communion cups of 1551, among the earliest to have survived in
England.

Almost opposite the entrance to the Pyx Chamber, at the east
end of the south cloister, a black slab set into the floor, known as
'Long Mey', marks the remains of twenty-six monks who are
believed to have died from the Black Death in 1349.

At the opening of the Dark Cloister is another part of the
Norman undercroft, which now forms the **Undercroft Museum
(4.22)**. Displays in this magnificent vaulted room centre around
a unique collection of royal death masks and wooden, plaster
and wax effigies made for lying-in-state and funeral processions.
From the late 13th century onwards effigies, generally attired in
full coronation regalia, were carried on the coffin beneath a
canopy. After burial, the effigy was displayed for several weeks
and became the property of the Abbey. Today these effigies
provide accurate portraits of great historical significance.

Of the medieval effigies, which are carved in wood with

plaster or gesso features, only two have survived intact: Edward III (1312–77), whose slightly distorted mouth is thought to have indicated a stroke, and Catherine de Valois (1401–37), wife of Henry V. The face of Edward III is believed to be an actual death mask, making it the earliest such mask in Europe.

Later effigies, which have wax heads, include an 18th-century replacement for the original effigy of Elizabeth I (1533–1603), and one of Charles II (1630–85), are thought to have been cast from life. Charles II's effigy is dressed in contemporary clothes, a mantle of blue silk velvet lined with white silk taffeta, a surcoat and hood of red silk velvet and a black velvet Garter hat with a plume of ten white ostrich feathers. One of the most interesting characters in the exhibition is Frances Stuart, Duchess of Richmond and Lennox (1647–1702). Known as 'La Belle Stuart', she was rumoured to have been a mistress of Charles II. Alongside is her West African grey parrot, for forty years the Duchess's companion. It outlived her by only a few days and is thought to be the earliest example of taxidermy.

Two later additions, introduced to attract the public and not for funereal purposes, are effigies of the statesman William Pitt, first Earl of Chatham (1708–78), and Lord Nelson (1758–1805).

The Undercroft museum also houses various insignia carried at Henry V's funeral in 1422, including his helm, limewood shield and lightweight saddle; General Monck's armour; two panels of white alabaster sculpted by Arnold Quellin from a design by Grinling Gibbons for an altar-piece at the Palace of Whitehall, and a bronze relief of Sir Thomas Lovell (d. 1504) by Florentine sculptor Pietro Torrigiano.

Continue east along the 11th-century Dark Cloister and take the passageway to the left leading to **Little Cloister (4.23)**. The monastery's hospital stood here in the 12th century. On Thursdays entry to the **College Garden (4.24)** is possible through the passage in the south cloister. This peaceful and charming garden, established for 900 years, is certainly the oldest garden in London, and possibly in England. It is enclosed on the south side by a part of the Abbey's wall, built *c.* 1372, and on the west side by Westminster School.

Privacy is requested in **Little Dean's Yard (4.25)**. Immediately on the left is the stone archway entrance to the **Great Hall** of Westminster School (by appointment only). Dating from 1090–1100, it was once part of the monastic dormitory. Between 1602 and 1884 the entire school was taught in this one room, which is still referred to as 'School'. In the Great Hall on Shrove Tuesday the school observes the old custom of tossing a pancake into the air, which the pupils then fight over. The one who ends up with the largest piece after a minute's scrum receives a guinea from the Dean of Westminster.

On the north side of the yard is the 17th-century Ashburnham House, accommodating the school's library (open during Easter week, otherwise by appointment only). This stately red brick house was built for the Ashburnham family and sold to the Crown in 1730. It is notable chiefly for its impressive staircase, above which an ornate plaster ceiling opens into a lantern.

Return along Dark Cloister and turn left on to the south side of Great Cloister. Straight ahead is the parlour where visitors were received in the 14th century. Further along, to the right, a passage leads to the Deanery Courtyard (private). The vaulted ceiling of the passage displays bosses that could be removed for defensive purposes to repel invaders with boiling liquid. In Deanery Courtyard are Collège Hall (by appointment only), the Deanery (private) and the 16th-century Jericho Parlour, which leads to the 14th-century Jerusalem Chamber (both can be entered only on a Super Tour).

Immediately left is the 14th-century east range of the yard, the oldest medieval domestic terrace in London. The archway in the northwest corner of the **Dean's Yard (4.26)** leads out on to Broad Sanctuary.

Jewel Tower (5), designed by Henry Yevele *c*. 1365 and constructed during Edward III's reign, was used until the time of Henry VII (1485–1509) as part of the Royal Wardrobe, a place of safety for jewels, clothes, furs and gold vessels. Later used to store parliamentary records and then inhabited by the Weights and Measures Office, Jewel Tower was restored after the Second World War and opened to the public. Various objects discovered in local excavations, including 11th-century capitals found buried in Westminster Hall, are on display, as well as drawings submitted for the redesign of the Houses of Parliament in 1834.

Victoria Tower looms from the north over **Victoria Tower Gardens (6)**, which house Auguste Rodin's bronze *Burghers of Calais* (1895), a bronze of suffragette leader Emmeline

Pankhurst (A. G. Walker, 1930) and a memorial fountain to social reformer Sir Thomas Fowell Buxton.

To the west of Victoria Tower Gardens is Smith Square. **St John's, Smith Square (7)** (Thomas Archer, 1728) is known nationally for its BBC lunch-time concerts, which are open to the public. This beautiful concert hall has been described as the 'sanctuary of harmony in the discord that comes out of the rest of Westminster', clearly a reference to the fact that in Smith Square's south-east and south-west corners respectively are Transport House, where the Labour Party has its headquarters, and Conservative Central Office.

St John's had its origin in the Fifty New Churches Act of 1711. When Queen Anne was asked how she wished the church to look, it is said she kicked over her footstool and said 'like that'. Distinguished by the four towers at its corners, this magnificent Baroque-style church was nicknamed 'Queen Anne's footstool'.

From Smith Square return towards Victoria Tower Gardens. At the south end of the gardens cross over Lambeth Bridge. To visit the Imperial War Museum go eastward along, or take bus nos. 3, 44, 109, 159, 510 from the north side of, Lambeth Road to beyond the junction with Kennington Road; the museum is on the right. Otherwise bear left towards St Mary's Church to visit the Museum of Garden History (*see* 9).

The **Imperial War Museum (8)** is devoted to the story of war in our century. All aspects of conflict, both civil and military, allied and enemy, involving British and Commonwealth troops since 1914 are recorded here. It is an essential visit for anyone interested in the military history of modern times.

Through the entrance hall is the spectacular, high exhibition hall, offering dramatic views of more than fifty of the museum's most historically significant large exhibits. Suspended in the atrium are six famous aircraft, including a First World War Sopwith Camel, an American P51 Mustang and a Battle of Britain Spitfire. Rising vertically from the central space are a German V2 rocket and a Polaris missile. Other items on show include: the 13-pounder gun that fired the first British shell on land in the First World War; a 4.7 ton shell from the Schwerer Gustav railway gun, the largest gun ever made; British, German, Soviet and American tanks, including the M3A3 Grant used by Montgomery at El Alamein; a V1 'doodlebug'; a

German midget submarine; the fishing boat *Tamzine*, the smallest craft to take part in the Dunkirk evacuation, and an Argentinian anti-aircraft gun captured during the Falklands conflict. Interactive video stations located around the gallery show exciting archive footage of many of these exhibits in action.

In the lower ground floor galleries are four exhibition areas – the First World War, the Inter-War Years, the Second World War, and Post-War Conflicts – some undergoing redevelopment and, therefore, temporarily closed. Exhibits include: material from the Spanish Civil War; the Munich Agreement signed by Chamberlain and Hitler in 1938; escape aids used by prisoners of war held in Colditz; the surrender document signed by Germany at Luneberg Heath in 1945; a section on the notorious Burma-Siam railway; and relics from Hiroshima. The range of material is enormous, from uniforms and equipment to clothing, personal items, letters, diaries, newspapers, cigarette cards and much more.

Alongside these exhibitions are two carefully researched reconstructions: one, a front line trench in the First World War; the other a London street, complete with air raid shelter, during the Blitz. In the Blitz Experience visitors are caught in an air raid – bombs explode, the ground trembles and smoke fills the air.

The Imperial War Museum also has, perhaps surprisingly, the second largest collection of 20th-century British art in the country. One part of the collection emphasizes the shock of the new 20th-century methods of warfare through modernist works, for which the collection is best known. Elsewhere, casualties of war are evoked by the paintings of Sydney Carline, Henry Tonks, Eric Kennington and Stanley Spencer. The key work, showing the silence and grief of the immediate end of the war period, is Sir George Clausen's *Youth Mourning*. Other works are by Paul Nash, Epstein, Sutherland, Piper, Moore and Topolski.

The museum has a fine collection of Victoria Crosses, and material relating to Victoria and George Cross winners. It also possesses the three campaign caravans used by Field Marshal Viscount Montgomery of Alamein in the Western Desert and north-east Europe. Behind the scenes the museum has film archives comprising more than 40 million ft/12 million m, more than 5 million photographic prints and negatives, a Department of Sound Recordings set up in 1972 to amass oral histories, and a Department of Documents.

The building itself is the surviving central part of the former Bethlem Royal Hospital, the lunatic asylum popularly known as Bedlam. Much redevelopment is taking place to improve space and public facilities and consequently, some areas of the museum may be temporarily closed.

The John Tradescants, father and son, were famous 16th-century collectors and gardeners who supervised some of the great gardens of their day and were royal gardeners to Charles I. At their home in South Lambeth they founded the first public museum in England, as well as a botanic garden stocked with exotic plants collected during their extensive travels. Father and son are buried in a finely carved tomb in the churchyard of St-Mary-at-Lambeth.

In 1977 the Tradescant Trust was established to save this derelict church and establish the **Museum of Garden History (9)**. Six years later the Queen Mother officially opened the Tradescant Garden, part of which has been designed as a replica of a 17th-century garden, containing trees, shrubs and flowers known to have been grown by the Tradescants. The church houses exhibitions and offers lectures on many aspects of horticulture.

For nearly 800 years **Lambeth Palace (10)** has been the London residence of the Archbishop of Canterbury. The palace holds an important collection of portraits of former archbishops painted by leading artists of the day; these are hung in the Guard Room, the Picture Gallery and the Great Corridor. The palace has a magnificent theological library of more than 150,000 books and manuscripts, and the finest collection of archives relating to the Church of England. Priceless treasures include the famous *Lambeth Bible* of *c.* 1150, richly illustrated and a superb example of English Romanesque art; a fine edition of Sir Thomas More's *Utopia*; and King Henry VII's treatise against Martin Luther, which gained him the title 'Defender of the Faith'.

The Great Hall, rebuilt by Archbishop Juxon in 1663, with its magnificent oak hammer-beam roof, was the scene of Henry VIII's special Commission, which intended to extort the support of the London clergy into acknowledging his, rather than the Pope's, supremacy over the Church. The Hall, now converted into a library, hosts the Lambeth Conference, an assembly of Anglican bishops from all over the world held every decade.

The Guard Room retains its 14th-century roof timbers despite extensive restoration in 1829, and the Palace's Tudor gatehouse, known as Morton's Tower and visible from Lambeth Palace Road, still contains a prison cell with heavy iron rings and wall inscriptions from the period when it housed Royalist prisoners during the Commonwealth. Kept in a showcase in the Chapel's Cloister Gallery is a set of Eucharistic vestments that belonged to Cardinal Pole, the last Roman Catholic Archbishop of Canterbury. The palace can be visited by prior appointment only, but the gardens may be opened to the public in the future.

Opposite Lambeth Palace is the Albert Embankment. Take the riverside walk northwards towards Westminster Bridge, passing St Thomas's Hospital on the right. This walk affords a familiar and spectacular view of the Houses of Parliament. In the under-croft of St Thomas's Hospital in Lambeth Palace Road is the **Florence Nightingale Museum (11)**, a tribute to one of the nation's great ladies and the inspirer of the nursing profession. The first major public monument to the 'Lady with a Lamp' was publicly unveiled in Waterloo Place at seven in the morning of 24 February 1915, five years after her death at the age of 90. But after the slaughter of Mons and Ypres, Asquith's Government judged the event untimely and left workmen to unveil the statue.

The museum's centre-piece display concerns her two years in the Crimea at the hospital at Scutari. When she arrived, the hospital was overrun with rats and lice, and there were no medicines, beds, food, fuel, or blankets. The Army had done nothing except whitewash the walls. Miss Nightingale trans-formed conditions for the wounded, taking total control of the hospital. However, the sentimentalized image of Miss Nightingale with her little lamp belied a will of iron. Scutari formed only two years of a busy life. Later, she established the first nurses' training school, revolutionized medical care in India (viceroys never embarked for the sub-continent without first consulting her), turned hospital construction into a science, and appealed for funds for the newly founded National Society for Aid to the Sick and Wounded in War, which subsequently became the British Red Cross Society. Her prized possessions, a lamp from the Crimean War, soldiers' tributes and an original nurse's uniform, are displayed for the first time.

Westminster Bridge (12) was built by Thomas Page in 1862. The Coade Lion, or South Bank Lion, was placed on the south side of the bridge in 1966, having been erected in a number of other locations previously. It has since been adopted as the emblem of the South Bank Arts Centre (*Embankment* ⊖). Constructed of artificial stone, a kind of terracotta, Coade stone was reportedly the most waterproof ever made. The secret of its manufacture was lost after the Coade Manufactory closed in 1840.

Near the lion lies County Hall, once the headquarters of the now defunct Greater London Council (GLC). It is to be converted into a hotel, leisure facilities, shops, homes and offices. The bridge leads to Parliament Square.

On the north side, Parliament Street leads into **Whitehall (13)**. This area was once the site of Whitehall Palace, the principal royal residence for about 160 years from the reign of Henry VIII until that of James II. The name may have derived from the light colour of some new buildings built then or, more probably, from the custom of naming any festive hall a 'whitehall'. Banqueting Hall (*see* **16**) is the only building to have completely survived the fire that razed Whitehall Palace to the ground in 1698.

Today Whitehall is the administrative centre of Britain. It houses the Foreign and Commonwealth Office, the Admiralty, the Ministry of Defence, the Civil Service Department, Cabinet Office, Welsh and Scottish Offices and, in Downing Street (*see* **15**), the Chancellor of the Exchequer's and the Prime Minister's official residences.

The **Cenotaph (14)**, in the centre of Whitehall, is the national memorial to those who lost their lives in the two world wars. A dignified monument designed by Sir Edwin Lutyens (1869–1944), it is the focal point of the annual Remembrance Day service held in November and attended by members of the royal family and prominent political leaders. Poppy wreaths are laid. Glance opposite to William Whitfield's Richmond House, a modern building with stripy brick towers joined by windows, a marvellous romantic foil to Lutyens' classical austerity.

No. 10 Downing Street (15) has been the official residence and office of the British Prime Minister for over 250 years. Most

premiers have lived here during their term of office. Downing
Street itself is a cul-de-sac ending in a flight of steps leading to St
James's Park. No. 10's simple façade belies the fact that it is the
nerve centre of the British Government, containing more than
40 rooms for the 140 or so people who work there.

Britain's first premier, Sir Robert Walpole, moved here in his
capacity as First Lord of the Treasury after accepting the house
from King George II in 1732. No. 11 is the official residence of
the Chancellor of the Exchequer, and in the ground floor and
basement of No. 12 are the offices of the Whips, members of the
Government responsible for seeing legislative policy through
Parliament.

By the time Walpole vacated No. 10 in 1742 the building was
much as it is today. However, a new façade was added in 1766,
the State Dining Room and Breakfast Room by Sir John Soane
were added in 1825 and there was some restoration in 1963. Its
most famous room, the Cabinet Room, with its long table, looks
out over Horse Guards Parade and St James's Park. No. 10 is not
open to the general public.

Banqueting House (16), designed by Inigo Jones, is one of the
finest and earliest examples of the classical style in England. It
was completed in 1622 and is the only important building
remaining from the Royal Palace of Whitehall, which was
destroyed by fire in 1698.

The building is entered at the north end. At the top of the
staircase vestibule, built by James Wyatt in 1809, is the main
apartment. The Banqueting Hall's proportions are exactly a
double cube; 110 ft/33.5 m long and 55 ft/16.75 m in breadth and
height. It has been called the grandest room in England.

Banqueting House contains beautiful ceilings by Peter Paul
Rubens (1577–1640). Charles I, who was later beheaded outside
this building, commissioned Rubens's nine allegorical paintings
in commemoration of his late father, James I. They were painted
on canvas and completed in Belgium in 1634. The paintings are
best viewed from the south entrance doorway to the hall. They
depict the benefits of James I's government; the apotheosis of
James I (central oval), flanked by processions of cherubs symbolizing Joyous Prosperity; and the union of England and
Scotland. The oval pictures in the corners show the triumphs of
Virtues over Vices; Royal Bounty bestriding Avarice (SW),
Wise Government curbing Intemperate Discord (SE), Heroic
Virtue clubbing Rebellion (NW) and Heroic Wisdom impaling

Ignorance (NE). These paintings are among the finest in the possession of the Crown, and Rubens received a knighthood and a payment of £3,000 for them.

Together with Banqueting House, **Henry VIII's Wine Cellar (17)** is the only major structure to have survived the fire at Whitehall Palace in 1698. It was probably built by Cardinal Wolsey, Archbishop of York, in 1514–29, as part of his palace, York Place. Wolsey often entertained Henry VIII and when the Cardinal fell from power, Henry VIII took possession of York Place, creating Whitehall Palace and this wine cellar. The cellar's vaulted roof, bays and central piers, and the stillages upon which the barrels were set, remain an evocative relic of Henry's palace. Entry is by appointment only.

Ceremonial Britain at its most colourful can be seen at **Horse Guards (18)**, on the west side of Whitehall. Horse Guards, an 18th-century building that surrounds three sides of a shallow forecourt, is guarded each day by two mounted Life Guards and two dismounted sentries. Life Guards, in their red tunics and white-plumed helmets, and the Royal Horse Guards (the Blues and Royals), in their dark blue tunics and red plumes, together form the Household Cavalry Regiment (Mounted), which in peacetime escorts the Queen on many ceremonial occasions. The statuesque Guards are not allowed to converse while on duty, but they will allow themselves to be photographed.

The daily ceremony of the Changing of the Mounted Guard takes place at 11 a.m. (noon on Sundays). The New Guard of twelve men is marched to Horse Guards from Knightsbridge Barracks along The Mall. If the Queen is in residence in London, the New Guard is accompanied by an officer, a standard-bearer and a Queen's trumpeter.

The **Cabinet War Rooms (19)**, located in an underground bunker, are the place from which Winston Churchill, his War Cabinet and the Chiefs of Staff governed Britain during air raids in the Second World War. Now open to the public, this extensive bomb-proof command centre in the basement of the Government's Offices in Great George Street remains an evocative and eerie complex of offices, living quarters and dark claustrophobic corridors.

The Cabinet Room has been laid out as it was for the War Cabinet meeting held at 5 p.m. on 15 October 1940. There are eighteen other rooms on display. From the Transatlantic Telephone Room, Churchill once spoke directly by the 'scrambled'

telephone link to President Roosevelt in the White House. The
Telephone Room's outer door, which came from a lavatory,
displayed 'engaged' when the hotline was in use. The Map
Room was manned day and night throughout the war. Here the
latest information about operations on all fronts was collected
and presented. All the maps seen here today were in use in the
last months of the war and were left in place when the Map
Room was closed in August 1945. The Prime Minister's Room
served Churchill both as an office and a bedroom. Churchill
made some of his most important wartime broadcasts from this
room, including his invasion warning on 11 September 1940.

Embankment ⊖

Victoria Embankment stretches in a magnificent sweep for nearly a mile and a half/2.4 km along the north bank of the Thames between Westminster Bridge and Blackfriars Bridge, affording spectacular views of riverside London.

A short walk north up Northumberland Avenue lies Trafalgar Square, the geographical centre of London. All distances from London, from Land's End to John O'Groats, are measured from the Charles I statue in the south of the square. Named by William IV after the Battle of Trafalgar to mark Admiral Nelson's decisive naval victory over the French in 1805, the great Lord Nelson's statue looks down on the square from atop a 170-ft/52-m column. Converging on Trafalgar Square are some of London's great thoroughfares: Whitehall, lined by the buildings of Britain's powerful government ministries; The Mall, a processional highway through St James's Park to Buckingham Palace; Pall Mall, with its gentlemen's clubs; and the Strand, linking Westminster to the City.

Facing south on to the square is the long imposing façade of the National Gallery, behind which lie some of the world's greatest paintings, and perhaps the most perfectly balanced and representative of all national collections of European painting. The National Portrait Gallery, a unique collection of pictures of the great men and women of Britain, is situated next door. Also facing on to the square is St Martin's-in-the-Fields, considered by many to be London's parish church.

The Hungerford Bridge pedestrian walkway leads south over the Thames to the South Bank's music, arts and theatre complex. The National Theatre, Royal Festival Hall, National Film Theatre and Hayward Gallery are located here. The acoustics of the Royal Festival Hall are among the most marvellous of any auditorium in Europe, and many of Britain's most acclaimed plays have been premiered at the National Theatre. The remarkable Museum of the Moving Image charts the dramatic influence of cinema and television on our times.

Standing next to the Thames near Embankment ⊖ is Cleopatra's Needle, London's most ancient piece of architecture, first erected 3,500 years ago in Egypt.

⊖   ⊖   ⊖

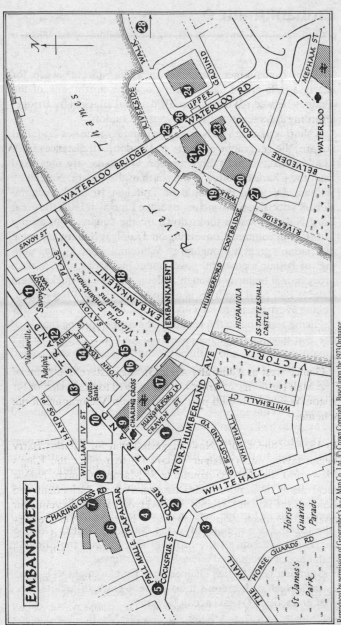

EMBANKMENT

West from Embankment ⊖, lying off Northumberland Avenue, is the **Sherlock Holmes Pub (1)**, whose first floor restaurant is a re-creation of the great detective's study in 221B Baker Street. Displayed are Holmes's large bowl pipe, violin, microscope, deerstalker, magnifying glass and handcuffs. A bust of Holmes, the one that reportedly decoyed an assassin's bullet, is next to the window. And, to complete this contemporary fantasy of Sir Arthur Conan Doyle's famous character and his life, there is a sample of soil from the Reichenbach Falls, scene of Holmes's fateful encounter with the evil Professor Moriarty. Only the great detective and his loyal companion, Dr Watson, are missing.

From the west end of Northumberland Avenue, the equestrian statue of **King Charles I (2)** (Hubert le Sueur, 1633) looks down towards Whitehall (*Westminster* ⊖), the site of his execution. After the King's death, Oliver Cromwell ordered the statue to be sold to a brazier and destroyed. Although in 1649 John Rivett was reported to be carrying on a roaring trade in souvenirs allegedly made from the statue, Charles I and his horse were in fact buried in his back garden. After the Restoration, Rivett unearthed the statue and returned it to the royal family. On 30 January, the anniversary of Charles's execution, the Royal Stuart Society lays a wreath at the base of the statue.

Glance west at **Admiralty Arch (3)**, the eastern end point of The Mall (*St James's Park* ⊖). Built in 1910 to the design of Sir Aston Webb, it formed part of the Queen Victoria memorial scheme.

In 1824 architect John Nash suggested that Sir Charles Barry began laying out **Trafalgar Square (4)** to replace the King's Mews and the slums surrounding St Martin's Church. Now a focal point of London, with its own Act of Parliament and Behaviour Code, it is second only to Hyde Park as the venue for political demonstrations. Each year it hosts New Year revelry and, for help rendered to Norway during the Second World War, it receives a giant Christmas tree from the Norwegian government.

Rising from the centre of the square is **Nelson's Column**, designed in 1843 by William Railton. Perched aloft is E. M. Baily's 17-ft/5.2-m statue of Nelson. The statue was unveiled nearly forty years after the great admiral's death, and received much contemporary criticism for its daring disregard of personal resemblance: unlike the man himself, the statue has two good eyes and two arms. Nelson put his blind eye to good use on at least one occasion. .To ignore an order during the Battle of Copenhagen, he placed his telescope to his blind eye and declared: 'I have the right to be blind sometimes . . . I really do not see the signal!' Turning a blind eye, it could be said.

At the base of the column bronze reliefs illustrate Nelson's major battles during the Napoleonic Wars: Trafalgar, 1805 (to the south); Cape St Vincent, 1797 (west); Nile, 1798 (north); and Copenhagen, 1801 (east). An account of the Battle of Trafalgar and the death of Nelson (22 October 1805) can be seen at the Public Record Office Museum (*Temple* ⊖). The quartet of bronze lions surrounding Nelson's column is said to represent the calm resolve that made Nelson the saviour of his country. Sculpted by Sir Edwin Landseer, they were finally positioned in 1868. Despite being described by contemporary naturalist Richard Jeffries as 'the true spirit of nature', it went unnoticed that the paws of the beasts were in fact those of the domestic cat.

Trafalgar Square's fountains were first installed in 1845, and were then supplied with water from two wells beneath the National Gallery. Now relocated facing the Canadian Parliament in Ottawa, they were replaced just before the Second World War by fountains designed by Sir Edwin Lutyens. Civil servants from government offices in nearby Whitehall have often been accused of only 'working from ten to four, like the fountains in Trafalgar Square'.

Sunk into the wall of the terrace is a set of imperial standard measures engraved on a bronze bar. Alongside are busts of Admirals Cunningham, Jellicoe and Beatty. Two columns at the southern corners of the precinct are surmounted by lanterns supposedly from Nelson's flagship *Victory*.

Plinths stand at each of the four corners of the square's precinct, three having statues of national heroes. In the north-east corner is an equestrian statue of George IV. It was commissioned in 1829 by the King to surmount Marble Arch (*Marble Arch* ⊖), when the arch was positioned in front of Buckingham Palace. The King, however, died before Sir Francis Chantrey completed the work, and it was later felt the site was inappropriate. Trafalgar Square was selected as its new 'temporary' home. The other two statues are of Sir Henry Havelock (SE corner), who suppressed the Indian Mutiny, and Sir Charles Napier,

Conqueror of Sind (SW corner). The fourth plinth is empty, pending the future choice of another intrepid Briton.

Canada House can be seen to the west from Trafalgar Square, and South Africa House to the east. The **George III monument (5)** (Matthew Cotes Wyatt, 1836), another equestrian statue, is to be found in nearby Cockspur Street. George III would be surprised to learn that just 100 yds/91 m behind him there now stands a statue to his erstwhile subject George Washington.

Dominating the north side of Trafalgar Square is Britain's **National Gallery (6)**, which houses one of the most superb collections of paintings in the world. A cross-section of the creative heights of European painting, almost all the great schools of art are represented, from Early Italian masterpieces to those of the early 20th century.

The National Gallery opened in 1824 with an initial collection of thirty-eight pictures. In 1838 the gallery moved to its present site, a building designed by William Wilkins with a long façade and magnificent portico. It was nicknamed then 'The National Cruet Stand', after its cupolas. Today the gallery's collection has swelled to more than 2,000 pictures, all of which are on permanent display (excepting those loaned to regional museums and loan exhibitions). Most of its British collection, however, is now held at the Tate Gallery (*Victoria* ⊖).

The gallery's first director, Sir Charles Eastlake, travelled annually in Europe in search of suitable pictures and as a result the National has outstanding works from the Early Italian Schools (Early Italian, Rooms 1 and 3; Italian 15th century, Rooms 2, 4, 5 and 6; North Italian 15th century, Rooms 10, 12 and 13). Works by Duccio, in the Byzantine style of early-14th-century Siena, are among the gallery's earliest pictures and include the *Virgin and Child* and the predella panels, *The Annunciation*, *The Transfiguration* and *Jesus Opening the Eyes of a Man Born Blind* from his masterwork, the high altar-piece of Siena Cathedral, called *The Maestà*, executed between 1308 and 1311. The more naturalistic and 'realistic' vision of Giotto, the first great painter of the neighbouring Florentine School, can be seen in his *Pentecost*. Thereafter, the progression towards an understanding of perspective, anatomy, light and shade, which characterizes the Italian Renaissance, can be traced through the works of Masaccio (*The Virgin and Child*); Uccello's 'fairy-tale' *St George and the Dragon* and his detailed *The Battle of San*

Romano; Piero della Francesca's carefully composed and time-less *Baptism of Christ*; Filippo Lippi; the Pollaiuolo brothers (*Martyrdom of St Sebastian*); Botticelli (*Adoration of the Kings*, *Mystic Nativity* and *Venus and Mars*) and others. In addition, there are noted works by Giovanni Bellini (*The Madonna of the Meadow* and *The Doge Leonardo Loredan*, with its remarkable diffused lighting), the sculpture-like *Samson and Delilah* by Mantegna, and the remarkable *Wilton Diptych*, painted in the decorative courtly style known as International Gothic.

The three great masters of the Italian High Renaissance, Leonardo, Michelangelo and Raphael, are all represented in the gallery, although the National is less well endowed with pictures of the Italian 17th century (Italian 16th century, Rome and Florence, Room 8; Italian 16th century, Venetian, Room 9; North Italian 16th century, Room 14; Italian 16th century, Room 30, and Italian 17th century, Room 29). Both Leonardo's the *Virgin of the Rocks* (Room 8) and the cartoon *The Virgin and Child with St Anne and St John the Baptist* (Room 7) are compositional groups of two adults and two children in a pyramidal structure, their characters cast with haunting shadows and bearing mysterious smiles not entirely of this world. Michelangelo is represented by an unfinished work, *The Entombment*. None of the ten works by Raphael are late works. They include his celebrated *Pope Julius II*, the *Ansidei Madonna*, the *Mackintosh Madonna*, the *Madonna and Child with St John* and the *Procession to Calvary*.

From Venice are works by Giorgione (*Sunset Landscape with Saints, 'Il Tramonto'*); many by Titian, including his disturbing *Allegory of Prudence*, mythologies *Bacchus and Ariadne* and *Death of Acteon*, as well as early and late religious works and portraits; and works by Titian's successors Tintoretto (*The Origin of the Milky Way*) and Veronese (*The Family of Darius before Alexander* and *An Allegory*). The dramatic lighting characteristic of the work of Caravaggio is to be seen in his *Supper at Emmaus*.

The symbolism and domestic detail to be found in the paintings of the Early Netherlandish (Rooms 24 and 25) and German Schools (Room 23) stand in contrast to the classical influence on the Italian Renaissance. Symbolism suffuses Jan van Eyck's masterpiece *The Arnolfini Marriage*, in which Arnolfini, an Italian merchant from Lucca in the service of the Duke of Burgundy and living in Bruges, is seen with his Paris-born Italian wife solemnly taking their matrimonial vows. Arnolfini has removed his clogs because he is standing on holy ground, the little dog is a symbol of faithfulness, the single burning candle in the chandelier is a symbol of the all-seeing Christ, whose Passion is represented in the ten roundels around the mirror, and a figure of St Margaret, patron saint of childbirth, is carved on the chair by the bed. Jan van Eyck himself can be seen in the mirror as a witness to the betrothal and he signed the portrait with the calligraphic fullness of a contemporary legal signature. Also by van Eyck are his *Portrait of a Young Man* and *Man in a Turban*.

Rogier van der Weyden was the most important painter working in Flanders in the mid-15th century and had been taught by van Eyck's contemporary Robert Campin. Campin is represented by his *Virgin and Child before a Firescreen*, and van der Weyden by *St Ivo*. Although nudity was almost unknown in Northern painting of this time, the National possesses Cranach's most famous erotic full-length female nude, *Cupid Complaining to Venus*, whose thin elongated figure is far removed from the voluptuous women portrayed in contemporary Italian art.

Painters of the 17th-century Dutch School (Rooms 15, 16, 17, 18, 26, 27 and 28) are well represented in the works of Rembrandt, Aelbert Cuyp, Frans Hals and Vermeer. From seeming darkness into a compassionate light emerge many of Rembrandt's graceful yet saddened portraits. *Margaretha Trip* is painted in the twilight of her life. Rembrandt's *Old Man in an Armchair* reclines, tired and reflective, a work of valediction yet conveying a timeless humanity. Of the sixty or so surviving self-portraits by Rembrandt it is possible to compare in Room 19 the *Self-Portrait Aged 34* with that aged 63. The affluent families then populating many Dutch villages are well expressed in Hals's *A Family Group in a Landscape*.

The influence of close family relationship among European rulers is evident from the gallery's other 17th-century French, Spanish and Flemish paintings (Flemish, Rooms 20, 21, 22; French, Room 32; Spanish, Room 41). King Charles I appointed Van Dyck as his court painter in 1632 and is immortalized in the canvas *Charles I on Horseback*. Rubens also worked in England, notably at Banqueting House, Whitehall (Westminster ⊖). He painted Charles I's unworthy favourite *The Duke of Buckingham Conducted to the Temple of Virtue*, and the gallery also possesses his *Judgement of Paris*, *Samson and Delilah* and *Minerva Protects Pax from Mars*, the latter painted after

Rubens, as ambassador to Philip IV, had successfully negoti-
ated a peace treaty between Spain and England in 1629, and
been knighted by Charles I for his services.

Philip IV is to be seen 'in brown and silver' in a portrait by
Velázquez, Philip's court painter from 1623 until the painter's
death in 1660. Other works from Spain include Velázquez's
Toilet of Venus and *Kitchen Scene with Christ in the House of
Mary and Martha*, El Greco's *Christ Driving the Traders from
the Temple*, a popular Counter-Reformation subject, and
Murillo's *Two Trinities*.

From France there are works by Claude as well as Philippe
de Champaigne's portrait of *Cardinal Richelieu*, the immense
grandeur of the picture reflecting Richelieu's immense power as
the country's chief minister under the youthful Louis XIII.

From the 18th century (French, Room 33; Italian, Room 34;
British, Rooms 36, 37, 38, 39; Spanish, Room 42) there are
works by Boucher (*Pan and Syrinx*); Jacques-Louis David
(*Jacobus Blauw*); Drouais (*Madame de Pompadour*); Tiepolo
(*The Banquet of Cleopatra* and *An Allegory with Venus and
Time*); views of Venice by Canaletto, and Goya's grand portrait
of *The Duke of Wellington*, dating from 1812 when the Iron
Duke entered Madrid after winning the Battle of Salamanca.
The affluence of English aristocratic life and empire, its classical
aspirations, is reflected in the works of Gainsborough (*Mr and
Mrs Andrews*); Stubbs (*The Melbourne and Milbanke Families*);
Lawrence (*Queen Charlotte*) and Reynolds (*General Sir
Banastre Tarleton*).

Such is the fame of the National's more modern paintings
(Rooms 35, 40, 43, 44, 45 and 46) that most need no description.
The gallery possesses Constable's *Haywain*; Turner's *'Fighting
Téméraire'*; Ingres' *Madame Moitessier Seated*; *Ovid among the
Scythians* by Delacroix; Courbet's *Les Desmoiselles des Bords
de la Seine*; *The Waitress* by Manet; *Tropical Storm with a Tiger*
by Rousseau; the *Water-lily Pond* and *The Beach at Trouville*
by Monet; *Woman Drying Herself* by Degas; Seurat's *Une
Baignade, Asnières*; *Les Grandes Baigneuses* by Cézanne;
Hermine Gallia by Klimt and Van Gogh's *Sunflowers*.

The museum provides informative lunch-time lecture tours of
its galleries.

Around the corner from the National Gallery, in St Martin's
Place, is the **National Portrait Gallery (7)**, a unique collection

devoted to the portraiture of the nature of human personality in art. The most comprehensive portrait survey of historical personalities in the world, with some 9,000 items, its works range from medieval times to the present day and include kings and queens, statesmen and scholars, soldiers and poets, as well as scientists and explorers. Some works are great masterpieces, such as Reynolds' *Laurence Sterne* and the sketch of the Earl of Arundel by Rubens. Others possess a unique documentary significance, like the Brontë sisters by their brother Branwell – a primitive work of art yet almost the only visual record of the literary trio. The medium of the portrait is not restricted. The collection contains oil paintings, watercolours, drawings, miniatures, even silhouettes. Photographs have been shown since 1968, and caricatures, disregarded in the early years of the gallery as not ennobling, have been rightly recognized as a searching form of portraiture. The standards for admission to the collection are the importance of the sitter and the authenticity of the portrait as contemporary likeness. The gallery now has an active policy of commissioning portraits of living persons.

The Gallery's permanent collection is now arranged as an illustration of themes in British history, with some related material to complement the portraits. The collection starts on the top floor with the Tudors, then the early Stuarts and the Civil War; 17th-century arts and sciences, the Restoration; the Glorious Revolution; the Marlborough Wars; the Kit-cat Club; arts and literature in the 18th century; the beginnings of imperial expansion and the American Revolution; the poets and writers of the Romantic Age; science and industrial revolution, the Regency; the Napoleonic Wars, and the age of political reform. Descending to the first floor there are illustrations of the court of Queen Victoria; literature and theatre in the age of Dickens; the Chartists and social reform; the Crimea and the Indian Mutiny; Victorian science and technology; the age of Gladstone and Disraeli, and the arts, literature and politics of the Edwardian era. On the ground floor are galleries devoted to most recent history.

Famous portraits include: Geoffrey Chaucer, the creative literary genius of the 14th century; Richard III, known as 'Crookback' because of his physical deformity; Henry VIII and his father, Henry VII, a full size working drawing for part of the great fresco painted to surmount the throne in the Privy Chamber in Whitehall Palace; Hans Eworth's *Mary I*, the

daughter of Henry VIII and Catherine of Aragon; three portraits of Elizabeth I, each portraying different facets of the
character of this intelligent and inscrutable woman; William
Shakespeare, the first picture to enter the gallery's collection
and the only one with any claim to be a likeness; Sir Francis
Drake by miniaturist Nicholas Hilliard; a stylized full-length
portrait of the bon viveur George Villiers, first Duke of Buckingham; Oliver Cromwell in Samuel Cooper's miniature of this
masterly military technician, Lord Protector and Puritan country gentleman; Nell Gwyn by court painter Sir Peter Lely; diarist
Samuel Pepys; Sir Christopher Wren; composer Henry Purcell;
Sir Isaac Newton, the discoverer of the law of gravity; John
Wesley, founder of the Methodist movement; William Hogarth,
a self-portrait; explorer Captain James Cook; a sketch by James
Barry of man-of-letters Dr Samuel Johnson; Sir Joshua
Reynolds, a self-portrait; George Gordon, Lord Byron; Admir-
al Horatio Nelson; 'Iron Duke' Arthur Wellesley, first Duke of
Wellington; Jane Austen by her sister Cassandra; Charles
Dickens by Samuel Lawrence; Florence Nightingale, the 'Lady
with a Lamp' at the hospital at Scutari in the Crimea; naturalist
Charles Darwin; philosopher-historian Thomas Carlyle, the 'sage
of Chelsea'; the famous Victorian photograph of Isambard
Kingdom Brunel before the chains of his legendary vessel, *Great
Eastern*; Benjamin Disraeli by Sir John Millais; a cartoon of
Oscar Wilde by Carlo Pellegrini; Augustus John's drawing of T.
E. Lawrence; James Joyce; Gwen John, a self-portrait; the royal
family at Buckingham Palace by Sir John Lavery in 1911; the
royal family at Royal Lodge, Windsor, by James Gunn in 1950;
Walter Sickert's Winston Churchill; Emmeline Pankhurst;
Margaret Thatcher by Rodrigo Moynihan; the famous image
of Her Majesty the Queen by Pietro Annigoni in 1969; Her
Majesty Queen Elizabeth, the Queen Mother; His Royal Highness, the Prince of Wales; Admiral Earl Mountbatten of Burma,
and Her Royal Highness, the Princess of Wales.

Opposite the National Portrait Gallery in St Martin's Place is the
church of **St Martin-in-the-Fields (8)**, once an 11th- or 12th-
century chapel standing in green fields. Its patron saint, a soldier
who became the Bishop of Tours, is said to have encountered a
beggar in bitter weather and, having nothing to offer him, drawn
his sword and cut his cloak in two, giving one half to the beggar.
The scene is depicted, in what is now an early-18th-century

church, in a stained-glass window, a painting and in the bas-reliefs on the parish's ancient lamp-posts.

James Gibbs's masterful combination of a steeple and classical portico, highly controversial at the time (1726), has often been copied, particularly in the United States. A delighted King George I decided to become St Martin's churchwarden, the only monarch ever to have adopted such a role. All royal births are recorded in the church's registers, a mark of its links with English sovereignty. It is now also the parish church of the Admiralty and its bells are first to announce a naval victory.

The BBC's first church service was broadcast from St Martin's in January 1924, and the church is known for its lunch-time classical music concerts. It now houses the London Brass Rubbing Centre, with kings, merchants, knights, squires and courtly ladies among the medieval company of monumental brasses. This enterprising church has opened a craft market in its courtyard and a restaurant, bookshop and visitors' centre in the crypt, all managed by a limited company – the first time that the Church of England has become involved in such a commercial venture. Money raised generates income for the church and its work, especially for the homeless.

An article published in a London newspaper in 1983 sums up St Martin's reputation as a caring church. The Post Office, upon receiving a letter addressed 'To God Somewhere in London', added 'Try St Martin's'.

A hamlet called Charing once stood where the **Charing Cross Monument (9)** (E. M. Barry & T. Earp, 1864) is now located, at the west end of the Strand. In 1290 Edward I erected a memorial in the form of a cross, the last of a series of thirteen crosses marking the stages of the funeral procession of his wife, Queen Eleanor, from Harby in Nottinghamshire to Westminster Abbey. The statue of Charles I, mentioned earlier, now occupies the original site of the Old Charing Cross.

A later version of the Charing Cross Monument was erected in the forecourt of **Charing Cross Railway Station**. Above the station is the Charing Cross Hotel, a fine building constructed in 1864 by E. M. Barry, and one of the first to be faced with artificial stone.

The song 'Let's All Go down the Strand' was written at the end of the last century, when the **Strand (10)** had the most theatres in

London. Now only the **Savoy**, **Vaudeville** and **Adelphi** theatres remain. Originally a bridle path alongside the river, the Strand later became lined with the large mansions of the affluent. Today, the well-to-do stay at the world famous **Savoy Hotel (11)** at the eastern end of the Strand. The Savoy's forecourt is the only highway in England where driving on the right is permitted. Originally, this was to allow carriages to pull up more easily outside the Savoy Theatre.

Adjoining the Savoy is Simpson's-in-the-Strand, world renowned for its traditional English fare. Further west is the imposing **Shell-Mex House (12)**, once the exclusive Cecil Hotel, which, when built in 1886, was the largest hotel in Europe. On the corner of Strand and Agar Street is **Zimbabwe House (13)**. In the 1930s, when the former Southern Rhodesian High Commission took over the building, orders were given for brutal dismemberment of the controversial nude figures forming Jacob Epstein's façade, *Ages of Man*. Near by, on the north side of the Strand are the premises of **Coutts' Bank**, bankers to the Queen, resplendent with a modern glass façade.

In the mid-18th century the area that today is surrounded by Villiers Street, the Strand and Victoria Embankment Gardens was a ruinous slum. The enterprising Adam brothers – John, Robert, James and William – leased the land for a grand riverside housing development called the **Adelphi** (*adelphoi* is Greek for brothers). No expense was to be spared during construction. Arches and subterranean streets were constructed to counteract the slope to the river. In 1773, beset by financial difficulties, the brothers were forced to request the government's approval to hold a lottery and development was completed only after 4,370 tickets were sold at £50 each.

The extent of the Adelphi has now been greatly reduced by new buildings, but a few parts survive, of which the most delightful is No. 8 John Adam Street, occupied by the **Royal Society of Arts (14)** (Robert Adam, 1774). Distinctive string-moulding around the society's doorway embellishes the building's elegant neo-classical exterior.

The society was founded in 1754 to encourage the 'Arts, Manufactures and Commerce'. Prince Albert was president of the society from 1843 until 1861, during which time it was instrumental in organizing the Great Exhibition of 1851. In 1867 the society instigated the practice of putting up memorial plaques on buildings where famous people had once lived. Byron's house was the first to be commemorated. This function was later taken over by local government, and 'blue plaques' are now liberally scattered on buildings throughout London. Note one such plaque commemorating the artist and cartoonist Thomas Rowlandson, who once lived at No. 16 John Adam Street. Members of the public may visit the Royal Society of Arts by prior appointment only.

Behind the main garden of Victoria Embankment, in Watergate Walk, is a reminder of the location of the former river bank. **York Watergate (15)** (1626) is all that remains of the great riverside mansions of the 16th and 17th centuries. Built in 1626 in the form of three stone arches, it has the arms and motto of the once powerful Villiers family. In the garden there are statues to Scotland's best loved poet, Robert Burns; the Imperial Camel Corps; Henry Fawcett, the blind Postmaster-General who developed the parcel post; Robert Raikes, founder of the first Sunday School, in 1780; and composer Sir Arthur Sullivan.

At the end of Watergate Walk, in Villiers Street, is **Gordon's Wine Bar (16)**. Modest and somewhat dilapidated on the outside, this belies a vintage inner charm. Until recently Gordon's traded with Royal Sanctions as a Free Vintner. In 1364 King Edward III granted Royal Letters Patent to the Mistery of the Vintners. As a result these worthy merchants were allowed to open premises and sell wine without applying for a licence.

Opposite Gordon's, on the west side of Villiers Street, are the Charing Cross Arches, the very arches celebrated in Flannagan and Allen's famous music hall song *Underneath the Arches*. **The Players' Theatre (17)** has celebrated the good old days 'enchanting, enthralling, enticing, expostulatory, entertaining evenings' in the style of our Victorian forebears for many years in arches 173 and 174 under Charing Cross Station. That same nightly banter and repartee, witty sketches and songs are again to be heard, following redevelopment of the area. Certain conventions are strictly observed, such as toasting the Queen – Queen Victoria! And the audience is again to sup on bangers and mash after the show.

To the south, through Embankment ⊖ station, is Victoria Embankment. The land on the north side of the Thames from Westminster Bridge to Blackfriars was artificially created between 1864 and 1870 under the supervision of Joseph Bazalgette. The original suggestion for this improvement came from

Sir Christopher Wren. Its creation narrowed the Thames by 394 ft/120 m, thereby increasing the speed of the river's flow and preventing it from freezing over in winter. The tree-lined Victoria Embankment affords excellent riverside views, especially at night.

Standing next to the Thames is **Cleopatra's Needle (18)**, the oldest monument in London. Carved from rose-pink granite and first erected in the city of On in Egypt nearly 3,500 years ago, the obelisk once stood outside Cleopatra's palace in Alexandria, although it pre-dates her birth by 1,500 years. The Needle was donated by Mohammed Ali, Viceroy of India. Inscribed with hieroglyphs recording the achievements of Rameses the Great, this 69-ft-/21-m-tall, 186-ton obelisk was erected on its present site in 1878. A time capsule containing the morning newspapers, Bradshaw's *Railway Guide*, photographs of the twelve most beautiful Englishwomen of the day, coins, razors, Bibles in different languages and a portrait of Queen Victoria were buried beneath its base. Sadly, city grime has effaced the hieroglyphs and dulled its colour. Its twin obelisk was presented to America and stands in Central Park in New York.

Across the Thames by the Hungerford Footbridge is the **South Bank (19)**, a complex of rather unattractive water-stained concrete post-war buildings dedicated to the arts. The **Royal Festival Hall (20)** is the one jewel among this neo-brutalist jungle and the sole survivor of that 'tonic for the nation', the Festival of Britain in 1951. It is artistically and acoustically one of the finest concert halls in Europe, with a stage capable of holding 100 musicians and a seating capacity for an audience of more than 3,000. The building's spatial delight, its great staircases rising to landings with wonderful views across the river through vast windows, is in marked contrast to the **Queen Elizabeth Hall (21)** and **Purcell Room (22)**, respectively used for small orchestra and chamber music concerts, and the **Hayward Gallery (23)**, housing Arts Council exhibitions, all stark gloomy structures now at the nadir of fashion.

The Greater London Council, before its demise, had begun to bring life to the South Bank by establishing a number of bars, restaurants and bookshops at the Royal Festival Hall. Extensive improvements to the South Bank are planned, including proposals to 'wrap' buildings like the Queen Elizabeth Hall and the Purcell Room with shops.

Outside the Royal Festival Hall are two sculptures by Sieg-fried Charoux, a bronze, *The Motorcyclist* (1962), and the cement and fibreglass *The Cellist* (1958). The stainless steel abstract *Zemran* (1972) outside the Queen Elizabeth Hall is by William Pye. The wooden peacock at the end of the waterfront terrace is by Brian Yale (1978).

Britain's **National Theatre (24)**, also on the South Bank, comprises three separate theatres, the Lyttelton, Olivier and Cottesloe. Daily tours of the theatre include visits backstage and to workshop areas. Drama of the highest standard, ranging from the Shakespearean classics to the controversial avant-garde, form the theatre's extensive repertoire. Live music can usually be heard echoing through the restaurant and exhibition areas. The playwright William Somerset Maugham donated his collec-tion of theatrical paintings, which now adorn the theatre's halls and corridors.

Next to the **National Film Theatre (25)**, underneath Waterloo Bridge, is one of the latest additions to the South Bank Arts Centre, the **Museum of the Moving Image (26)**. MOMI tells the story of man's instinctive love of making pictures move, from the earliest Chinese shadow plays of 2,500 BC to the satellite television revolution and beyond. The museum is more than just a scientific chronicle of film and television, showing the develop-ment of the projector, photo-electric cell, cathode ray tube, CinemaScope lens through to possible future TV technologies; it also stimulates the imagination with timeless and magical images and reflects the medium's influence on our attitudes, manners and appreciation of life through a juxtaposition of artefacts, memorabilia, images, costumes, designs, posters and programmes. Displayed are the tailcoat worn by Fred Astaire in his classic RKO films of the 1930s, the cane and hat worn by Charlie Chaplin in *The Gold Rush*; even a detail of one of the Odeon's foyer carpet tiles, specially crafted from original designs.

On MOMI's outer wall Oscar-winning animator Chuck Jones, creator and developer of Bugs Bunny, Daffy Duck and The Roadrunner, has drawn a 40-ft-/12-m-high mural featuring thirteen of Warner Brothers' favourite characters in a chase sequence. Inside, a staircase transformed into 'The Temple of the Gods' – statues of Valentino, Pickford, Gish and others support a Graeco-Roman pediment whose frieze is dedicated to Charlie Chaplin – stands in tribute to the silent era, when stars were worshipped as near deities.

The short and incredibly dramatic history of the moving image – barely longer than one lifetime – is told chronologically in fifty permanent exhibition areas, commencing with pre-cinema devices, such as zeotropes, phenakistoscopes, praxinoscopes, thaumascopes and other 'persistence of vision' experiments. Working models tell the story of the Lumière brothers, who first displayed films to a paying public in the basement of the Grand Café in Paris on 28 December 1895. At first, Auguste Lumière had declared his invention purely 'a scientific curiosity' with 'no commercial value whatsoever'.

The museum's guides are unlike ordinary guides. A Hollywood 'director' takes visitors around a re-created movie studio and behind the scenes to look at the casting, make-up, editing and publicity departments. Soviet cinema – Lenin declared it the art of the revolution – is presented by a 'Russian soldier' aboard a replica of the 1919 Lenin agit-train cinema carriage. Agit-prop footage of such directors as Vertov and Eisenstein is shown. From France comes the magic of the work of Georges Meliès, Surrealist creations by Spaniards Buñuel and Dali, and the New Wave of Truffaut, Resnais and Godard. Contributions from Germany include the haunting perceptions and perspectives of Murnau's *The Cabinet of Dr Caligari* as well as Lang's *Metropolis*, a futuristic critique of industrial oppression.

A box office 'commissionaire' at a 1930s' cinema is the guide to the major British Cinema exhibit, which also has an accompanying display about the birth of television in that decade. Elsewhere, an animator is at work in space devoted to cartoons. In a TV studio visitors can edit, mix, read the news, conduct a live interview and apply video effects to images of themselves.

A Dalek from the *Dr Who* series directs visitors on to the next exhibit. The latest in interactive video disc technology enables visitors, for example, to ask Alf Garnett on screen for his opinions and get answers. The Moving Image Workshop is the world's first four-screen unit: four screen surfaces (for flat, rear, Perlux and 3D projection) are mounted on a travelling gantry, enabling perfect projection of different film image ratios and light intensities.

The museum's finale portrays a futuristic 'Brave New World' fantasy where visual images come directly to the brain, the eye bypassed by an electronic implant.

Other additions to the South Bank are the **South Bank Crafts Centre (27)**, where craftsmen in jewellery, ceramics and fabrics can be seen at work, and **Gabriel's Wharf (28)**, east of the National Theatre, a market square with craft workshops, a restaurant bar and garden centre, all open for a colourful weekend market.

Temple ⊖

'He who enters Temple's quiet courtyards and open staircases,' Dickens once wrote, 'leaves noise behind.' That hallowed atmosphere, reminiscent of an Oxford or Cambridge college, still remains in Temple's precincts. For centuries Temple has been a major legal centre in Britain. It contains Middle and Inner Temple, two of the four Inns of Court. Barristers dressed in their customary long black gowns and horsehair wigs can be seen on most weekdays striding through Temple's cloisterly alley-ways on their way to the nearby Royal Courts of Justice.

Temple was named after the Knights Templars, an order founded to protect pilgrims visiting the Holy Land. By the early 12th century the Templars were established in High Holborn, but in 1162 they moved south to the area now known as Temple. There they constructed a complex of buildings, of which only their wonderful round Temple Church now remains. When King John was resident in Temple, he signed Magna Carta, kept today in the nearby Public Record Office.

The Templars' white tunic with its red cross proclaimed their immunity from all temporal jurisdiction, save that of the Pope. For their services, the Templars were showered with gifts and became property owners and wealthy bankers. But such power aroused envy: Philip the Fair of France brought charges of sodomy, heresy and blasphemy against the Templars and finally persuaded Pope Clement to suppress the order in 1312.

In London the Templars were arrested, incarcerated in the Tower of London and their properties confiscated. Temple passed into the hands of the Knights Hospitallers, who leased it to lawyers as a hostel, thus beginning Temple's long and fascinating connection with the law.

The earliest records of the lawyers' Inns of Court date from the 15th and 16th centuries, but the Inns existed earlier as societies teaching apprentices in the law, partly because of the lack of English Common Law tuition at universities. Today there are four Inns of Court: Middle Temple, Inner Temple, Gray's Inn (*Chancery Lane* ⊖) and Lincoln's Inn (*Chancery Lane* ⊖). However, students no longer live here and neither are the Inns now major centres of legal instruction. Temple is today occupied by the chambers of practising barristers, although

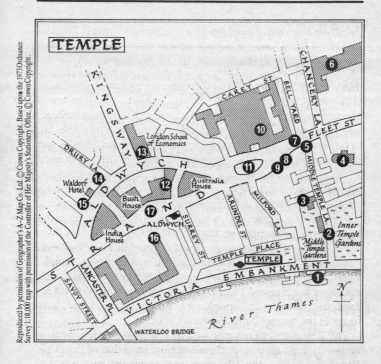

before joining an Inn of Court, students are required to 'keep term' by dining in their future hall. Aimed at fostering comradeship in the legal profession, 'eating dinners' is obligatory on a specified number of occasions before entering pupilage at an Inn of Court.

Almost wholly self-governing and fully independent, each Inn is administered by Masters of the Bench ('Benchers'), generally senior barristers, Queen's Counsel and judges. Barristers have a near monopoly in pleading cases in the higher courts of England and Wales, 'briefed' by solicitors on each client's case. To spend a morning in the public galleries of the Royal Courts of Justice watching members of the legal profession at work can be a fascinating experience.

Also located in the Temple ⊖ area is St Catherine's House, where people of English and Welsh descent can research their family ancestry, and Somerset House, which houses the Probate Registry, a register of wills and testaments dating back to 1382.

⊖   ⊖   ⊖

Walking east from Temple ⊖ past a section of Victoria Embankment Gardens, glance across at the ship moored at King's
Reach, off the Embankment. **HQS Wellington (1)**, once a
Second World War destroyer, is the floating hall of the Honourable Company of Master Mariners, the only livery company
outside the City (*Cannon Street & Mansion House* ⊖*s*).

Walking north up Middle Temple Lane is the area known as
Temple (2); Inner Temple predominantly to the east, and
Middle Temple mainly to the west. Officially, Temple is private
land, but, with the exception of its gardens, the area can be
accessed freely by the public. It is the only remaining part of
London illuminated by gas lamps, lit each night by a lamp-
lighter. Notice the emblems of these two Inns of Court; the
sacrificial Paschal Lamb of Middle Temple, and Pegasus, the
winged horse, of Inner Temple.

In **Middle Temple Hall (3)**, off Fountain Court, students, after
passing their final examinations, are 'called to the Bar' to
become barristers. The hall is predominantly Elizabethan, with
a rare oak double hammer-beam roof of that period. In front of
the bench table, which is 29ft/8.8 m long and made from a single
oak tree, is a small table traditionally known as 'the cupboard'.
In former days students would gather around it while debating a
topic under the tutelage of a senior barrister, known as a
Reader. The present cupboard is reputedly made of wood from
the hatch of Sir Francis Drake's ship, the *Golden Hind*. Many
former Readers' coats of arms are rendered in stained-glass and
adorn the walls, including those of a Mr Jekyll and a Mr Hyde,
names made infamous in Robert Louis Stevenson's famous
novel. Middle Temple Hall has been used to stage lavish entertainments, and it was here that Shakespeare's *Twelfth Night*
received its first performance on 2 February 1601.

At the heart of Temple's alleys and courts is Inner Temple
Hall, a building of relatively recent construction and not open to
the public. Its buttery and crypt are medieval. During dining
terms a horn is blown at 6.45 p.m. to summon members to
supper in the hall.

Temple Church (4) is one of the hidden architectural treasures
of London. Built *c.* 1185, it miraculously escaped the Great Fire
of 1666 and, despite being grievously burned during the last, and
worst, night of the Blitz, the fabric of this extraordinary round
church has survived. It was the first of several round churches in
England, and is probably the finest. Although some have said it

was modelled on the Holy Sepulchre in Jerusalem, it is more probably fashioned after Jerusalem's Dome of the Rock.

Temple Church was built at a time when exciting innovations, following the introduction of the pointed arch, were transforming the heavy semicircular Romanesque style into a new heavenward-aspiring architecture, which came to be known as Gothic. It is a fine example of this transitional style. Purbeck marble was used lavishly and there are some interesting carved grotesque stone heads. An Early English rectangular choir was added early in the 13th century. The crypt survives where once secret initiation ceremonies were performed.

Another relic from the days of the Crusaders is the penitential cell, less than 5 ft/1.5 m long, on the north side where the round church and chancel are joined. Here Walter-le-Bacheler, the Grand Preceptor of Ireland, was left to starve to death for disobeying the Master of the Order. The nine medieval effigies on the floor of the church are thought to be powerful associates of the order rather than Templars themselves. It is argued that the cross-legged position of some of the figures signifies their presence at the Crusades.

In a recess in the south wall of the chancel lies a fine 13th-century sepulchral monument, a Purbeck marble effigy of a bishop fully robed, his feet resting on a dragon. It is thought to be Sylvester de Everdon, Bishop of Carlisle (d. 1255). When the stone coffin was opened in 1810, the bones of a child were found at the foot of the skeleton. These were thought to be the remains of William Plantagenet, infant son of Henry III, who was buried in the church in 1256.

After the power of the Knights Templars was broken, Temple passed into the hands of lawyers. In 1608 James I presented the Benchers with the freehold of the church, the southern half to the Inner Temple, and the northern half to the Middle Temple, on condition that they maintain the church and its services for ever. By custom, members of each Inn continue to sit on separate sides.

The appointment of Temple Church's chaplain, or Master, remains the prerogative of the monarch and is independent of the Bishop of London.

Middle Temple Gateway (5), the 17th-century entrance at the north end of Temple, is open between 8 a.m. and 8 p.m. Note the Latin inscription stating that the gateway was built at the expense of the Middle Temple Society. Inner Temple also has a gateway. This is located below Prince Henry's Room (*Blackfriars* ⊖). Most of this gateway's Jacobean woodwork was renewed in 1906, although the carved panels between the windows are original (1610).

North along Chancery Lane is the massive **Public Record Office (6)** (James Pennethorne, mid-19th century), whose archives contain the records of the British government and English courts of law and include documents dating back to the Norman Conquest. The Public Record Office Museum shows a tiny, but fascinating, fragment of the PRO's collection of millions of documents, which now occupy nearly 90 miles/145 km of shelving.

At the centre of the museum is the Domesday Book, the result of a general survey of England ordered by William the Conqueror in 1085. A detailed inventory of the lands and resources of his newly conquered kingdom, the book is a remarkable fiscal record, noting taxable values; a feudal statement, stating the estates in each county; and a legal record, establishing which tenant rightfully held which estates. In the second half of 1086 at Winchester, a single scribe, under the supervision of an unknown royal official who masterminded the project, summarized the work carried out by groups of commissioners across the country. The survey was originally known as the 'Book of Winchester', but it soon acquired the name Domesday (Day of Judgement), as its evidence was not subject to appeal.

Other exhibits are grouped into ten display cases. The first is called Chancery and the Great Seal. Chancery originated in the writing office of the king's court, presided over by the Lord Chancellor, the king's principal secretary and adviser, and custodian of the great seal used to authenticate all important documents. On show are enrolment letters of patent granting lands in America to William Penn in 1861 as well as the enrolment of the charter of the British Broadcasting Corporation of 1952. In the Exchequer: Taxes and Accounts case are the death-duty account for William Wordsworth (1850–59), a letter from Charles Babbage to the Treasury about progress on his calculating machine (1820) and a letter from John Maynard Keynes reporting the conclusion of the Bretton Woods Conference (1944), which laid the foundations of the post-war international monetary system. In the Law Courts case are documents relating to the special commission for the trial of Sir Walter Ralegh (1603), and minutes of the proceedings at Dorchester Assizes recording the trial and sentence of the Tolpuddle Martyrs (1834). In the display about war is the journal of the English and Spanish Fleets (19–31 July 1588), Admiral Collingwood's account of the Battle of Trafalgar and the death of Nelson (22 October 1805), a plan of the Battle of Waterloo (15 June 1815) and a report on the German use of gas in the First World War. Other cases are Diplomats and Treaties; From Colonies to Commonwealth; Trade, Industry and Transport; The Welfare State, and Modern Policy-Making: the Education Act 1944.

In the last display case, Tracing Your Ancestors, are various census returns and registers. The PRO is a mine of information for tracing the family tree, although not the place to commence research, since the main collections of birth, marriage and death records are held elsewhere (see St Catherine's House, p. 77). There is no central index of names and the PRO does not undertake genealogical research, but records include census returns for the years 1841–81; the Nonconformist registers of baptisms, marriages and burials before 1837; records of service of those who have served in the armed forces, the civil service or the merchant marine; records of criminal trials, imprisonment and transportation, and records of wills and the payment of death duties.

Prior to 1838 official records were located in about fifty different buildings. Although many extensions have been added to the Public Record Office since it first received deposits in the 1860s, the growing problem of storage and public accessibility gave rise to a decision in 1968 to divide the records between here and a new office at Kew (*Outer London*). More than 120,000 visitors a year study some 750,000 documents from the PRO's repository.

Opposite the Public Record Office, the legal wig-making department of Ede and Ravenscroft, robe maker and tailor since 1689, displays a barrister's wig in its rear shop window.

Topped by a bronze griffin, the unofficial badge of the City, **Temple Bar Memorial (7)** (H. Jones, 1880) stands at the point where Strand and Fleet Street meet, marking the boundary between the City and Westminster. Various barriers have stood here since the Middle Ages. The most memorable was Wren's

Temple Bar, a triple gateway built in 1672 and dismantled in 1870 because it obstructed traffic.

Today statues of royalty stand below the griffin. Whenever the sovereign wishes to enter the City, permission is always asked of the Lord Mayor. The Lord Mayor will then present the Mayoral Sword of State to the sovereign, representing his loyalty and the armed might of the City. The sword is immediately returned to him and carried before the royal procession to show that the sovereign is in the City and under protection.

Until the 18th century the severed heads of people executed for treason were displayed here. For a half penny, telescopes could be hired to spy out the expressions on the dead men's faces.

The gatekeeper of Temple Bar once lived in No. 229 Strand, a 17th-century timber-framed, stuccoed building. A neighbouring building, No. 230, built at a slightly later date, has been joined internally to form the **Wig and Pen Club (8)**, a society for lawyers and writers (not open to the general public).

In 1716 **Twining's (9)** the quality tea merchants established premises here; the current building, erected in 1787, is claimed to be the narrowest in London. Above the doorway is the figure of a brightly coloured Chinaman and a lion – the company's trade mark. Every imaginable blend of tea is sold and there is a fascinating museum of tea memorabilia, including the world's largest teapot (*c.* 1850), 30 in/760 mm in height and 13.5 gal/ 61.4 l in capacity, made for the Great Exhibition of 1851, a spectacular example of mid-Victorian exhibitionism with rococo ornamentation. A range of other items dating from 1706 onwards are on display, including a 19th-century Russian samovar, a collection of tea caddies and a TIP – 'to ensure promptness' – box. Tea and coffee houses once nailed TIP boxes to the wall, and patrons desirous of special service would *first* put in their money, hence the word 'tip' for a gratuity.

The cathedral-like proportions of the **Royal Courts of Justice (10)** (G. E. Street, 1882), a dramatic Victorian Gothic style building containing over 1,000 rooms and 3.5 miles/5.6 km of corridors, dominates the east end of the Strand. Opened by Queen Victoria in 1882, it is the Supreme Court of Judicature, consisting of two courts: the High Court of Justice and the Court of Appeal. The High Court consists of three divisions, dealing mainly with civil disputes: the Chancery Division; the Queen's Bench Division and the Probate, Divorce and Admiralty Division. The High Court may, and does, sit at various provincial centres (Scotland and Northern Ireland have their own legal systems), but the majority of cases are heard within this building. In 1972 a third branch of the Supreme Court, called the Crown Court, was created by Parliament. The Crown Court, which deals with the more newsworthy criminal matters, does not sit at the Royal Courts of Justice but at a number of permanent centres throughout England and Wales. The best known of these is the Central Criminal Court, usually referred to as the Old Bailey (*St Paul's* ⊖).

Visitors to the law courts commence their visit in the Great Hall, off which, in galleries, are situated many of the Chancery and Queen's Bench courtrooms. Entering from the Strand, the steps on the left lead to the Lord Chancellor's Court, and to the right, the courtrooms of the Lord Chief Justice and the Master of the Rolls. When the courts are sitting, during legal terms, the public is admitted to the galleries. A morning spent in the public galleries can provide a fascinating insight into the English legal system.

At the right of the entrance from the Strand in the main hall on the ground floor is a small display of judicial dress. Upstairs in this labyrinthine building is a portrait of Lord Stowell, a famous Admiralty judge of the early 19th century, who appears with the silver Admiralty Ceremonial Mace of Office in the shape of an oar. During Admiralty hearings in the Queen's Bench Division this silver oar is placed before the judge, but at other times it is on display with the collection of judicial dress. In the 'Bear Garden' Queen's Bench Masters deal with a constant stream of 'short' applications.

The association of **St Clement Danes (11)** (Wren, 1682) with the Danes is obscure, although it is possible that the first church was built in the 9th century for a colony of Danes, and named after St Clement, the patron saint of Danish mariners. It is known that the church was rebuilt by William the Conqueror, and again in the Middle Ages.

St Clement's escaped the Great Fire, but little more than a decade later it was pronounced structurally unsound, pulled down and rebuilt by Wren. In 1941 the church was completely gutted by bombs. It has since been superbly restored to its former glory. The interior of the church is light and colourful, dark wooden panelling and galleries contrasting with tunnel-vaulting richly decorated with ornate plasterwork. The pulpit has been restored and, like many others of the period, its intricate carving is attributed to Grinling Gibbons (1648–1720). In 1958 St Clement Danes was reconsecrated in the presence of the Queen, and her signature can be seen in the visitors' book at the front of the church.

St Clement Danes is now the official church of the Royal Air Force, who contributed greatly to its restoration. More than 750 slate badges of squadrons and units of the RAF are set into the church floor. On its pillars are the badges of all the Royal Air Force's Commands, and there are many shrines to various foreign air forces. Memorial books list the names of more than 125,000 airmen who have died in action. A chair at the east end of the nave is dedicated to Thelma Bader, wife of Battle of Britain hero Douglas Bader. The crypt has now been converted into a chapel, whose font was donated by the Norwegian Air Force and furnishings by the Royal Netherlands Air Force.

A former rector of the church, the Reverend William Webb-Ellis, invented the game of rugby. As a boy at Rugby school, he achieved notoriety in 1823, when 'with a fine disregard for the rules of football as played in his time, first took the ball in his arms and ran with it, thus originating the distinctive feature of the rugby game'.

Although the bells of St Clement Danes occasionally peal the tune of the nursery rhyme 'Oranges and lemons, say the bells of St Clements', the church actually referred to is probably St Clement, Eastcheap (*Monument* ⊖).

The **Aldwych (12)** area, further to the east, was laid out in 1905. Its name derives from the 'Aldwic', meaning old settlement, an area that King Alfred generously donated to the Danes he had vanquished. Aldwych's half-moon island of buildings, mid-stream of today's heavy traffic, includes the imposing façades of **Australia House**, a very grand piece of *beaux arts* architecture by A. Marshall Mackenzie and A. G. R. Mackenzie, built in 1911–12; **India House** (Sir Herbert Baker, A. T. Scott, 1928–30), and the headquarters of the BBC's famous World Service at **Bush House**. The BBC's External Services broadcast to the world in English and thirty-six other languages. Today 120 million people throughout the world tune regularly to these broadcasts, of whom some 35 million listen to programmes in Hindi, 10 million in Pakistan to the Urdu Service, and more than 2 million in America to the 24-hour-a-day BBC World Service.

St Catherine's House (13) contains important archives for the family historian with English or Welsh ancestors. All records of births, deaths and marriages registered in England and Wales, and deaths at sea, since 1 July 1837 are kept here. Family trees may be difficult to reconstruct, as records are held as individual events, not grouped by family pedigree. If applied for in person, for which a small fee is charged, certificates are normally available in 48 hours. Indexes may be searched free of charge. Fruitless searching can be reduced if family documents, such as a family Bible or baptismal cards, are obtained. It is open to those wishing to trace their family trees into the more distant past to consult the Society of Genealogists (*Farringdon* ⊖) and, if the family concerned is thought to have had a coat of arms, information can be obtained from the College of Arms (*Blackfriars* ⊖).

Behind St Catherine's House is the internationally renowned London School of Economics, in Houghton Street. Further west on the northern side of Aldwych, the **Aldwych Theatre (14)** has two distinct and diverse claims to fame. During the period from 1925 to 1933 a series of farces by Ben Travers were performed, the theatre becoming recognized as the home of farce. From 1960, for 21 years, it was the London base of the Royal Shakespeare Company before the company moved to its present home in the Barbican Centre (*Barbican* ⊖).

The **Strand Theatre (15)**, near by, was designed by Sprague to match the Aldwych, and is known for its long-running production of *No Sex Please We're British*. Sandwiched between the Aldwych and Strand theatres is the **Waldorf Hotel**, with its impressive Ionic columns.

Somerset House (16), a vast Palladian-style quadrangular building designed by Sir William Chambers and allocated for government offices, was the first large office block in England. Built in 1790, it has housed a number of illustrious tenants since then, including the Royal Academy (*Bond Street* ⊖), the Royal Society (*St James's Park* ⊖), the Society of Antiquaries, the Navy, the Stamp Office and even the Hackney Coach and Barge Master. Today the Inland Revenue occupies most of the building.

The Probate Registry's register of wills and testaments, which dates back to 1382, is also housed in the building. It includes the wills of Lord Nelson, Charles Dickens, Sir Winston Churchill, Noel Coward and even the spy Donald Maclean. For a small fee, these and other documents can be examined. Within the building's massive courtyard is a statue (1778) by John Bacon the Elder, depicting George III in a toga with Father Thames at his feet. Somerset House's principal façade faces south on to the Thames, and is best viewed from Waterloo Bridge or the South Bank (*Embankment* ⊖).

In its earlier manifestation Somerset House, the first Renaissance palace in England, had a complex and chequered history. To make way and provide materials for it, many other buildings were demolished. It was built for Lord Protector Somerset in 1547–50. Somerset was later executed and the house given to Princess Elizabeth. In 1603 it was presented to Anne of Denmark. During her residence the house was the scene of many spectacular masques organized by playwright Ben Jonson and architect Inigo Jones. In the late 17th century Italian opera was performed here for the first time in England. In 1775 Queen Charlotte considered living here, but chose Buckingham House instead. The original Somerset House was then demolished.

The most recent arrival at Somerset House is the Courtauld Institute Galleries, the main body of which is a remarkable collection of Impressionist paintings bequeathed to London University by textile magnate Samuel Courtauld in 1931. Housed in the Strand block of the north wing, it includes Manet's *A Bar at the Folies Bergère*, Renoir's *La Loge*, *The Card Players* by Cézanne and a self-portrait by Van Gogh in one of the finest collections of Impressionist and Post-Impressionist paintings outside France.

The superb Princes Gate Collection, bequeathed in 1978 by Count Antoine Seilern, is a vast and scholarly collection spanning more than 600 years of art, with outstanding Italian and Flemish paintings – not least thirty-two by Rubens – and Old Master drawings, including works by Bellini, Tiepolo, Michelangelo and Leonardo. Roger Fry donated his collection of pictures and other works of art by the Bloomsbury Group and the Omega Workshops.

The move of the Courtauld Institute to Somerset House has helped to realize its founder's aim to enable students to study art history alongside original works of art.

London University's King's College adjoins the east wing of

the present Somerset House. Founded in 1829, primarily for members of the Church of England, it was incorporated into the university in 1910.

St Mary-le-Strand (17) (James Gibbs, 1717), a delicate and charming baroque church, beautifully proportioned with a graceful steeple, stands isolated on an island site in the middle of the Strand. A church first stood here in 1147. St Mary-le-Strand was the first church built under the Fifty New Churches Act of 1711. In 1750 Bonnie Prince Charlie is said to have been received into the Anglican Church here during a secret visit to London. The church's interior was remodelled in 1871, and in 1977 the then Poet Laureate, Sir John Betjeman, launched a restoration appeal. However, the church's structure is still in need of repair from the combined effects of time, weather, heavy traffic and the blast of a wartime bomb. Note the decorative plasterwork ceiling, Italian in style but executed by English craftsmen.

Fleet Street, the 'Street of Ink', has been the centre of the printing industry in Britain for nearly 500 years. Until recently nearly all the country's famous national newspaper titles were printed here. Now, however, the newspaper industry has largely deserted the area, the last great manufacturing industry to depart the centre of London.

In medieval times Fleet Street connected London's commercial centre in the City with king, court and council at Westminster. Blackfriars, the area, gained its name from the Dominican monks who settled here in the 13th century. Together with the Knights Templars and the Carmelites of Whitefriars near by, they almost certainly encouraged literacy. Later, the rise of the Inns of Court at Temple, with their enormous capacity for legal documentation, brought additional need for the written and printed word. Fleet Street and its surrounding alleys became densely populated with clerks and scriveners.

Printing began to evolve at the end of the 15th century after the invention of the Gutenberg press. Wynkyn de Worde, an appropriately named printer and apprentice to the father of modern printing, William Caxton, established in the early 16th century the English-speaking world's first commercially run movable-type press 'at the Sign of the Sun' near some of his principal clients, the clergy at St Bride's Church. Other printers followed. Fleet Street soon became the industry's shop window, its back streets crammed with printers and their hand presses. The need for proximity to this flourishing industry brought such characters as Dr Samuel Johnson to the Fleet Street area. His house in Gough Square, where the first edition of his great dictionary of the English language was created, is now a museum.

Until the early 19th century the trades of printing, publishing and bookselling were closely associated. Although Britain's first newspaper, the *Daily Courant*, appeared from an address near Ludgate Circus in 1702, newspapers were then essentially by-products of the printing industry. However, in the second decade of the 19th century printing was revolutionized by the steam-driven rotating cylinder press. Newspapers became economically feasible. After 1855, when the prohibitive Stamp

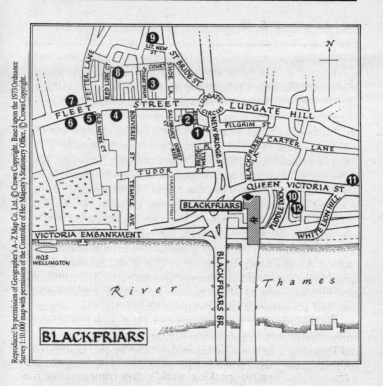

Duty on newspapers was repealed, they flourished, aided by increased literacy, the railways, telegraphy and a fall in paper prices. Print works were then dirty, unhealthy and dangerous; machine rooms thundering in their basements, proof-readers shoehorned into little closets above, with engravers and compositors occupying the best-lit rooms at the top. But as newspapers prospered, proprietors began to build substantial purpose-built works, many as grand monuments to the prestige of their titles as well as to themselves.

At the end of the last century, printing was again revolutionized, this time by mechanical typesetting machines, called 'linotype' by their inventor, Ottmar Mergenthaler. Linotype machines enabled all the words and spaces in a line to be cast in one continuous unit, or 'slug', with automatic space adjustment. At a stroke they did away with the printer's traditional method of stick and frame. In Fleet Street these remarkable pieces of mechanical engineering have only in the last decade been replaced by modern computer and photosetting techniques – a difficult and bitter transition.

The Linotype machine and other archaic techniques had engendered a somewhat fixed, rigid and archaic system of production and labour relations in the printing industry. After a number of trials of strength between printing unions and newspaper managements, a financial crisis was brought about when the *Today* newspaper threatened to break the stranglehold of traditional Fleet Street working practices from the outside.

On 26 January 1986, all Fleet Street changed. That day, the News International group moved their titles – *The Times*, *Sunday Times*, *Sun* and *News of the World* – from Fleet Street to Wapping in London's Docklands (*Outer London*). There, the company introduced a system of direct input, called single key-stroking, by which reporters, sub-editors and advertising staff could keyboard their own material into a central computer without the assistance of a printer. This posed an immediate threat to the livelihood of Linotype operators, the best paid and most highly organized labour group in printing. It precipitated a long and acrimonious labour dispute. By the time the dispute was resolved, a year later, most other Fleet Street titles had announced plans to relocate their printing works, encouraged by the advantages of the new technology and by the substantial property gains their premises had made during the 'Big Bang' financial boom. The *Observer* moved to Battersea. Others have opted for split-site production, with editorial and advertising in one place, and printing works located on cheaper property sites. The *Daily Mirror*, *Sunday Mirror* and *Sunday People*, however, still occupy a tower block to the north of Fleet Street overlooking Holborn Circus, and the editorial offices of the *Daily Mail* at Ludgate House are just south of Blackfriars Bridge.

⊖   ⊖   ⊖

From Blackfriars ⊖ a subway exit leads on to New Bridge Street. The area to the west of New Bridge Street, between Tudor Street and Victoria Embankment, was bought by the Harmsworth empire and is now the best place to appreciate the printing world of late Victorian London. The *Daily Mail* and *Daily Mirror* were born here, and although no single building amounts to great architecture, most are pleasant compositions of brick and stone. Some still have loading bays and gantries revealing their former use. Alfred Harmsworth's Carmelite House was built between 1897 and 1899 by leading newspaper building architects Ellis and Clarke on the corner of Carmelite Street and Tallis Street.

Bride Lane leads to the west from New Bridge Street. Situated here is the **St Bride's Printing Library (1)**, which houses extensive material on all aspects of the printing industry and its history. The library also gives occasional exhibitions.

It was at **St Bride's Church (2)**, quietly tucked away down St Bride's Avenue on the south side of Fleet Street, that church and printer forged their unique relationship – spreading the word. Printing terminology today still reflects those ecclesiastical links. Printing trade unions use the word 'chapel' to denote an organized group of workers, with a 'father' rather than a shop steward at its head. At work a printer 'justifies' a line of type, meaning that he makes it fill a space neatly. In theology, justification is to have all one's 'spaces' filled with Christ's righteousness and thereby be freed from the penalties of sin.

The elaborate steeple of St Bride's, brilliantly lit at night, was designed by Sir Christopher Wren. It inspired local pastry cook William Rich (1755–1811) to invent the modern tiered wedding cake. The church's interior, with its gilt, coloured stucco walls and rich wooden panelling, is a stunning sight during daylight hours. Then, the crown glass of its well-proportioned windows refract the sun's rays into every corner of the building.

Near the font is an effigy of Virginia Dare, who, in 1587, was the first English child to be born in the New World. London's celebrated diarist Samuel Pepys was christened in this font. His graphic 1.25 million word day-by-day account of nine years in the city's life forms the best contemporary record of two terrible disasters that befell London, the Great Fire (*Monument* ⊖) and the Plague.

Underground, the church's crypt contains an historical microcosm of the Fleet Street area: a pavement from the ancient Roman city of Londinium; a Norman altar tomb, and manuscripts from old Fleet Street. It also contains a gruesome 19th-century coffin. To discourage body-snatchers, who once sold cadavers for medical research, corpses were incarcerated in more secure coffins of iron, not wood.

North of Fleet Street in Wine Office Court is one of London's most famous pubs, **Ye Olde Cheshire Cheese (3)**. Rebuilt in 1667, the pub retains many original features and a time-honoured atmosphere. Following Dr Johnson and his contemporaries, then Dickens and his friends, the Cheshire Cheese remembers among its *habitués* a parrot, called Polly. This African grey parrot arrived in a cigar box presented by a Liverpool skipper and went on to achieve world-wide notoriety. Swearing like a cavalry sergeant-major, Polly once interjected some profanity into the conversation of two of Britain's Prime Ministers, Lord Asquith and Neville Chamberlain. Known by a succession of American ambassadors, this cheeky parrot also exchanged tittle-tattle with top press and theatrical celebrities. It is said that on Armistice night at the end of the First World War Polly imitated the sound of 400 champagne corks being pulled without stopping, then fainted from exhaustion. When asked about the Kaiser, she is reported to have retorted, 'To . . . with the Kaiser!' Sadly, this gifted conversationalist is now stuffed and inhabits a glass case mounted in the pub. She died, it is claimed, of apoplexy when women were first allowed to drink at the bar. Polly's obituary appeared in more than 200 newspapers world-wide and was broadcast over the BBC.

The practice of refusing to serve women at the bar continued elsewhere until recent times, notably at **El Vino's (4)**, an exclusive wine bar at No. 47 Fleet Street. Women's rights campaigners, however, finally took the matter to the High Court of Appeal. In November 1982 the Court ruled that El Vino's was breaking the law by continuing to refuse to allow women to stand and be served at the bar.

The smoke-filled, wood-panelled world of furtive conversations at El Vino's does not invite the casual customer and the bar's standards of dress are formal. To be served, gentlemen must wear ties and jackets; ladies, a dress or skirt. Barmen will politely decline to serve ill-attired customers. Clientele are advised to order food to complement the wine, not vice versa. Do not ask for beer.

A few yards west down Fleet Street lies the **Cock Tavern (5)**, yet another of London's famous taverns and the oldest in Fleet Street. Samuel Pepys found Ye Olde Cock Tavern a convenient rendezvous for his flirtations with a certain Mrs Knipp, an actress. It is known that on at least one occasion he lingered too long and felt the unwelcome lash of his wife's hot curling tongs on returning home. The tavern's original frontage is a pleasant reminder of what 'The Street' must have looked like 400 years ago.

A little farther west along Fleet Street, at No. 17, is **Prince**

Henry's Room (6), named after the eldest son of James I. This timbered Tudor room projects out over Fleet Street and was once the Council Chamber of the Duchy of Cornwall. The house's greatest treasure is a rare Jacobean enriched plaster ceiling, which has at the centre of its design the Prince of Wales's feathers, and the letters P H (Prince Henry) in a star-shaped border.

The room now contains the Samuel Pepys Exhibition, a collection of items, prints and paintings about this great man of letters and the lively events of Charles II's London. Samuel Pepys was born in 1633 in Salisbury Court off Fleet Street, the son of a tailor. He was educated at St Paul's School, London, and Trinity Hall and Magdalene College, Cambridge. In 1656 he entered the household of Sir Edward Montagu and his subsequent success was due largely to Montagu's patronage. In June 1660 he was appointed Clerk of the Acts to the Navy Board, one of the principal positions in the Navy, and in 1665 he became the surveyor-general of the victualling office. Seven years later Pepys was appointed to the Admiralty and in his own lifetime he was best known as a great naval administrator, 'the right hand of the Navy'. It was not until 1825, when his remarkable diary was published in heavily abbreviated form, that he earned his widest fame.

The diary had been kept for his own private enjoyment without any thought of publication; hence its unselfconscious charm, vividness and frankness. It began on 1 January 1660, the day General Monck moved troops over the Tweed to begin the march south from Scotland and start the process towards a free parliament. On 11 May Montagu, made General-at-Sea with Monck, set sail to bring Charles II home from exile in Holland. Pepys's diary relates his work at the Navy Board as well as the tension between his convivial life of philandering, music and theatre-going and the domestic demands of his wife, Elizabeth. Sadly, he was forced to abandon his diary in May 1669, fearing that eye-strain was causing him to go blind.

Across the road, a few yards east down Fleet Street, glance up at the ancient clock tower of **St Dunstan-in-the-West (7)**. In Dickens's most famous novel, David Copperfield and Betsy Trotwood stopped to gaze at it. Every quarter of an hour two strange-looking figures, Gog and Magog, move together to strike the chime. They represent the legendary giants, originally

known as Gogmagog and Corineus – the former an ancient
inhabitant of Britain, the latter a Trojan invader – the leading
warriors in a fictional conflict that resulted in the founding of
Albion's (England's) mythical capital city, New Troy, in 1000
B C. Below the clock is a statue of Queen Elizabeth I, which,
before the Great Fire of London, stood upon Lud Gate at the
foot of Fleet Street.

More than one great genius has found inspiration within St
Dunstan's cold stone walls. John Donne, the poet, was the
church's vicar between 1624 and his death in 1631. One of his
closest companions was a local ironmonger, Izaak Walton, a
vestryman here from 1629 until he felt obliged to flee from
London following the defeat of the Royalist forces at Marston
Moor in 1644. Walton found time to write a biography of
Donne, as well as one of the enduring masterpieces of English
literature, *The Compleat Angler*, published in St Dunstan's
churchyard in 1653.

Those who venture through the portals of this little church will
find an unexpected sight. This Anglican house of worship has
been lent to the Romanian Eastern Orthodox community in
London, who have erected a beautiful iconostatis across the
nave. The stark contrast between the dark and introspective
Gothic interior of St Dunstan's at one end of Fleet Street, and
the classical brilliance of St Bride's at the other could not be
more marked.

North of Fleet Street in a maze of narrow courts and alleys lies
Dr Johnson's House (8). Another of England's famous 18th-
century literary figures, Dr Samuel Johnson wrote the first
edition of his great dictionary of the English language in this
house at No. 17, Gough Square. Published on 15 April 1755, it
immediately took its place as the standard authority, a great
improvement on its predecessors. His dictionary's most obvious
defect, however, arose from Johnson's ignorance of the early
forms of the English language. He failed to trace its growth
historically, but simply defined the actual senses of words as
employed by the 'best authors'. He held that fullest development of English had been reached in the days of Shakespeare,
Spenser and others, and that it was needless to go back further
than Sidney.

While the dictionary was still in preparation, Johnson published his *Vanity of Human Wishes* in January 1749, a collection

of poems scarcely rivalled in their peculiar style of grave moral
eloquence. They were profoundly admired by Byron and Sir
Walter Scott. Also that year, David Garrick, his friend and
manager of the Drury Lane Theatre, put on Johnson's play
Irene. Johnson, however, proved not to be a dramatic author,
then the most profitable form of authorship, and his play was a
failure.

Johnson loved London, of which he said, 'By seeing London,
I have seen as much of life as the world can show.' He later
added, 'When a man is tired of London, he is tired of life; for
there is in London all that life can afford.' Now a museum, his
house contains a pleasant variety of Johnsoniana. Books, 18th-
century engravings and mezzotints adorn the walls, and there is
a fascinating collection of literary memorabilia.

Tucked underneath the London International Press Centre at
the northern end of Shoe Lane is the **Cartoonist (9)**, another of
Fleet Street's plentiful supply of ale houses. Its walls are covered
with hundreds of original cartoons from Britain's famous daily
newspapers.

Returning to, and just to the east of, Blackfriars ⊖, British
Telecom have established their **Telecom Technology Showcase
(10)** to commemorate 200 years of progress in telecommunications. Displays range from the earliest forms of naval telegraph
systems to futuristic new developments. A 'fun-to-play' push
button exhibition, the showcase also looks back fondly at the old
call boxes, manual exchanges and telephone paraphernalia of
yesteryear.

Further east is the **College of Arms (11)** (M. Emmett and F.
Sandford, 1678). Since the time of the Crusades, heralds have
carried their masters' coats of arms on banners, shields and
surcoats. Eventually, heralds came to be responsible for the
regulation of these ancient marks of identification. In 1484
Richard III granted the heralds a charter of incorporation as the
College of Arms, requiring them to keep records of arms and
family descents. Today, in addition to researching family history, processing applications for new coats of arms and adjudicating on such matters, the thirteen Officers of Arms forming
the College are also involved in the great ceremonies of state,
such as coronations and the State Opening of Parliament.

The College's premises, Derby House, were granted in 1555. After the Great Fire, they were built as an open quadrangle. Only the Court Room and the adjoining waiting room are open to the public. The best exhibition about heraldry is to be found in the Heralds' Museum at the Tower of London (*Tower Hill* ⊖.)

In 1956 the City gained the **Mermaid Theatre (12)**, its first new theatre since the 16th century. Founded five years earlier by Bernard Miles and wife, Josephine Wilson, in their St John's Wood home, its success prompted the Corporation to grant Miles and 'other poor players of London' the lease of a war-damaged Victorian warehouse in Puddle Dock, south of Queen Victoria Street. It has a children's theatre and a restaurant overlooking the Thames. Return to Blackfriars ⊖ by the raised walkway.

Cannon Street ⊖ & Mansion House ⊖

Since the 12th century craftsmen have banded together into trade guilds, known in the City as livery companies, a name that derives from their distinctive livery, or uniform. The colourful halls of many of the ninety or so surviving livery companies are situated in the Cannon Street ⊖ and Mansion House ⊖ area. Based originally on religious, trade or fraternal lines, the companies' enterprise has spread far afield and many are still highly active in their respective trades. They also own some of the most valuable secular treasures of gilt and plate to be found in the City.

Guilds, or mysteries (via misteries from the Italian *mestiere*, a trade), once wielded sweeping power over their trades. Not only did they control prices, wages, working conditions, welfare and admission, but their monopoly powers also extended to exercising rigorous quality control with wide powers of inspection and confiscation, together with severe punishment, for poor workmanship.

All liverymen receive the Freedom of the City. Lowest ranking liverymen, known as freemen, swear an oath of loyalty to their company and are granted a certificate of freedom. This is taken to the Chamberlain of the Corporation of London. There, a further oath is sworn, the roll signed and the right hand of friendship extended before a certificate of Freedom of the City is presented in a red case. By seniority, freemen become eligible to join the Court of Assistants and thereafter, rising through various degrees of warden, to be master. Liverymen still form the sole electorate for the appointment of the sheriffs and the Lord Mayor of London. Women can gain freedom of a company or the City.

Most livery companies engage in substantial charitable and educational activities promoting their industry, if it still exists, or a modern successor.

Many members of the royal family today have both substantive and honorary connections with livery companies. The Queen is a freeman and is associated with the Drapers; the Queen Mother with the Shipwrights, Grocers, Merchant Taylors and Musicians, and the Prince of Wales with the Fishmongers, Master Mariners and Shipwrights.

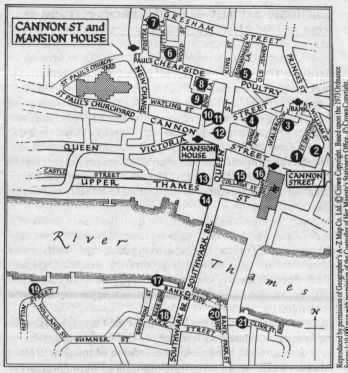

Of the companies now in existence, just over a third possess handsome halls and other treasures. Unfortunately, these halls are not generally open to the public except on special days during the summer. Visits are co-ordinated by the City of London Information Centre (*St Paul's* ⊖). Admission is also possible by written application. To view treasure collections is normally a lengthy business, involving obtaining permission from each company's governing body, or 'Court'.

True Londoners, or Cockneys, must be born within the sound of Bow Bells, the bells of the church of St Mary-le-Bow. Cockneys, recognizable by their distinctive accent and vernacular, gained their name from contemptuous country folk, who derived 'cockney' from 'cock-ey', meaning 'cock's egg' the derogatory term for a misshapen egg. Bow bells also persuaded pantomine hero Dick Whittington, a real person and four times Lord Mayor of London, not to forsake the city. Whittington first made his way to London after hearing its streets were paved with gold. Ballads tell that Whittington, after rising to serve three terms as Lord Mayor, determined to leave London. But on hearing Bow Bells chime and interpreting them as saying 'Turn again, Whittington, thrice Mayor of London', he returned for a fourth term. His extensive public benefactions are remembered to this day.

South of the Thames across Southwark Bridge is an area known as Bankside, where bear-baiting, brothels, inns and famous Elizabethan playhouses – the Globe, the Rose, the Swan – once flourished outside the City Council's strict jurisdiction. The Shakespeare Globe Museum contains reconstructions of the theatre and the plans for a full-scale working replica.

Mansion House, the Lord Mayor's residence, is situated directly opposite Bank ⊖, some way from Mansion House ⊖.

⊖   ⊖   ⊖

Across from Cannon Street ⊖, in a niche in the wall of the Overseas-Chinese Banking Corporation, is an irregularly shaped piece of stone, known as **London Stone (1)**. Its origin and purpose are uncertain. Recent excavations immediately behind the original position of this stone, which uncovered the gateway of the Roman governor's palace, suggest that it may have been a *milliarium*, a distance-measurement point on Roman roads.

A few yards to the east of the London Stone lies **St Mary Abchurch (2)**, the site of a church since the 12th century. After the Great Fire, Sir Christopher Wren gathered some of his most talented associates to rebuild the City's churches, all of which, save one, had been damaged. His main contribution to the new St Mary was an architecturally challenging dome resting unaided by buttresses. Grinling Gibbons (1648–1721), the most prolific and talented woodcarver of his day, created the dominating reredos beneath the dome. In 1708 William Snow depicted the worship of Heaven on the dome's ceiling. At its centre, the Divine Name written in Hebrew characters is surrounded by rays of glory, angels and cherubs in worship beneath. It took five painstaking years to reassemble the beautiful decorative reredos after a bomb blast in the last war fragmented it into 2,000 pieces. William Gray built the canopied pulpit (1685); the door cases, font cover and rails. James II's royal coat of arms (*c.* 1686) are by William Emmett, and Robert Bird created the gilded pelican weather-vane now situated above the north door.

In many ways **St Stephen Walbrook (3)** was the forerunner to
Wren's great masterpiece, St Paul's Cathedral (*St Paul's* ⊖).
Both churches combine a cross-in-square plan with a large
centralized dome. Views of the dome's pretty copper exterior
and lantern can be glimpsed between buildings. William Newman carved the unusual semi-elliptical altar table, communion
rails, the reredos, canopied pulpit and font cover (1679). Benjamin West (1738–1820), the only American to become President of the Royal Academy, painted *The Martydom of St
Stephen* on the north wall of the church. Sir John Vanbrugh
(1664–1726), dramatist and architect of Castle Howard and
Blenheim Palace, is buried in St Stephens. A controversy raged
over whether a 10-ton marble altar, sculpted by Henry Moore
and described by opponents as a 'giant piece of cheese', should
adorn the church. It was agreed that the sculpture will stay.

The Reverend Dr Chad Varah founded the Samaritans here
in 1953. It is now a world-wide organization, with more than 100
branches overseas and nearly 200 in Britain.

In 1953 in nearby Victoria Street archaeologists uncovered a
Roman temple dating from shortly before AD 200. Its existence, on the east bank of the Walbrook stream, had been
suspected since the discovery in 1889 of a relief of Mithras, a god
of light popular among Roman legionnaires. The Walbrook
stream, which now flows underground, is thought to have once
been sacred, judging from the number of votive offerings recovered from its depths. What is left of the **Temple of Mithras (4)**
has been reconstructed in front of Temple House, a short
distance from its original site. Its sculptures and other finds are
now at the Museum of London (*Barbican* ⊖).

During the Middle Ages the great trade guilds vied among
themselves for power and influence. Eventually twelve companies emerged as the 'Great Companies', with the Mercers
having the greatest civic precedence among them. **Mercers' Hall
(5)** (E. Noel Clifton, 1958), in Ironmonger Lane, is at the eastern
end of Cheapside, an area that once was medieval London's
chief market place – *ceap* or *chepe* being the Old English for
'market'. The term 'mercer' is derived from the French *mercier*,
a dealer in small wares. Since the 14th century Mercers had been
leading merchants in London, trading in a variety of goods, but
mainly textiles.

The 250 or so Mercers possess a major plate collection dating from the 15th century, a series of 18th- and 19th-century English crystal chandeliers, and the Leigh Cup, given by a former Master and mentioned in an inventory of 1569. The present hall and chapel were rebuilt after the Second World War, incorporating fittings from its predecessor.

Saddlers' Hall (6) (L. Sylvester Sullivan, 1958) is located at the west end of Cheapside, in Gutter Lane. The Guild of Saddlers dates from 1272. For the election of its Master, Saddlers make use of a ballot box made in 1619 for the East India Company. The painted and inlaid box is designed to carefully conceal how members cast their votes. The company also possesses a funeral pall dating from 1508.

Many exhibitions of gold, silver and porcelain ware are given at **Goldsmiths' Hall (7)** (Philip Hardwick, 1835), which is located on a magnificent island site in Foster Lane, north of Cheapside. The Goldsmiths' Company, the oldest of the country's four hallmarking authorities, assays and hallmarks up to a million items each month, and maintains a technical advisory service on the manufacturing and research of precious metals. It has statutory responsibility for upholding the standard of gold, silver and platinum items and ensuring that the precious metal content of the coin of the realm does not fall below a legally prescribed minimum at the annual trial of the pyx ceremony. The Goldsmiths were also the first bankers in London.

A Roman stone altar to Diana is displayed in the Hall's Court Room, and the Exhibition Room's splendid collection of gold and silver plate includes a gilt dish and ewer by Paul de Lamerie (1741), and the famous Bowes Cup, a 16th-century cup and cover of silver gilt and rock crystal with the armorial bearings of Alderman Sir Martin Bowes in coloured enamel. It is believed that this cup was used by Elizabeth I at her coronation banquet in 1558.

In 1334 the bells of **St Mary-le-Bow (8)**, Bow Bells, announced a nightly curfew beginning at 9 p.m. and ending at 5.45 a.m. and, until 1847, they continued to peal out at these times. To be a Cockney, one must be born within earshot of Bow Bells. It was their sound that inspired Dick Whittington to return to London and serve a fourth term as mayor. During the Second World War the B B C broadcast the church's twelve-bell chime to bring hope to millions throughout the world. The chime achieved the accolade 'the most famous peal in Christendom'.

The Normans built the first stone church in London here in 1087, a decade after the original wooden Saxon church on this site was destroyed by fire. The Norman arches, or bows, which give the church its name, can still be seen in the crypt standing among roughly constructed Saxon foundations and Roman bricks. The Court of Arches, the chief judicial court of the Archbishop of Canterbury since the 12th century, at one time sat in this crypt, adjudicating cases of ecclesiastical law and confirming the election of bishops.

After the Great Fire, Wren produced a magnificent tower and steeple for the church. Together with the church's walls, they were the only parts to survive bombing during the Second World War. The tower, however, was later found to be unsafe and was rebuilt stone by stone. The weather-vane for Wren's steeple is a winged dragon 8 ft 10 ins/2.69 m long. In 1674 daring stuntman Jacob Hall rode upon it as it was hoisted 239 ft/72.8 m to the top.

The church's restoration was completed in 1962. A carved wooden rood designed by John Hayward, a gift from the people of Germany, hangs from the renovated ceiling. Hayward also designed the etched glass screen at the entrance to the crypt and one of his modern stained-glass windows in the east wall shows the bombed City churches grouped around Mary cradling St Mary-le-Bow in her arms. The Norwegian Chapel on the north side is dedicated to Norwegian resistance fighters. The key-stones of the arches in the church, once the faces of angels, are now likenesses of those responsible for the church's restoration.

Just off Bow Lane, in Groveland Court, is **Williamson's (9)** pub and restaurant. Once the residence of Sir John Fastolff, Shakespeare's model for the dissolute bon viveur, Falstaff, the building has also been the official residence of the Lord Mayor of London. One Lord Mayor entertained William III and Mary here, and was presented with the pair of wrought-iron gates now to be seen at the end of the alley. In 1739 Robert Williamson, a silk merchant of Bow Lane, founded a hotel here, which was run by his family for generations.

Further south down Bow Lane is **Ye Olde Watling (10)**, built by Wren in 1668 and reportedly frequented by him while he designed St Paul's Cathedral. Britain's most famous Roman road, Watling Street, once ran near by.

St Mary Aldermary (11) (Wren, 1682), the older Mary, stands opposite Mansion House ⊖. Rebuilt by Wren after the Great Fire, it possesses an interesting fan-vaulted ceiling. One unusual feature is a blank monument near the altar, which, the story goes, was installed by a woman in memory of her husband – she remarried before she could think of an epitaph for him.

On the corner opposite St Mary Aldermary is **Sweetings (12)**, one of London's oldest fish restaurants and a 150-year-old bastion of the City. Its four bars have a delightful Edwardian atmosphere, with high ceilings and marble counters, one bar exclusively for sandwiches and three for oysters, shellfish salads and a range of soundly prepared traditional English fish dishes.

Situated south of Mansion House ⊖, at the foot of Garlick Hill, is the church of **St James Garlickhythe (13)** (Wren, 1683). Known as 'Wren's Lantern' because of its large expanse of clear glass windows, the church was originally founded in the 12th century. It has a magnificent organ case containing a Father Smith organ of 1697. A mummified body, at least 400 years old and in an almost perfect state of preservation, was discovered here in 1839. It now stands in a glass case near the porch.

Vintners' Hall (14) (Roger Jarman, 1671) is across the road in Vintners Place. Vintners celebrate with five cheers instead of the customary three, this tradition, according to legend, marking the occasion, in 1363, when they entertained five kings: Edward II of England, David of Scotland, John of France and the kings of Denmark and Cyprus.

Together with the Dyers' Company and the Crown, the Vintners own all the swans on the Thames. Each year, in late July or early August, at the ceremony of 'Swan Upping', Her Majesty's Swan Keeper, the Vintners' Swan Marker and the Dyers' Swan Marker, assisted by the swanherds, round up new cygnets to mark their beaks – one nick for the Dyers, two for the Vintners and none for the Queen. A small fleet of boats, banners flying and bearing this colourful entourage, travel up the Thames from Tower Bridge to 'up' the birds, sometimes in lively scrimmages. The voyage ends at Henley with a traditional banquet at a riverside inn, the main course a dish of swan meat.

One of the twelve 'Great' livery companies, the Vintners' received its charter in 1364 and still plays an important role in its trade. In 1973 the company was authorized to set up a Wine Standards Board to enforce new EEC wine laws. Some free vintners are privileged to sell wine on their premises without an excise licence. Each July, after the Master's election, the company's procession to St James Garlickhythe is preceded by the white-smocked wine porters sweeping the way.

The present Vintners' Hall has a beautifully carved Jacobean staircase (Woodroffe, 1673), one of the finest in London. The company also has an impressive collection of glass and wine labels, an ancient tapestry dating from 1466 and a painting after Van Dyck of the Vintners' patron saint, St Martin, dividing his cloak with the beggar. A more unusual possession is a 17th-century silver-gilt vessel in the form of a milkmaid. New members are expected to drink from its two 'cups' without spilling the contents.

St Michael Paternoster Royal (15) (Wren, 1694) combines the name of an old thoroughfare, Paternoster Lane, and a corruption of La Reole, near Bordeaux, the source of local vintners' wine. Records date the church from the middle of the 13th century. It was rebuilt by Wren and renovated after the Blitz. The church's tower, completed in 1713, is noted for its elaborate three-stage octagonal lantern. Dick Whittington, who lived in nearby College Hill, is buried here and a fountain and garden commemorate him. A modern stained-glass window depicts this munificent public benefactor standing with his cat on one of London's legendary golden streets.

Around the corner in Dowgate Hill is **Skinners' Hall (16)**. The wearing of furs was once strictly controlled by various sumptuary laws stipulating the dress to be worn by different ranks of society. As furs were once the exclusive province of aristocracy, Skinners gained a high degree of importance, but it also brought conflict with other 'Great' livery companies. In 1484 the Lord Mayor was required to settle a dispute about the order of civic precedence with the Merchant Taylors Company. He decided that the companies should alternate annually between sixth and seventh positions and to bury the hatchet, he required that they should regularly entertain each other, an arrangement that continues today. The expression 'at sixes and sevens' derives from this ruling.

The Skinners' Company received its first charter in 1327 and a hall has probably existed on this site since 1380. Rebuilt after the Great Fire, a handsome new front was added in 1778. The Skinners' Dining Hall contains a series of fifteen panels by Frank Brangwyn showing scenes about the fur trade and the company's history. The staircase is *c*. 1670, as is the Virginia cedar panelling in the Court Room. An 18th-century Russian glass chandelier hangs in the Outer Hall, and over the chimney piece in the Great Hall are the Royal Stuart Arms, set up originally in April 1660 to commemorate the Skinners' daring in entertaining Royalist General Monck more than a month before Charles II returned to the throne.

During the Middle Ages and the 16th and 17th centuries, **Bankside (17)**, on the south side of Southwark Bridge, was the equivalent to today's West End. Flourishing out of reach of the City Council's strict jurisdiction, this raffish area was notorious for bear-baiting, brothels, inns, gardens and the famous Elizabethan playhouses – Shakespeare's Globe Theatre (1599), the Rose (1595) and the Swan (1595). However, the austerity of the Puritan era brought Bankside into decline, and the playhouses were closed in 1642. The area rose again in the 18th and 19th centuries as a thriving commercial centre. Two 18th-century houses still stand on Bankside. No. 49, called Cardinal's Wharf (*c.* 1710), occupies the site of a famous Elizabethan brothel called the Cardinal's Hat, and Nos. 51–2 (1712), called Provost's Lodgings, is now the residence of the Provost of Southwark Cathedral (*Monument* ⊖).

In 1992 a replica of Shakespeare's Globe is to open within yards of its original Bankside location – the third Globe Theatre to occupy this site. The original Globe quickly became London's most popular theatre, attracting the greatest playwrights, actors and audiences. Shakespeare owned a share of the Globe and it saw the first performance of many of his plays, among them *Hamlet*, *Othello* and *King Lear*. On 29 June 1613 a 'prop' cannon ignited the thatched roof of the first Globe during a performance of *Henry VIII* and the theatre burned down in two hours. By the time it was rebuilt, with a tiled roof, Shakespeare had retired to Stratford. The Globe survived until its closure by the Puritans in 1642, and two years later was pulled down to make way for tenements.

A converted Georgian warehouse in nearby Bear Gardens houses the **Shakespeare Globe Museum (18)**, containing exhibits about the history of Bankside during the Bard's day, models of Elizabethan and Jacobean theatres, and a reconstruction of a 1616 stage. It also contains an exhibition about the world-wide effort to establish the International Shakespeare Globe Centre at Bankside. King George IV, Sir Walter Scott, Coleridge,

Thackeray, Garrick and Nash all tried and failed to rebuild the Globe, but current plans for the rebirth go further, including: the Inigo Jones theatre, an elegant private theatre of the period, based on two surviving drawings by this the earliest English Renaissance architect; an audio-visual archive and library; an education centre, and a grand piazza surrounded by shops, apartments and restaurants.

Shakespeare described the Globe as 'this wooden "O"'. Ever since the discovery of the copy of Dutchman Johannes de Witt's sketch of the interior of the Swan, made during a visit to London in 1596, scholars have been collating such fragmentary information in the hope of arriving at an acceptable three-dimensional reconstruction of a Shakespearean public playhouse. The new Globe will be built using traditional methods with seasoned oak, wattle and daub. It will be a pure 24-sided oak-framed polygon with stark whitewashed external walls and timbers. The theatre will hold 1,500 people, with seating arranged on three tiers and standing room in a yard open to the skies around the apron-like stage.

Bankside Gallery (19), the home of the Royal Society of Painters in Watercolours and the Royal Society of Painter-Etchers and Engravers, is the national centre for the appreciation of watercolours, prints and drawings, maintaining permanent diploma collections as well as hosting a wide variety of loan exhibitions.

A few paces from the river, and with excellent views over to St Paul's, is the **Anchor Inn (20)**, a tavern that dates back to Shakespearean times. Burned in the great conflagration that destroyed the borough of Southwark in 1676, a decade after the Great Fire, the pub now has a rambling 18th-century exterior, a minstrels' gallery, oak beams and tiny bars and snugs. In 1939 the fabric of the inn was considered unsound and condemned for demolition, but the outbreak of war prevented its destruction. The pub contains a collection of Elizabethan objects found during renovations. A plaque in the Ale Bar records the great high tide of 1928.

Wherever the English language is spoken today, the phrase 'in the clink' conjures up the image of prison. It derives from reputedly the oldest prison in England, the Clink, built over 850 years ago within Winchester Palace, the London residence of the Bishop of Winchester. For more than 500 years the Clink operated as a private prison, its prisoners treated according to how much they could afford to pay – the higher the fee, the lighter the shackles.

The Clink Exhibition (21) is housed on the actual site where numerous prostitutes, debtors and religious martyrs were confined and horribly tortured. Amongst its exhibits are the 'Stewehouse' Room, devoted to the history of Southwark's brothels, and a selection of unusual plates (adults only) depicting all kinds of unseemly goings-on.

Monument ⊖

The Great Fire destroyed almost all the medieval City. It began shortly before 2 a.m. on 2 September 1666. A workman in Farriners, bakers to the king, in Pudding Lane, smelled burning and aroused the household. They hurried to safety over roof-tops but their maid, too timid to follow, was engulfed in the flames. Aided by strong easterly winds, the fire spread quickly, although City authorities initially underestimated the serious-ness of the blaze. Informed about it, the Lord Mayor declared the matter unworthy of his attention and returned to bed. 'Pish!' he said, 'A woman might piss it out.'

In only a few days, however, more than 400 acres/162 ha. inside and outside the City walls had been destroyed, including 89 churches, 44 livery halls and 13,200 houses. Although only 9 lives were lost, 80,000 citizens were made homeless. The Tower of London was saved only because the navy blew up nearby houses as a fire-break. Today, sadly, nearly all that remains of the medieval city are quaint street names and their layout.

Although the Great Fire destroyed one London, the catas-trophe gave architect Christopher Wren (*St Paul's* ⊖) his extra-ordinary opportunity to create an entirely new city. To mark the Great Fire, he was commissioned to construct a marvellous column towering 202 ft/61.5 m above the ground, called simply 'Monument'. Appointed one of the three Royal Commissioners for the rebuilding of the City, then Surveyor-General of the King's Works, Wren transformed the City's skyline with new stone churches replacing the predominantly wooden structures of the Middle Ages. Some of the most beautiful, especially St Magnus the Martyr, can be seen from Monument ⊖.

South of the Thames over London Bridge is Southwark Cathedral, London's first complete Gothic church and, apart from Westminster Abbey, its largest survivor in that style. Its airy and colourful interior, despite many years of neglect and damage, has been restored to much magnificence. A remarkable 'time capsule' has been discovered in the cathedral's Chapter House: the 19th-century St Thomas's Hospital operating theatre, a chilling reminder of the early days of surgery.

Even more gruesome, and not for the faint-hearted, is the London Dungeon, a vivid re-creation of the darker chapters of

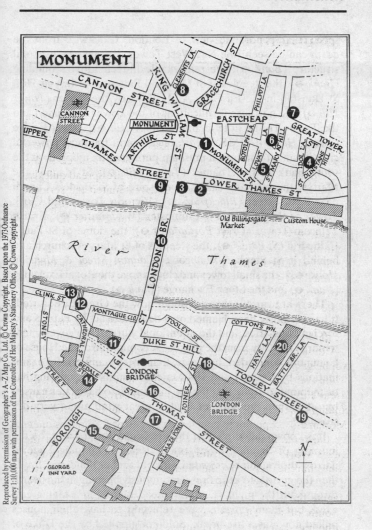

British history. Visitors enter a three-dimensional reconstruction of Pudding Lane during the Great Fire to be bombarded by the cries of fleeing Londoners and the smell of burning timbers.

⊖   ⊖   ⊖

Monument (1), the tallest isolated stone column in the world, commemorates the Great Fire. For a small sum, the 311-step climb to perch on the windy caged ledge at the top gives a spectacular panoramic view of London. Clockwise from the north can be seen: the Nat West Tower, Britain's tallest solid structure (*Bank* ⊖); the remarkable hi-tech Lloyd's building (*Bank* ⊖); the steeples of St Margaret Pattens, St Mary-at-Hill, St Dunstan-in-the-East and All Hallows-by-the-Tower (*Tower Hill* ⊖); the northern fortifications of the Tower of London and the Tower Thistle hotel behind (*Tower Hill* ⊖); Tower Bridge (*Tower Hill* ⊖); HMS *Belfast*, once one of the most powerful cruisers afloat and now a museum permanently moored on the south bank of the Thames (*Tower Hill* ⊖); St Magnus the Martyr; the wedding cake-shaped spire of St Bride's Church near Fleet Street (*Blackfriars* ⊖); Victoria Tower and Clock Tower at the Palace of Westminster (*Westminster* ⊖); British Telecom Tower (*Great Portland St* ⊖); the dome of St Paul's Cathedral (*St Paul's* ⊖); the steeples of St Mary Abchurch and behind it St Stephen Walbrook (*Cannon Street & Mansion House* ⊖s); the small tower and clock above the Royal Exchange (*Bank* ⊖) and the Stock Exchange (*Bank* ⊖).

There are various theories about how the Great Fire started. It has variously been blamed on a deliberate act by Papists and foreign emissaries, and the intentional work of the government to purge the City from the plague. A committee of the House of Commons concluded, however, that 'after many careful examinations by Council and His Majesty's ministers, nothing has been found to argue that the fire in London to have been caused by other than the hand of God, a great wind and a very dry season.'

It is known definitely that the fire began about 2 a.m. on the morning of Sunday, 2 September 1666, in Pudding Lane, a narrow thoroughfare crowded with old timber buildings. It was then the custom to keep fires continuously burning in the hearth throughout the night. The fire spread rapidly in a raging east wind, but many citizens were reluctant to have their houses pulled down as a fire-break. Soldiers supplied by the Duke of York, however, began blowing up buildings, enabling the progress of the fire eventually to be stopped. *The London Gazette* of 8 September 1666 recorded:

> By the favour of God, the wind slackened a little on Tuesday night and the flames meeting with Brick-buildings at the Temple, by little and little it was observed to lose its force on that side, so that on Wednesday morning we began to hope well, and his Royal High-

ness never despairing nor slackning his personal care, wrought so well that day, assisted in some parts by the Lords of the Council before and behind it, that a stop was put to it at the Temple Church, neer Holborn Bridge, Pie Corner, Aldersgate, Cripplegate, neer the lower end of Coleman Street, at the end of Basinghall Street, and by the Postern, at the upper end of Bishopsgate Street, and Leadenhall Street, at the Standard in Cornhill, at the Church in Fanchurch Street, near Clothworkers' Hall in Mincing Lane, and at the Tower Dock. On Thursday, by the blessing of God it was wholly beat down and extinguished.

The toll of damage was considerable. Of approximately 448 acres/181 ha. inside the City walls, only about 75 acres/30 ha. remained unburnt. An Act of Parliament was passed for the rebuilding of the City. The King ordered a survey and prohibited the erection of 'hasty and unskilful buildings' or the use of any material other than stone or brick for building. To raise the finance the City was empowered to levy a duty on all coals brought into the Port of London. The Act of 1666 also ordered the fire to be commemorated:

And the better to preserve the memory of this dreadful Visitation, be it further enacted, That a Colume of Pillar of Brase or Stone be erected on or as neere unto the place where the said Fire soe unhappily began as conveniently may be in perpetuall Remembrance thereof, with such Inscription thereon, as hereafter by the Maior and Court of Aldermen in that behalfe be directed.

Several designs were prepared. Finally, a design by Sir Christopher Wren in collaboration with Robert Hooke was selected and building began in 1671 and was completed in 1677. Monument was erected on the site of the former St Margaret's Church, the first church to perish in the fire. It was built there and its height of 202 ft/61.5 m was made equal to its distance from the King's baker's house in Pudding Lane where the fire began.

Monument is a fluted Doric column constructed of Portland Stone. Its consists of a pedestal about 21 ft/6.4 m square and 40 ft/12 m high, with a plinth 28 ft/8.5 m square, and a shaft 120 ft/36.5 m high and 15 ft/4.5 m in diameter; on the abacus is a balcony encompassing a moulded cylinder, which supports a flaming urn of gilt bronze, symbolizing the fire. On three of the pedestal's panels are Latin inscriptions recording the City's destruction (north), its restoration (south), and the years and mayoralties in which Monument was constructed (east). On the west panel is a sculptured design by Caius Gabriel Cibber, showing the King affording protection to the desolate City, and freedom to its rebuilders and inhabitants. At first Monument was used by the Royal Society for scientific experiments.

Suffocating in the grimy traffic of Lower Thames Street near Monument, **St Magnus the Martyr (2)** (1671–6) has one of the most spectacular interiors of any Wren church in the City, as well as an impressive bronze of its patron saint. In *The Wasteland* author and poet T. S. Eliot described its 'inexplicable splendour of Ionian white and gold'. Light bursts through the church's brilliant circular stained-glass windows. Double gallery stairs with turned balusters, panelled Corinthian columns and glass screen form the entrance to its richly furnished interior. Tall, fluted Ionic columns support the barrel-vaulted nave. Sword-rests, candle brackets and shrines abound, and a painting of Moses, Aaron and cherubs overlooks the church's splendid altar-piece. Above the altar is a carved pelican. According to legend, the pelican plucks its breast to feed its young with blood, a symbol of Christ's sacrifice for mankind. In the early years of the English Reformation a former rector of the church, Miles Coverdale, became the first man to publish a complete Bible in the English language. His psalter has remained in the Book of Common Prayer, much loved by generations of Anglicans to the present day.

Leaving the church, to the left of the main door by the stairs to the organ loft, are some high shelves on which it was once the custom to place bread for the poor – high enough for the needy, but too high for the thieving hands of mischievous children (or the City's teeming rat population). Donated by a former Lord Mayor of London, who as a young apprentice had frequently been scolded for poor timekeeping, the clock of St Magnus looks out from the City to remind the thousands of commuters who cross London Bridge each day not to be late for work.

Beneath the approach to London Bridge, through an inconspicuous doorway lies the **City F.O.B. (3)** (Free-on-Board). Only those customers 'respectably attired' will be served at this old ale and port house. Down a staircase is the candlelit bar, where old wine and port barrels are piled on the sawdust-sprinkled stone floor. Customers giving 24-hours' notice can have the port of their choice specially decanted. Ale, notably Davy's Old Wallop, can be served in traditional metal mugs from large copper jugs. Beware the 'lead shot hazard' in the FOB's game pie.

Returning west along Lower Thames Street is the site of the famous **Old Billingsgate Market**, where fish was traded since the 10th century, when Billingsgate began life as a Saxon wharf. The beautiful façade and market hall have been preserved in a multi-million pound redevelopment around Sir Horace Jones's 110-year-old building, but the hard leather hats used by porters to carry loads of more than a 100 lb/50 kg have disappeared for ever from this part of London. The new development is to include a riverside walkway. The historic market has moved to a 13-acre/5·3-ha. site at West India Dock on the Isle of Dogs.

Dominating Lower Thames Street is the headquarters of Her Majesty's Customs and Excise, **Customs House**, designed by Robert Smirke, architect of the British Museum. Sometimes it is possible to see the beautiful Georgian Long Room. At one time every ship's captain arriving in the Port of London had to report here to pay the appropriate duties.

Along Idol Lane, where it meets St Dunstan's Hill, are the ruins of Wren's **St Dunstan-in-the-East (4)**, which now watch over a quiet garden, a tranquil haven from the City's bustle.

Nearby, in St Mary-at-Hill road is the **Watermen and Lightermen's Hall (5)** (Blackburn, 1780). Until the 19th century the Thames was London's main thoroughfare. Watermen ferried passengers, and lightermen carried cargo from ships. Between Gravesend and Windsor there were over 40,000 watermen during the reign of Elizabeth I (1558–1603), but by the end of the 18th century, that number had been halved as a result of the building of new bridges. Roughly 1,300 watermen are still involved with the river, and their company examines apprentices on behalf of the Port of London Authority. At the end of each July watermen contest the Doggett's Coat and Badge Race (*Sloane Square* ⊖), which starts from London Bridge. Note the Hall's handsome stone front with its coupled Ionic pilasters and large three-part Palladian window.

A Dutch-style church incorporating the tower and parts of the walls of its 15th-century predecessor, Wren's **St Mary-at-Hill (6)** (1676) has undergone much restoration. Sadly, it has been damaged by fire and will be closed until 1991. This richly decorated church is cross-shaped inside, with a shallow dome over the intersection. Its delicate Adam-style vaulted ceiling contrasts with the dark woodwork of the carved pulpit and

sounding board, organ case and altar-piece. The box pews are
the only surviving such examples in a Wren church. A glass
case in the vestibule contains the trombone of the Reverend
Prebendary William Carlile (rector here, 1892–1926), founder
of the Church Army. On the church's east side St Mary's elegant
clock is driven by complex lever mechanisms, a staggering 100 ft
distant from the clock face.

Further up St Mary-at-Hill road is **St Margaret Pattens
Church (7)** (Wren, 1687), which owes its name to wooden shoes
called 'pattens'. These shoes consisted of a wooden sole fitted
with leather straps and mounted on a large iron ring, thereby
raising the wearer above the filth of London's streets. Two pairs
are preserved in the church. The noise made by the iron rings on
the church's stone floors explains a notice in the vestibule asking
women to 'leave their pattens before entering'. For posterity, Sir
Christopher Wren left his monogram, 'C.W. 1686', on the
ceiling of one of the two magnificent canopied pews inside the
church.

St Clement, Eastcheap (8) (Wren, 1687) is probably the church
referred to in the nursery rhyme 'Oranges and Lemons say the
bells of St Clements', as it stands near the wharves where citrus
fruit from the Mediterranean was once unloaded. St Clement's,
dedicated to the martyred Bishop of Rome who was thrown into
the sea with an anchor around his neck, was rebuilt by Wren
after the Great Fire and pleased the parishioners so much that
they sent the illustrious architect one-third of a hogshead of
wine.

Fishmongers' Hall (9) stands, appropriately, near the Thames.
Fish had considerable religious significance in the medieval diet,
bringing wealth and influence to the Fishmongers' Company.
First established in the 13th century, officials of the Fish-
mongers', called fishmeters, still ensure fitness for consumption
of all fish sold in the City today. In 1381 the most famous fish-
monger, Sir William Walworth, then Lord Mayor, broke the
Peasants' Revolt by stabbing its leader, Wat Tyler. The dagger
Walworth allegedly used is on display in the vestibule of the
Hall, as well as a statue of him by Pearce (c. 1685).

The Fishmongers', one of the twelve 'Great' livery companies, have owned a hall on this site since 1434. The first was
destroyed by the Great Fire and the second demolished to

accommodate the new London Bridge in 1827. The third and present hall was built by Henry Roberts in 1834. In addition to an excellent collection of 17th- and 18th-century plate, the company is known for Annigoni's portraits of Queen Elizabeth II and the Duke of Edinburgh.

Each year, at the end of July, the Fishmongers organize the Doggett's Coat and Badge race rowed by Thames watermen.

London Bridge (10) has existed in various forms since Roman times. For many centuries it was the only bridge in London to straddle the Thames. The first stone bridge, which took thirty-two years to construct, was built at the end of the 12th century. In 1305 the Scottish patriot William Wallace was hanged, drawn and quartered by the English and his severed head was hung above the portico of the bridge's gatehouse. In one of the gatehouse rooms his head had been parboiled and dipped in tar for preservation.

A new but somewhat dreary bridge was built in 1832, but was replaced in the mid-1970s with a new structure more suited to London's rush-hour traffic. The old bridge was sold for more than £1 million to some American tycoons. It is said that after the deal was completed the tycoons admitted, somewhat red-faced, that they had thought they had bought London's magnificent Tower Bridge, further downstream! Nevertheless, the bridge was dismantled slab by slab, each of its 10,000 pieces meticulously numbered, shipped and reassembled over a man-made lagoon in the desert heat of Lake Havasu, Arizona. There it is now a remarkable tourist success.

Across London Bridge is **Southwark Cathedral (11)**, London's first complete Gothic building and, apart from Westminster Abbey, its largest survivor in that style. Like the surrounding area, Southwark Cathedral has been restored after years of neglect. Officially known as the Cathedral and Collegiate Church of St Saviour and St Mary Overie, three successive churches had existed on the site before the present building was constructed in the 13th century. Extensive renovation took place in the 19th century and most of the external features are from this period, although there are parts from earlier centuries.

Many of its treasures are inside the cathedral, which is entered by the south-west door. There is a 13th-century chancel and in the south wall a section of arcading survives from the same period. Medieval roof bosses are displayed in the north-west, including one of the Devil swallowing Judas Iscariot. The rounded arched doorway in the north aisle is from the earlier 12th-century Norman church. The brightly coloured canopied tomb of John Gower (d. 1408), poet laureate to Richard II and Henry IV and friend of Geoffrey Chaucer, has an effigy of the man with his head resting upon representations of his three books.

The north transept has genuine 13th-century Purbeck marble shafts against 12th-century base walls. There are also two magnificent Jacobean communion tables with twisted legs. Off the north transept is the Harvard Chapel, dedicated to John Harvard, founder of the world-renowned American University, who was born in Southwark in 1607 and baptized here.

The unusual stilted arch passing into the chancel north aisle contains one of the earliest wooden effigies in England (*c.* 1275), which may depict a member of the de Warenne family, noted benefactors. On view in the retro-choir is an intricately carved and inlaid Elizabethan nonsuch chest, presented *c.* 1588, so-named because chests of this kind depict the former Nonsuch Palace, a hunting residence of Henry VIII. The retrochoir once served as the courtroom of the Bishop of Winchester, who lived near by. It now contains four chapels.

In the south aisle of the chancel, before the steps to the south transept, a tessellated (mosaic) pavement has been laid. It came from a 7th-century Roman villa discovered in the churchyard. The sanctuary is divided from the retrochoir by a magnificent three-tiered stone reredos presented in 1520 by Bishop Fox. The choir has a floor slab in front of the central stalls commemorating the burial of Edmund Shakespeare (d. 1607), younger brother of William. The south transept was rebuilt in 1420 by Cardinal Beaufort, whose coat of arms surmounted by his hat can be seen on the vaulting shaft. Suspended at the crossing under the central tower is a rare brass candelabrum, donated in 1680. In the south aisle of the nave is a modern memorial window to William Shakespeare (1554–1616), designed by Christopher Webb in 1954 and depicting characters from Shakespeare's plays. Beneath it, carved by Henry McCarthy in 1912, is a recumbent Shakespeare in front of a 17th-century relief of Southwark, which includes the playwright's Globe Theatre (*Cannon Street & Mansion House* ⊖).

Today Southwark Cathedral offers lunch-time events,

including organ recitals, choral and instrumental music as well as exhibitions of artists' work.

Moored in St Mary Overy Dock, the **Kathleen and May (12)** is the last remaining wooden three-masted topsail schooner. Built at the beginning of the century, this coastal sail trader has recently been restored and refitted by the Maritime Trust with a donation from Hong Kong multimillionaire Sir Yue Kong Pao. Aboard ship is an exhibition about the history of the coasting trade. The **Old Thameside Inn (13)** near by has an outlook across the Thames to the City.

A market is said to have existed on the site of **Borough Market (14)** since 1276. Today this traditional fruit and vegetable wholesalers' market, smaller but more friendly than New Covent Garden or Spitalfields, is centred on an area of ground known as the Triangle. Trading starts at 5.30 a.m. and pubs are open for salesmen from 6.30 a.m.

The 17th-century **George Inn (15)** (1676) is the only surviving galleried coaching inn in London. Many such inns once accommodated travellers arriving too late at night to cross London Bridge into the capital and were also patronized by pilgrims on their way to Canterbury. In one of the George's bars is an 'Act of Parliament' clock dating from 1797. A short-lived piece of legislation once taxed five shillings on timepieces, thereby forcing people to rely on these public clocks. In the summer occasional performances of Shakespeare's plays are given in the inn's delightful cobbled yard.

Old St Thomas's Hospital Operating Theatre (16) at Southwark Cathedral Chapter House in St Thomas Street is the sole surviving example in England of an early 19th-century operating theatre and a monument to operative surgery before the days of Lister. In 1956 this amphitheatre-shaped room was unexpectedly discovered in Chapter House tower, which had been bricked up and sealed since 1862. The Chapter House was formerly the Church of St Thomas, a parish church within the old hospital. When the church was rebuilt in 1702 under the supervision of Sir Christopher Wren, the loft was designated a 'herb garret' in which the hospital apothecary could store and dry medicinal plants. In 1821 half of the herb garret was turned into an operating theatre for women, which was used for forty years until the hospital finally left Southwark.

St Thomas's ceased to be a parish in 1898 and the theatre was forgotten. After some detective work, the theatre was rediscovered and restored to its original condition by Guy's and St Thomas's Hospitals. The theatre is ringed by five rows of 'standings' for students. Beneath the operating table, a contemporary wooden structure with raised head-rest, is a box of sawdust once pushed by the surgeon to where most blood was spilling. 'The floor was separated by a partition from the rising standing places,' wrote John Flint South, surgeon at St Thomas's from 1831 to 1863, in his *Memorials*, 'and behind the second partition stood the pupils, packed like herrings in a barrel, but not so quiet . . . I have often known the floor so crowded that the surgeon could not operate till it had been partially cleared.'

Inside the Chapter House porch through a tiny door and up a steep and narrow spiral staircase is the herb garret, with an exhibition about the apothecary's work.

Across St Thomas Street is the large 1,000-bed **Guy's Hospital (17)**, founded in 1721 by publisher and printer benefactor Thomas Guy. It was the first purpose-built hospital, its predecessors having evolved mainly from earlier religious establishments. Richard Bright, Thomas Addison and Thomas Hodgkin, each of whom have medical conditions named after them, were medical researchers at Guy's, and the hospital has since established a world-wide reputation for medical and dental inquiry.

Not for the squeamish (some exhibits are unsuitable for young children), the **London Dungeon (18)** offers a nightmarish experience, with waxworks depicting events ranging from Boudicca, Queen of the Iceni in ancient Britain, spearing a Roman soldier to death to the beheading of Anne Boleyn as well as the victims of the Great Plague (1665). Lit by candles in a dingy 19th-century warehouse beneath the northern part of London Bridge railway station, the tableaux vividly re-create scenes of torture, witchcraft, death, disease and the grisly practices of early surgery.

Space Adventure (19), situated in Tooley Street, is one of London's hi-tech attractions. It uses sophisticated flight simulator technology to alarmingly authentic effect with the sensation of G-force during take-off. Under blazing lights, in a smoke-laden atmosphere tinged with the odour of rocket fuel, the space adventurer boards a ramp into the belly of Starship *3001* for a trip 'from the heart of London to the edge of the universe'. After gliding across the surface of Mars, rescuing the crew of a crippled starship and bringing laser torpedoes to bear on a formidable meteorite storm, the space traveller lands to receive a written commendation from the vice-admiral of the red sector command, Earth sector, that he acted 'with exemplary courage and skill in the rescue of the crew aboard the badly damaged starship in sector 9.7 while on a flight to the planet Mars via satellites Deimos and Phobos'.

On the opposite side of Tooley Street is **Hay's Galleria (20)**, a shopping and eating complex created out of the former Hay's Wharf and sealed over with a glass and steel roof. Stall-holders change throughout the week, and there is much street theatre as well as a giant kinetic sculpture, *Navigators*, by David Kemp.

Tower Hill ⊖

Her Majesty's Royal Fortress and Palace of the Tower of London, to give it its full name, is a mirror to the people and events that have shaped England since the Norman Conquest in 1066. Its numerous buildings house many unique treasures. More than a million people come here each year to see the world-famous Crown Jewels and one of the greatest collections of armour in the world.

The Tower, as it is simply known, has been famous as a fortress, a palace and a prison. During the turbulent political struggles of the Middle Ages custody of the Tower was often equivalent to possession of the throne. King John lost the city and had to agree to the Magna Carta in 1215. His son, Henry III (1216–72), was also brought to heel by his barons after losing the Tower. During the Peasants' Revolt of 1381 Richard II was put at risk and the Tower looted after the monarch left it to negotiate with some of the rebels. In 1460, during the Wars of the Roses, the garrison again surrendered rather than fight for a lost cause.

Ranulf Flambard, Bishop of Durham, arrested for selling benefices, became the Tower's first prisoner in 1100 and in 1399 Richard II became the first king to be incarcerated here. Other famous inmates have included the Infant Princes, Sir Walter Ralegh, Guy Fawkes, Henry VIII's wives Anne Boleyn and Catherine Howard, as well as Princess Elizabeth later Queen Elizabeth I, and even Samuel Pepys. During the reign of Henry VIII the Tower became the state's chief prison. Hitler's deputy, Rudolph Hess, kept here for a few days in 1941, was the last man to be imprisoned in the Tower. Contrary to popular belief, few inmates were tortured or kept in harsh conditions. Whether they were foreign nobles, rioting London apprentices, victims of religious disputes or court rivalries, most were sooner or later released. The last execution carried out here was in 1747.

During the reign of Henry VIII the Tower declined as a royal residence and James I (1603–25) was the last monarch to have lived here. Although Charles II did not take up residence here following the Restoration in 1660, he renovated the Tower as a fortress, garrison and show-place, thereby underscoring the renewal of the strength and splendour of the monarchy.

The Royal Mint was housed in the Tower from 1300 to 1810,

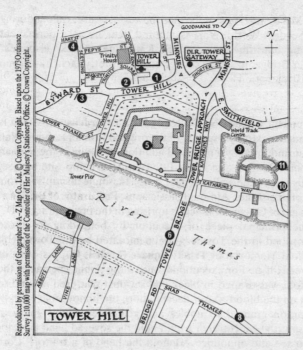

TOWER HILL

strategically positioned adjoining the commercial capital. It was the largest of the royal mints and the only one to coin in both gold and silver. The Royal Observatory once occupied one of the Tower's turrets and, from 1235, it was the home of the Royal Menagerie until 1834, when the collection was moved to form the basis of London Zoo. It was also once the country's chief arsenal, storing and assembling armaments for the royal armies and fleets.

The Yeomen Warders, or 'Beefeaters', in their colourful Tudor dress, guide people visiting the Tower. Today they still perform several traditional functions, notably the Ceremony of the Keys and the Changing of the Yeoman Guard.

Tower Bridge, near by, is perhaps the most instantly recognized landmark of London. When it was opened, nearly a century ago, it was hailed as one of the great engineering wonders of the world. Its original hydraulic machinery, which continued to operate until 1976, is now displayed in the Tower Bridge Museum. Wonderful river views can be seen from the bridge's high walkways.

HMS *Belfast*, one of the most powerful cruisers afloat during the Second World War, is moored near by as a permanent floating maritime museum. St Katharine's Dock, also near Tower Bridge, has been converted into a pretty yacht haven and tourist attraction.

⊖   ⊖   ⊖

Tower Hill ⊖ leads out on to **Wakefield Gardens (1)**, which is bounded in part by a section of the original Roman London Wall and surmounted by a medieval addition. A statue of the Roman Emperor Trajan, cast in the 19th century in composite bronze, stands before the wall and near by is a facsimile inscription from the tomb of Julius Alpinus Classicianus, Procurator of Britain at the time of Queen Boudicca's uprising in the first century A D.

The principal place of execution by beheading for those imprisoned in the Tower is commemorated by the Tower Hill Scaffold Memorial in **Trinity Square Gardens (2)**, just west of Tower Hill ⊖. For executions, once a big public spectacle, the scaffold was draped in black and sawdust scattered around to soak up the blood. After decapitation, the honourable form of execution granted to nobles and gentlemen found guilty of treason, the executioner would hold the severed head aloft for all to see and announce, 'Behold the head of a traitor!' Lord Lovat, in 1747, was the last of a total of some 125 Tower prisoners to have lost their lives on this spot since 1388. Two other memorials in the gardens, one by Sir Edwin Lutyens (1928) and the other by Sir Edward Maufe (1955), commemorate the 36,000 men of the merchant navy and fishing fleets who lost their lives during the two world wars.

North-west of the gardens a statue of Old Father Thames gestures towards the mouth of the river from the topmost tier of the extravagant Edwardian façade of the former Port of London Authority building. Beside it is the pretty Trinity House, home of the Guild, Fraternity and Brotherhood of the Trinity, first granted a charter by Henry VIII and now the chief pilotage authority in Britain and responsible for maintaining lighthouses, lightships and other sea marks.

All Hallows-by-the-Tower (3) is the central church of Toc H, a world-wide charitable movement and religious fellowship first forged during the First World War. Set into the 15th-century canopied stone tomb of Alderman Croke (d. 1477) is a casket containing the Toc H lamp. The fellowship was established by the Reverend 'Tubby' Clayton, vicar of All Hallows between 1922 and 1963. Clayton first established this fellowship for the physical and spiritual needs of troops during the First World War when he was stationed in Talbot House at Poperinghe, near Ypres, Belgium. In the signallers' language of that time Talbot House became 'Toc H', to avoid any misreading of the letter T.

It was from All Hallows that Samuel Pepys made his graphic descriptions of the progress of the Great Fire of London (*Monument* ⊖) in 1666. His celebrated diary records that he ascended the tower and gazed upon 'the great Fires, oyle cellars and brimstone and other things burning' until he 'afeared to stay there longer'. All Hallows, which dates from AD 675, survived the Great Fire, but was reduced to an empty shell by bombing in 1940. Only the crypt and undercroft, tower, and north and south walls remained standing. Happily, the church is now restored to its former glory, with a distinctive copper spire, the only shaped spire to be added to a City church since Wren rebuilt the City churches in the aftermath of the Great Fire.

Attributed to Grinling Gibbons and situated in the south-west corner of the church is a limewood font cover (1682), one of the most exquisite pieces of carving in any London church. It stands next to a 7th-century Saxon arch supporting the south wall of the tower. Second World War bombing revealed an early aisleless Saxon church. All Hallows' pulpit (*c.* 1670) is from the former church of St Swithun, London Stone.

The Lady Chapel in the north aisle contains all that remains of a winged altar-piece said to have been commissioned by Sir Robert Tate, Lord Mayor in 1488. Although lost in 1547, four panels later reappeared minus their centre section. The altar-piece was obtained for All Hallows by the famous sugar manufacturers Tate & Lyle, one of whose partners was descended from Robert Tate.

All Hallows' site was once a Roman villa, and a near-perfect tessellated pavement from the late 2nd century is on view in the undercroft museum. Also here are fragments of Saxon crosses and an altar made up of stones from the Crusader castle at Athlit in Palestine, possibly even from its Templar church. Church registers surviving from the 16th century show the baptism of the founder of Pennsylvania, William Penn, born at Tower Hill. The registers also record the marriage of John Quincy Adams, who was to become the sixth president of the United States.

Following executions, decapitated bodies were often laid to rest in All Hallows. The church's register records just such a burial of Archbishop William Laud of Canterbury, beheaded on Tower Hill in 1645.

All Hallows provides some of the finest brass rubbing in London. Of its seventeen brasses, the earliest is 14th-century and for a small charge visitors may make their own rubbings.

Across Byward Street, at the north end of Seething Lane is St Olave's church. Otherwise, proceed directly to the Tower of London (see 5).

From the south side, **St Olave's (4)** churchyard is entered under an iron-spiked gate adorned with skull and cross-bones, which prompted Dickens to nickname the church 'St Ghastly Grim'. It is named, however, after Olave Haraldson, who fled his native Norway in the early years of the 11th century after the King of Denmark seized the Norwegian throne. In 1013 Olave helped Saxon King Ethelred vanquish the Danes then holding the bridge in London. Two years later Olave returned to Norway to claim the country's throne, and pledged to drive out paganism.

Pepys worked near St Olave's and it was thanks to his vigilance that the church was saved from the Great Fire. In his position as Clerk of the Acts, Pepys became a Commissioner of the Navy Board in 1660 and lived next door to the Navy Office in Seething Lane. He constructed an outside stairway and small gallery for easy entrance to St Olave's. Although they have since been removed, a monument to Pepys by Sir Arthur Blomfield marks their former location on the south side of the church. Pepys and his wife are buried in the church.

St Olave's, which was built in 1450, was badly damaged during air raids in 1941. Renovated, its restoration stone was laid by King Haakon of Norway, who worshipped here and carried on his country's resistance during the German occupation of Norway. Set into the restoration stone is a small fragment of St Olave's tomb from the cathedral of Trondheim, Norway.

On Christmas Day 1066, two months after the defeat of Saxon King Harold at the Battle of Hastings, William the Conqueror ordered the construction of fortifications to secure London, the capital of his new kingdom. Ten years later this earth-and-timber fort was transformed into a massive palace-fortress, which became known as the **Tower of London (5)**. The original great central stone tower came to be called White Tower.

Between 1190 and 1285 the Tower was enlarged, transformed and completed. In 1189, while Richard I, the Lion-heart, was away on crusade, the Tower's defences were expanded. Ten years later, Richard's brother and successor, John, completed a doubling of the area of the bailey, a new curtain wall and ditch beyond. Henry III, John's son, loved fine buildings and lavish decoration, improving the Tower with a royal palace and establishing the royal menagerie. There he kept an elephant given to him by King Louis of France in 1255, as well as three leopards presented by the German emperor and a polar bear donated by the King of Norway. Henry, like his father, came into dispute with his barons and ordered a further expansion of the Tower's fortifications, again doubling its area. A new curtain wall round the enlarged bailey was guarded by towers at regular intervals and by a wide moat. Henry III's son, Edward I (1272–1307), determined to master his new kingdom, transformed the Tower into one of the great castles of the age with a new moat and curtain wall. A curtain wall was also constructed by the river bank.

Most of Tower Hill outside the Tower's fortifications was once part of the Liberties of the Tower, an area under the jurisdiction of the Tower and independent of the City. The Liberties are now marked by thirty-one boundary stones, each bearing the broad arrow of royal ownership. Every third year, on Ascension Day, the Tower's authority is reasserted in the ceremony of the Beating of the Bounds, when local choirboys armed with willow wands literally 'beat the bounds'. The ceremony dates back to at least 1381.

Built in 1280, **Middle Tower (5.1)** originally stood between the second and third drawbridges near the site of the former Lion Tower. Carved above the arch are the arms of George I (1660–1727), dated 1717, when this tower was largely refaced with Portland stone. Richard I (1157–99) excavated the **Moat (5.2)**, which was improved by Henry III and Edward I. In 1834, however, the Duke of Wellington had it drained due to its insanitary condition. It remains dry today, although in 1928 the moat was filled by a freak tidal wave on the Thames. Assemble here for tours by the Yeoman Warders.

Byward Tower (5.3), a gatehouse built in 1280 and housing guardrooms and a defensive portcullis, stands 'by the ward', the

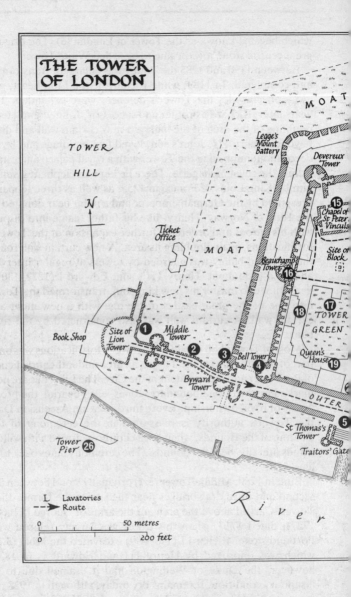

THE TOWER
OF LONDON

TOWER

HILL

N

MOAT

Legge's
Mount
Battery

Ticket
Office

MOAT

Devereux
Tower

15 Chapel of
St Peter
Vincula

Site of
Block

Beauchamp
Tower

16

18 **17** TOWER
GREEN

19

Queen's
House

Book Shop

Site of
Lion
Tower

1

Middle
Tower

2

3

Bell Tower

4

Byward
Tower

OUTER

Tower
Pier **26**

St Thomas's
Tower

Traitors' Gate

5

River

L Lavatories
➝ Route

0 _____ 50 metres
0 _____ 200 feet

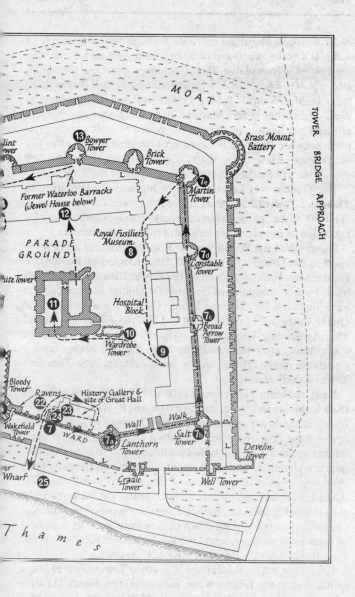

MOAT

TOWER BRIDGE APPROACH

TOWER

13 Bowyer Tower

Brick Tower

Brass Mount Battery

7e Martin Tower

Former Waterloo Barracks
(Jewel House below)

12

PARADE
GROUND

Royal Fusiliers
Museum

8

7d Constable Tower

White Tower

11

Hospital
Block

7c Broad Arrow Tower

10

9

Wardrobe Tower

Bloody Tower

Ravens

22

History Gallery &
site of Great Hall

24 23

Wakefield Tower

7

WARD

Wall

7a Lanthorn Tower

Walk

Salt Tower 7b

Develin Tower

Wharf

25

Cradle Tower

Well Tower

Thames

outer ward, as the main entrance through the outer circle of walls. It was the innermost of three gate-towers and at one time the last of a formidable line of defences. Princess Elizabeth, later Queen Elizabeth I, was imprisoned in **Bell Tower (5.4)** from 18 March until 19 May 1554 for suspected complicity in plots against her sister, Mary I (1516–58). Close confinement affected her health, so she was permitted to walk on the ramparts between Bell and Beauchamp Towers, known to this day as Princess Elizabeth's Walk. London's oldest curfew bell sounds here twice daily, once for the closing of the Tower.

The Thames was London's major highway for centuries. **St Thomas's Tower (5.5)** stands above the Tower's river entrance, 'Traitors' Gate', named after the many prisoners landed here for execution or incarceration following trial at Westminster.

During the First World War Sir Roger Casement was imprisoned in St Thomas's Tower and later hanged at Pentonville Prison, found guilty of planning the Easter Rising with German help. Earlier occupants of this tower's palatial accommodation have included Sir Thomas More, Queen Anne Boleyn and Queen Catherine Howard. Built in 1276, the Tower was named after Archbishop Thomas Becket, later canonized St Thomas of Canterbury, after his murder in 1170. He had earlier been a Constable of the Tower, and a small oratory in St Thomas's Tower is dedicated to him.

Built by Henry III between 1220 and 1240, **Wakefield Tower (5.6)** is the largest tower in the castle after White Tower, and stands at the heart and strong point of Henry's new palace. Its upper floor contains a single vaulted chamber of some magnificence, once a comfortable apartment, and the king's inner, or privy, chamber. The small oratory, opening off the east of this chamber, was the alleged scene of Henry VI's murder in 1471. A marble tablet marks where he fell. Henry VI, the last king of the House of Lancaster, founded two distinguished institutions. On the anniversary of his death he is remembered by members of both Eton College, who lay lilies here, and King's College, Cambridge, who lay the white rose of Lancaster.

Encircling White Tower from Wakefield Tower are the towers of the Wall of the Inmost Ward, mostly built by Henry III after 1238. From a defensive standpoint this towered curtain wall commanded practically all the ground inside and surrounding, its limits. The **Wall Walk (5.7)**, which gives fine views of the Tower and the river, passes through a number of these towers.

Lanthorn Tower (5.7a) was rebuilt after a fire in 1788. It contains a model of the Tower as it was in 1890 during Queen Victoria's reign, as well as the colourful figure of a Yeoman Warder in state dress. In Tudor and Stuart times prisoners on treasonable or religious charges were held in **Salt Tower (5.7b)**, so named after the saltpetre once stored here for making gunpowder. Inmates have left behind some noteworthy inscriptions. Hugh Draper, for example, imprisoned in 1561 on suspicion of conspiring to use magic, carved an astrological chart on the wall. **Broad Arrow Tower (5.7c)** has been re-created as the chamber of a late-14th-century knight. The arms of a particular knight, Sir Simon Burley, tutor to the young Richard II, have been chosen to illustrate the period. The furnishings, reproduced from medieval manuscripts, have a surprisingly modern appearance. Beyond **Constable Tower (5.7d)**, rebuilt in the 19th century and now a Yeoman Warder's residence, is **Martin Tower (5.7e)**, the largest and most comfortable of Henry III's wall towers. The upper chamber contains a fine collection of reproduction prints and maps of the Tower and a carving of the infamous Colonel Blood. In 1671 Blood attempted to steal the Crown Jewels from the Keeper of the Regalia, Talbot Edwards, and almost succeeded. But he and his accomplices, leaving Edwards for dead, were disturbed in the act and captured. Blood's refusal to speak to anyone but the king, Charles II, and his subsequent pardon have led many to suspect that Charles himself, in need of money, had commissioned Blood to steal the treasures. Blood's enigmatic remark that 'it was a brave attempt, for it was for a crown' has only deepened the mystery.

The **Regimental Museum of the Royal Fusiliers (5.8)** records the 300-year history of the body of men once armed with a musket known as a 'fuzil', and originally formed to guard the guns in the Tower. On display are weapons, uniforms, dioramas, silver, china and captured trophies. Housed in a red brick building, the **New Armouries (Board of Ordnance Gallery) (5.9)** contains an exhibition devoted to the history of all the weapons issued by the Board of Ordnance to the army and navy from the reign of Charles I (1625–49) until the Crimean War (1853–6). Included in its collection are the original models of the revolutionary percussion lock, which superseded the flintlock in firearms development.

When the Crown Jewels were moved from Westminster Abbey to the Tower in 1303, they were deposited in **Wardrobe**

Tower (5.10). Only a few remnants of this late-12th-century tower remain. Lying behind it are fragments of London's ancient Roman wall.

Dominating the Tower of London is **White Tower (5.11)**, a superb example of a hall keep, unique in England and to the early Norman period. It is the oldest visible part of the fortress and one of the earliest and largest keeps in Western Europe. Commenced by William the Conqueror around 1078 and completed by his son William 'Rufus', its construction was entrusted to Gundulf, a Norman monk and Bishop of Rochester. Everything about this inner sanctum of the Tower complex, surrounded by its quarry of towers and gates, emphasizes solidity and security. Constructed of limestone brought from Caen in Normandy and Kentish ragstone, the keep's walls are 15 ft/4.6 m thick at their base. Housing four floors, it was once possible to remove the stairs from the first floor level in time of danger. Originally, the only staircase was in the north-east corner. It spiralled in a clockwise direction to give defenders the advantage in right-handed sword play. It is interesting to note that the other three turrets are square, not circular.

In 1241 Henry III whitewashed the royal apartments in the White Tower as well as the building's exterior, hence its name. The ground floor, intended as a store, was later used as a dungeon; the first floor served as soldiers' and servants' quarters; the second floor contained St John's Chapel, the banqueting hall and the bedrooms of the nobility; and the third floor, royal bedrooms and the council chamber. In 1358 the King of France, John the Good, and his son, the Dauphin, were lodged in White Tower; and after the Battle of Agincourt in 1415, Charles, Duke of Orleans, began his 25-year imprisonment in England here.

White Tower is now the home of an enormous and unique collection of arms and armaments from the age of the Saxons and Vikings up to modern times. Arms from Asia and the Islamic world are on show in the Oriental Armoury, housed in the Tower's Waterloo Barracks. The Armouries' present collection owes much to Henry VIII, who first opened the Tower to show it. Public displays were improved and continued during the reign of Charles II. The Tower Armouries can claim to be the oldest museum in England and contains many examples of high artistic and technical achievement.

Through the first floor south entrance is the **Hunting and**

Sporting Gallery, which contains weapons of sport, ranging from crossbows used in the Middle Ages to elephant guns used at the end of the 19th century. Jousting and tournament equipment from the 15th and 16th centuries in the **Tournament Gallery** includes an unusual pair of foot-combat armours for small boys. The nearby Crypt of St John's Chapel is now a shop.

The stairs in the south-east corner lead up to the **Chapel Royal of St John the Evangelist**, the oldest surviving piece of Norman ecclesiastical architecture in London, dating from about 1080. It possesses a rare English example of tunnel vaulting and solid Romanesque pillars and arches. The chapel's simplicity is misleading. It was once richly decorated with painted stonework, stained glass and a painted rood screen, removed during the Reformation.

Through the north doorway of the chapel is the **Medieval Gallery**, which contains arms and armour from the Dark Ages to the late 15th century. Much prized is some German armour for man and horse. In the south-west corner of this chamber is an original garderobe (a lavatory). The **Renaissance Gallery**, originally the banqueting hall, houses 16th-century European arms and armour, including two longbow staves found in the wreck of the *Mary Rose*, which sank in 1545 and has recently been raised.

The stairs at the north-west angle lead to the **Tudor Gallery**, which contains four of the personal armours of Henry VIII, as well as other 16th-century English pieces. Among the 17th-century armour in the **Stuart Gallery** is the gilt harness of Charles I and the richly decorated armour of Charles II when he was Prince of Wales. Leave this gallery by the north stairway and descend to the basement.

Re-created in the **Mortar Room** is the atmosphere of an 18th-century arsenal. Row upon row of muskets, rifles, cuirasses, swords and lances are displayed as well as bronze mortars and other pieces of ordnance. The barrel-vaulted **sub-crypt of the Chapel of St John** houses finely decorated small cannon of the 16th and 17th centuries and a gilded wooden Lion of St Mark brought in 1809 from the Venetian fortress of Corfu. Through the west wall is the **Cannon Room**, which contains English and foreign guns, some made for Henry VIII and one from the wreck of the *Mary Rose*. The well on the east side dates from the 12th century.

The **Oriental Gallery (5.12)**, across Broad Walk in the Old Waterloo Barracks (1845), houses an extensive collection of armour and weapons from the Far and Middle East. Its colossal centre-piece is a unique set of elephant armour brought from India by Lord Clive and thought to have been captured at the Battle of Plassey in 1757.

The Heralds' Museum's rich and colourful exhibition charts the function and development of heraldry in a fascinating collection of manuscripts, weapons, helmets, shields and banners. The opening of this museum has enabled the College of Arms (*Blackfriars* ⊖) to display some of the magnificent treasures it has collected over the centuries.

Displayed in the **Bowyer Tower (5.13)** are some of the most gruesome torture instruments devised by man. They include a gibbet, and the block and axe used in 1747 to execute Simon, Lord Lovat, the last man to be executed by beheading in England.

More than a million people come each year to the **Jewel House (5.14)**, the Tower's underground stronghold, to see the Crown Jewels. This famous collection of regalia rightly qualifies as one of the great wonders of Britain, if not the world. Its historic and religious significance dates back to the reign of Edward the Confessor, who became king in 1042. Essentially, the ornaments used then for coronations are the same as those today, although few of the original pieces have survived. Much of the contemporary regalia originated in 1661, when a new set was created for Charles II's coronation. The previous set was almost entirely destroyed during the period of Oliver Cromwell's Commonwealth following the execution of Charles I.

The Crown Jewels have been kept in the Tower ever since the Royal Treasury at Westminster Abbey was robbed in 1303. Today the ground floor of Jewel House has on display plate, medals, orders of knighthood, maces and coronation robes as well as ten gleaming silver state trumpets. The Crown Jewels themselves can be seen in the Lower Chamber, a strong-room in the basement protected by two large steel doors.

The **St Edward's Crown**, the earliest sovereign's crown, is thought possibly to be that of Edward the Confessor. There is no record that it was melted down during Cromwell's time. At any event, it is suspected that parts of the original survive in today's crown, which has been used at every coronation bar three since that of Charles II. It is the heaviest crown, weighing 5 lb/2.26 kg, and is worn only during the coronation ceremony.

The **Imperial State Crown** is worn by the sovereign on leaving

Westminster Abbey after the coronation and on all subsequent major state occasions. This crown, made in 1838 for Queen Victoria, is set with over 2,800 small diamonds as well as the ancient Black Prince's Ruby. This balas ruby, said to have been given to the Black Prince by Pedro the Cruel after the Battle of Najara in 1367, and later worn by Henry V in the coronet surrounding his helmet at the Battle of Agincourt in 1415, has appeared in the state crowns of more than twenty generations of British sovereigns. Immediately below this ruby is the Second Star of Africa, cut from the great Cullinan diamond; Edward the Confessor's sapphire, by tradition worn by him in a ring and buried with him in 1066; and four large drop-shaped pearls known as Queen Elizabeth's Ear-rings.

The **Crown of Queen Elizabeth the Queen Mother** was made for the Queen Mother when she was crowned queen consort of King George VI in 1937. Set mainly with diamonds, this crown boasts the outstanding Koh-i-noor (mountain of light) diamond of 108 carats, discovered before the 16th century and brought to England in 1839. Legend has it that the owner of this diamond rules the world and that it must be worn only by a woman. Interestingly, many of its male owners have met untimely deaths. No King of England has ever worn this fateful stone.

Among the other crowns are **Queen Mary's Crown**, made for her when she was crowned queen consort of George V in 1911; the **Imperial Crown of India**, made especially for George V when he was acclaimed Emperor of India; **Queen Victoria's Small Diamond Crown** of *c*. 1877, made at her own expense because she found the Imperial State Crown too heavy; and **Mary of Modena's Crown**, the oldest in the Tower, which was made for the second wife of James II and worn at her coronation in 1685.

The collection holds what is believed to be the largest cut diamond in the world. It came from the largest diamond ever found, an incredible 3,106 carats, a model of which is on display. It was named the Cullinan, after the president of the mining company that found it. The diamond was presented to King Edward VII on his birthday in 1907 by the Transvaal government. Because of its size the King had the diamond split into four. The largest stone and the largest cut diamond in the world, a pear-shaped brilliant of 530 carats called the Star of Africa, is now set in the head of the **Royal Sceptre with the Cross.**

The two oldest objects used in the coronation ceremony are

the **ampulla**, in the shape of an eagle, made for Charles II's coronation in 1661, and the silver gilt **anointing spoon**, believed to date from the 12th century. The Ampulla and Spoon represent the most solemn moment of the Coronation, when holy oil is poured from the beak of the eagle into the spoon, and the sovereign's head, breast and palms are anointed.

The **Sovereign's Orb**, a globe of gold surmounted by a jewelled cross, symbolizes the extent of the Christian religion throughout the world. The most elaborate of the five Swords of State is the gem-encrusted **Jewelled State Sword**, and the most important of the coronation rings is the **Sovereign's Ring**, made for William IV (crowned 1831) and used at the coronation of every succeeding monarch except Queen Victoria. An ancient tradition says that the tighter the ring fits at the coronation, the longer and more successful the reign. Queen Victoria had a coronation ring made especially for her little finger, but the Archbishop insisted on following the rubric and forced it on to her fourth finger; Victoria's reign lasted sixty-four years.

The aptly named **Chapel Royal of St Peter ad Vincula (5.15)**, or 'St Peter in Chains', close to the scaffold site, is the last resting place of those who died there. Its name is derived from the Church of San Pietro in Vincoli, Rome, where St Peter's chains are displayed each year on April 1, the date on which this chapel was consecrated. St Peter ad Vincula enshrines the memory of many royal and noble individuals who met untimely deaths. Their bones have been buried in unmarked graves beneath its altar, and include those of two of Henry VIII's wives: Anne Boleyn, executed on Tower Green in 1536, and Catherine Howard, in 1542. In the crypt wall lie the remains of Sir Thomas More and Bishop John Fisher, Roman Catholic saints, both executed in 1535 for refusing to acknowledge Henry VIII as supreme head of the Church of England. Floor tiles in the chancel bear the family crests of some of the Tower's other unfortunate victims.

This early Tudor chapel is of simple design, with a slender flint tower surmounted by a delicate bell turret. The date of the bell is unknown, but it was recast in 1697 and almost certainly tolled at executions on Tower Hill and Tower Green. This Chapel Royal dates from about 1518, when it was rebuilt by Henry VIII, although the original church was probably built for Henry I in the early 12th century, and a second for Edward I in the late 13th century. Its fine organ, built by Bernard Smith in 1699 for the

Banqueting House in Whitehall, and adorned with carvings by Grinling Gibbons, was installed in 1890.

Residents of the Tower and soldiers of the garrison worshipped here, and it is still the Chapel of Her Majesty's Body of Yeoman Warders and their families. There are fifty families living in the Tower, forty-one of the Yeoman Warders, and three of the governors, three Jewel House curators, a doctor, a padre and an engineer. The Chapel may be visited only as part of a Yeoman Warder tour.

Man's instinct to write his name or leave his mark is as ancient as civilization. Various inhabitants of the Tower over the centuries have left a variety of inscriptions, varying from idle scratchings to profound moral reflections and specific aids to devotion. Some of the most interesting are to be found in the **Beauchamp Tower (5.16)**, and have been the subject of antiquarian study for nearly 200 years. Beauchamp Tower dates from the reign of Edward I (1272–1307), its interior revealing an extensive use of brick characteristic of Edward I's work and an innovation in English castle-building. Its name probably derives from Thomas de Beauchamp, Third Earl of Warwick, imprisoned here by Richard II in 1397.

A paved square on **Tower Green (5.17)** marks the former site of the execution block. Inscribed on a board are the six names of those who had the 'privilege' to be executed on this semi-private spot rather than in public on Tower Hill. They were Anne Boleyn; Margaret, Countess of Salisbury; Catherine Howard; Jane, Viscountess Rochford; Lady Jane Grey; and the last victim, in 1601, Robert Devereux, Earl of Essex. William, Lord Hastings, was also executed nearby.

The present early-17th-century brick houses of the **Yeoman Gaoler's House (5.18)** have replaced the previous Yeoman Gaoler's residence in which Lady Jane Grey, 'Queen for nine days', was imprisoned in 1553. From here she witnessed the return of her husband's corpse from Tower Hill following his execution on 12 February 1554. Later that day she met a similar fate on Tower Green.

The Tudor **Queen's House (5.19)** building was constructed in 1540 and originally called the Lieutenant's Lodgings. Distinguished prisoners were placed in the Lieutenant's keeping and some dined at his table. In the building's Council Chamber in 1605 the conspirators of the Gunpowder Plot were interrogated. Also detained here was Lord Nithsdale, condemned for his part in the Stuart rebellion. Nithsdale escaped on the eve of his execution, rouged and dressed in smuggled woman's clothing. More recently, Hitler's deputy, Rudolf Hess, the last man to be imprisoned in the Tower, was kept briefly in Queen's House in 1941.

Queen's House is now the home of the Governor of the Tower. It is not open to the public because of the building's delicate fabric.

Built in 1225 and once called the Garden Tower, **Bloody Tower's (5.20)** gruesome name may derive from the suicide here in 1585 of Henry Percy, Earl of Northumberland, who shot himself to escape conviction for treason and the forfeiture of his family lands to Elizabeth I. By tradition it is also the site of the murder in 1483 of Edward V, and his brother, the Duke of York, customarily known as the 'princes in the Tower'. They were allegedly smothered to death on the order of their uncle, who subsequently ascended to the throne as Richard III.

Bloody Tower's most notable internee was Sir Walter Ralegh, who occupied it with his family from 1603 to 1615. In a seemly set of rooms with a little laboratory built in the garden, Ralegh went about his work, distilling medicines and receiving social visits from the Queen. The tower is now furnished as it might have been in Ralegh's day. On display is a copy of his *History of the World*, written during his confinement. In 1616, the King released Ralegh for what turned out to be a disastrous expedition to South America. On his return Ralegh was once again lodged in the Tower before his execution in 1618 at Westminster. The walkway between the Bloody Tower and the Queen's House is still called Ralegh's Walk. Bloody Tower's ancient portcullis and winch on the ground floor are still in working order.

Running north from Wakefield Tower (*see* 5.6) is **Old Palace Wall (5.21)**, from Henry III's 13th-century royal palace. Its north end terminates where Coldharbour Tower, the main gateway to the Inmost Ward, once stood.

The **Ravens' Cages (5.22)** are just north of Wall Walk (*see* 5.7). Superstition dating from Charles II's time prophesies that if the ravens leave the Tower both the White Tower and British Commonwealth will fall. After the Great Fire, ravens fed off the bodies of dead horses and people that had been piled high at the Tower. Charles II was petitioned to have them removed after the carnage was over. However, his soothsayer warned that this would bring about the end of royalty. Henceforth there have always been at least six ravens kept in the Tower by a raven-master. The birds are adopted as fledglings and have their wings clipped. The ravens are let out every morning at 8 a.m. and called by the raven-master each evening with his 'secret' whistle. Recently, the ravens' names were Moonin (Danish for memory), Hoogin (Danish for future), Rys, Charlie, Hardie (after Thomas Hardy because the raven came from Dorset) and Larry as well as two young 'guests', Cedric and Katy. Some have been known to attain great age. One, John Crow, was a resident for forty-four years during Queen Victoria's reign.

The history of the Tower of London is illustrated on wall panels and in models in the **History Gallery (5.23)**, on the site of the great hall of the palace and adjoining the Lanthorn Tower. It was opened in 1978 to commemorate the 900th anniversary of the White Tower.

Part of the 4th-century Roman riverside defence is visible from **Riverside Wall (5.24)**. Royal salutes are fired from modern guns on state occasions at **Tower Wharf (5.25)**. A number of guns of historic interest are also on display, among them a battery of French field guns from the Battle of Waterloo. The wharf closes at dusk. In the summer a ferry service runs across the Thames from **Tower Pier (5.26)** to HMS *Belfast* (no. 7).

On the opposite side of the river from the Tower, at Hay's Wharf, archaeologists have discovered remains of the long-lost palace of King Edward II, a large moated building about 80 yds/73 m square built around 1325 and known to historians as the 'Rosary'. The King, who enjoyed a reign of dissolution with his catamite, Piers Gaveston, used it as a retreat to escape the Tower and its cares of office.

The symbol of **Tower Bridge (6)** (Sir Horace Jones), is synony-mous with London. It is a world famous landmark and now a museum and major tourist attraction. When the bridge was opened in 1894, it was hailed as one of the great engineering wonders of the world. It took eight years to build and cost more than £1 million. Tower Bridge is an important river crossing. Its great bascules, however, now open no more than a dozen times each month. Its twin towers and elevated walkways give wonderful views upstream and downstream on the Thames.

This 800-ft-/244-m-long bridge is made of steel and clad in stone to harmonize with its surroundings. Until 1976 its twin

1,000-ton bascules were raised by the original water hydraulic machinery dating back to 1894, a tribute to their Victorian engineers and designers. Now, for economic reasons, the bascules are raised by an electrically operated installation, although the original machinery was reliable and still in good working order after eighty-two years of faultless performance. The Tower Bridge Museum, on the south side of the bridge, contains the mechanism's original boilers, steam and hydraulic engines and accumulators. On level 3, in the north tower, is an exhibition explaining the working of the mechanisms of the bridge. On the glass-enclosed walkways between the towers, 140 ft/42.6 m in the air, there are display panels identifying famous landmarks. Small sliding windows allow unobstructed views for photographers.

Along the south side of the river to the west is **HMS** *Belfast* **(7)**, now a permanently moored floating museum, but once one of the most powerful cruisers afloat. She is the first warship since HMS *Victory* to be preserved for the nation.

In November 1939, just one year after she was launched, HMS *Belfast* was hit by a German mine in the Firth of Forth. Three years later she rejoined the British fleet and went on to play a key role in the sinking of the *Scharnhorst* (1943) and in the D-Day landings (1944). In the Korean War she provided fire support for United Nations' forces, and ended her days as the flagship of the Royal Navy's Far East station. Her active career was concluded in 1963, and in 1971 the HMS *Belfast* Trust was formed to save her from the scrapyard. Later that year *Belfast* was opened to the public. The Imperial War Museum (*Westminster* ⊖) is now responsible for her upkeep and running.

A full tour of the seven decks can take up to two hours, and to avoid getting lost it is advisable to follow the directional arrows to be found on the vessel's many decks. HMS *Belfast* has been preserved as nearly as possible in her original state. She provides a vivid impression of the confined conditions, economy of space and complexity of life on a battleship. Areas open to the public start with the Flag Deck, high above the water level, and progress downwards into the boiler and engine rooms, deep in the bowels of the vessel. Most aspects of a naval life at sea are on view: the bridge, operations room and gun-turrets, sick bay and wireless office, punishment cells and the more domestic activities of the bakery, mess deck, ship's laundry and chapel. Special displays cover mines, D-Day, conflict at sea, diving, ships' crests and cruisers.

To the east of Tower Bridge on the south side of the river at Butler's Wharf is the **Design Museum (8)**, a cross between the Bauhaus and the Museum of Modern Art in New York and guided by Le Corbusier's inspiration for such a museum sixty years ago. Concerned with the history, practice, theory and future of design ('the planning of man-made things') in mass-produced consumer products and services, the organizers claim it will take the concept of the museum out of the 19th century and into the 21st. 'Industry is our culture,' says its director, Stephen Bayley. Bayley, the originator of the Victoria and Albert Museum's highly successful Boilerhouse project, has been quoted as saying that, by comparison, traditional culture, opera, ballet, orchestral music and literature are all 'bankrupt, finished, empty. Only subsidy keeps them alive.' As a prophet of the culture of material things, Bayley believes the museum's mission is to explain the function and appearance of mass-produced consumer goods, to become a showcase, a market-place and an auditorium, a 'highly visible bridge between two cultures', and a 'clinic' where manufacturers can assess popular reaction.

The building contains the Boilerhouse space for 'features' – temporary, thematic exhibitions; the museum itself, devoted to a permanent collection of distinctive designs; the Design Review, for 'news and current affairs', a shop window on inno-vation, featuring new and speculative designs; and a lecture theatre, library, restaurant, shop, café and bar. Arranged as a history of design and designers, the museum shows products in a commercial, social and technical context. Works include a series of pictures showing the evolution of the Ford Sierra (1981); Niels Diffrient's 'Jefferson' chair (1985); the Olivetti ET111 electronic typewriter by Mario Bellini (1984); Harley Earl's Buick 'Y' Job (1934); 'Bodyworks' by Issey Miyake (1985); table by Eileen Gray (*c*. 1929); fabric by Collier-Campbell (1987); a *chaise-longue* by Le Corbusier (1927); the familiar milk Tetra-pak; Luxo light (1936); the Jeep (1940) and the Sony Walkman Sports (1985). It is hoped that material retained from Design Reviews will continuously enhance the permanent collection.

Returning north over Tower Bridge, on the east side of Tower
Bridge Approach is **St Katharine's Dock (9)**. In 1824 Thomas
Telford began clearing and excavating this area to construct
docks and warehouses to cope with trade from the expanding
British Empire. These docks were finally abandoned, having
first fallen victim to heavy bombing during the Second World
War and then to the introduction of large container ships unable
to navigate so far upstream. Today St Katharine's Dock has
been converted into a pretty yacht haven surrounded by shops,
restaurants and offices, including the World Trade Centre.

In front of the massive riverside Tower Thistle Hotel is one of
David Wynne's *Girl with a Dolphin* bronzes (1973), and a
massive stainless steel *Sundial* (1973) by Wendy Taylor. On the
dockside is the Coronarium Chapel, constructed from a circle of
seven metal Doric columns from a former warehouse. It was
consecrated in 1977 in memory of the medieval hospice of St
Katharine, founded here in 1146 by Matilda, wife of King
Stephen.

Yachts enter the marina via tidal lock gates from the River
Thames and pedestrians are occasionally required to wait while
the walkways are raised or opened. Beside the dock is the **SS
Yarmouth (10)**, built in 1895 as a double-ended river ferry and
pleasure steamer. Now on dry land and displaying her original
steam engine, she has been converted into an ice-cream parlour
and coffee shop. Near by is the lightship *Nore*.

Dickens Inn (11), a charming three-storey wooden building
dating from the late 18th century, once a brewery, then a
warehouse, now houses two restaurants and a public bar. The
Dickens Room inside specializes in fish dishes and the Pickwick
Room in traditional English fare.

Between West and East Docks is the Italianate Ivory House,
created from a mid-19th-century warehouse. Once the centre of
London's ivory trade, it now houses luxury flats, yacht club
headquarters and a restaurant and shops.

North-west of St Katharine's Dock, on Tower Hill, is the
Docklands Light Railway's (DLR) Tower Gateway station, so
far the westernmost terminus of this distinctive high-level rail
link to Docklands (*Outer London*).

Aldgate ⊖ & Liverpool Street ⊖

A motley and fascinating assortment of London's most famous street markets are held on Sundays in the shadow of the City's skyscrapers near Aldgate and Liverpool Street ⊖. For the seasoned market-goer, Petticoat Lane and Brick Lane are musts, but there are others. Near Petticoat Lane, in Cutler Street, there is a self-contained Sunday market with stalls selling gold and silver. At the western end of Bethnal Green Road, to the north of Club Row, in Columbia Road, a market specializes in plants, flowers and gardening equipment. The large Spitalfields wholesale fruit and vegetable market still springs to life early on weekday mornings, although the market is set for redevelopment.

Spitalfields, the area around St Mary Spital, remained basically agricultural until French Huguenot silk-weavers and Calvinists arrived in the 17th century. After a temporary period of prosperity at that time, the genteel quality of the area declined and it became noted for poverty, poor housing and its rapidly changing population. Germans arrived to work here in the sugar refineries of Whitechapel. The Irish concentrated around the Royal Mint Street area. And in the 19th century the Jewish community took control of the second-hand clothes trade. Between 1880 and 1914 the Jewish community was swollen by an enormous influx of refugees from eastern Europe. Parts of the area then came to look like foreign towns.

Since the Victorian era, the expansion of the prosperous yet scruffy Spitalfields Market has dominated the architecturally distinguished early-18th-century houses near by. In more recent years Bangladeshi immigrants have largely superseded the Jewish community, especially in the clothing industry. But London's most famous kosher restaurant, Bloom's, and the Beigel Bakery remain in the area as a reminder of the days of Jewish domination. Now, ironically, with the impending departure of Spitalfields and a slump in the rag trade, the threat to the heritage of the area is not of poverty but of wealth – from a property boom, the encroaching City, office development and from those who *can* afford to live here.

Today Spitalfields is a far cry from the empty streets, dark alleys and shadowy doorways that were once the haunt of Jack

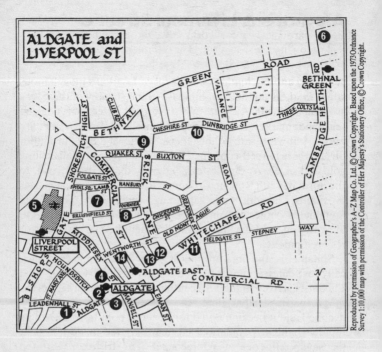

the Ripper. This vicious killer is thought to have brutally murdered six women, five of whom were prostitutes, within a square mile of Whitechapel. After the killings, this cold-blooded murderer wrote confessions to the police signing himself 'Jack the Ripper'. The Whitechapel Murders were never solved; nobody was even charged. They occurred within a period of three months and ended as suddenly as they had begun. Although this mystery has obsessed generations of criminologists and new evidence keeps emerging, the riddle of Jack the Ripper's identity has never been solved.

A little east, beyond Whitechapel ⊖, is The Blind Beggar pub, site of another black incident from the East End's past. Here in 1966 Ronnie Kray, one of the infamous gangland twins, gunned down George Cornell during one of the most bloody incidents of East End gang rivalry.

The Aldgate was one of six original gates to the City built by the Romans. Routes through it went to the east and Colchester, once Roman Britain's capital. The Saxons called it Ealdgate, old gate. Whitechapel was originally a suburb of the City, named after the parish church St Mary Whitechapel. Noisy or noxious trades, particularly metalwork, considered a nuisance in the congested City, moved here. The Whitechapel Bell Foundry, which cast Big Ben and America's original Liberty Bell, is still located in Whitechapel and in nearby Bethnal Green is Engelfields, the finest and probably the oldest remaining cast pewter manufacturer in the world.

At the eastern end of the area is the Bethnal Green Museum of Childhood, a unique collection of children's objects, including marvellous displays of dolls and toys.

⊖   ⊖   ⊖

West along Aldgate, at the junction of Leadenhall Street and Fenchurch Street, is **Aldgate Pump (1)**. The present stone pump, whose spout is a brass dog's head, dates from 1871, although a well has existed here since the time of King John (1166–1216).

Four churches dedicated to St Botolph, the English patron saint of travellers, were built near the old City gates. The architect of Mansion House (*Bank* ⊖), George Dance the Elder, completed the present **St Botolph-without-Aldgate (2)** in 1744, although a church has existed here since the 10th century. During Dance's reconstruction the body of a boy was found in a standing position in one of the vaults. People once paid two pence to see the spectacle. Towards the end of the 19th century St Botolph's was remodelled by J. F. Bentley, architect of the Roman Catholic Cathedral at Westminster (*Victoria* ⊖).

Off Aldgate, the church is entered through the baptistry, which contains an 18th-century domed front cover and busts of two of St Botolph's benefactors, Robert Dowe (1552–1612) and Sir John Cass (1661–1718). Cass, a prosperous master of two livery companies and a Member of Parliament, earnestly desired to found a school bearing his name. It was built in St Botolph's churchyard in 1710. On his deathbed, eight years later, while preparing to sign a large endowment to the school, Cass suffered a pulmonary haemorrhage, which stained with blood the quill pen in his hand. In his memory, on the nearest Friday to his birth date, 20 February, a service known as Red Feather Day is held at St Botolph's. A symbolic turkey feather quill, dyed red, is worn by the children of John Cass School, who attend the ceremony.

Bentley's remodelling of the church created a curved ceiling with fine decorative plasterwork. Side screens to make the chancel and new gallery fronts with a pierced balustrade were also added. The Renatus Harris organ in the west gallery is the oldest in London and dates from 1676. Its early-18th-century casing is in the style of Grinling Gibbons.

After the Great Fire in 1666, an Act of Parliament forbade the building of new timber-framed structures in the City to avoid any further such 'dreadful Visitation' upon London, and the **Hoop and Grapes (3)**, perhaps London's oldest licensed establishment, is the only remaining 17th-century timber-framed structure of its kind in the City of London, retaining an atmospheric charm despite recent restoration and extension. Legend has it that a secret underground passage once connected the Hoop and Grapes to the Tower of London, less than 880 yds/ 804 m to the south.

Petticoat Lane Market (4), in the heart of the East End, is held on Sunday mornings in Middlesex, Wentworth and Goulston Streets. Once called Hog's Lane, it became Petticoat Lane in the 1680s, a time when French Huguenot silk-weavers made ladies' lingerie here. Later, a flourishing market, primarily for clothes, was established by the predominantly Jewish community in the 18th century. Petticoat Lane was renamed Middlesex Street during the prudish Victorian era, although the market has continued with its old name.

Today rough-and-ready Londoners, proud of their salesmen's spiel, man the hundreds of stalls that line Middlesex Street and its tributaries and are famed for their 'bargains'. There are plenty of market pitchers, traders who rely on their spiel to gather a crowd to whom to sell their products. Pitchers refer to other silent traders as gazers or lurkers. Gazers may shout out: '50p a cabbage, 50p a cabbage', thereby becoming shouters, but this repetitive use of language does not make them pitchers, who regard themselves as the cream. The use of plants, or ricks as they are called, in the audience is evidently less widespread than popularly imagined. Pitchers often offer goods at give-away prices to gather a crowd, and then request the audience to move forward for a closer look to commit them to buying something. Reluctant-looking members of the crowd are often embarrassed into buying the pitcher's goods. The sight of other customers buying is turned to good effect by 'twirling the edge', prolonging the handing over so more people see a person purchasing.

Beware of pickpockets. It is said that a watch can be stolen at one end of the lane and sold back at the other!

Broadgate Square (5), next to Liverpool Street Station on the site of the former Broad Street Station, is the first new square in the City for many years. Inside the square, which is largely occupied by the premises of finance houses, is a circular amphitheatre of shops, restaurants and public facilities on many interlocking levels. At its centre is the only outdoor ice-skating rink in Britain, which is used as an amphitheatre during the summer months.

To visit the Bethnal Green Museum of Childhood, take the Central Line east from Liverpool St ⊖ to Bethnal Green ⊖. Exit Bethnal Green ⊖ and go north up Cambridge Heath Road. The museum is on the right. Otherwise, proceed to **7**.

The joy of childhood through the art, craft and design of toys is beautifully created in the **Bethnal Green Museum of Childhood (6)**. Spanning about four centuries to the present day, the museum's exhibits range from the simplest marbles, balls and hoops to elaborately fashioned wooden models and doll's houses, and more recently, to metal cars, mechanical toys and clockwork railways.

Its collection of dolls begins with a finely attired example from England in the 1680s. Popular 19th-century dolls with papier-mâché or wax-coated heads are plentiful, as well as those in more expensive porcelain. From the 1920s, there are dolls made entirely of cloth. Some fine examples have come from Queen Mary's collection, including 'Princess Daisy' with her layette. Ladies' fashions from the generations between 1754 and 1912 have been recorded in a fascinating collection of thirty-nine dolls that once belonged to a single family. The Nuremberg house of 1673 is the oldest and most valued of the collection of doll's houses.

Other holdings include soft toys, board games, books, model theatres and puppets, and 18th-century children's dress. On the upper level 19th-century Continental furniture and decorative art are displayed. The museum is a branch of the famous Victoria and Albert Museum (*South Kensington* ⊖) and its building, erected in 1872, is of archetypal Victorian design.

Spitalfields Fruit and Vegetable Market (7) wholesale market galvanizes into action before dawn, handling around 1,500 tons of fruit and vegetables each weekday. In 1682 Huguenot silk-weaver John Balch was granted a charter to hold a market here. Spitalfields assumed its vast proportions 200 years later, when a former farm labourer, Robert Horner, used the fortune he had acquired in the horticultural wholesale business to acquire the present site and to erect a £80,000 new market building. Horner's gabled façade on Commercial Street survives today, although the City Corporation took over his market at the beginning of this century. Local pubs open at 6 a.m. for the market's folk, and there is a jellied eel stand inside the market building.

The initiative for **Christ Church (8)** came from the Fifty New Churches Act of 1711, which levied a tax on coal to pay for the building of 'fifty new churches of stone and other proper materials, with towers or steeples to each of them'. Architect Nicholas Hawksmoor's largest and grandest church lies almost directly opposite Spitalfields, amidst 18th-century brick houses once built for the Huguenot weavers. Many of the church's remaining gravestones bear the names of members of that once prosperous French community. Hawksmoor's design admirably fulfils its statutory brief; an oblong tower and high octagonal spire looming over the body of the church and its great barrel-vaulted portico.

Despite the ravages of time and a lack of money, Christ Church still emanates a respectful and hallowed atmosphere. Enthusiasts are gradually restoring this fine example of what has come to be known as 'English Baroque'. Apply at the crypt door to view the interior.

Adjacent to Christ Church is Fournier Street, once the home of merchants and Huguenot silk-weavers. Their houses retain 'weaving' attics, with deep rear windows to give maximum light. No. 2 was designed as the church's rectory. The large building at the end of the street reflects the changing nature of the East End. Built as a church for French Protestants in 1743, it later became a Wesleyan Methodist chapel, then a synagogue, and is now a mosque serving the Asian community.

Left, north along Brick Lane, is Truman's Brewery, whose premises tastefully combine an 18th-century warehouse with a modern glass façade. Truman's have recently returned to the pleasant tradition of using horse-drawn drays for local deliveries of beer.

A visit to **Brick Lane Market (9)** is a must for the keen market-goer. Every Sunday morning a thriving general market, perhaps the last genuine survivor in London of a market for the working classes, occupies the north end of Brick Lane, Sclater Street and Cheshire Street. New and second-hand goods are on sale, as well as fruit and vegetables, electrical equipment, crockery, clothes, furniture, general junk and even bicycles in nearby Chilton Street. Cockney crockery salesmen can be seen mesmerizing their audiences by juggling plates while prices fall lower and lower. A recent bargain here was an authentic manuscript of Wordsworth's sonnet 'When Severn's Sweeping Flood Had Overthrown'. The Beigel Bakery, selling its hard, ring-shaped bread rolls, echoes the days when the Jewish community dominated the East End. Today the demography of this area has changed and many Bangladeshi and Indian shops now proliferate in the southern half of Brick Lane.

The finest and probably the oldest remaining cast pewter manufacturer in the world is **Englefields (10)**. Modestly tucked away at the east end of Cheshire Street, the firm maintains a remarkable tradition, continuing to fashion pewter using the same methods, in many cases from the original 18th-century moulds, employed by Thomas Scattergood, who founded the company 300 years ago. Since the beginning of the 16th century London's pewterware has been certified with the mark of a crown and rose as well as the maker's mark, or touch-mark. As the last London pewterers, Englefields have been granted the exclusive right to use the crown and rose trade mark. Historically, the touch-mark could be applied only by master pewterers following a rigorous apprenticeship and admission to the Worshipful Company of Pewterers.

To share their craft with the public, Englefields has recently introduced guided tours around its workshops. After the pure metals – gold, silver and platinum – pewter is the most valuable alloy metal in commercial use. Crown & Rose pewter is entirely lead-free, containing 94 per cent tin, 4 per cent antimony and 2 per cent copper. At 572 °F/300 °C, pewter is cast into bronze or steel moulds coated with a traditional binding of egg white, red ochre and pumice powder. Casting by hand requires great skill and dexterity to ensure no air remains in the mould, and that the feed carrying the molten alloy is the last part to harden. A mould carved by John Townsend and dated 1790 has been used since

that date to form the body of the bell tankard with hinged lid, a
popular Georgian design. The company has recently produced
some replicas based on items recovered in 1982 from the
sunken wreck of the *Mary Rose*, once Henry VIII's vice-
flagship.

The **Whitechapel Bell Foundry (11)**, which cast Big Ben (*Westminster* ⊖), America's original Liberty Bell in Philadelphia,
'Bow Bells' (*Cannon Street & Mansion House* ⊖s), the bells at St
Clement Danes (*Temple* ⊖) and Great Tom of St Paul's (*St
Paul's* ⊖), is located on Whitechapel Road. Established in 1420,
the foundry moved to Whitechapel in 1583, and to its present
site in 1738. Thanks to its impressive antecedents, the foundry
has continued at the forefront of its craft. It has promoted bell
frames in steel and, later, in reinforced concrete, as well as
introducing sophisticated electronic bell-tuning and supplying
computerized chiming devices. It also makes handbells for tune
ringing and cast the new set of thirteen bells for St Martin-in-the-
Fields, Trafalgar Square.

   Although the foundry proper is not open to the public, there is
a small museum to its work. Inside its entrance, look back to see
how the door is framed by the enormous template of the 13½ ton
Big Ben.

The **Whitechapel Art Gallery (12)** (Charles Harrison-Townsend,
1901), in its striking art-nouveau building, has a widespread
reputation for its avant-garde exhibitions. Its policy is commit-
ted to bringing contemporary art to the people of East London
and to showing the work of local artists.

   Bloom's (13) is said to be London's most famous kosher
restaurant. Originally opened in Brick Lane in 1920 by Morris
Bloom, who devised a method of making salt beef that once
drew customers from all over London, it is now in Whitechapel.
Bloom's counter and dining room are immensely popular on
Sundays.

The **Fawcett Library (14)**, in the City of London Polytechnic
in Old Castle Street, is Britain's main reference and lending
collection on women, with more than 50,000 books, pamphlets
and leaflets and over 700 periodical titles. The collection is

directly derived from the London Society for Women's Suffrage, founded in 1867, which was at the centre of the non-militant campaign for women's suffrage under the leadership of Millicent Garrett Fawcett.

Moorgate ⊖

Moorgate once led out of the City on to Moorfields, open fens on which, in early times, archery was practised. The gate was built in 1415 by Thomas Falconer, a mercer, but it was demolished in 1762. During the Great Plague it was one of the main exits for those fleeing the City. Just north of Moorgate, in Bunhill Fields, the Corporation of London interred the plague's victims.

Following the rebuilding of London Bridge in 1831, the present Moorgate road was laid out as a link route. A few houses of that period survive, but to the south of London Wall the street has now become a centre of banking and insurance. Opposite Moorgate ⊖ on the east side of Moorgate is Finsbury Circus, laid out in the early 19th century with tall, handsome houses by William Montague to the designs of George Dance the Younger. Its fine oval garden contains the only bowling green in the City.

Opposite Bunhill Fields on the east side of City Road is the house and chapel of the founder of Methodism, John Wesley. Now a museum, it contains much interesting Wesleyana and an illustrated history of Methodism. A small museum about the Honourable Artillery Company, the oldest regiment in the British Army, is nearby.

⊖   ⊖   ⊖

Between 1315 and the final burial carried out here in 1854 120,000 corpses were interred at **Bunhill Fields (1)**. Many were victims of the Great Plague. Called 'the cemetery of Puritan England', it is doubtful that the ground was ever consecrated. Consequently, many Nonconformists were able to bury their dead here without the use of the Book of Common Prayer. Beside the main path of the graveyard is the tomb of John Bunyan (d. 1688), author of *Pilgrim's Progress*, and on a side path to the north are the graves of Daniel Defoe (d. 1731), author of *Robinson Crusoe*, and William Blake (d. 1827), the poet and artist. Susanna Wesley, John Wesley's mother, is also buried in Bunhill Fields.

Across City Road is **Wesley's House and Chapel (2)**. John Wesley (1703–91), the founder of Methodism, underwent a vivid inner experience, a feeling that his heart was 'strangely

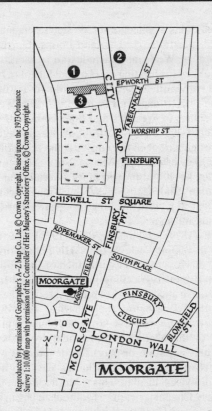

Reproduced by permission of Geographer's A–Z Map Co. Ltd. © Crown Copyright. Based upon the 1973 Ordnance Survey 1:10,000 map with permission of the Controller of Her Majesty's Stationery Office, © Crown Copyright.

warmed', at a meeting in the City's Aldersgate Street on the eve of 24 May 1738. Thenceforth his life was transformed into one of extraordinary missionary zeal, an enthusiastic ministry completely at variance with the arid and soulless theology of the contemporary Anglican Church. A year later, on 11 June, he wrote in his journal: 'I look upon the world as my parish.' An inspired preacher and brilliant organizer, Wesley led the evangelical revival in 18th-century Britain and created the system of 'connections' and 'circuits' that became the Methodist Church, now a world-wide organization of 54 million people, which has recently celebrated the 250th anniversary of its founder's conversion. Though Wesley travelled some 250,000 miles throughout Britain in his lifetime, preaching and founding chapels, the Foundery in Moorfields and the City Road chapel were the hub of his mission.

His house contains a collection of Wesley's personal belong-
ings; furniture, portraits, clothes, and books. On the second
floor a museum of Wesleyana includes an advanced electric-
shock machine used for treating cases of melancholia, his baptismal gown and baby rattle, examples of commemorative pottery
and the gallon (4.5 l) teapot given him by Josiah Wedgwood.
Above the fireplace in Wesley's first floor bedroom, where he
died on 2 March 1791, is a portrait of Wesley aged 86 by
Romney. Through a door in the corner is the tiny prayer room
known as the 'Powerhouse of Methodism'. At 4 a.m. every
morning Wesley knelt and prayed in its quietude 'far from the
busy ways of man'. In his study is Wesley's magnificent walnut
bureau and, next to it, his travelling robe, three-cornered hat,
preaching bands and shoes.

Despite fire (1879) and restoration (1978), the chapel is
essentially as it was in Wesley's time. His pulpit, originally a
three-decker, survives together with much of the woodwork in
the apse. The Adam-style ceiling has been copied from fragments. Deliverance and healing are represented by the dove and
the snake in the frieze below the galleries. The Museum of
Methodism in the crypt tells the story of John and his brother
Charles, and of the Methodist movement from the 18th to
the 20th century. Separate displays are devoted to Methodist
ceramics and chapel architecture. Charles Wesley's hymns are
part of the audio-visual display 'This is Methodism'.

The Foundery Chapel is near by. Methodism began in 1738 in
the original Foundery Chapel, which once stood a short distance
to the south. Wesley is buried in ground to the rear of its present
successor.

The Honourable Artillery Company (HAC) proudly boasts
that it is the oldest regiment in the British Army. Its precise date
of origin is unknown, but in 1537 Henry VIII granted a charter
to a body of citizen archers known as the Guild of St George,
later, the Gentlemen of the Artillery Garden. As the only
trained unit stationed permanently in London during the 18th
century, the HAC was called upon to police the Gordon Riots
in 1780. The HAC's role in peacetime includes firing salutes and
providing a bodyguard for the Lord Mayor as a company of
pikemen and musketeers.

Past a guard post on the west side of City Road, the **HAC
Museum (3)** contains uniforms, weaponry, medals and other

associated military memorabilia associated with the regiment. This includes early 18th-century grenadier caps, which enabled grenades to be thrown overarm unimpeded by their brim; the impressive Tarleton helmet, complete with leopard-skin chained turban and black fur crest; and a life-size model of a member of the crack Yäger company of marksmen (*c*. 1810) resplendent in the company's distinctive dark-green uniform and armed with a Baker rifle.

The first great cricket match in England was contested on the artillery ground outside the HAC's headquarters. James Love's 'Cricket, A Heroic Poem' described the match, which was played on 18 June 1774, between All England and Kent.

Barbican ⊖

The Romans encircled Londinium with a long and high stone wall pierced at certain points by gateways, one of which was Aldersgate. Today the boundary of the City of London still follows roughly those same Roman fortifications. In the south-east corner the Normans built the Tower of London on the site of a former Roman fort. Barbican, the fort in the north-west corner, kept its Latin name. Barbican was partially demolished in 1267 by Henry III and thereafter became a watch-tower. In the 16th and 17th centuries a high-class residential area developed, but nearly all traces of it were obliterated by either the Great Fire or an air raid in 1940. A road named London Wall, a small section of Roman stonework near by and the name Barbican are all that now reveal the area's ancient origins.

During the 1950s a massive redevelopment project was conceived to repopulate the City at Barbican. Architecturally, it was to provide a vivid, lively, high-density type of urban living for some 6,000 people, replacing the 'cats and caretakers' reality of City life, a life that died in the evenings and at weekends. The Barbican Centre was finally completed in the early 1980s and stands as a lasting monument to the gigantism and uniformity of architectural vision of the 1950s. It is enlivened by the presence of a concert hall, the permanent venue of the London Symphony Orchestra and a theatre, the London base of the Royal Shakespeare Company.

At the nearby Museum of London the story of London and Londoners is told in a sequence of galleries covering, 2,000 years of the capital's history. Everyday life in Londinium is recreated in a reconstructed Roman kitchen and dining-rooms, sculptures from the Temple of Mithras and a Roman bikini. The horror of the Great Plague of 1665 is tolled with an original plague bell and the Great Fire of the following year is experienced with readings from the diary of Samuel Pepys and a full range of sound and visual effects. The violence of 18th century London is reflected in the iron-clad doors of Newgate Prison.

⊖   ⊖   ⊖

Great Britain, and particularly London, is renowned throughout the world for its royal heritage. More than a millennium of

royal history is celebrated at **Royal Britain (1)**, a dream-like
journey through the lives of fifty-one monarchs since Edgar, the
'First King of All England', took the throne in AD 973.

Edgar's coronation ceremony is read out in rich tones of
Latin. Monks chant prayers for Henry V (reigned 1413–22),
hero of Agincourt, his body gently illuminated through medieval stained glass. Weapons clash as the white rose of the House
of Lancaster and the red rose of York fight for the throne. Rivals
Henry VIII of England and Francis I of France meet amidst the
unparalleled scenes of feasting, jousting and pyrotechnics that
formed the pageantry of The Field of Cloth of Gold (1520). The
dark panelled corridors of Fotheringay Castle echo with the
footsteps of Mary Queen of Scots on her journey to the executioner's block (1587). Elizabeth I gives her famous rallying
speech at the height of the Spanish Armada crisis (1588).

Turbulent episodes in the lives of the Stuart monarchs (1603–
1714), among them the beheading of Charles I, are staged in a
large mechanized toy theatre. Statues of the Hanoverians
underscore the new symbolic role of royalty. A gigantic bronze
statue of Queen Victoria dominates a busy foundry in the

industrial North of England, celebrating both Britain's industrial prowess and the Queen's Diamond Jubilee year, 1897. A
recording of Edward VIII's abdication speech counterpoints
with the celebrations of Elizabeth II's coronation (1953), the
first time the ceremony was broadcast live on television. Royal
Britain concludes with a computerized montage of facts and
figures about the modern royals, including an electronic voting
system inviting visitors to give their views on whether the press
today gives them fair treatment.

The tale of a city and its people, from pre-history to the present
day, is encapsulated within the remarkable **Museum of London
(2)** (Powell and Moya, 1975). Appropriately sited amidst the
remains of London Wall, the oldest standing feature of urban
life in the metropolis, the museum is laid out as a walk through
the social history of the capital. A reconstructed Roman kitchen
and dining-rooms leads through to a dramatic recreation of the
Great Fire, enlivened for the visitor by a blast of hot air and the
sounds of the howling wind that fanned the flames across the
stricken city. The Medieval Gallery, spanning the period from
the 5th to the 15th century, contains Saxon jewellery, medieval
leather shoes and scabbards, pilgrim badges and an early pair of
spectacle frames. Period music echoes through the Medieval
and Tudor London galleries. The museum's Newgate Prison cell
recaptures Hogarthian London and the appalling degradation of
18th-century prison conditions, and contrasts it with the elegant
finery of contemporary Georgian figures. Shops from the late
Victorian and early Edwardian period nestle together – a tobacconist, barber, pharmacist, tailor, and Mr Bugg's Grocery, with
his ingenious overhead pulley system for sending money to the
cashiers. On display from the present century are the art-deco
elevators once installed at Selfridges department store, a Wool-
worth's counter from the 1930s and a black Model Y Ford car,
which cost just £100 in 1936.

The 'living' quality of this museum is emphasized each year in
November during the Lord Mayor's Show (*Bank* ⊖). The Lord
Mayor's State Coach (1757), resplendent in red and gold, is
taken from its home in the museum and drawn by six grey horses
through the streets of London as the centre-piece of this annual
pageant.

Near the main entrance to the museum is a monumental metal
flame inscribed with a passage from John Wesley's journal

describing his mystical conversion, an experience that changed his life and led to the formation of the Methodist Church (*Moorgate* ⊖).

To the north of the museum is **Ironmongers' Hall (3)** (Sydney Tatchall, 1925). Since the 13th century London has accommodated iron dealers, or ferroners, in and around Ironmonger Lane, Cheapside. Ferroners plied their trade mainly in iron bars and rods, horseshoes and cart-wheels. Such was their status that the Ironmongers were incorporated by charter in 1463 and, despite their small membership, became a wealthy and influential livery company. The hall's pretty Tudor-style exterior, built with hand-made bricks and iron fittings, dates from 1925. The Ironmongers' panelled banqueting hall contains a minstrels' gallery and a fine Waterford glass chandelier. Viewing is by appointment only.

St Botolph Aldersgate (4) (Nathaniel Wright, 1791) is reached via a raised walkway across the traffic island in Aldersgate Street. Four London churches dedicated to Abbot Botolph, the 7th-century patron saint of travellers, are situated next to the sites of four old City gates. A church of this dedication has stood at Aldersgate since the mid-11th century, but the one seen today is from the late 18th century and contains an interesting period plasterwork ceiling, galleries and organ case. It boasts the only surviving painting-on-glass window in the City, created in 1788 by James Pearson and depicting Christ's agony in the Garden of Gethsemane. Outside, note the unusual angle at which the tower is set to the main body of the church.

On the south side of St Botolph's is Postman's Park, opened in 1880 and named after the General Post Office. In 1887 artist George Frederick Watts conceived the idea of a substantial wall plaque to commemorate Britain's unsung everyday heroes. An example of the many men and women commemorated on the plaque is railway foreman Daniel Pemberton, aged 61, who, in hurling his workmate from the path of a railway train, forfeited his own life.

Return past the museum entrance and take the raised walkway east along London Wall. Many sections of the old Roman and medieval London Wall are visible below. East of Wood Street a fine part of this boundary is exposed in the garden of the ruined St Alphage Church.

At the north end of Wood Street, is the church of **St Giles-without-Cripplegate (5)**. In 1545 fire destroyed much of the

Gothic church on this site, causing it to be rebuilt. The brick tower, which was added in 1682 still stands today, though somewhat ill-matched with the rest of the stone construction. The first bomb to be dropped over the City by enemy aircraft during the Second World War fell within paces of St Giles. Later, during the blitz, the church was burnt out and its roof collapsed.

Over the north door stands a figure of St Giles with a hind. Tradition has it that St Giles lived as a hermit in a cave in Provence, France, beside the River Rhône. On a hunt, a Goth king chased a hind into St Giles's cave and mistakenly wounded the hermit with an arrow. The king subsequently revisited the cave several times and St Giles urged him to build a monastery. The king agreed only on condition that St Giles became its abbot. St Giles is the patron saint of cripples and beggars, and the church carries out charitable and welfare work for physically and mentally handicapped children. In Anglo-Saxon, however, the word 'crepelgate' actually meant covered walkway.

Parish registers dating back to 1561 show that on one day during the Great Plague, 18 August 1665, a total of 263 burials took place in the churchyard. A floor tablet beside the communion rail records the burial place of writer and poet John Milton (d. 1674). Milton, who lived nearby, sold his great work *Paradise Lost* to an Aldersgate printer. Oliver Cromwell was married in this church in 1620. A plaque at the right of the entrance door records the church's many notable parishioners.

On the north side of St Giles is the **Barbican Centre (6)** (Chamberlin, Powell and Bon, 1982). Finding the best entrance to this multi-level complex is notoriously difficult. Ground-level entry, at the Centre's level 5, is via Silk Street, reached by taking Fore Street east, then north along Moor Lane. Alternatively, the steps opposite the east end of St Giles lead up to a high walkway, which connects with the Barbican at level 7.

The Barbican was conceived in the 1950s as affordable housing for clerks and business people wishing to live near their work. Some 6,000 people now live in Barbican's twenty-one towers; an exclusive and highly concentrated clan of City professionals, bankers, accountants, solicitors and civil servants, almost a state within the City, they form around three-quarters of the City's total resident population.

The centre is a monument to the singlemindedness and con-formity of the architectural vision of the 1950s, to a Corbusian type of urban living. Finished in the early 1980s across a 60-acre/ 24-ha. site, the mammoth development occupied the lives of a whole generation of architects, contractors and workers. This concrete monolith shows few signs of wit, no light touches; all is big, bold and very serious. It lacks the diversity of Covent Garden, but locked into a part of its vast subterranean area are a distinctively striped pine-veneered 2,000-seat concert hall, the permanent venue of the London Symphony Orchestra, and a 1,200-seat theatre, the London base of the Royal Shakespeare Company. The development also contains exhibition centres, conference facilities and a new home for both the Guildhall School of Music and Drama and the City of London School for Girls, as well as a smaller studio theatre, cinema, art gallery with open-air sculpture court, library and a number of bars and restaurants. In the Terrace Foyer there are often free exhi-bitions and performances at lunch-time and in the early evening.

A little to the north, in Chiswell Street, below the great glass office block of the Whitbread redevelopment, is the remainder of **Whitbread's Old Brewery (7)**, which began ale production in 1750. Samuel Whitbread's beer proved so popular that King George III and Queen Charlotte visited the brewery in 1787. In 1798, the year Whitbread died, a record total of 200,000 gallons/ 909,082 litres left the premises. Production ceased here in 1976, but the site still serves as the company's headquarters. By request to the commissionaire, it is possible to gain access to the courtyard of the Old Brewery, which houses the beautiful coach, originally made in Holland for William III in 1698, in which the Speaker of the House of Commons now rides on state occasions.

Whitecross Street Market (8), a quaint Victorian street that leads north from the junction of Beech Street and Chiswell Street, houses a busy and friendly lunch-time market, although it lacks the size of the East End markets.

Farringdon ⊖

Clerkenwell, one of London's hidden villages, grew up in the 12th century serving two monastic institutions, the Priory of St John of Jerusalem, the English headquarters of the famous Knights Hospitallers, and St Mary's Nunnery. Two centuries later, following the Black Death, another monastic foundation, Charterhouse, was established here. The area takes its name from the ancient *fons clericorum*, or Clerk's Well, from which the Benedictine nuns of St Mary's drew their water. The well was also once the site for performances of mystery plays by the Worshipful Company of Parish Clerks in the Middle Ages. Both the well and the Worshipful Company still survive.

The nunnery and St John's Priory, however, have not survived, broken up by Henry VIII during the Dissolution of the Monasteries. Today all that remains of the nunnery is a wall in the gardens situated behind Clerkenwell's parish church, St James. Fortunately, the splendid Gatehouse of St John's Priory still stands and, in the 19th century, the Order of St John (the Knights of Malta) was revived as a Protestant order. Inside the Gatehouse is a fascinating museum encompassing the history of these Knights Hospitallers, who, together with the Knights Templars, defended Christendom in the Holy Land during the Crusades. On display are ecclesiastical, hospitaller and military objects. Also in the gatehouse is a small museum to the St John Ambulance Brigade, Britain's voluntary first aid organization and an offshoot of the order.

Although Clerkenwell's other great monastic institution, Charterhouse, was also dissolved by Henry VIII, its buildings survived to house one of Britain's leading public schools and a home for pensioners. Charterhouse School has since left London, but pensioners remain in the quiet and pleasant surroundings of Charterhouse's predominantly 16th-century precincts, some of the most wonderful yet relatively unknown groups of buildings of London.

The pursuit of ancestry has become a leading national pastime in Britain. Thousands of people now enjoy the study of genealogy, with its deeply personal insight into history. The unique library of the Society of Genealogists, with its millions of references, is a focal point for such study. The society also has

collections of material on English people living abroad in the
Commonwealth and in America.

The Marx Memorial Library, established in 1933 to mark
the fiftieth anniversary of the death of Karl Marx, founder
of communism, holds a unique collection on the history of
socialism.

⊖   ⊖   ⊖

East from Farringdon ⊖, Cowcross Street joins Charterhouse
Street, which runs to the north of Smithfield Market (*St
Paul's* ⊖). A little further east the road forks to the north.
Through the gate is Charterhouse Square, a quiet, leafy haven
surrounded by Georgian houses. The gateway on the north side
of the square forms the entrance to **Charterhouse (1)**.

Founded in the mid-14th century as a Carthusian priory by Sir
Walter de Manny, Charterhouse's name is a corruption of the
French monastery of the Grande-Chartreuse to which Sir
Walter owed allegiance. It was intended as a centre of prayer
for the souls of the thousands who had died that century during
the Black Death. Until the dissolution of the monasteries in
1537, Carthusian monks lived here as hermits. During the

Dissolution, Prior John Houghton refused to accept Henry VIII as supreme head of the English Church and was tried for treason and hanged and quartered at Tyburn (*Marble Arch* ⊖). On the oak doors of the outer gatehouse, still in place today, Houghton's right arm was once nailed to discourage further 'treason'. After the Dissolution, the building passed into various hands before becoming a home for eighty male pensioners and a school for forty-four boys, founded in 1611 by Thomas Sutton, a pioneer investor in the newly discovered Durham coalfields. Charterhouse School, which moved to Godalming in Surrey in 1872, has become one of Britain's foremost public schools. Pensioners remain in the old Charterhouse buildings.

The predominantly 16th-century buildings of Charterhouse, which are open only for guided tours between April and July on Wednesday afternoons or by prior appointment, are formed round a succession of quiet courts. However, parts of the ancient priory remain. In Wash House Court much of the stonework is 14th-century, and in the Great Cloister a section of the original monastery wall, including the entrance to a Carthusian hermit's 'cell', dates from Sir Walter de Manny's lifetime.

Beyond the 15th-century gatehouse is Master's Court. The original monastic church lay here, but it was pulled down by Sir Edward North when he constructed a mansion here in 1545. Master's Court was gravely damaged during the Second World War, but has since been restored. In 1947, during the reconstruction, the lead coffin of Charterhouse's founder, Sir Walter de Manny (d. 1372), was found near the site of the altar.

Beyond Master's Court to the north is the Great Hall, still used today as a dining hall by the elderly 'brethren', as the pensioners are known. It incorporates the hammer-beams from the 16th-century roof. The Great Chamber, a fine Elizabethan room, has a rich gilded plaster ceiling and is decorated with some handsome Flemish tapestries. Both Elizabeth I and James I were once entertained here. Charterhouse also contains a library from the 17th century and a chapel, the latter containing the tomb of Thomas Sutton.

Carthusian Street leads off from the south-east corner of Charterhouse Square. North along Aldersgate, which continues into Goswell Road, at the junction with Clerkenwell Road are Charterhouse Buildings. At No. 14 is the **Society of Genealogists (2)**. Thousands of people, naturally curious about their ancestors, are now members of this society, which was founded in

1911 to promote and encourage the study of genealogy and heraldry. The society's resources are unique. It has the largest national collection of parish registers. These cover mainly the period from the 16th century to 1812. Transcripts of parish registers are arranged by county with local histories, copies of monumental inscriptions, poll books and trade directories, other topographical material and the publications of county record and archaeological societies.

There is also a general slip index with about 3 million references, as well as a marriage index of over 7 million names, covering about 3,000 parishes in England between 1538 and 1837; an index of apprentices from 1710 to 1774; and calendars of wills and marriage licences. An index of Chancery and other court proceedings, the Bernau Index, contains about 4.5 million references prior to 1800. There is a microfiche index (International Genealogical Index) of over 88 million baptisms, and some marriages, within the British Isles and other parts of the world. The society also holds many printed and typescript family histories. Many journals, works relating to the professions, the military forces, schools and other genealogical periodicals are also held. Collections of material are maintained on English people living abroad, in the Commonwealth and in America.

Non-members may use the library for a fee, and the society will undertake a limited amount of research for members and non-members. The society emphasizes in the strongest terms that it is absolutely essential to get the fullest possible information about the family or the individual under investigation before the library is consulted.

Records of births, deaths and marriages in England and Wales since 1 July 1837 are held, but not by family pedigree, at St Catherine's House (*Temple* ⊖). The College of Arms (*Blackfriars* ⊖) hold records for identifying coats of arms and to ascertain whether families are by descent entitled to arms.

St John's Square is west along Clerkenwell Road, beyond St John Street. At its south-east corner is the **Clerkenwell Heritage Centre (3)**, which provides information for visitors to this area. To the south, in St John's Lane, are **St John's Gate** and the **Museum of the Order of St John (4)**.

The castellated St John's Gate was once the main gateway to the Priory of the Order of St John of Jerusalem. The priory was founded around 1144 on land donated by a Norman knight,

Jordan de Bricet, and formed the headquarters of the order in England. The order itself had developed as the military Knights Hospitallers during the Crusades, although its origins may stretch back to the 11th century, when the merchants of the Italian city of Amalfi re-endowed the hospital in Jerusalem used by prilgrims to the Holy Sepulchre. The Knights Hospitallers, who wore a black habit with a white eight-pointed cross on the left breast, cared for pilgrims and the sick and, together with the Knights Templars (*Temple* ⊖), defended the Christian kingdoms in the Holy Land. However, after its expulsion from Palestine by the infamous Saladin, the order became much less international. In England it became increasingly wealthy.

The knights' first priory was destroyed during the Peasants' Revolt of 1381. The present gatehouse, probably the third to occupy the site, was built in 1504 by Prior Thomas Dowcra. Although the loss of its headquarters, Rhodes, to the Turks, albeit heroically, did nothing to deflate the panache of the English knights, the order was suppressed in 1540, shortly after Henry VIII's Act of Dissolution. Reinstated by Queen Mary in 1557, all its possessions were again confiscated by Queen Elizabeth I. At Malta, where the main body of the order had moved after the loss of Rhodes, a shadow of the organization was still continued.

In England the order's buildings then fulfilled various functions. In the 18th century the celebrated *Gentleman's Magazine* was published here and Dr Johnson (*Blackfriars* ⊖), a contributor to the magazine, once occupied one of its rooms. It then became the parish watch house and, later still, the Old Jerusalem Tavern.

In 1874 the gate came into the possession of The Most Venerable Order of the Hospital of St John of Jerusalem, established in 1831 as a revival of the old institution but as a Protestant order. In 1888 Queen Victoria granted it a Royal Charter and it became a British Royal Order of Chivalry, which has the sovereign at its head. The present Grand Prior is the Duke of Gloucester. Until a rapprochement in the 1960s, it remained a national and independent order from the Order of Malta because of religious difficulties.

It was at St John's Gate that the St John Ambulance Association was founded in 1877. The St John Ambulance Brigade, formed a decade later, today provides voluntary first aid assistance at public gatherings.

The entrance to the museum and other rooms is on the south side of the gatehouse. Some parts of the interior and the priory church have limited opening hours and can be seen only with a guide. The museum contains the widest range of exhibits about the order outside Malta, illustrating its rich ecclesiastical, hospitaller and military history. Of special interest are two panels of a Flemish triptych, one of which portrays the coat of arms of John Weston, prior 1476–89; a 16th-century processional cross; and the Rhodes Missal, an illuminated service book of the mass presented to the Convent at Rhodes in 1504, upon which the knights swore their oath of allegiance.

The Chapter Hall is part of an extension to the gatehouse built in 1903 and now used for meetings of the order's governing body. The Chancery, in the east tower of the gatehouse, displays a finely sculptured Elizabethan stone chimney piece. The Council Chamber is situated above the arch. The library, in the west tower, houses an important collection of books relating to the history of the order. A small St John Ambulance museum is also located in the building.

St John, Clerkenwell (5), the priory church of the Order of St John, is now separated from St John's Gate by Clerkenwell Road, and stands on the east side of St John's Square. Consecrated in 1185, the church originally possessed a circular nave and short choir extending eastwards, similar to that of the Knights Templars' round church at Temple.

The church fell victim, like St John's Gatehouse, to Wat Tyler's rebels during the Peasants' Revolt. It underwent rebuilding, and had a chequered history as a secular building following the Dissolution. Henry VIII stored his hunting tents here, and during Edward VI's reign (1547–53) the nave was destroyed to provide stone for the construction of the first Somerset House (*Temple* ⊖). During the Elizabethan era the remainder of the chancel provided offices for the Master of the Revels, an early form of censor, who, among other duties, granted licences for the performance of many of Shakespeare's plays. After a spell as a private chapel, it was restored and sold to the Commissioners of the Fifty New Churches, thereby becoming the parish church of St John.

In 1931 the church reverted to the Order of St John, but bomb damage during the Second World War has left little evidence of its historic past. The present church was rebuilt and rededicated in 1958. The major surviving ancient feature is a magnificent

12th-century crypt. Three of the nave's five bays are late
Norman round-arched, and the eastern two are in the pointed
transitional style. The memorial chapel in the south aisle is in the
Early English style that followed the transitional period. The
crypt contains two tomb sculptures: the emaciated effigy of
William Weston, the last prior before the Reformation, and a
16th-century Spanish alabaster effigy of Knight of the Order
Don Juan Ruiz de Veraga (d. 1567). This knight had been
proctor of the order's League of Castile. His effigy has beautifully sculpted armour with the order's characteristic cross on the
breastplate.

Today the Priory Church is used for the order's major services
and for investitures.

On the north side of St John's Square, Jerusalem Passage leads
towards Clerkenwell Green, the heart of Clerkenwell village.
Standing in a spacious grassy churchyard to the north of
Clerkenwell Green is the parish church, **St James Clerkenwell
(6)**. It was built on the former site of the Benedictine nunnery of
St Mary, dissolved by Henry VIII in 1539. The site and church
were in various hands until 1656, when it was bought by
parishioners. With it they also bought the advowson, the right of
presentation to benefice and, like the people of other parishes
during the Commonwealth, they began to elect their own vicars.
This practice, however, did not cease at the Restoration, and
Clerkenwell continued as a sort of Congregationalist enclave
within the Church of England. The practice of free ecclesiastical
election, and of much colourful electioneering as well, continued until early in the present century. The present church
dates from 1792. The wall of the medieval nunnery can,
however, still be seen in the gardens behind the church.

Now used as a Masonic conference centre, the **Middlesex Court
of Sessions (7)** (John Rogers, 1882) was constructed in 1779–82
as a court building. Its handsome Portland stone façade, decorated with sculptured plaques representing Justice and Mercy
and showing the arms of the County of Middlesex, dominates
the west side of Clerkenwell Green.

The green was once the centre of a semi-rural village and a
little of that atmosphere lingers today. During the Victorian era
the green became a centre for radical political activity. And on

Sunday, 13 November 1887, Clerkenwell Green was the departure point for a fateful Socialists' demonstration known as Bloody Sunday, in which two people died.

The **Marx Memorial Library (8)**, on the north side of the green, was established in 1933 to mark the fiftieth anniversary of the death of the founder of communism, Karl Marx. It was also seen as a gesture against the burning of books in Nazi Germany. Today the library houses more than 100,000 books, manifestoes, pamphlets and periodicals associated with Marx.

Marx, an impoverished German refugee, lived in London with his family from 1849 until his death in 1883. During that time he wrote his greatest work, *Das Kapital* (1867). His grave in Highgate Cemetery (*Outer London*) bears the inscription 'Workers of all lands unite'.

The building was once a charity school for Welsh children. Its long association with the Socialist movement began in 1872, when the London Patriotic Club took up residence. William Morris addressed the club before setting off on the ill-fated Bloody Sunday demonstration in 1887. Five years later Morris backed the establishment in this building of the first Socialist press in Britain. From here, Lenin, leader of the Russian Revolution, edited and published seventeen issues of *Iskra* ('The Spark') during 1902–3. His works are housed in a room named after him, along with specialized works on the Spanish Civil War, the hunger marches, the peace movement and Chartist literature.

Russian premiers Nikita Khruschev and Mikhail Gorbachev have visited the library.

St Mary's Nunnery drew its water supply from the *fons clericorum*, or **Clerks' Well (9)**, which gave its name to the parish. The well gained its name from the medieval parish clerks, who came here to perform 'miracle plays' on the banks of the River Fleet. The well, however, became polluted and clogged with debris, but was rediscovered in 1924. Together with an iron pump and plaque dating from around 1800, it can still be seen today behind the window of No. 16 Farringdon Lane. For closer inspection inquire at Finsbury Reference Library.

Clerkenwell has been home to many members of the Italian community, particularly in the area around **St Peter's Church (10)** in Clerkenwell Road, which is sometimes called 'Little Italy'. Every year on the Sunday following the Feast of Our Lady of Mount Carmel (16 July) Italians from all over Britain congregate for the colourful street procession at the *sagra* (fête) centred around the church. The Italian procession concludes the week-long Clerkenwell Festival.

The connection with Italy began in 1836, when Italian revolutionary Giuseppe Mazzini made Clerkenwell his home. It was also the first port of call for Giuseppe Garibaldi, the Italian general and patriot, on his visit to London in 1836. The famous singers Caruso and Gigli used to perform on the church's steps on Sunday mornings.

St Peter's stands on a site acquired in 1852 for the construction of an international Roman Catholic cathedral to be designed by Francesco Gualandi of Bologna. Work was soon abandoned, but ten years later a modified design by J. M. Brydon was erected by Italian immigrant workers.

Farringdon Road runs south from Clerkenwell Road. To its south in Cowcross Street is Farringdon ⊖.

King's Cross/St Pancras ⊖

A Saxon altar dating from AD 600 found at the site of the St Pancras Old Church, Pancras Road, indicates that this was one of the oldest Christian sites in Europe. Pancratius (Pancras in English), the boy martyr, was born into a noble family in Asia Minor and was converted to Christianity while visiting Rome. During the Diocletian persecution Pancratius refused to give up his beliefs and was beheaded on the Aurelian Way in AD 304, aged 14.

Today the St Pancras area is best known for the remarkable Victorian Gothic façade of St Pancras railway terminus. This truly astonishing architectural fantasy of brick and stone towers over Euston Road. Nearby is the busy King's Cross Railway Station, which was named after the monument to George IV that once stood at a crossroads close to its site.

To the south of King's Cross and St Pancras stations, among acres of flats, houses, shops, hospitals and offices, lie Coram's Fields, now a tree-lined children's playground. Here, the Foundling Hospital stood for nearly 200 years, home for the abandoned children of London and a memorial to the tenacity of purpose and kindliness of philanthropist Captain Thomas Coram. Commemorated now by a remarkable small museum located near the site of the former hospital, its exhibits unfold the hospital's history, and comprise works of art by Hogarth, Gainsborough, Reynolds and Rysbrack. The staircase, gallery and Court Room are the originals from the old hospital.

⊖　⊖　⊖

The façade and decor of the astonishing **St Pancras Station (1)** would appear more suited to an archbishop's palace or a castle than to a railway terminus. Disliked for many years for its Victorianism, size, pretension, colour and ornamentation, it has now found favour again. There remains, however, an element of the ludicrous in this tall, Gothic fantasy of brick and stone.

In 1863 the Midland Railway Company, which was then using nearby King's Cross as its London terminus, obtained powers to build a new station. The constraints of the site forced architect W. H. Barlow to build a great iron shed over the platforms and tracks, with its iron lattice ribs projected in a single span, an

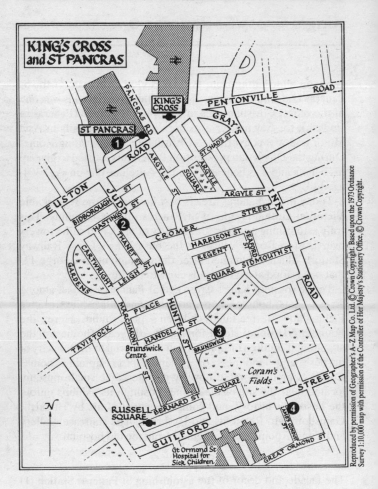

unprecedented 240 ft/73 m. The ribs met at a point like a four-centred Gothic arch, not for aesthetic reasons, but to resist lateral wind pressure.

Space was left for a hotel at the head of the tracks. If the roof design manifests extreme rationality, the hotel stands as a testament to an incredible feat of irrationality in English architecture, a monument to the Victorian Gothic revival. George Gilbert Scott's design for this extraordinary and unique building, which cost a staggering £316,000, was executed between 1865 and 1871. Its façade is best seen from the south side of Euston Road. Scott, a believer that 'architecture should decorate construction', used a whole repertoire of stylistic effects, an amalgam of Italian and early French Gothic with outcrops of English and other styles. Motifs spring up at every juncture. Decorations on the capitals of pillars in the booking hall tailor medieval style to Victorian railway themes. The building is almost ridiculously tall, adorned by turrets and pinnacles and a high dormered roof. The confident sweeping curve of the west wing shows an uninhibited use of colour. Its interior is adorned by a grand staircase.

At the time of its opening, St Pancras was thought by many to be the most magnificent of London's hotels, and in his autobiography Scott stated that it was 'possibly too good for its purpose'. It was the first hotel to have lifts, called 'ascending rooms', which worked by hydraulic power. In 1890 the first ladies' smoking room in London was opened here. In 1935 the hotel was closed and has since been used as offices, known as St Pancras Chambers. However, plans have now been laid for a multimillion-pound restoration of the building as a hotel. Ambitious schemes are also in hand for the development of a massive 100 acres/40 ha. of rundown railway land to the north of St Pancras and King's Cross stations.

The 'Christian soldiers' of the Salvation Army have marched to the four corners of the world, and their movement is now active in nearly ninety countries. Its story is told in the **Salvation Army International Heritage Centre (2)**, located on the third floor of the organization's publishing and supplies building in Judd Street. Photographs, documents and objects belonging to General William Booth, the Salvation Army's founder, are included among the museum's exhibits. There is a section on the movement's distinctive uniform, with special attention paid to the famous bonnet, headgear that Mrs Booth deemed should be 'cheap, strong and large enough to protect the heads of the wearers from cold as well as from brickbats and other missiles'. There are also some idols used by a West African witch-doctor who later became a Salvationist.

At its southern end, Judd Street becomes Hunter Street, named after John Hunter, a physician and Vice-President of the Foundling Hospital (*see* 3), who lived here in 1803–9.

Still further south is Brunswick Square, on whose western side are the modern terraced and cantilevered apartments, shops, restaurants and cinema of the Brunswick Centre, referred to locally as the 'Hanging Glasshouses of Babylon'.

On the north side of the square is the **Thomas Coram Foundation for Children (3)**. Captain Thomas Coram, mariner, pioneer and colonizer of New England, was granted a royal charter by George II in 1739 to found a hospital 'for the maintenance and education of exposed and deserted children'. Coram, on his frequent business trips to London from his home in Rotherhithe, had been shocked at how many unwanted babies were abandoned in the capital's streets and alley-ways. His perseverance to establish a foundling hospital gained the support of many prominent citizens, notably composer George Frederick Handel and painter William Hogarth. Six dukes, eleven earls and a great assembly of lords, merchants and bankers were present when the royal charter was finally received. Hogarth, one of the hospital's first governors, encouraged many of his artist contemporaries to donate works for display in the Governors' Court Room to attract visitors and funds. He gave many paintings himself, including a portrait of Coram, and designed the hospital's arms. Handel, who gave an organ to the chapel, wrote the Foundling Hospital Anthem, and frequently played and conducted performances of his own works here.

Today, in a remarkable small museum, the story of the early days of the Foundling Hospital is unfolded through a series of contemporary engravings and documents. The Thomas Coram Foundation for Children, whose work now centres around the adoption and fostering of children, has also loaned a number of unique exhibits, including the original and wonderfully illustrated Charter of Incorporation, the keyboard of Handel's organ, two costumes worn by foundling children and Hogarth's own splendid punch bowl.

The original Foundling Hospital was built on Lamb's Conduit Fields, but in 1926 the governors decided to move the hospital to the cleaner air of the country. The old hospital was demolished. The present building, which dates from 1937 and is near the original site, incorporates the staircase, gallery and beautifully panelled Court Room from its predecessor.

On the landing at the top of the stairs is Hogarth's masterpiece *Captain Thomas Coram* (1740). A lobby leads into the Court Room, reconstructed with red walls and white-and-gilt plasterwork as Hogarth and his friends had decorated it in the 1740s.

Four large canvases illustrate biblical incidents on the theme of pity for neglected children, including Hogarth's *Moses Brought before Pharaoh's Daughter*. There are also Rysbrack's relief *Charity* (1746), and Gainsborough's *The Charterhouse*, an important landmark in the history of English landscape painting. A glass case contains a touching display of tokens left by mothers to identify their abandoned children. A passage off the landing leads to the Picture Gallery, whose treasures include the *Massacre of the Innocents*, the largest surviving fragment of a cartoon for one of three panels of a tapestry in the Vatican woven in the early 16th century. Originally attributed to Raphael, it is now thought to be by Giulio Romano. The portrait of the Second Earl of Dartmouth, vice-president of the hospital between 1755 and 1801, was donated by Reynolds.

To the east of Brunswick Square, in Guilford Street, is Coram's Fields (formerly Lamb's Conduit Street), where the original Foundling Hospital stood. Now a playground, it is still devoted to the needs of children.

Opposite, beyond Guilford Place, is **Lamb's Conduit Street (4)**, named after an Elizabethan dam made in one of the tributaries of the Fleet River and restored in 1577 by engineer William Lamb. Lamb also provided 120 pails for the poor women of the area, and although the conduit no longer exists, a statue in Guilford Place shows a lady with an urn. **The Lamb** public house at No. 94 Lamb's Conduit Street, once a meeting place of members of the Bloomsbury Group, is a typical, old-fashioned Victorian London pub, noted for its mahogany panelling and attractively engraved screens. Further south, at No. 73, is the **Cartoon Gallery**, which sells, at affordable prices, many original cartoons by noted cartoonists.

To the west of Lamb's Conduit Street is the Great Ormond Street Hospital for Sick Children, founded in 1851 by Dr Charles West, who saw around him then an appallingly high rate of infant and child mortality and a lack of medical treatment.

Euston Square ⊖ & Russell Square ⊖

The influence of the University of London, Britain's first 'open' university, permeates the area to the south of Euston Square ⊖. The university was founded in 1836, largely inspired by the nearby University College, a separate institution founded a decade earlier. The university grew from a need to provide higher education that was free from the influence of the Church; at that time the admissions policy of the country's older universities excluded Dissenters. London University and University College eventually combined and their many buildings and institutes now line Gower Street and stretch south and east towards Russell Square.

University College's Flaxman Gallery houses a superb collection of sculptor John Flaxman's original neo-classical plaster models, which were used to create many church monuments. On the south side of the college's precincts is the Petrie Museum of Egyptology, the finest collection of Ancient Egyptian archaeological material in any university in the world. The outstanding collection of Chinese ceramics acquired by Sir David Percival, a former governor of London University's School of Oriental and African Studies, is housed in a small museum in Gordon Square.

The rich heritage of the Jewish community in Britain is displayed at the Jewish Museum in Tavistock Square. Its centrepiece is a superb 16th-century Venetian synagogue ark.

To the north of Euston Square ⊖ is Euston British Rail Station, the oldest of London's mainline termini, now housed in the newest premises.

⊖ ⊖ ⊖

University College (1) was the first great secular establishment to challenge the power of the Church in higher education. Founded in 1826, it was the first university institution in England to admit students irrespective of religion, race and, some years later, sex. Known by its detractors as 'the godless college in Gower Street', it provided university education to non-Anglicans, who were at that time excluded from Oxford and Cambridge.

Passing into the college's courtyard from Gower Street, the original central range (1827–9) by William Wilkins (1778–1839)

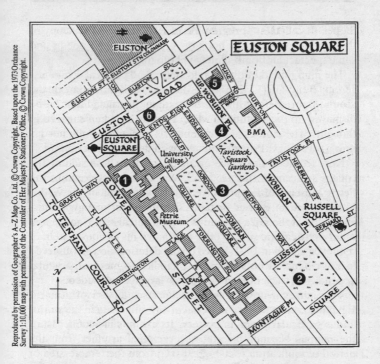

Reproduced by permission of Geographer's A-Z Map Co. Ltd. © Crown Copyright. Based upon the 1973 Ordnance Survey 1:10,000 map with permission of the Controller of Her Majesty's Stationery Office, © Crown Copyright.

is immediately visible ahead. The dome, Corinthian portico and fine flight of steps are reminiscent of Wilkins' other great London landmark, the National Gallery (*Embankment* ⊖). To the left of the portico, a door leads up to the first floor, where, located under the dome in a marvellous architectural setting, is the **Flaxman Gallery**. On display here are 120 original plaster models for church monuments made by the distinguished English sculptor and illustrator John Flaxman.

The **Strang Print Room** in South Cloisters contains a collection of prints and drawings, including fine Old Master etchings, engravings and early English mezzotints; the Grote bequest of 16th-, 17th- and early-18th-century German drawings, Turner's *Liber Studiorum*; Lucas's prints after Constable; and a large collection of drawings by Flaxman.

In the North Cloisters is **The College Exhibition**, a tribute to famous members of staff and students, whose number includes Ambrose Fleming, inventor of the thermionic valve; painter Augustus John, economist Sir Stafford Cripps; and Marie

Stopes. Its changing programme of exhibits includes a copy of the first X-ray picture, a book of A. E. Housman's poems and some spectacular bomb-damage photographs.

The mummified body of philosopher and political economist Jeremy Bentham (1748–1832) is on view during term time on the ground floor. Before his death Bentham instructed that he be displayed 'in the attitude in which I am sitting when engaged in thought'. The clothes are the thinker's original, but the head is now a wax effigy. Porters will help with detailed directions.

Next to the Malet Place entrance, on the south side of the college's precincts, the D. M. S. Watson Library contains the **Petrie Museum of Egyptian Archaeology**, formed by Sir W. M. Flinders Petrie. Petrie, Britain's first professor of Egyptology, excavated at the Giza pyramids in 1880 and also at Naqada and other pre-dynastic sites. Petrie originated his famous system of sequence dating in 1901, based on the deterioration he observed in wavy-handled pots from true handles to mere ornamental appendages, a scientific method now largely superseded.

This museum now houses the finest collection of Ancient Egyptian archaeological material of any university in the world, and is particularly rich in pottery. Its exhibits include a cast of the famous Narmer palette, a ceremonial artefact from the period of unification (3200–3050 BC) from the temple area of Hierakonopolis; amulets, beads, ivories, votive objects, stone vessels from many periods; the granulated gold spell case and the first faience figure of Ptah-Sokar from Harageh; a fascinating range of material from the capital city of Akhetaten built by Akhenaten (Amenophis IV); material from the Roman cemetery at Hawara in the Fayum (post 30 BC); weights, measures, tools, weapons, household objects and glassware, and Graeco-Roman wax mummy portraits. The museum has been given the fragmentary limestone lions, monumental Early Dynastic lions, excavated by Petrie in the temple at Koptos in 1894. It also possesses garments from Tarkhan and Deshasheh and a child's linen tunic, dating from the First Dynasty (c. 3100 BC), the oldest known linen garment in the world.

University College, which in many ways served as the inspiration for the University of London, was formally incorporated into it in 1907. The University of London's main buildings lie to the south in Malet Street. The west side of Gower Street, south from University College, is one of London's longest unbroken, but far from the prettiest, stretches of late-Georgian houses.

Also situated in Malet Street is the Royal Academy of Dramatic Art (RADA), the leading drama school in the country. At the south end of the street is Montague Place, which leads east into Russell Square.

Russell Square (2), at the heart of Bloomsbury, is one of the largest and leafiest squares in London. Developed in 1800, the square was named after the local landlord, the head of the Russell family, the Duke of Bedford. The statue on the south side of the gardens by Westmacott is of Francis, Fifth Duke of Bedford, in whose lifetime the square emerged.

The **Percival David Foundation of Chinese Art (3)**, situated at the south-east corner of Gordon Square, is entirely devoted to an outstanding collection of Chinese ceramics. Each item in this small museum is of superb quality and some pieces once belonged to emperors of China. Poems and historical notes from the brush of Emperor Qianlong (1735–95) appear on a number of artefacts. Sir Percival David (1892–1964), a former governor of London University's School of Oriental and African Studies, presented some 1,400 pieces to the university in 1950. This connoisseur's collection spans a period from the 9th century to the 19th century, covering the Song, Yüan, Ming and Qing dynasties. The Song period is especially noted for Ru, Ding, Jün, Guan and Longquan celadon wares, with their pale greenish-grey glaze. The earliest known dated pieces of classic underglaze blue-and-white porcelain are a pair of temple vases, the 'David' vases, from 1351. Polychrome wares of great variety are well represented from the 15th century onwards. Sir Percival's Foundation also includes a library of Chinese and Western books dealing with Chinese art and culture, available by application.

East of Gordon Square lies Tavistock Square, named after the Marquess of Tavistock, who was also Duke of Bedford. In the garden, near a cherry tree planted in memory of the victims of Hiroshima, stands a statue of Indian independence leader and pacifist Mahatma Gandhi. Dominating the east side of the square is Tavistock House, built in 1913 by Edwin Lutyens for its present occupant, the British Medical Association.

The rich and diverse heritage of Anglo-Jewish culture is spread out in the **Jewish Museum (4)**, which occupies one large room in Woburn House, on the corner of Tavistock Square and

Upper Woburn Place. The museum was the first permanent collection of Jewish ritual art and antique items in England when it opened to the public in 1932. It now contains more than 1,000 items of Anglo-Jewish history. The nucleus of the collection, on loan from the United Synagogue, consists mainly of ritual objects from early City of London synagogues.

Jews have lived in England since the Norman invasion – and perhaps before – but were expelled by Edward I in 1290. Usury was forbidden to Christians by the medieval Church and social laws excluded Jews from all occupations except money-lending, in which capacity they became the property of the Crown and acted as its bankers. The museum possesses two 'tallies', wooden objects that were notched to indicate the amount the Exchequer had received. Until 1656 no Jews officially lived in Britain, but during Cromwell's Protectorate Jews were readmitted and a group of Sephardic Jews opened a synagogue in the City. The importance of this Spanish and Portuguese Jewish group to the history of London is evident from the Lord Mayor's Salver (1702). The salver and two cups were once presentation pieces accompanying annual gifts of chocolates or sweetmeats to the City's figurehead.

One end of the room is dominated by the museum's centre-piece, a richly carved and painted 16th-century Venetian synagogue ark in which the Scrolls of the Law were once kept. The ark had previously been used as a servant's wardrobe before a Jewish bookseller discovered it in an auction sale at Chillingham Castle, Northumberland. Sabbath lamps hang from the ceiling of the room and there are many superbly crafted objects of religious and ceremonial significance, including antique circumcision sets. One of the earliest treasures is a gold votive plaque from the 7th or 8th century, with a Greek inscription from the Byzantine period. The Jewish life-style and the Jewish year are illustrated through videos and the objects on display.

Woburn Walk is a delightful pedestrian thoroughfare on the east side of Upper Woburn Place. It was designed by Thomas Cubitt in 1822 as a small shopping centre and today still possesses some of the best late-Georgian bow-windowed shopfronts in London.

When **St Pancras New Church (5)** was completed in 1822, it was, at £90,000, the most expensive church erected in London since St Paul's Cathedral (*St Paul's* ⊖). Built of brick faced with

Portland stone, its rich, grand and civilized Neo-Grecian design, London's first in the style, was based by architects father and son William and Henry Inwood on a clever rearrangement of the layout of the Acropolis Erechtheum in Athens. Instead of one of its porticoes, however, they gave it a segmental apse. They also put the caryatid tribunes on both sides instead of only one and, for the spire, put up a stack of three diminishing towers – the Tower of the Winds, based on the one in Athens. The tower terminates in a simple cross. Draped female terracotta caryatids by Charles Rossi, which support the roofs of the two pavilions, were found to be too large when originally installed. Sections from their middles were removed, hence their present squat appearance.

The church's interior also displays many of the rich decorative features of the Greek revival, notably the lotus-leaf capitals copied from the Elgin Marbles on the slender columns supporting the galleries. Around the apse stand a series of Ionic columns made of *scagliola*, a mixture of plaster, marble chippings and glue.

Friends' House (6), the British headquarters of the Religious Society of Friends, is west along Euston Road. Its library, founded in 1673, contains a fine collection of Quaker literature, including George Fox's journal and documents relating to the foundation of the American state of Pennsylvania.

Great Portland Street ⊖

South and east from Great Portland Street ⊖ and the busy
Euston Road lies Fitzroy Square, one of London's finest squares
and once a centre for writers and artists. Two sides of this fine
square were designed by Robert Adam. Telecom Tower, just to
the south, rises high above the square. Charlotte Street, further
to the south-east, was once an artists' quarter, although it is
today famed for its restaurants, notably those specializing in
Greek cuisine. Off Charlotte Street in Scala Street is Pollock's
Toy Museum, two connecting Georgian houses containing a
dainty collection of toys, dolls and toy theatres.

⊖   ⊖   ⊖

Fitzroy Square (1) is one of London's finest squares. Its stone-
faced south and east sides were built in the 1790s to the designs
of Robert Adam (1728–92). The designs are typically Adam,
light and elegant with protruding accents in the centre and at the
ends. The rusticated ground floor façade, with its recessed
columns in these accents, gives a contrast in texture.

Early this century the area around Fitzroy Square became a
centre for writers and artists. Virginia Woolf, a leading member
of the 'Bloomsbury Group', lived at No. 29, once also the home
of writer George Bernard Shaw. Unrecorded by any memorial
plaque are the former Omega Workshops, at No. 33, the
distinguished creative centre run by painter and connoisseur
Roger Fry. Fry scandalized the art world with the first exhibition
of French Post-Impressionist work in Britain, which the establishment then took to be a disgraceful display of bad painting.
Painter William Sickert had a studio in Fitzroy Street and
other illustrious residents living nearby included Whistler and
Rossetti. Poet Dylan Thomas was a familiar figure in the local
pubs. Fitzroy Square is now a pedestrian precinct.

Telecom Tower (2), formerly the Post Office Tower, at
580 ft/176.8 m vies with the Nat West Tower (*Bank* ⊖) as the
tallest building in Britain. It all hinges over whether Telecom
Tower's 39-ft/12-m aerial mast is eligible for inclusion. Unfortunately, the splendid views from the top of the tower are now
closed to the public following a terrorist bomb attack in 1971.

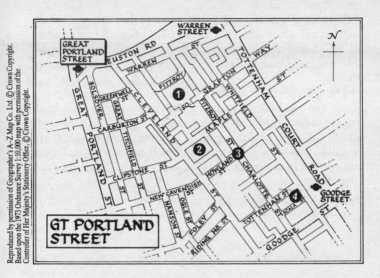

Some of those galleries now accommodate equipment for the many dishes and aerials that transmit and receive radio, television and telephone calls in and out of London. It is still possible, however, to dine in the tower's revolving restaurant. The restaurant completes a circle every 23 minutes, giving a unique panorama of the capital. A short distance away in Cleveland Street is the house where Samuel Morse, inventor of Morse Code, once lived.

From the late 18th century, **Charlotte Street (3)** was an artists' quarter. Landscape painter John Constable lived at No. 76. Today this street, named after Queen Charlotte, wife of George III, is noted for its numerous restaurants. There is much alfresco eating in the summer, and many Greek restaurants at its southern end. Charlotte Street also houses the headquarters of Britain's Channel Four television network.

Pollock's Toy Museum (4), now an educational charitable trust, takes its name from Benjamin Pollock (1856–1937), who devoted his life to keeping alive the tradition of English toy theatre. Pollock's shop in East London was so well known and loved that Robert Louis Stevenson was moved to write: 'If you love art, folly or the bright eyes of children, speed to Pollock's.'

Pollock's toy collection forms the basis of this museum, which now occupies two Georgian houses (No. 1 Scala Street and No. 41 Whitfield Street), connected by narrow winding staircases. The museum also continues Pollock's work in keeping alive toy theatre.

The collection contains toys from around the world and many ingenious mechanical creations. Particular attention has been paid to the acquisition of English dolls and toys. The museum is ideally suited for children aged 7–12 and many of the exhibits are at child's eye-level. Miniature cardboard cut-out theatre scenes are on sale in the premises through Pollock's Theatrical Print Warehouse.

Baker Street ⊖

Millions of people come to Madame Tussaud's each year to see the museum's incredible collection of waxworks. Created by a remarkable Frenchwoman, Madame Tussaud's is the best known waxworks in the world. Its figures, tableaux and Chamber of Horrors are famed for their uncanny and eerie realism. The collection, whose earliest figure is from the 18th century, is kept up to the minute with contemporary effigies of the famous and infamous. At the Planetarium next door visitors can take a seemingly magical journey through the stars. On most evenings the Planetarium's massive and spectacular auditorium is transformed into the Laserium, an audio-visual fantasy of pop and classical music concerts accompanied by pulsating laser beams.

Regent's Park, by contrast, is a much more natural environment. John Nash designed the park and surrounded it with fine terraces, enhancing its feeling of space. The park houses London Zoo, the world's oldest zoo, with its collection of more than 8,000 animals.

Baker Street itself was laid out in the mid-18th century as a broad thoroughfare and today is lined with shops and offices. The street's most famous resident, the fictional detective Sherlock Holmes, lived at 221B, today the offices of the Abbey National building society. An exhibition about Sir Arthur Conan Doyle's celebrated character, held in 1951 as part of the Festival of Britain celebrations, is now housed in the Sherlock Holmes pub off Northumberland Avenue (*Embankment* ⊖).

⊖   ⊖   ⊖

London Transport's Lost Property Office is situated on the west side of Baker Street ⊖. East along Marylebone Road are Madame Tussaud's and the London Planetarium.

Madame Tussaud's (1) is the most famous waxworks in the world. Its lifelike exhibits of the living and the dead form a weird, wonderful and sometimes terrifying collage. Great emphasis is placed on accuracy, and a number of figures wear clothes donated by their subjects.

The earliest figure, dating from 1765, is of Madame Du Barry, the last mistress of Louis XV, now shown as the ingenious 'breathing' Sleeping Beauty. Madame Tussaud (1761–1850)

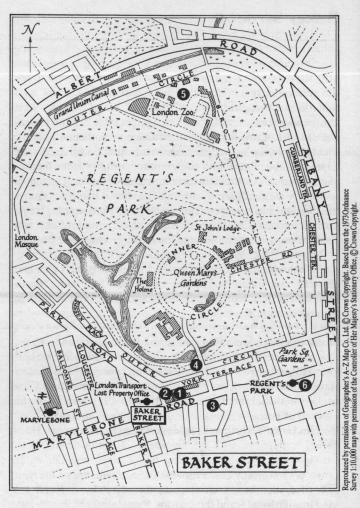

herself worked at the Court of Louis XVI. During the French Revolution she was commanded to take death masks of victims of the guillotine. In 1802 Madame Tussaud moved her waxworks business to Britain and presented her exhibition across the country. She established her permanent collection in 1835 in London when she was 74. At the age of 81, and by then a stiff and small figure, she sculpted a mercilessly accurate self-portrait, now to be seen in the Great Hall.

When she brought her exhibition to Britain, Madame Tussaud included a separate section for the notorious political characters of the day, as she could not juxtapose effigies of men like revolutionary leader Robespierre with those of members of the British royal family. The satirical magazine *Punch* was quick to nickname this room the Chamber of Horrors, and it was rapidly made popular by the public.

A new version of the chamber opened in 1980. The death masks of Louis XVI and Queen Marie Antoinette can still be seen beside the actual guillotine blade that decapitated them. The chamber's gallows were acquired in 1878 from Hertford Gaol. The chill Victorian cobbled street where the Ripper's last victim was murdered has been re-created. So, too, has 10 Rillington Place, where John Christie killed and concealed seven women victims. Elsewhere, special audio-visual techniques are used to show the murderer Gary Gilmore before and after the firing squad.

The museum's tableaux show Mary Queen of Scots preparing for the executioner's block, and Guy Fawkes in the cellars of Parliament preparing for his infamous Gunpowder Plot. In the Conservatory the scene is set for film stars, sportsmen, writers and television personalities. Agatha Christie presented clothes for her effigy; Larry Hagman provided a stetson as well as a piece of turf from Southfork, Dallas, for his JR, and Liza Minnelli donated a pair of her false eyelashes. In another gallery superstars Michael Jackson, David Bowie, Sylvester Stallone and others have been brought to life with sound, light and special effects.

The Great Hall houses statesmen, artists and royalty. Henry VIII is depicted with his six wives. Winston Churchill was modelled thirteen times during his lifetime, highlighting the museum's concern to achieve contemporary likeness. Margaret Thatcher has already been modelled four times.

The Battle of Trafalgar display, opened in 1966, has become one of Madame Tussaud's most popular exhibits, with its reconstruction of the atmosphere on the gun deck of Nelson's flagship, HMS *Victory*.

Recent additions to the museum are Sir Francis Drake, Paul Hogan as Crocodile Dundee, Grace Jones, Bob Hoskins, Anneka Rice, Boris Becker, Fatima Whitbread, Archbishop Tutu and Prince Edward.

Madame Tussaud's remarkable success has depended on the

considerable skills of its sculptors, moulders, hairdressers and costumiers, as well as its research department. New portraits can take anything up to three months to complete. Exhibits are dusted every day, and at least twice a year the hair of each model is washed, the wax recoloured and the clothes cleaned.

The **London Planetarium** (2), with its large green copper dome, adjoins Madame Tussaud's and is a place of unique entertainment and learning. The Astronomers' Gallery beneath the Planetarium auditorium portrays some of the great scientists responsible for many major breakthroughs in man's long search for an understanding of the universe. The discoveries of Ptolemy, Copernicus, Galileo, Newton and Einstein are represented in three-dimensional structures with sound, light and special effects. On the circular wall of the exhibition area are two murals summarizing various philosophies about the nature of the Universe.

The Planetarium, or 'theatre of the skies', is entered up a ramp winding round the outer wall of the Gallery. Its complex Zeiss star projector, weighing over two tons and containing 29,000 parts, travels backwards and forwards in time and space illustrating the dramatic and mysterious movements of the heavens. On the building's inner aluminium dome, perforated with over 18 million small holes for acoustic purposes, this giant projector can create the images of no less than 9,000 stars.

In the evening the Planetarium is transformed into the Laserium, the first of its kind in Europe. It presents a fantasy of music and light, combining pop and classical concerts accompanied by pulsating laser beams.

In the early Middle Ages a church dedicated to St John was built on the banks of the River Tyburn, the Tye Bourne, near what is now the western end of Oxford Street. In 1400 a new church was erected on the present site and named St Mary by the Bourne, hence **St Marylebone** (3). Thomas Hardwick began building the present church in 1813 as part of John Nash's plans for the Regent's Park area. Soon afterwards, it was decided to elevate Hardwick's building to become Marylebone's parish church. In recognition, the church was given a magnificent Corinthian portico. Nash also provided the church with a fine vista along York Gate into the park. The church's distinctive cupola is supported by gilt caryatids. The Browning Room, where poet

Robert Browing secretly married Elizabeth Barrett, contains souvenirs to their memory.

Regent's Park (4) was originally part of Middlesex Forest. In the mid-16th century, at the time of the Reformation, an area was set aside here as an enclosed hunting park for Henry VIII. In the early 19th century a competition was held to determine the best design for a new Crown Estate for what had by then become a patchwork of farms and fields. John Nash (1752–1835), with the patronage of the Prince Regent (later George IV), produced the most original and grand design. Nash's grand plan was for a park 500 acres/200 ha. in size and roughly circular. Wishing to avoid creating a grid of residential squares and streets, and desiring to retain the spaciousness of the parkland, Nash designed fine terraces to be built around the park. The park was to be landscaped with trees, a serpentine lake, a royal summer house, numerous neo-classical villas and an inner circus ringed with houses. In sum, it was to be a truly exquisite garden suburb linking a proposed royal country home in the park by an impressive processional thoroughfare, later known as Regent Street, to Westminster and George IV's Carlton House (*St James's Park* ⊖).

Nash's grand plan was never fully realized, although an expansive park with trees, a lake and terraces had been created by 1825. Terraces built around the Outer Circle from the north-east to the south-west were named after the sons of George III. On the east side of the park **Chester Terrace** has a long unbroken façade designed under Nash's supervision by the young architect Decimus Burton, son of financier and developer James Burton. North of Chester Terrace, **Cumberland Terrace** has been judged the most impressive of Nash's designs, once intended to provide a pleasant vista for the park's proposed royal summer palace. Of the many terraces, **Sussex Place**, on the south-west side of the park, is the most extraordinary, with its curved wings and ten-pointed cupolas. Fifty-six neo-classical villas were also planned, of which only eight were built. Today, three remain: Hanover Lodge, the Holme and St John's Lodge.

Regent's Park is entered on its south side through York Gate, which bisects Nash's York Terrace. Immediately north, bounded by the Inner Circle, **Queen Mary's Gardens**, named after George V's consort, are noted for their wonderful roses. During summer months Shakespeare's plays and other great classics are performed in the **Open Air Theatre** on the north-west side of the Inner Circle. To the west of Queen Mary's Gardens is **Regent's Park Lake**, fed by the Tyburn stream now channelled underground. There is a special boating pond and playground for children on the west side of the park. Opposite the playground is the distinctive dome and minaret of the London Mosque.

London Zoo (Zoological Society Gardens) (5) occupies the northern portion of Regent's Park. It is the oldest, as well as the most famous and prestigious, zoological garden in the world. First opened to the public in 1827, it now houses more than 8,000 animals in its 36-acre/14.5-ha. compound. London Zoo is famed not only for its lions, giraffes, elephants, birds, reptiles, amphibians, fish and insects, but also for the many buildings of architectural merit in its confines. The zoo was founded by the Zoological Society of London in the 1820s, and the society still maintains a high reputation for scientific research, particularly in the conservation and breeding of endangered species.

A notice-board by the main entrance shows feeding times for pelicans, penguins, sea-lions, polar bears, lions, piranhas and many other creatures, each a popular public spectacle. On Fridays snakes are fed on whole (dead) animals. Elephants' bath time and weighing are among the favourite events and young elephants walk round the zoo each day. Rides are given on camels, ponies and donkeys, as well as in a llama cart. The Children's Zoo has a wide variety of farm animals and pets, and its cows are milked daily.

Gorillas, orang-utans, chimpanzees and gibbons inhabit the Pavilion for Apes and Monkeys, and other mammals, including bears, sheep and goats, each live in terraces built specially for them with pits and moats. The tanks of the Aquarium are stocked with fish from fresh and sea waters from all over the world, including the deadly piranha with its razor-sharp teeth.

The Reptile House has some particularly venomous snakes, but visitors can touch one of the totally harmless species. In the Moonlit World, night is created during the day to encourage nocturnal animals such as badgers, bats and the only species of nocturnal monkey, the douroucouli, to come forward. Some of the animals in Moonlit World are crepuscular, active at dawn and dusk; others, like lorises and bushbabies, have large eyes, a common adaptation to nocturnal life. The Insect House contains

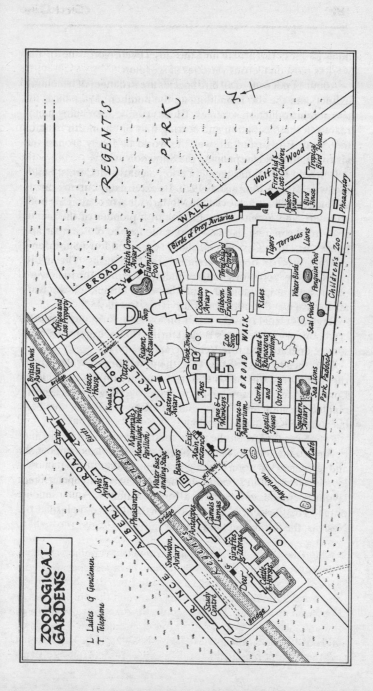

ZOOLOGICAL GARDENS

L Ladies   G Gentlemen   T Telephone

REGENT'S PARK

Wolf & Wood
First Aid & Lost Children
Peafowl Aviary
Tropical Bird House
Bird House
Pheasantry
BROAD WALK
Birds of Prey Aviaries
Tigers
Terraces
Lions
British Crows' Aviary
Flamingo Pool
Penguin Pool
Water Birds
Children's Zoo
Seal Ponds
Cockatoo Aviary
Gibbon Enclosure
Rides
Zoo Shop
Offices and Lost Property
Shop
D
Regent Restaurant
Clock Tower
Zoo Shop
Elephant & Rhinoceros Pavilion
Park Paddock
Sea Lions
British Owls' Aviary
Bridge
Insect House
E. TUNNEL
Otters
Koala's
Apes
Apes & Monkeys
Eastern Aviary
BROAD WALK
Storks and Ostriches
Southern Aviary
CIRCLE
Mammals Moonlight World Pavilion
Entrance to Aquarium
Reptile House
Café
Exit
Main Entrance
Beavers
N. TUNNEL
Aquarium
Exit
Owls' Aviary
Water Bus Landing Stage
BIRDS
ALBERT ROAD
Pheasantry
Bridge
OUTER
Camels & Llamas
Snowdon Aviary
Regent's Antelopes
Giraffes & Zebras
Study Centre
Deer
Cattle & Horses
Bridge
PRINCE ALBERT ROAD

dung beetles, tarantulas and the desert scorpion, one of the world's most dangerous varieties of scorpion.

About 11 per cent of all bird species are in danger of becoming extinct, and the zoo is building up the number of rare birds for use in reintroduction schemes. Chicks can be seen being hand-reared in the incubation and rearing unit on the north bank of the canal. Birds from all over the world fly freely around the visitor on the bridge spanning the Snowdon aviary.

Berthold Lubetkin's penguin pool, an early Modernist building, was listed as long ago as 1970. Its extensively curving ramps are judged to have achieved the Modern ideal of combining both sculpture and architecture. Lubetkin, a pioneer of the use of reinforced concrete, is also responsible for the old circular ape house. Sir Hugh Casson's elephant house and Lord Snowdon's aviary are other notable architectural landmarks. The entire plans of the zoo's original architect, Decimus Burton, were never fully implemented, but the east tunnel, clocktower, raven's cage and giraffe house survive to this day.

Regent's Canal runs through London Zoo, forming the northern boundary of Regent's Park. During summer months a boat service operates to Little Venice (*Paddington* ⊖).

To return to Baker St ⊖, take the grand **Broad Walk**, which runs parallel to the park's eastern boundary on the east side of London Zoo. In summer its wayside overflows with flowers planted in giant urns and, south of Chester Road, the herbaceous beds are a riot of colour.

Park Square Gardens lie at the south end of Broad Walk, and beyond to the south is **Park Crescent (6)**. The grace, proportion and elegance of John Nash's crescent makes it one of the loveliest terraces in London. Its classical curve and uncluttered layout is emphasized by paired Ionic columns in a continuous porch. The crescent is divided by Portland Place, regarded by Nash as 'the finest street in London'.

Edgware Road

Edgware Road follows the course of the old Roman road, Watling Street, which once ran north from Londinium to Verulamium, near St Albans, and Chester (Deva). It later became a turnpike road, which ran north from Tyburn Gallows (*Marble Arch* ⊖). Edgware Road is now a busy modern thoroughfare, lined with the neon lights of hi-fi and electrical shops.

⊖　　⊖　　⊖

There are few features of sight-seeing interest to be viewed here, except perhaps **Bell Street Market (1)** north of Marylebone flyover. This rather shabby Saturday market, the bottom of the antiques pyramid, sports a lot of junk and what could only politely be described as house clearance bric-à-brac. Its wares comprise second-hand furniture, books, jumble and some interesting toys, as well as cheap and not-so-cheerful clothes. A few minutes' walk northward is **Church Street Market (2)**, one of London's more lively, all-purpose, open-air bargain areas for fruit and vegetables, household goods and clothes. Near the

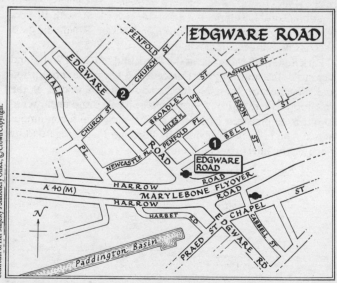

Lisson Grove end of Church Street there are a number of fine antique shops and Alfie's, which houses many smaller antique shops and stalls.

Paddington ⊖

Two hundred years ago Paddington was a small village set around a green. Little of the original village remains, and the area is now bisected by the busy Westway flyover. The famous Great Western Railway Company had its London terminus here, and it was to Paddington that Queen Victoria made her first railway journey. Isambard Kingdom Brunel's Paddington Station in Praed Street, a light and airy structure, still forms the essential fabric of today's station. The world's first underground railway was opened at Paddington in 1863.

In a small laboratory overlooking Praed Street Sir Alexander Fleming, apparently by accident, revolutionized modern medicine by discovering *Penicillium notatum*. By chance a mould spore blew in through an open window on to a culture plate; Fleming later noted its remarkable anti-bacterial properties.

Little Venice, north of Westway, is an unexpected area of glinting white stuccoed buildings, greenery and water. From here canal trips can be taken in the summer to Regent's Park and London Zoo.

The London Toy and Model Museum has one of the finest collections of toy and model trains, cars, dolls, boats, planes and teddy bears.

⊖ ⊖ ⊖

Paddington Station (1) in Praed Street is where the Great Western Railway, or 'God's Wonderful Railway' as it was affectionately known to railway enthusiasts, had its London terminus. Queen Victoria made railway travel respectable in 1842 when she took a train from Slough to Paddington. The 17-mile/27-km journey took 23 minutes at an average speed of 44 mph/70 kmph on Brunel's broad-gauge track. Travelling on the footplate was the Great Western Railway's celebrated engineer, Isambard Kingdom Brunel. In 1851 the company appointed Brunel to design a new station. Drawing on ideas from Paxton's Crystal Palace, Brunel designed a light, airy building with a graceful triple roof of wrought-iron and glass, supported by slender cast-iron pillars. Elegant iron-work decoration embellishes the roof and the capitals of the columns. On a wall by platform No. 1 a plaque with a picture of Brunel

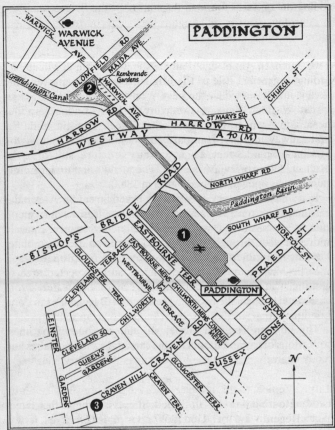

PADDINGTON

wearing a stovepipe hat and dangling a cheroot was put up to mark the station's centenary in 1954. The world's first underground railway was opened here in 1863 by the Metropolitan Railway Company.

Paddington Station now covers 13 acres/5.2 ha. Each weekday some 50,000 passengers pass through its portals. The station has latterly been immortalized by Paddington Bear, the principal character in Michael Bond's children's novel *A Bear Called Paddington*. Paddington Bear travelled from 'darkest Peru via

Paddington' and was found at the station by the Brown family. An enormous stuffed Paddington Bear is to be found on the station concourse.

At the northern end of Eastbourne Terrace, on the west side of Paddington Station, Bishop's Bridge Road crosses east over the railway and Grand Union Canal. On the far side of the bridge, round to the left beneath the Westway dual carriageway, a footpath leads northward beside the canal to the carefully maintained Rembrandt Gardens next to **Little Venice (2)**, one of London's most unexpected beauty spots.

Reflected through trees on the triangular-shaped stretch of water and pool at the junction of the Grand Union Canal and Regent's Canal are the white stuccoed mansions of Little Venice. In the early 1800s nearby Paddington Basin was a busy commercial wharf lined with warehouses used for storing goods brought by canal from the Midlands and industrial North. In the 1820s it was linked to London's docks by John Nash's Regent's Canal, running across Regent's Park to Limehouse. But by the middle part of the century this area had become a fashionable Italianate suburb of the capital. Poet Robert Browning was the first to compare it with Venice, but the name Little Venice seems not to have been generally used until after the Second World War. The graceful mansions of Park Place Villas constitute some of the best examples of early Victorian domestic architecture in London.

Little Venice, with its tree-clad island, houseboats and Cascade Floating Art Gallery, is linked in the summer by canal trips to Regent's Park and London Zoo (*Baker Street* ⊖). The Rembrandt Gardens were named to mark the 750th anniversary of the founding of Amsterdam, which has links with the City of Westminster. Plans are currently being considered to develop the Paddington Basin area.

Return to Paddington Station and proceed to the southern end of Eastbourne Terrace, then turn right on to Craven Road and continue west to the **London Toy and Model Museum (3)** at No. 23 Craven Hill. This private museum contains one of the finest collections of toy and model trains, boats, cars, planes, dolls and teddy bears. Spread throughout two Victorian houses, it includes more than 3,000 toys and models dating from the 18th century to the present day. A ride-on train runs in the garden each day, and on Sundays they are pulled by steam locomotives. Older children can become special junior railwaymen. Also outside are model electric and clockwork trains, a boating pond, a playbus and a 1920s Orton and Spooner children's roundabout for under-10s. A café opening out on to the garden allows parents to take a rest while keeping an eye on the children.

The Train Room is devoted to toy and model trains from all over the world covering the period 1850–1980. The room has an operating miniature railway and there is also a model of the 1903 'Tu'penny Tube' – the CLR Steeplecab, London's first tube train.

The Tin Toy Room has hundreds of exhibits, including many elaborate clockwork toys and characters from *Alice in Wonderland* and *Snow White and the Seven Dwarfs*.

In the basement is a nursery, an animal house and three replica toyshops. A section added in 1984, named 'Two Centuries of Dolls' (1750–1950), reflects both the British and Continental history of toy dolls and it contains a whole case devoted to Paddington Bear.

Various special events take place throughout the year, including open days on the museum's railway tracks in April, the annual model boat regatta in June, and a Teddy Bears' picnic in July. The museum can arrange birthday parties and quizzes for children's groups.

Bayswater ⊖

News-stands bursting with magazines and newspapers in Arabic, Greek, Chinese and other scripts greet the visitor emerging on to Queensway from Bayswater ⊖. Pizza parlours jostle with Cantonese restaurants, Greek kebab houses and tavernas vie with American ice cream shops, and Indian restaurants are to be found to the north in Westbourne Grove, emphasizing the cosmopolitan nature of the Bayswater area. In Queensway alone at least ten different cuisines are on offer, and there are a number of 24-hour supermarkets and much late night eating.

A variety of different places of religious worship also reflect Bayswater's shifting, polyglot community. In earlier days a large number of churches were built, like St Matthew's in St Petersburg Place. Later on, as the area became increasingly cosmopolitan, Bayswater produced a large synagogue, also in St Petersburg Place, and the even larger St Sophia's Greek Orthodox Church, with its marbled and mosaic interior, in nearby Moscow Road.

Bayswater Road, which is at the south end of Queensway, was once a countryside lane crossing the pretty Westbourne Green. There were gravel pits near by. In the 18th and early-19th centuries the area gradually developed into an elegant and fashionable district. Around 1815 Edward Orme, a Bond Street print-seller who had made a fortune from the area's gravel pits, built St Petersburg Place, Moscow Road and Coburg Place, so named to mark the visit the previous year of sovereigns of allied countries to London.

There were still green fields to the north until 1837, when John Whyte turned 200 acres/80 ha. of land near Notting Hill into a racecourse known as the Hippodrome, advertising it as 'a racing emporium more extensive and attractive than Ascot or Epsom'. Both high life and low life were attracted to the area, and a property boom ensued. An entire district of terraces, squares and crescents flourished, reflecting every change in Victorian architectural style and catering for the newly rich businessmen of that era. For John Galsworthy, who once lived at 100 Bayswater Road, the area was the ideal setting for the snobbish upper

Jim + Joanne Newell
Flat E, 31 Porchester
Square London W2 6AN
Tel 071-727-2804
P.x

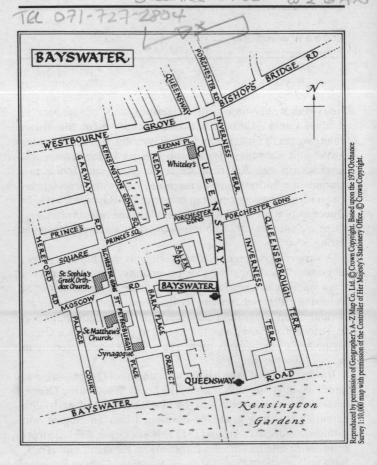

Reproduced by permission of Geographer's A-Z Map Co. Ltd. © Crown Copyright. Based upon the 1973 Ordnance Survey 1:10,000 map with permission of the Controller of Her Majesty's Stationery Office, © Crown Copyright.

middle class characters in his most famous novel series, *The Forsyte Saga*.

At that time the affluent shopped at William Whiteley's store in Westbourne Grove. Its proprietor was a man who styled himself 'The Universal Provider', capable of supplying 'from a pin to an elephant at short notice'. By 1899 the store had an annual turnover of more than £1 million and was a more fashionable place to shop than establishments in Kensington or Knightsbridge. The business was eventually bought by Selfridge's (*Marble Arch* ⊖) but became unviable and was closed in 1981. The site changed hands and was completely rebuilt behind the famous exterior, and re-opened in 1989 as a shopping centre, housing a wide variety of shops and restaurants as well as a multi-screen cinema.

After the Second World War, when the area was damaged by bombs, Bayswater went into decline and gained a reputation as an area of ill-repute. Some evidence of this still remains, but the area is rapidly being given a face-lift.

Bayswater ⊖ and Queensway ⊖ (*Central Line*) are very close to each other. Kensington Gardens, with their intimate atmosphere, can be seen from Queensway ⊖. Situated in the gardens is Kensington Palace, chosen by the Prince and Princess of Wales as their London residence. The palace contains the wonderful Court Dress Collection.

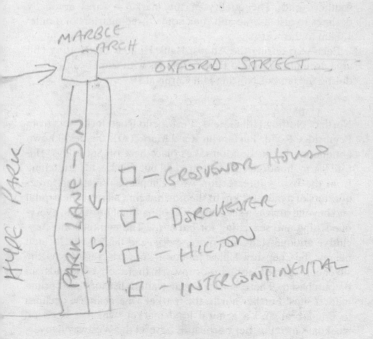

Notting Hill Gate

Notting Hill Gate is named after the toll gates that once stood here on the main road from London to Bath. The road dates from Roman times, which is clearly visible in the way that Bayswater Road runs in a straight line into Notting Hill Gate and Holland Park Avenue. During Victorian times the Notting Hill Gate area developed rapidly. Today it includes a number of listed buildings and architectural conservation areas, notably the Ladbroke Estate. A walk through this estate and the Campden Hill Square area reveals a fine selection of Victorian classical architecture.

Portobello Road Market is the best known antiques market in London. On Saturdays hundreds of stalls stretch along its length, the most exclusive wares on display at the market's southern end. The quality of the market's wares gradually declines to bric-à-brac and junk some three-quarters of a mile/1.2 km to the north.

Each year during the August Bank Holiday the Notting Hill area around Portobello Road explodes with Caribbean culture during the famous Notting Hill Carnival.

North of Notting Hill Gate , Portobello Road forks west from Pembridge Road. **Portobello Road Market (1)**, the best-known antique market in London takes place here on Saturdays. Before 8 a.m. hundreds of stalls are laid out side by side stretching from the road's intersection with Chepstow Villas for three-quarters of a mile/1.2 km to the north. From all over the capital and beyond arrives a seething mass of habitual browsers, everyone sifting and searching for bargains. The market's most exclusive antique stalls and more specialized dealers are located nearest the Chepstow Villas' junction, known by regulars as 'the silver end'. Here Georgian silver worth thousands of pounds can be purchased. There is a five-year waiting list for these prime market sites. Further north, the market's merchandise declines to bric-à-brac and a general food market, which is open on weekdays too. Further north still, beyond the Westway flyover, Portobello Road's stalls and pavements contain a miscellany of domestic junk. The wide variety of goods on sale attracts the

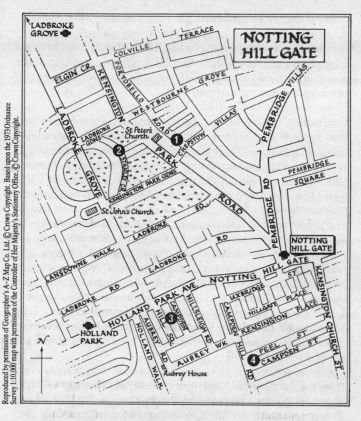

widest miscellany of visitors – dealers and tourists, the old and the young, buskers and flower sellers.

The name of Portobello Road came from a farm once situated near by. It was called 'Porto Bello' in patriotic commemoration of the Spanish town in the Gulf of Mexico captured in 1739 by English sailors under Admiral Vernon. A market was established here in the late 1830s, when trading was dominated by gypsies dealing in horses at the nearby Hippodrome racecourse, a relatively short-lived and ill-fated sporting venture abandoned in 1841. It was not until the 1880s that a street market began to develop in Portobello Road. In 1926 the market gained legal status and twenty years later, when the old Caledonian market in Islington closed, Portobello Road was flooded with antique dealers.

Portobello Road also hosts the annual **Notting Hill Carnival**. Founded in 1966 as a local pageant to bring black and white communities together, the Notting Hill Carnival now attracts approaching a million visitors for its extended weekend offering of colourful carnival floats, steel bands, calypso singers, eating, drinking and dancing in the streets.

Contrasting sharply with the crooked terraced houses of Portobello Road, Notting Hill also encompasses a distinctive district of wealthy residential crescents and squares, rich in classical Victorian architecture. Most of this area was developed in the mid-19th century during the great suburban expansion of Victorian London. At the western end of Westbourne Grove, which bisects Portobello Road, and beyond Kensington Park Road lies the heart of the Ladbroke Estate, a collection of grand sweeping terraces and semi-detached villas dating from this period.

In the 1820s James Weller Ladbroke began developing his family's predominantly agricultural estate, which surrounded Notting Barn and Portobello Farm. This coincided with the opening in 1837 of the ambitious Hippodrome racecourse project, an enterprise intended to rival Ascot and Epsom. The Hippodrome closed four years later, but new housing development continued and by the 1870s the area's population had grown fifty-fold.

On the south side of Ladbroke Gardens, which leads east from the junction of Westbourne Grove and Kensington Park Road, lie **Stanley Crescent** and **Stanley Gardens (2)**. These two streets represent the finest planning and architecture in the Ladbroke Conservation Area. Architect Thomas Allom was employed from about 1850 by Charles Henry Blake, a retired Calcutta merchant, to design this group of large Italianate houses. His skilful plans and designs are most apparent in Stanley Gardens, a street closed in at each end; in Nos. 10 and 11 Stanley Crescent, with their complementary roof towers, and in St Peter's Church, opposite the east end of the crescent in Kensington Park Road. His houses are designed in an elaborate classical manner with stuccoed exteriors. Allom made use of the newly discovered building material, cement, whose properties were particularly suitable for creating an abundance of embellishments in cornices and window architraves. Kensington Park Gardens, again largely designed by Allom, have suffered slightly from alterations and additions.

The summit of Notting Hill is at the west end of Kensington
Park Gardens. In the days of the Hippodrome, spectators stood
here and watched the races take place below them. It is now
transected from north to south by the estate's axis, Ladbroke
Grove. **St John's Church** was the first development on the hill.
Designed in 1845 by John Hargrave Stevens and George Alexander, St John's spire can be seen for miles around from its
commanding position. The upper reaches of Notting Hill, with
their grand stuccoed mansions, were once truly 'society hill', but
further, and lower, to the north and west were the simpler brick
houses of the poorer classes, an area known as 'The Potteries'.
Today nearly all the area is a desirable residential area.

Opposite the southern end of Ladbroke Grove, south of
Holland Park Avenue, is **Campden Hill Square (3)**, a prestigious
address when it was laid out by Joshua Hanson in 1826, and still
so today. A plaque on a tree on the north side of its garden reads:
'J. M. W. Turner R A, landscape painter, born 1775, died 1851,
often painted sunsets near this tree.' To the west of the square
Aubrey Road rises steeply towards the south. The view down
the hill is dominated by the spire of St John's.
    During the 17th century Campden Hill saw the building of a
number of country mansions, notably Holland House (*High
Street Kensington* ⊖); Campden House, demolished in 1900; and
Aubrey House, named after Aubrey de Vere, the first lord of
Kensington Manor. Aubrey House was built in 1698 near a
newly discovered medicinal spring known as the Kensington
Wells, located at what is now the corner of Aubrey Road and
Aubrey Walk. The appearance of the present Aubrey House
dates from the mid-18th century, when Sir Edward Lloyd transformed it into an impressive Georgian mansion. The house is
known for its association with the Alexander family, philanthropists and art collectors. The family still resides there, and
the fine-art collector W. C. Alexander, a patron of the painter
Whistler, bequeathed his collection to the nation in 1965.
    The coach houses of the Campden Hill Square mansions line
Aubrey Walk. They are now some of the most sought after
studio residences in London. Further west are some 20th-
century Dutch-style houses and beyond is the Gothic-style St
George's Church (1864).
    The delightful country-style inn, the **Windsor Castle (4)**, was
built in 1835 in Campden Hill Road, at the highest point of

Campden Hill. The real Windsor Castle lies over 17 miles/27 km
to the west, and it is claimed that on a fine day it was once
possible to see the distant royal residence from the bar of the
inn, hence its name. The Windsor Castle has an intimate atmosphere, with wood-panelling, original screens and open fires.

Returning north, opposite Aubrey Walk, is a small neigh-
bourhood of two-storey artisans' cottages, bounded by Kensington Place to the south and Uxbridge Street to the north. Built in
the mid-19th century, they quickly became overcrowded, with
one house reportedly occupied by as many as thirty-two residents. It typifies what was once the contrasting nature of the
Notting Hill area, with fine residences situated close to poorer
housing. However, much transformation has recently taken
place.

High Street Kensington ⊖

The Kensington area was once thought a healthy spot, close to mineral sprinngs at Notting Hill, Kensington Gardens and Earls Court. William III came to live here at Kensington Palace in 1689 on account of his chronic asthma. Inevitably, the area became fashionable, and many courtiers and members of the nobility came to live at Kensington Square, one of London's oldest squares.

Kensington's main urban development took place, however, between 1800 and 1881, when the area's population grew from 8,600 to over 160,000. Kensington became a Royal Borough in 1901 at the request of Queen Victoria, a gesture to mark her birthplace and her childhood at Kensington Palace. From the Victorian era come two of Kensington's most successful artists, Edward Linley Sambourne, *Punch* magazine's principal cartoonist, and Lord Leighton, President of the Royal Academy. The houses of both men survive, complete with their furnishings, offering remarkable yet differing monuments to Victorian taste and aesthetic.

Linley Sambourne's house is a perfectly preserved example of an upper middle class 'artistic' family home, crammed with an amazing mixture of furniture, statuary, clocks, stained glass and patterned carpets. Its great decorative richness – framed pictures are close hung wall-to-wall and floor-to-ceiling – makes the house a compendium of the educated taste of the era.

Lord Leighton's fastidious, classical, and exotic taste is manifest in the house he designed for himself, one of the first purpose-built studio houses in Britain. The rich and harmonious result, centring on the house's decorative and exotic Arab Hall with its magnificent array of ancient tiles and black marble fountain and pond, displays both the marked individuality of its owner and the influence of an aristocratic Victorian aesthetic.

Today the nations of the British Commonwealth encompass about a quarter of the world's population. The Commonwealth Institute, through its wide and varied programme of exhibitions, education, arts and debates, attempts to reflect the rich diversity of, and the issues facing, this great association of peoples.

High above the busy Kensington High Street 1½ acres/0.6 ha. of landscaped gardens with fountains, cascades of wisteria and

roses, peach and apple trees, and flamingoes form the surprising and charming Roof Gardens.

⊖   ⊖   ⊖

Nearly two hundred years after William III moved to Kensington Palace **Kensington High Street (1)** developed into a busy shopping thoroughfare when its Underground railway station opened in 1868. Although its large department stores have gone, with the exception of Barkers, most of Britain's well-known high street chainstores are represented. At the east end of the street there are two youth fashion markets.

Situated at the west end of Kensington High Street is **Edwardes Square (2)**, laid out in 1811–19 by Louis Changeur in elegant late-Georgian style and named after Lord Kensington's father, William Edwardes. In 1819 an Act of Parliament was passed to regulate lighting, watching, watering, cleansing and planting in the square. Failure to clean the doorstep before 9 a.m. was punishable by a five-shilling fine. The square's private residents' garden was laid out in 1820 together with its classical-style gardener's cottage, known as the Temple. The Scarsdale Arms, with its antique prints and pleasant paved terrace, was established in the south-east corner of the square in 1867.

Behind the simple red brick exterior of No. 12 Holland Park Road, to the north of Kensington High Street, lies the fascinating domestic interior of **Leighton House (3).** Lord Leighton (1830–96), the accomplished artist and President of the Royal Academy, collaborated with his friend the architect and master of decoration George Aitchison (1825–1910) during 1866 to construct one of the first purpose-built studio houses in Britain. The house, with its decorative and exotic Arab Hall, ancient Persian and Saracenic tiles, Victorian ceramics and furniture, and important paintings by Burne-Jones and Millais, is the wonderful legacy of this classical and fastidious man. The rich and harmonious blend of house and contents displays both the marked individuality of its owner and the influence of contemporary Victorian design.

Tall ebonized doorways in the vestibule are decorated with gilt rosettes, a recurring motif throughout the house. The Inner Hall, lit by a skylight, with its striking blue wall tiles by William De Morgan, leads into the Hall of Narcissus. Further along, large columns of red Caserta marble precede the Arab Hall, a rich evocation of the Moorish Spain which Aitchison had once visited. The Arab Hall is adorned with a sparkling array of vividly coloured Mediterranean and Middle Eastern tiles of 13th-, 16th- and 17th-century origin. The hall's spectacular effect is heightened by a single fountain that gently trickles into a black pool made from a single block of marble. Tiles set into a wooden alcove, or *alhacen*, include two examples from 13th-century Persia. Birds are depicted on other tiles, each with an incision in the throat to represent death, thereby conforming with the Muslim edict that no living thing be represented. The dome, high above, was brought from Damascus and once gilded. The Drawing Room's marble fireplace is located, unusually, beneath a window. The Dining Room leads into the garden, which contains Leighton's large bronze *Athlete Struggling with a Python* (1877).

Leighton's *Elisha Raising the Son of Shunamite* (1881) is one of the paintings decorating the staircase. The upstairs landing, known as the Silk Room, has been rehung in green silk. The Arab theme in the house is again repeated in a lattice window, or *zenana*, created in intricate *musharabiyeh* work. It overlooks the Arab Hall, the type of vantage point built in the world of Islam for women to see without being seen. On the north side of the landing is Leighton's Great Studio, measuring 60 × 25 ft/ 18 × 7.6 m. A cast of part of the Parthenon frieze runs along its south wall and there is also a plaster cast of Michelangelo's roundel *Taddei Tondo*. A tall, narrow door was built in the studio's west wall to enable large canvases to be lowered out. The first floor is hung throughout with examples of High Victorian art. The Winter Studio and Upper Perrin Gallery at the east end of the Great Studio house temporary exhibitions.

Approximately 1,000 million people live in the forty or so sovereign states that make up the Commonwealth. The **Commonwealth Institute (4)** (Sir Robert Matthew and Johnson-Marshall, 1962) situated on the north side of Kensington High Street, endeavours to demonstrate the continuing relevance today of the Commonwealth association and thereby to increase understanding and respect for other cultures. The rich diversity of the Commonwealth peoples is celebrated throughout the year in the Institute's imaginative and informative programme of events.

Founded as the Imperial Institute to commemorate Queen Victoria's Golden Jubilee in 1887, it became the Commonwealth Institute in 1957. The Institute moved in 1962 to the present building, with its diamond-shaped exhibition block and striking five-peaked roof clad in Zambian copper. Other materials for the building were donated by various Commonwealth countries. Spacious galleries on three floors accommodate continuous and changing exhibitions, many of which recreate in great detail typical scenes from the daily lives of the Commonwealth's peoples. Major exhibitions of paintings, sculpture, textiles and other crafts are mounted in the art galleries on the middle floor. The cinema often doubles as a theatre for the Institute's lively programme of performing arts. A festival of traditional music and dance, 'Ancestral Voices', is held regularly, as well as a summer 'Music Village' in nearby Holland Park. The Institute's educational facilities cater for school par-

ties, and there is a bookshop, a comprehensive library and
resource centre, and a restaurant. The Institute's programme of
conferences covers international, political, social, economic and
artistic issues, and there are also more detailed workshops and
seminars. A recent innovation in the main exhibition area is the
Today Gallery, focusing on current topics such as health, the
environment and the role of voluntary agencies. North of
the Commonwealth Institute is Holland Park.

Holland House (5), a Jacobean mansion built in 1605 for James
I's Chancellor of the Exchequer, Sir Walter Cope, occupies the
south side of Holland Park. Originally known as Cope Castle, it
became Holland House in 1624 when Sir Walter's son-in-law
became the first Earl of Holland. The Earl, a Royalist, was
executed and the house occupied by Parliamentarians until the
Restoration in 1660.

A distinguished artistic and political salon developed here in
the 18th and 19th centuries. During the patronage of the third
Baron Holland (1773–1840), the essayist and historian Thomas
Babington Macauley described the house as the 'favourite resort
of wits and beauties, of painters and poets, of scholars, philosophers and statesmen'. Famous figures associated with the
house include author Sir Walter Scott, politician William
Wilberforce, poet Lord Byron and playwright and politician
Sheridan.

In 1850 the fourth Baron Holland constructed the Garden
Ballroom, now the luxurious Belvedere Restaurant. He also
added the Orangery, which he connected to the house by a series
of arcades and terraces. Both the Orangery and the 18th-century
ice-house are now used as exhibition venues. Most of Holland
House was destroyed by bombing during the Second World
War. In 1952 the London County Council acquired the decaying
ruins and started restoration work. Least damaged was the east
wing, which has now become part of the King George VI
Memorial Youth Hostel. The gardens were opened as a park.

In summer the Holland Park Theatre arranges a mixed programme of open-air plays, ballets, operas and concerts on the
front terrace. The terrace is surrounded by the surviving lower
storey and the arcades of the central section. Near the terrace
stand the original stone gateway piers dating from 1629 whose
design is attributed to Inigo Jones.

Between the house and the Belvedere Restaurant lie three

small formal gardens; the Rose Garden, the Dutch Garden and the Iris Garden. The Dutch Garden's precise geometric layout, designed in 1812, is in complete contrast with the rest of the park. A dense rambling wood occupies the northern part of the 60-acre/24-ha. Holland Park. In enclosed areas, semi-domesticated species such as peacocks and emus have been introduced. Holland Walk, which defines the eastern boundary of the park, leads south back to Kensington High Street.

'Mr Linley Sambourne is not at home' reads the brass letterplate on the door of No. 18 Stafford Terrace. Sadly, Edward Linley Sambourne (1845–1910), once the principal cartoonist of the satirical magazine *Punch*, will never now be at home but, miraculously, **Linley Sambourne House (6)** and its contents have been preserved, intact in every detail. This late Victorian home, typical of an 'artistic' upper middle class family on the fringe of smart London society, is open to anyone who cares to visit on Wednesdays and Sundays during the summer.

Every inch of its walls, every table, every ledge, even every chair and bed is covered with a typically cosy Victorian clutter of paintings, photographs, ceramics, books, pens, shells, ornaments, memorabilia and endless assorted bric-a-brac. Clocks tick, brass glints in the light filtering through Linley Sambourne's own stained-glass window and door panel designs, and a fountain tinkles in the water garden. The fashionable William Morris wallpapers are still there. In the hall Morris's *Willow* pattern adorns the walls and his *Pomegranate* is set in panels on the ceiling. There are ninety-four framed photographs hung on the staircase alone. Linley Sambourne was obsessed with photography and took some 10,000 pictures of family and friends, many of which were then moulded into cartoons. His coachman, adorned with coronet and robes, poses as the Duke of Westminster. Some cartoons adorn the hall.

The centre-piece of the house is the L-shaped Drawing Room, featured in the film *A Room With a View*, which occupies the entire first floor. Its walls are decorated in gilt-embossed wallpaper, which is sandwiched between a gold ceiling and dado. Drawings by Sambourne and his friends abound. A shelf running round the room at frieze level displays ceramics. Elsewhere there are Chinese cloisonné enamel vases, a French *boulle* clock and many small bronzes. The furniture is in the style of Louis XVI and the Regency period.

Lady Rosse, whose bedroom is on the second floor, was the last member of the family to occupy the house. Hanging here are two of Sambourne's most impressive drawings: *Heralding the New Century* (1900) and *Look Before You Leap: the Twentieth Century* (1901). The house was acquired by the Greater London Council in 1978. Two years later it was opened to the public under the auspices of the Victorian Society. Linley's great-grandson is Lord Snowdon.

The celebrated **Roof Gardens (7)**, laid out 100 ft/30 m above busy Kensington High Street, were opened in 1938 by the former Derry and Tom's department store. Derry and Tom's was succeeded by the chic Biba fashion store and by Régine's Club in the 1970s. Today the Roof Gardens are occupied by the Gardens Club, a nightspot and restaurant.

During the week members of the public can visit, via the Club's Derry Street entrance, the three themed gardens that extend over the rooftop. The Rose Garden is enclosed by brick-built Elizabethan arches supporting cascades of wisteria and fragrant roses. The Spanish Garden, with its pure white Court of Fountains, Granada red tiles and palm trees, is overlooked by a minstrels' gallery. Peach and apple trees in the English Woodland Garden surround a stream with strutting pink flamingoes.

The Roof Gardens have hosted the first-night parties for *Indiana Jones*, two James Bond films and *Beverly Hills Cop* as well as the 1,000th edition of *Top of the Pops* and the launch of the Channel Four television network.

Kensington Square, at the south end of Derry Street, dates from 1681. It became a fashionable residence for courtiers and the nobility following William III's arrival at Kensington Palace. Artists, writers and members of the intelligentsia moved in after the Court left Kensington Palace in 1760. Philosopher John Stuart Mill once lived at No. 18, composer Sir Charles Parry at No. 17 and painter Sir Edward Burne-Jones at No. 41. Many of the houses on the south and west sides date from the original development, but the majority are Georgian brick and stucco. Some are in late 18th-century Flemish style.

To the north of Kensington Square is **Barkers (8)**, the last survivor of the many department stores once occupying Kensington High Street. Further east, six Romanesque caryatids form the unusual façade of **Hyper Hyper** (9), a fashion emporium specially for up-and-coming designers. At the rear of its ground floor a shiny Pullman railway carriage from 1900 has been converted into a café. Opposite Hyper Hyper is **Kensington Market** (10), a comparatively down-market labyrinth of tiny clothing shops dealing in every trend from the 1930s to the 1980s.

Sir George Gilbert Scott, commissioned to design a church on a 'scale proportioned to the opulence and importance of this great Metropolitan parish', gave **St Mary Abbots** (11) the highest spire in London, rising 250 ft/76 m above the southern end of Kensington Church Street. The church, Kensington's parish church, is reached by passing along a bent and sloping cloister walk. Like most of Sir George Gilbert Scott's ecclesiastical architecture, St Mary Abbots is rigid and simple, a characteristic of the Early English Gothic style employed extensively in churches between 1850 and 1880. A leading exponent of the style, his plain ecclesiastical works differ dramatically from the energy and exuberance of his secular buildings, notably the astonishing and decorative Great Midland Hotel building at St Pancras Station (*King's Cross/St Pancras* ⊖) and the Albert Memorial (*South Kensington* ⊖)

During the Middle Ages Kensington parish church belonged to the Abbey of Abingdon, hence the name St Mary Abbots. Founded in the 12th century, St Mary's was rebuilt in 1370 and, except for its 14th-century tower, rebuilt again in 1696. William III, residing at nearby Kensington Palace, contributed to the construction of this earlier church and donated the pulpit still seen today.

To the east of St Mary Abbots, a line of quality antique shops on **Kensington Church Street** (12) rises north towards Notting Hill Gate.

Gloucester Road ⊖

The area around Gloucester Road ⊖ is one of London's more select residential districts. Although its residents are not as affluent as those in Belgravia or Mayfair, this part of Kensington claims some prestigious addresses. The Boltons, for example, to the south of Old Brompton Road are two fine mid-19th-century crescents with palatial semi-detached mansions separated by a central garden and its Neo-Gothic church. Elsewhere the area contains some high and grand Victorian terraces.

A number of houses along the Cromwell Road and its immediate tributaries have been converted or replaced by hotel accommodation. As one of the main westbound routes in and out of London, many of these hotels house guests arriving at Heathrow Airport.

Two of London's main exhibition venues, Earl's Court and Olympia, are within easy reach of Gloucester Road ⊖ by changing from the Circle Line to the District Line and travelling one station to the west. All westbound District Line trains from Gloucester Road ⊖ stop at Earl's Court ⊖. When a major exhibition is in progress, there is also a special Underground service that travels via Earl's Court ⊖ directly to Kensington (Olympia) ⊖.

⊖   ⊖   ⊖

Many of Britain's most famous exhibitions and events take place in the vast main hall of the **Earl's Court Exhibition Centre (1)** (C. Howard Crane, 1937). The International Boat Show in January is followed each year in February by Cruft's, the world-famous championship dog show. One of Earl's Court's most popular events is the Royal Tournament, held in July. This spectacular and colourful pageant of massed bands, field-gun races and military expertise is staged by Britain's armed forces and customarily ends with the mast-manning ceremony. Earl's Court also hosts the Ideal Home Exhibition and the Royal Smithfield Show. On Sundays there is an open-air market behind the centre.

At the time of its construction Earl's Court was the largest reinforced concrete building in Europe, with a site covering 12

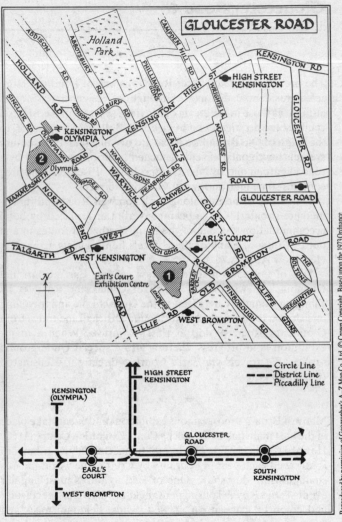

acres/4.8 ha. The Earl's Court area itself is a sprawling cosmopolitan district with plenty of inexpensive hotel accommodation.

Opened in 1884, **Olympia (2)** in its early days regularly hosted circuses. Its first, the 'Paris Hippodrome', featured 400 animals, a stag hunt and a chariot race. Olympia, in Hammersmith Road, also hosted the first Motor Show as far back as 1905. The first International Horse Show was held here two years later. Olympia's National and Empire Halls were built in the 1920s. In 1930 Olympia's striking, almost Cubist, entrance frontage was added by architect Joseph Emberton. In recent years the larger exhibitions have gone to Earl's Court, and Olympia has staged smaller events and conferences. However, art and antiques fairs, international show jumping competitions, trade fairs of all descriptions and the National Cat Club Show still take place here.

South Kensington ⊖

South Kensington is home to perhaps the most remarkable group of museums and educational institutions in the world. Whole lifetimes could be spent in studying and learning from the massive collections held at the Victoria and Albert, Natural History, Science and Geological museums.

The Great Exhibition of 1851, the first of its kind in the world, provided the financial profit that led to this unique development. Inside the Crystal Palace, built specially on 19 acres/7.6 ha. of Hyde Park, the Great Exhibition attracted a staggering 14,000 exhibitors. More than 6 million people visited the exhibition and a profit of £200,000 was achieved. The exhibition's patron, Prince Albert, proposed that the profits be spent building a great educational centre in South Kensington. The aim of the exhibition, to extend 'the influence of Science and Art upon Productive Industry', was to be realized here by building a group of museums, colleges, concert halls and premises for learned societies. Eighty-six acres/35 ha. of land were purchased, bounded on the north by Kensington Gardens and on the south by Cromwell Road.

In 1856 the 'Brompton Boilers' were built, later to become the Victoria and Albert Museum. Work started on the Albert Memorial five years later, after the death of Prince Albert. It is one of the finest monuments of mid-Victorian taste. Between 1867 and 1871 the Royal Albert Hall was built as a national memorial to the Prince Consort. It is now the venue of the world-famous Promenade Concerts. In 1862 an International Exhibition was held on the site of what is now the Natural History Museum. Today this museum houses one of the largest collections of plants, animals, fossils and minerals – in all, more than 65 million specimens. The Science Museum, formerly housed in the Brompton Boilers, moved to its present site in 1913. The Geological Museum, opened in 1935, has a collection of minerals and fossils numbering over a million specimens. Its Gemstones Gallery houses the most varied collection of precious, semi-precious and other translucent stones in the world.

Other learned institutions have sprung up in this area, including the Royal College of Music, with its small but outstanding museum of instruments; the Royal College of Organists; the

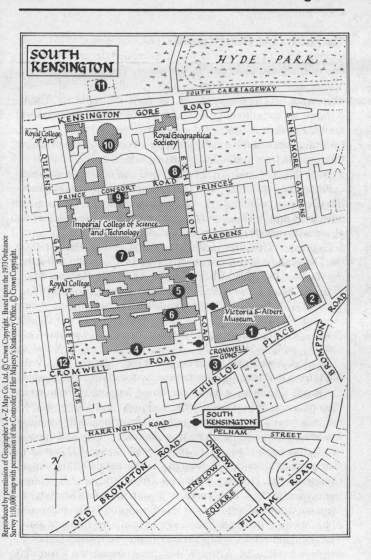

Imperial College of Science and Technology; and the Royal College of Art.

Many of the museums can be reached by an underground tunnel from South Kensington ⊖.

⊖　⊖　⊖

The **Victoria and Albert Museum (1)** (Aston Webb, 1913), with its magnificent collection of fine and applied decorative art, is one of the finest museums in the world. The sheer size of the V & A, as it is popularly known, is awe-inspiring. Several million objects are held by nine separate curatorial departments. The V & A, in its incredible 8 miles/12.8 km of gallery space on six floors, has one of the most extensive collections of English furniture ever assembled; the greatest collection of Italian sculpture outside Italy and of Indian art outside its sub-continent; as well as the National Art Library; and the country's national collections of sculpture, watercolours and miniatures. Fashion, interior decoration and musical instruments are also among the museum's multitude of special collections. Its maze of galleries gleam with marble, mosaics and coloured tiles.

Its greatest treasures include the Great Bed of Ware (1590), the Devonshire Hunting Tapestries (*c.* 1450), Rodin's *St John the Baptist* (1880), Boucher's *Jeanne Antoinette Poisson, Marquise de Pompadour* (1758), the Syon Cope (1320), *Tipoo's Tiger* (1790), the Gloucester Candlestick (*c.* 1105), the Akita Armour (1714), Turner's *Venice – The Salute and the Doge's Palace, from the Giudecca* (1840) and Constable's *Dedham Vale* (1802).

The V & A was born out of the Great Exhibition of 1851. With funds from Parliament and with Prince Albert's encouragement, the Royal Commissioners for the Great Exhibition included in their plans a museum to show the best in art and design. In 1857 two museums were brought together to form the South Kensington Museum: the Museum of Manufactures, which had opened in Marlborough House (*St James's Park* ⊖) in 1852, and the Government's School of Design, a forerunner of the Royal College of Art. Housed in a haphazard concourse of buildings, still evident in the V & A's present layout, the South Kensington Museum achieved notoriety as the 'Brompton Boilers' because of its immense structure of corrugated iron, cast iron and glass. Today's building is a combination of many schemes, the last of which is fronted by Aston Webb's main façade on Cromwell Road. In 1899, on the last public engagement of her reign, Queen Victoria laid the foundation stone for this impressive quarter-mile/0.4-km frontage. The museum acquired its present name at her request.

The Victorians' utilitarian policy of 'representing the application of Fine Art to manufactures' has given the museum much of its unique character. Under one roof such modern commercial objects as moulded plastic radios and outrageous fashion outfits coexist with great works of Renaissance art and Chinese pottery of 2000 BC.

The Art and Design galleries are divided into four walks: Through the Middle Ages to the Renaissance – the arts in Europe up to around 1600, mainly in England, France, Germany and Italy (Rooms 43, 22–4, 38, 25–9A, 16–21A, 48); Mannerism to Art Nouveau – the arts in Continental Europe from about 1600 to 1900, mainly in France and Italy (Rooms 1–9); British Art: Elizabeth I to Elizabeth II – the arts in Britain from about 1500 to the present day (Rooms 52–8, 74A–C, 118–126); and The Arts of the East – the arts of Islam, India, South-east Asia, China and Japan (Rooms 47A–C, 47E, 41, 42, 44, 45, 38A). Exhibits are displayed according to their period and style, and laid out in more or less chronological order. Each walk may easily last half a day or more.

Each curatorial department in the V & A has its own gallery, collectively known as the Materials and Techniques galleries. They are intended for both specialist and general audiences. These galleries are devoted to sculpture (Rooms 50 east and west, 46, 46A–B, 51, 62–4, 11–24, 43), furniture and interior design (Rooms 1–9, 48 east, 52–8, 74C–A, 103–6B, 118–126), ceramics and glass (Rooms 111–12, 116–17, 127–45), metalwork (Rooms 65–9, 70A, 81–4, 87–93, 114A–E), textile furnishings and dress (Rooms 32–3, 38, 52–3, 85, 94–102, 107–9), Indian art (Rooms 41, 47A–B), Far Eastern art (Rooms 38A, 44, 45, 47E, 129, 143–5) and the National Art Library (Rooms 77–8). The Department of Designs, Prints and Drawings, which also includes important paintings, has its own exhibition area in the Henry Cole wing, named after the man who both conceived the idea of the Great Exhibition and was the first director of the Brompton Boilers.

The Special Collections display important bequests, loans and especially outstanding or popular collections. These include the Jones Collection of French fine and decorative art, from the reign of Louis XIV to that of Louis XVI (Rooms 5–7); the Raphael Cartoons, a set of full-scale working designs of scenes from the lives of St Peter and St Paul for tapestries to hang in the Sistine Chapel (Room 48); the Dress Collection, examples of fashionable clothing from 1600 to the present day (Room 40); Musical Instruments (Room 40A); Sculptures by

VICTORIA and ALBERT MUSEUM

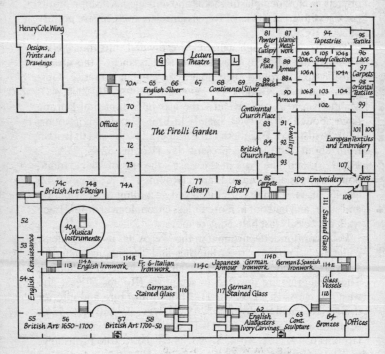

Henry Cole Wing

Designs, Prints and Drawings

G | Lecture Theatre | L

81 Pewter & Cutlery
82 Plate
87 Islamic Metalwork
88 Armour
88A
89 Enamels
90 Armour
94 Tapestries
95 Textiles
96 Lace
97 Carpets
98 Oriental Textiles

106 20th C. Study Collection
105
104B
106A
104A
106B 103 104

70A
65 66 67 68 69
English Silver   Continental Silver

70
71 Offices
72
73

The Pirelli Garden

Continental Church Plate
83
84 British Church Plate
85 Carpets

91 Jewellery
92
93

102
101 100 European Textiles and Embroidery
99
107
109 Embroidery   Fans
108

74C 74B 74A
British Art & Design

77 Library
78 Library

111 Stained Glass

52
English Renaissance
53
54

40A Musical Instruments

114A
113 English Ironwork
114B
Fr. & Italian Ironwork
114C Japanese Armour
114D German Ironwork
German & Spanish Ironwork
114E

Glass Vessels
112

55 British Art 1650-1700
56
57 58 British Art 1700-50

German Stained Glass
116

117 German Stained Glass

62 English Alabasters Ivory Carvings
63 Cont. Sculpture
64 Bronzes
Offices

FIRST FLOOR and UPPER GROUND FLOOR (52-64)

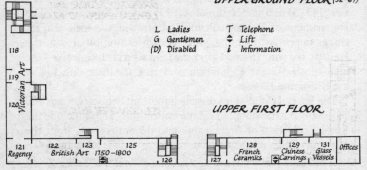

L Ladies	T Telephone
G Gentlemen	⇕ Lift
(D) Disabled	i Information

UPPER FIRST FLOOR

118
119 Victorian Art
120

121 Regency
122 123 125 British Art 1750-1800
126

128 French Ceramics
127
129 Chinese Carvings
131 Glass Vessels
Offices

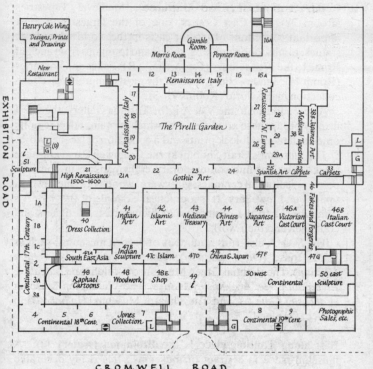

Henry Cole Wing
Designs, Prints and Drawings

New Restaurant

Morris Room
Gamble Room
Poynter Room

16A

11 12 13 14 15 16 16A

17 Renaissance Italy

Renaissance Italy

18

The Pirelli Garden

19

20

21 High Renaissance 1500–1600
21A
22 Gothic Art 23 24

Renaissance N. Europe

27 28
38 Medieval Tapestries
38B Japanese Art

29
26
29A
25 Spanish Art Carpets
32 33 Carpets

46 Fakes and forgeries

Sculpture
51
i

1A
40 Dress Collection
41 Indian Art
42 Islamic Art
43 Medieval Treasury
44 Chinese Art
45 Japanese Art
46A Victorian Cast Court
46B Italian Cast Court

1B
1C

Continental 17th Century

41A South East Asia
47B Indian Sculpture
47C Islam
47D
47E China & Japan
47F
47G

2
48 Raphael Cartoons
48 Woodwork
48E Shop
49 i
50 west Continental
50 east Sculpture

3A
3B

4
5 Continental 18th Cent.
6
7 Jones Collection
L
8 Continental 19th Cent.
9
Photographic Sales, etc.
G

CROMWELL ROAD

GROUND FLOOR and LOWER GROUND FLOOR (1–9)

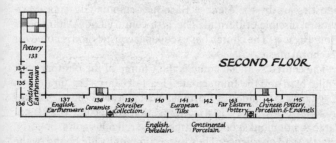

SECOND FLOOR

Pottery 133

134
135
136 Continental Earthenware

137 English Earthenware
138 Ceramics
139 Schreiber Collection
140
141 European Tiles
142
143 Far Eastern Pottery
144 Chinese Pottery, Porcelain & Enamels
145

English Porcelain
Continental Porcelain

Rodin (Exhibition Road Entrance); Medieval Tapestries (Room 38); the Cast Courts, one of the largest and most important collections of plaster casts in the world taken from statues, tombs, doors, pulpits, reliefs and fountains from ancient Rome to the 17th century (Rooms 46A–B); Fakes and Forgeries (Room 46); and Jewellery, in itself the most comprehensive such collection in the world (Rooms 91–3).

A new addition to the V & A is the Toshiba Gallery, the finest display of Japanese art in Europe, which contains tea ceremony objects, fine woodblock prints and a collection of lacquer work.

The museum's Craft Shop near the Cromwell Road entrance stocks works of fine contemporary craftsmanship in domestic pottery, sculptural ceramics, glassware, woodwork, metalwork, textiles and jewellery. It is a practical example of the V & A's commitment to the promotion of living artists, designers and craftsmen and their work.

The V & A also runs a number of branch museums, such as Ham House (*Outer London*), Osterley Park House (*Outer London*), The Bethnal Green Museum of Childhood (*Aldgate & Liverpool Street* ⊖), Apsley House, The Wellington Museum (*Lancaster Gate* ⊖), and The Theatre Museum (*Holborn* ⊖) in Covent Garden.

East along Thurloe Place is the **Brompton Oratory (2)**. 'A museum piece in a street of museums', this richly decorated church was built in Italian Baroque style by Herbert Gribble in 1896 and served as London's most important Roman Catholic place of worship until the opening of Westminster Cathedral (*Victoria* ⊖) in 1903. Its interior is even more Italian in style than its exterior. The more than life-size marble statues of the twelve apostles are by the Sienese Baroque sculptor Giuseppe Mazzuoli, a disciple of Bernini. The 17th-century Lady Altar comes from Brescia. The church has excellent acoustics and is noted for its choral music.

The church's official name is the Church of the Oratory of St Philip Neri and the Immaculate Heart of Mary. The Oratory in England was founded by Cardinal Newman and Frederick Faber in 1848. An oratory is a congregation of secular priests, or fathers, not monks, bound by the three religious vows, poverty, chastity and obedience. They live a community life bound by the internal bond of charity and the external bond of a common life.

Return west past the Yalta Memorial, a spherical cluster of bronze heads entitled *Twelve Responses to Tragedy* by Angela Conner. It was erected in memory of the hundreds of thousands of men, women and children repatriated by the Allies between 1945 and 1947 who suffered incarceration or death at the hands of the authorities in the Soviet Union and Eastern Europe.

Dedicated to the arts, architecture and culture of developing countries with an emphasis on Islamic cultures, the **Zamana Gallery (3)** holds three or four exhibitions a year, as well as lectures, seminars and meetings. The Gallery contains a book-shop stocking a wide range of material on the literature, art and architecture of the Third World. Its chief patron is His Highness the Aga Khan, who founded the gallery in 1985.

West along Cromwell Road is the **Natural History Museum (4)** (Alfred Waterhouse, 1881), whose twenty exhibition galleries are arranged over three floors, and which is also an international centre of scientific excellence for reference and research.

The main entrance leads into the Central Hall, which contains spectacular dinosaur skeletons and models, including the mass-ive diplodocus, the triceratops and the iguanadon. A video, *Dinosaurs and Their Living Relatives*, links these extinct crea-tures to today's reptiles and birds. On the ground floor to the west of Central Hall is a display area about spiders, mites, scorpions and some of their relatives. The Hall of Human Biology lies beyond and explains man's biological development from cell and chromosome through to birth and the develop-ment of perception and learning. Also situated in the western half of the ground floor are the displays: Whales and Their Relatives, with a full size model of the blue whale, around 90 ft/27 m long and more than the length of three London double-decker buses; Marine Invertebrates, such as squids, corals, crabs and many other sea creatures with no backbone; Insects, with some startling enlarged models and fascinating examples of insect 'architecture', and Birds.

To the east of Central Hall, a unique collection of plesiosaurs and ichthyosaurs is held in a display called Fossil Sea Reptiles. The Introducing Ecology exhibition, which explains the inter-action between plants, animals and their natural surroundings, includes a computer game following the course of a real ecologi-cal problem. Other displays on the ground floor are: Fossil Fishes, including the coelacanth – the amazing 'fossil fish' found in the Indian Ocean; Wildlife in Danger, Fossil Mammals, Fossil Invertebrates and Creepy Crawlies – the Good, the Bad and the Ugly, about arthropods, which include crabs, centipedes, spiders and scorpions, the most numerous and successful group of creatures in the world.

On the first floor, the Origin of the Species exhibition explores Darwin's theory of natural selection. Man's Place in Evolution explains how we are related to other living animals, and how our forebears, the 'fossil men', were found. Other displays are Mammals, African Mammals, Minerals, Rocks and Gemstones, and Meteorites.

On the second floor the British Natural History exhibit illustrates the main habitats of Britain and features some 2,000 plants and animals.

Lectures are given frequently at the museum and there is also a bookshop and cafeteria. Behind the scenes, the Natural History Museum holds a giant databank of carefully archived and classified specimens. Its five departments – Zoology, Entomology, Palaeontology, Botany and Mineralogy – are visited each day on average by more than 100 scientists from all round the world. With 800,000 volumes, the Natural History Library is the major collection of natural history literature in the world.

The museum originated in the collection of the distinguished physician Sir Hans Sloane (1660–1753) (*Sloane Square* ⊖), bequeathed by him to the British Museum. In 1880 the British Museum's collection was moved to its current premises.

Architect Alfred Waterhouse took 11th- and 12th-century Rhineland Romanesque cathedral architecture as his model for the Natural History Museum. His vast symmetrical building has twin towers above a rounded recessed entrance. The building's fabric is of buff and pale blue terracotta blocks, whose decoration includes mouldings of living and extinct animals, fish and birds.

Britain's foremost museum of science and technology, the **Science Museum (5)**, adjoins the Natural History Museum and houses treasures which include 'Puffing Billy', the earliest surviving locomotive; Stephenson's 'Rocket'; Amy Johnson's *Gypsy Moth*; the Benz three-wheel car of 1888; Fox Talbot's first camera; Edison's original phonograph; an early Bell telephone; the Vickers 'Vimy' aircraft, in which Alcock and Brown made the first Atlantic air-crossing; and the Apollo 10 space capsule.

Examples and illustrations of every landmark of scientific discovery are on display, and genius and ingenuity are not confined just to the museum's exhibits. The museum itself has invented wonderful and exciting display technologies; remarkable working models with hundreds of handles to pull and buttons to push; the amazing Launch Pad Gallery; the Space Gallery, a futuristic glimpse of a project to travel 35 billion miles/56 billion km to what may be the nearest planetary system to our own; and many more exciting exhibits.

The Science Museum is now one of London's major tourist attractions, visited each year by more than 3 million people. It covers an area of more than 7 acres/3 ha. and is spread over five levels.

At the museum's entrance, hanging from the ceiling of the stairwell high above the hall, is the stunningly simple Foucault's Pendulum, a model that demonstrates how the Earth moves on its axis.

The ground floor exhibition area is principally devoted to motive power, that is, the steam engines that laid the foundations of the modern world. There are engines by Newcomen, Watt and Trevithick. Electric power, exploration, railways, tunnels, bridges and fire-fighting (a fire engine from 1734) are also represented with displays.

On the lower ground floor is the Children's Gallery together with exhibits about fire-making (Bryant and May appliances and a Temple of Vesta fire machine); locks and fastenings; and 19th-century domestic appliances (a cosy Victorian kitchen, the New Family Sewing Machine of 1866). Exhibits in the Children's Gallery either involve participation by children or are dioramas showing how science and engineering have influenced life. The gallery is entered through a door operated by a photoelectric cell and motor, an exhibit which has perhaps been opened 50 million times. This noisy and crowded gallery, with its many working exhibits, also houses a full-size submarine periscope, through which it is possible to see other floors, as well as displays to test hearing and colour vision.

The first floor is devoted to telecommunications, hand and machine tools, iron and steel, glass, textile machinery, agriculture, gas, meteorological instruments, time measurement, map-making and surveying instruments, and astronomical instruments.

On the second floor galleries cover printing and paper-

making, weighing and measuring, chemistry, lightning, the
structure of matter, nuclear physics and power, computing,
navigation, ships, marine engineering, and docks and diving.

On the third floor exhibits are devoted to photography and
cinematography, optics, talking machines, heat and temperature, the early centuries of physics, electricity and magnetism,
geophysics, clothes for the job, and aeronautics.

The lower and upper Wellcome Galleries, on the fourth and
fifth floors, are respectively devoted to medical history, and the
science and art of medicine. Practical reconstructions show
prehistoric bone surgery, trepanning of the skull, a Roman
field hospital, the medical deck of Admiral Nelson's flagship
Trafalgar at the height of battle; and a field dressing-station of
the First World War. There is also an X-ray room, oculist's and
dentist's equipment, an iron lung, a full-size open-heart surgery
theatre and a 19th-century chemist's shop.

The Science Museum Library, an integral part of the main
museum, holds a total stock of 500,000 volumes and 19,000
periodicals, of which 6,000 are current. It also holds the
museum's Pictorial Collection of paintings, prints and drawings,
and the Archives Collection of historic and manuscript items.

Leave the Science Museum by the Exhibition Road exit. The
Geological Museum (6) is a short distance to the south. The vast
processes that shaped the Earth are portrayed here in majestic
images. Much quieter than the neighbouring Science Museum,
the Geological Museum's remarkable collection of minerals and
fossils now numbers over a million specimens. It developed as a
result of the Geological Survey of Britain in 1835. A century
later the organization moved its headquarters and collection to
the present Classical Revival-style building, and in 1985 it
became a constituent part of the British Museum. Three
floors are open to the public, the top floor housing the reserve
collection.

On the ground floor displays are concerned with the physical
structure of the Earth and its geological processes. Here the
museum's internationally acclaimed Story of the Earth opens
with a road cutting in Scotland showing rocks 1,000 million years
old. It continues at a cosmic level with the Galaxy cyclorama and
planet models. By pushing a button it is possible to watch the
'Birth and Death of Stars'. Subsequent chapters of the story
focus on the Earth. Volcanoes are represented with animated

models and stunning eruption sequences. The Great Alaskan Earthquake of 1964, which registered force 4 on the Richter scale, is re-created with the help of slides, and a section of the gallery floor is shaken by hydraulic rams to enhance the experience.

Also on the ground floor are the Britain before Man and Treasures of the Earth displays. Treasures of the Earth shows how we use the planet's minerals. By pushing coloured buttons in the exposed cross-section of an ordinary house it is possible to find out from which minerals domestic objects are made.

The mezzanine floor houses the British Fossils display and the remarkable Gemstones Gallery, the most varied collection of precious, semi-precious and other translucent stones in the world. Gems are shown in their natural state and at various stages during cutting. There are models of some of the world's most famous stones, including the Koh-i-nor and Cullinan diamonds. On display are a red ruby crystal in calcite from Burma; a very unusual octagonal orange sapphire; fine emerald crystal from Muzo, Columbia; rich iridescent opals from Australia; orange fire opals from Mexico; and the diamond-studded Murchison Snuffbox with its portrait of Tsar Alexander II presented in 1867 to Sir Roderick Murchison, a former director of the museum.

Exhibits on the first and second floors are more technical. The geology of Britain is dealt with region by region on the first floor. Geologically distinct areas are illustrated in bays with rock specimens, maps, models, dioramas and photographs. Exhibitions on the second floor deal with the economic geology of the world and include the world's largest display of metalliferous ores as well as models of large gold nuggets and a model of Stonehenge.

The museum pursues a wide range of educational activities and field excursions as well as lectures, demonstrations and films for the general public. Its shop sells maps, minerals and geological instruments.

North along Exhibition Road, turn west towards the Imperial College of Science and Technology, part of the University of London and one of the world's most prestigious institutions of advanced technological education. The 287-ft-/87-m-high **Queen's Tower (7)** at the centre of the college campus gives a marvellous panorama over this part of London. Its ten bells, a personal gift to Queen Victoria, each bear a name of a member of the royal family. The tower is all that remains of the Imperial Institute, the forerunner to the Commonwealth Institute (*High Street Kensington* ⊖), and was built to a design by T. E. Collcutt to mark Queen Victoria's Golden Jubilee in 1887.

Return to Exhibition Road, and turn north to the junction with Prince Consort Road to the **National Sound Archive (8)**, the national repository for sound recordings of all kinds, from wax cylinders to compact discs. Its current holdings amount to 1 million discs and over 45,000 hours of tape-recordings. It is the main point of public access to the BBC Sound Archives. The archive holds seasons of lectures and discussions, a free listening service by appointment and a reference library. Around 80 per cent of all discs commercially issued in this country are received here. There are also important collections of international traditional music, Western art music, wildlife sounds, jazz and popular music. The archive itself produces around 300 hours of original material through its own extensive live-recording programme, which includes coverage of all new productions at the National Theatre, the Royal Shakespeare Company and the Royal Court Theatre. The archive has also played a central part in the compilation of the National Discography and is a part of the British Library.

West along Prince Consort Road is the **Royal College of Music Museum of Instruments (9)**. This small museum, with around 500 instruments, has gathered a number of individual works of outstanding international significance since it was founded in 1883, at the opening here of the Royal College of Music. Most are European keyboard, stringed and wind instruments from the 16th to 19th centuries, but in its small ethnic collection there are works from India, Africa, China and Japan.

The museum's prized possession is a clavicytherium dating from around 1480 and believed to be the earliest stringed keyboard in existence. The museum also contains one of the earliest surviving harpsichords from Venice, which dates from 1531; a clavichord that might have belonged to Haydn; a regal, probably of German origin, from the early 17th century and the only such example in a public collection in Britain; English bedside spinets; a virginal built in 1593; a chamber organ by Bernard Smith (1702), the *Queen's Band*, a set of miniature instruments commissioned by Queen Mary; and early English and Viennese pianos. A series of full-size working drawings (dyeline prints), has been published by the museum for those wishing to make modern 'authentic' copies of some of these remarkable instruments.

Exhibits are on two levels, grouped mainly according to type, and there are examples of hurdy-gurdies, lutes, mandolins, citterns, guitars, dulcimers and harps as well as exotic 19th-century musical inventions. Many are beautifully decorated.

The Royal College of Music's Department of Portraits is sometimes not open to the public, but it holds a wonderful collection of some 120 portraits, 3,000 engravings and photographs, and sculpture representing the greatest composers, instrumentalists, singers and conductors from all nations. The department also holds a treasure trove of concert programmes, posters, letters and other musical ephemera.

Directly north is the **Royal Albert Hall (10)** (Fowke, 1871). In 1868 Queen Victoria laid the foundation stone of this red-brick circular hall, nearly a quarter of a mile/0.4 km in circumference. At her suggestion the name 'Royal Albert' was given to the building in memory of her late husband. A 42-ft/12.8-m-high memorial statue of the prince stands on the steps leading up the hall.

Today the hall is internationally known for the famous Sir Henry Wood Promenade Concert season, held on weekdays between mid-July and mid-September. On the last night of the Proms the hall is packed to its 7,000-people capacity with a cheering throng. Thousands of youngsters have been led to an enjoyment of classical music since Sir Henry Wood founded and conducted the first 'prom' in 1895.

The Royal Albert Hall is also a venue for pop and jazz music, exhibitions, regimental reunions, conferences and boxing contests. Its 150-ton organ with nearly 9,000 pipes and steam-driven bellows, was first played by the Austrian composer Anton Bruckner at the inaugural concert.

Surrounding the hall are buildings of the Royal College of Art, the Royal Geographical Society and the Royal College of Organists, with its dense and distinctive ornate decoration.

Opposite the Royal Albert Hall, on the north side of Kensington Gore, is the **Albert Memorial (11)**, completed in 1876. In shape and ornament the two are in sharp contrast. The Hall, with its shallow glass and iron dome, has only one decoration, an upper frieze illustrating the triumph of the Arts and Sciences. Marble, enamel, polished stone, bronze, mosaic, pinnacles, a cross and 200 sculpted figures arranged in seven tiers are incorporated in the 175-ft/53-m-high memorial – a monument to both Prince Albert and mid-Victorian taste. A bronze statue of a seated Prince Albert under this open-sided square temple shows him surrounded by allegorical figures and reading the catalogue of the Great Exhibition. The figures include Homer, Dante, Raphael, Michelangelo, Leonardo and Giotto as well as famous soldiers, scientists and statesmen of many nations.

Return to South Kensington ⊖ by walking west along Kensington Gore and turning south into Queens Gate. At the north-west corner of its junction with Cromwell Road is **Baden-Powell House (12)**, headquarters of the Scout movement in Britain. On the ground floor of this modern hostel is a small and interesting museum, which traces the life of Lord Baden-Powell (1857–1941), hero of the siege of Mafeking, and founder in 1907 of the Scout movement. It contains personal photographs, souvenirs and other memorabilia of this remarkable man.

Sloane Square ⊖ & Knightsbridge ⊖

At Sloane Square stately Belgravia meets fashionable Chelsea. North of the square, connected by Sloane Street, is Knightsbridge, with its famous shops.

Chelsea is a pretty part of London, earning the description in the 16th century as the 'village of palaces'. Today it has no great mansions, but instead a number of pleasing squares, terraces and individual houses from all periods. Through its centre runs the King's Road, the heartbeat of the 'Swinging Sixties' and, more recently, punk fashion. On Saturdays, at its busiest, the street's *habitués* form a kind of fashion parade of the trendy clothes found in the windows of its hundreds of boutiques.

King's Road is named after Charles II and was his official and private route to Hampton Court. It was reportedly also the route to the Fulham home of his mistress, Nell Gwyn. The Royal Hospital, Chelsea, home of the Chelsea Pensioners for the last 300 years, was built by Charles II. The Pensioners' soldier's uniform, which dates from the 18th century, seems incongruous with the rest of the King's Road's dedicated followers of fashion.

Chelsea first rose to prominence in 1520, when Sir Thomas More travelled upstream and built Beaufort House. In 1536, a year after More was executed, Henry VIII acquired the Manor of Chelsea and built a palatial new mansion. The Duke of Norfolk and the Earl of Shrewsbury also possessed grand houses here. After the Restoration, Charles II made Chelsea a fashionable resort and in 1712 Sir Hans Sloane, the famous physician and collector, bought the manor. Sloane, after whom Sloane Square is named, donated the land on which the Chelsea Physic Garden has today accumulated, behind its secluded walls, one of the finest botanical gardens. A statue of Sloane is at the centre of the garden. Sloane's tomb, as well as monuments to a number of other figures in Chelsea's early history, can be seen at All Saints, Chelsea Old Church.

Chelsea later became the home of writers Swift, Addison, Leigh Hunt and Carlyle, and was famed for its intellectual gatherings. The house of Scottish historian and philosopher Thomas Carlyle, the 'Sage of Chelsea', has been preserved almost intact and contains a wealth of personal items, books and portraits relating to his life as a member of the intelligentsia

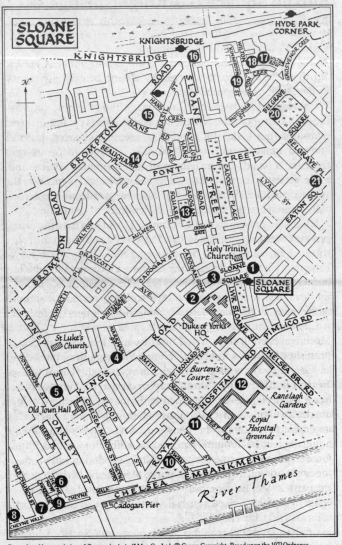

SLOANE SQUARE

of mid-Victorian London. Later still, many famous artists, including Turner, Whistler, Rossetti, Sargent, Wilson Steer and Augustus John, came to live in Chelsea, as well as writers Oscar Wilde, the Sitwells and Hilaire Belloc.

Situated next to the Royal Hospital is the National Army Museum, whose remarkable collection illustrates the history of the British Army since its foundation in 1485 by Henry VII as the Yeomen of the Guard.

Harrods and the shops of Knightsbridge are best reached from Knightsbridge ⊖ on the Piccadilly Line. Otherwise, take a pleasant walk towards Knightsbridge along Sloane Street through Cadogan Square and into Beauchamp Place. The words 'of Knightsbridge' added to a shop's name have become synonymous with the highest quality, and at the centre of Knightsbridge is Harrods, the most famous department store.

Belgravia, an area of grand houses, elegant terraces and pretty mews, is equalled only by Mayfair in its exclusivity.

⊖   ⊖   ⊖

Running above the Underground lines at Sloane Square ⊖, in a high-level cast-iron conduit, is the Westbourne, one of London's streams now channelled beneath the ground. Sloane Square ⊖ faces Sloane Square.

In 1956, the year rock 'n' roll hit the scene and the Suez Crisis diminished Britain's international role forever, the play *Look Back in Anger* burst on to the London stage at the **Royal Court Theatre (1)**. Many critics found the play distasteful, but Kenneth Tynan in the *Observer* acclaimed it the best young play of its decade. Twenty-seven-year-old John Osborne's play launched a movement that came to be known as the 'Angry Young Men' and challenged the complacency – one author has called it the 'decoratively arranged aspic' – of West End commercial theatre. Under the artistic direction of George Devine the English Stage Company at the Royal Court brought forward dozens of new works by British writers, changing the face of drama. In Devine's words, the Royal Court was not to be 'a producers' theatre, or an actors' theatre, but a writers' theatre', staging works that were serious, realist and of contemporary relevance.

Following Devine's death in 1966 this tradition has been carried forward by his successors. Works by Arnold Wesker, John Arden, Ann Jellicoe, David Storey, David Hare, Joe

Orton, Christopher Hampton, Edward Bond and Caryl
Churchill have been performed here, as well as plays by great
foreign writers, including Samuel Beckett, Bertolt Brecht, Jean
Genet and Jean-Paul Sartre. The Royal Court has fostered some
highly creative writer-director partnerships: John Osborne and
Tony Richardson, David Storey and Lindsay Anderson, Arnold
Wesker and John Dexter, Edward Bond and William Gaskill,
Christopher Hampton and Robert Kidd. Some of the great
actors were also attracted from the West End, starting with Sir
Laurence Olivier, who appeared in *The Entertainer* (1957), a
play written specially for him by John Osborne.

The present theatre, on the east side of Sloane Square next to
the Underground station, was opened in 1888. During the first
decade of this century many of George Bernard Shaw's controversial and iconoclastic plays were premièred here, and the
theatre began to gain its reputation. The Royal Court, with its
small experimental Theatre Upstairs, remains at the forefront of
the avant-garde, but it faces competition today from fringe
theatre and from the Royal Shakespeare Company's (*Barbican*
⊖) and the National Theatre's (*Embankment* ⊖) small auditoria,
which absorb much new dramatists' work.

Chelsea's main thoroughfare is the **King's Road** (2), which
stretches west from Sloane Square all the way to Putney. Its first
mile or so is lined with shops catering for the dedicated follower
of fashion. Music pounds from most doorways and on Saturdays
trendy shoppers mingling in and out of boutiques make up an
almost impromptu fashion parade – people there to be seen, as
well as to buy. It all began in the 'Swinging Sixties', when Mary
Quant opened her shop, Bazaar, at No. 138, changing the face of
fashion with her daring and unusual designs. Punks in the late
Seventies and early Eighties continued the King's Road's
reputation for radical fashion and, although Quant's shop is
gone, some of the most original clothes in London can still be
found in shops such as Boy (No. 153), Academy (No. 188A),
Hetherington (No. 289), Quasimodo (No. 239) and Review
(No. 81).

Peter Jones (3), at the head of King's Road, is a much more
conservative department store. Its site was acquired in 1877 by
Peter Rees Jones for his drapery and furniture business. After
his death in 1905, the store was bought by department-store
magnate John Lewis. Peter Jones is a quality department store,

noted for its excellent home furnishing and china and glassware departments.

Walking west, the Duke of York's Headquarters is on the south side of the King's Road. At the beginning of the last century it was erected as a school for soldiers' orphans, but now serves as the headquarters for Territorial Army and various other military units. A short distance west, Royal Avenue leads off to the south, lined by a series of late-Georgian terraces facing each other across a line of trees. It was originally intended as a leafy boulevard linking the Royal Hospital, Chelsea, with Kensington Palace, but it was not continued north of the King's Road. Author Ian Fleming chose the avenue for James Bond's London residence. In the distance through ornamental iron gates is a view of the Royal Hospital.

The King's Road's two main indoor antique markets are Antiquarius, at Nos. 135–41, and the Chenil Galleries, at Nos. 181–3.

The Pheasantry, at No. 152, is one of the most distinctive buildings in the King's Road, set behind a flamboyant gateway and façade. The building, now the **Pheasantry Restaurant (4)** and cocktail bar, takes its name from the pheasants bred here in the last century, but a house has existed on the site since 1769. The Joubert family, upholsterers and furniture makers, acquired the house in 1881 and remodelled its façade in the style of a 17th-century French mansion. It was here, between 1916 and 1934, that Princess Serafine Astafieva held her Russian ballet school, her pupils including Dame Alicia Markova, Dame Margot Fonteyn, Leonide Massine and Anton Dolin. In 1932 the basement became a bohemian club, which for the next 35 years was patronized by writers, painters, actors and politicians, including Augustus John, Dylan Thomas and Pietro Annigoni.

The **Chelsea Farmers' Market (5)** in Sydney Street is a collection of wooden chalet buildings occupied by various shops, including an extensive horticultural business, restaurants, a bakery, a dairy and a fruiterer. Three hundred years ago the King's gardener grew plants and flowers here for the Palace of Westminster as well as herbs for his master's apothecary.

Slightly further north along Sydney Street are the distinctive flying buttresses of St Luke's – Chelsea's parish church and London's first church in the Gothic Revival style.

Further west along the King's Road, just beyond the fire station, Glebe Place leads south into a picturesque collection of Georgian and early Victorian streets centred around Cheyne Row and Lawrence Street. Historian and philosopher Thomas Carlyle settled in No. 24 Cheyne Row in 1834 and lived here until his death in 1881. Such was his reputation that public subscription enabled **Carlyle's House (6)** to be purchased, and in 1895 it was opened as a museum. The house, built in 1706, and its decoration have remained largely as they were in Carlyle's time, each room containing a wealth of personal possessions, furniture, books and portraits relating to his life in mid-Victorian London.

Carlyle's hat still hangs on a peg at the far end of the hall. In the Sitting Room, or parlour, hangs *A Chelsea Interior* (*c.* 1857), a painting by Robert Tait showing the Carlyles in this same room. In the Back Dining Room hangs a portrait of Frederick the Great of Prussia, the subject of Carlyle's famous epic biography. In the tiny China Closet, off the Back Dining Room, is a cast of Carlyle's hands from life by Sir Edgar Boehm (1834–90). Carlyle would often retire to the basement kitchen to smoke, regularly accompanied by his friend the poet Tennyson. Its adjustable open fireplace is a delightful example of Victorian economy. Note the maid's bed in the kitchen dresser.

Leading intellectual and literary figures, including Dickens, Ruskin, Leigh Hunt, Browning, Thackeray and Darwin, were entertained in the first-floor Library. Its screen, a homely touch, is by Mrs Carlyle. Carlyle wrote *The French Revolution* (1837) here. In the rear room on the first floor stands Mrs Carlyle's four-poster bed and beyond it, in the Dressing Room, are the original washstands and an enamel hip-bath.

Carlyle demanded absolute silence in which to work, so he built his Attic Study as a sound-proof room at the top of the house. Unfortunately, his sound-proofing devices not only failed, but had quite the reverse effect, amplifying noise. None the less, for twelve years the great thinker persisted here with *Frederick the Great*. In a showcase by the door is a charred fragment of the manuscript of the first volume of the *The French Revolution*. Fellow philosopher John Stuart Mill had borrowed the manuscript to read, but his maid, mistaking Carlyle's only copy for waste paper, burned it. In a matter of weeks Carlyle recovered the situation, though he remarked he had 'nearly killed himself accomplishing zero'.

In the mid-18th century nearby Lawrence Street housed the Chelsea Porcelain Factory, makers of pastoral-style figures that are now highly valued antiques. Justice Walk leads into Old Church Street, the oldest thoroughfare in Chelsea. **All Saints, Chelsea Old Church (7)** stands at its southern end. Although it was largely destroyed during the Second World War, parts of the original survive, including sections of the medieval chancel and its adjacent chapels as well as the church's magnificent collection of monuments.

On the nave's north side is Pietro Bernini's reclining figure (1669) of Lady Jane Cheyne, whose family occupied Chelsea Manor House from 1660 to 1712. The family's name is preserved in Cheyne Walk, which now occupies the site of their former manor.

The Lawrence Chapel, on the north side of the chancel, dates from around 1325. Near the east arch is a small alabaster group of Sir Thomas Lawrence (1593), goldsmith and merchant adventurer of the City of London, and his family at prayer.

On the south side of the chancel is a monument to Sir Thomas More. Sir Thomas built nearby Beaufort House in 1520 and eight years later he had All Saints' south chapel rebuilt as his private place of worship. Its pillars, which support the arch from the chancel, are adorned with capitals allegedly designed by Hans Holbein the Younger. They represent symbols of the offices More held in the Church and the State, and constitute some of England's earliest Renaissance work.

After More was executed by Henry VIII, his Chelsea properties fell to Lord Dacre, whose monument is on the south side of the nave. Further west are the only examples of chained books in any London church. They date from the late 17th and early 18th centuries and were the gift of Sir Hans Sloane. Sloane's ornate tomb is outside at the east end of the church.

Crosby Hall (8), the Great Hall of Crosby Place – once the 15th-century City residence of wealthy wool merchant and grocer Sir John Crosby – was removed from its Bishopsgate site and rebuilt in Chelsea in 1909. It was erected on what had been part of Sir Henry More's Beaufort House gardens and, nearly twenty years after its arrival, the hall was incorporated into the international hostel of the British Federation of University Women.

Much of its external stonework has been renewed, but the

interior reveals a magnificently carved oak and chestnut roof, constructed on the scissor-beam principle. The oriel window and the splendid fireplace display Sir John's crest, the ram trippant. The minstrels' gallery is a replica. On the north wall, the painting *The Family of Sir Thomas More* is a copy of a Holbein original. Crosby Hall is entered via the garden gateway on Chelsea Embankment and through the hostel.

Cheyne Walk (9), one of Chelsea's most exclusive residential streets, is named after the Cheyne family, lords of the Manor of Chelsea between 1660 and 1712. It stretches along the Thames from Ballantyne Street in the west to Royal Hospital Road in the east. Its western section, beyond Beaufort Street, contains the oldest residence in Chelsea – Lindsey House, at Nos. 96–100, built in 1674. The house was divided in the 1770s and was later home to the painters Whistler and Turner. The latter lived here anonymously until his death in 1851. The Brunels, father Marc and son Isambard, lived at No. 98.

Albert Bridge divides the eastern section of Cheyne Walk. It was built in 1873 and is one of London's most beautiful bridges, particularly at night, when it is illuminated by hundreds of electric lights. To the east of Albert Bridge is Cadogan Pier, the finishing point of the Doggett's Coat and Badge Race, the oldest established annual event in the British sporting calendar. The race was instituted in 1715 by Thomas Doggett, a comedian and manager of the Drury Lane Theatre. Doggett loved the river and was inspired to create the race in honour of the accession of George I. Doggett died in 1721, but his will provided a legacy for prize money for the race, as well as a special reddish orange coat and a large silver badge bearing the white horse of Hanover to go to the best oarsman from among the Thames's Watermen (*Monument* ⊖). Doggett's bequest is conveyed by the Fishmongers' Company (*Monument* ⊖), the superintendents of the race.

Nos. 19–26, in Cheyne Walk's eastern section, today occupy the site of the former Chelsea Manor House, built by Henry VIII in 1537 and the home of his last wife, Catherine Parr. It was demolished after the death of its last occupant, Sir Hans Sloane, in 1753. No. 16 was once the home of Pre-Raphaelite painter Dante Gabriel Rossetti (1828–82). The menagerie of exotic animals kept here by Rossetti included a wombat that had a fondness for consuming visitors' floral hats. To this day a neighbouring landlord is said to stipulate in his lease that tenants are forbidden to keep wombats.

Lying behind a high wall at the southern end of Royal Hospital Road is **Chelsea Physic Garden (10)**, London's 'secret garden'. One of the oldest botanic gardens in Europe, it was founded as a teaching garden by the Worshipful Society of Apothecaries in 1673. It contains many rare and unusual plants and trees, including the largest olive tree in Britain, with a herb garden of culinary and medicinal plants, the earliest rock garden in the country (1772) and botanical order beds. In total there are more than 5,000 species. Many other gardens came in time to be termed 'botanic', but only Chelsea, with its strong tradition in medicinal teaching and research, retained its original title. 'Physic' was then the term used for the art of healing, and in those days apothecaries largely adhered to Parcelsus's theory that every plant was effective against some disease. None the less, since then thousands of specimens of both native and foreign origin have been introduced not only for their import-ance to pharmacology, but also for their industrial and horti-cultural value. It was via this garden that cotton seed was sent to Georgia in 1732, helping to establish the great cotton plantations of America's southern states.

The first curator, or Gardener, John Watts, started an inter-national exchange of seeds and plants, and imported four cedars of Lebanon, among the first in the country. Sir Hans Sloane, who as a young man had studied in the Physic Garden, virtually re-founded the garden by leasing it to the Society for £5 a year in perpetuity and guaranteeing tenure provided that 'it be for ever kept up and maintained as a physic garden'. His statue now stands at the centre of the garden. Sloane appointed Gardener Philip Miller (1691–1771), whose fifty years' curatorship brought the garden to international fame. Miller trained William Aiton (1731–93), the first Gardener at Kew, and Miller's *Dictionary of Gardening* became a standard reference work for generations.

Many parts of this secluded four-acre/1.6 ha. garden have been restored to their 18th-century layout. Some displays are based on plants introduced by various curators and collectors. The 'order beds' hold families of plants arranged in what is thought to have been their evolutionary sequence. The diversity of the Physic Garden's exotic species is remarkable, considering

England's temperate climate. Its sheltered grounds and the heat from surrounding buildings manage to sustain varieties of plants from South America, South Africa and the Mediterranean.

More than a hundred varieties of tree are also to be found, with exotic names like the Chinese willow pattern tree and the golden rain tree. In the hot summer of 1976 the 30-ft-/9-m-high olive tree produced a fine crop of edible fruit, an unexpected harvest in Britain's normally cool climate. But the forces of nature have not always been so kind. During the hurricane that struck southern England in October 1987 many rare trees were devastated. A thornless honey locust tree was ripped out of the ground and the garden's magnificent and ancient holm oak, believed to have been planted in 1772, was also among the casualties.

The Physic Garden also has the oldest rock garden in Britain adorned with basaltic lava brought by plant hunter Sir Joseph Banks from Iceland in 1772. Water plants grow in a delightful pond garden. Various research facilities are provided to academic institutions.

East along Royal Hospital Road is the **National Army Museum (11)**, which tells the remarkable story of the British Army. On the first floor, in Gallery One, the museum's main displays begin with the year 1485, when Henry VII raised the Yeomen of the Guard. History is taken through to the outbreak of the First World War in 1914. Some displays are devoted to campaigns and battles; others concentrate on the lives of important commanders, such as Wellington, Wolseley and Kitchener, or mark changes in army organization. The museum possesses Marlborough's gold-embroidered saddle-cloth, a French eagle and standard captured at Waterloo, and the order that sent the Light Brigade to destruction at Balaklava. Gallery Two, Flanders to the Falklands, completes the survey to the present day.

The Weapons Gallery, in the basement, traces the development of hand-held firearms. It includes a longbow retrieved from Henry VIII's ship the *Mary Rose*, which sank in 1545. The Uniform Gallery, on the second floor, illustrates the evolution of the colour and cut of army attire from the days of the 'Redcoats' through to contemporary combat wear. The museum's Art Gallery includes many portraits, including several by Reynolds and Gainsborough. The museum also holds records of the Indian Army up to that country's independence in 1947, as well as extremely comprehensive, and sometimes rare, collections of books, manuscripts, prints, maps and photographs.

The Royal Hospital, Chelsea (12) has been the home of the Chelsea Pensioners since 1692. Here today more than 400 of these colourful old soldiers receive board, lodging, clothing and nursing, as well as a small weekly allowance. Each wears the distinctive uniform of an 18th-century soldier, which comprises a black three-cornered hat worn on special occasions, and a navy blue coat in winter, a scarlet one in summer.

Charles II founded the 'hospital' in 1682 for regular army veterans aged 65 or over. On Oak Apple Day, 29 May, pensioners still celebrate their founder's birthday and receive double rations. Oak foliage is put around Grinling Gibbons's bronze statue (1676) of Charles II in South Court, which symbolizes the oak in which Charles hid while fleeing from Cromwell's troops.

Sir Christopher Wren designed the main buildings around three courtyards, with the main court open to the south and the Thames. His Great Hall and chapel are situated in the central block, which is surmounted by a lantern. The block has a Tuscan portico flanked by a low colonnade overlooking the grounds of this south side.

The Chelsea Pensioners dine in the panelled Great Hall. Note the old leather beer jugs. Charles II, on horseback, looks down on the Pensioners from a large mural, which was begun by Antonio Verro in 1687 and completed by Henry Cooke a decade or so later. Around the walls is a series of portraits of British monarchs and their consorts, from Charles II to Queen Victoria.

Flags captured in battle decorate the chapel, which has remained much as Wren designed it nearly 300 years ago. A dramatic painting, *The Resurrection* (*c*. 1715) by Sebastiano Ricci, hangs over the altar. On the east side of the Hospital, overlooking Light Horse Court, there is a small museum of objects about the history of the institution and its residents. The Great Hall, chapel and museum are open for two hours every morning and afternoon. The Royal Hospital has beautiful grounds, which include the Ranelagh Gardens. The Chelsea Flower Show has been held at the Royal Hospital every May since 1913.

From the crossroads at the east end of Royal Hospital Road, Lower Sloane Street continues north back to Sloane Square.

From the north side of Sloane Square, Sloane Street stretches long and straight, connecting Chelsea with Knightsbridge. At its southern end the General Trading Company, at No. 144, sells a stylish pot-pourri of furniture, gifts and household merchandise, and Partridge's, at No. 132, offers gourmet delights. Opposite is the Holy Trinity Church, rebuilt in 1888 at the height of the Pre-Raphaelite movement and the apotheosis of William Morris's Arts and Crafts movement. Many leading artists of the day contributed to its interior decoration.

From the west side of Sloane Street, Cadogan Gate passes into **Cadogan Square (13)**, an impressive red-brick development from the early 19th century. Pont Street, on the north side of the square, joins the western end of **Beauchamp Place (14)**. This pretty street has almost a village atmosphere. Below the iron balconies of its Regency housing nestle small fashionable boutiques, restaurants and antique shops – a *bijou* street for *bijou* gifts. They make an enchanting contrast to the large Harrods and Harvey Nichols department stores near by. Most are unusual and very individually run. Fouquet of Knightsbridge, at No. 58, is a branch of the famous old Parisian food shop, and ideal for finding food presents. San Lorenzo, at No. 22, is one of London's most beautiful restaurants and a place for society spotting.

On Brompton Road, at the north end of Beauchamp Place, is **Harrods (15)**, the best known department store in the world. Its motto is *Omnia, Omnibus, Ubique* – Everyone, Everything, Everywhere. The world's most comprehensive range of merchandise and special services is to be found in the 1.3 million sq. ft/120,000 sq. m of its six-storey premises. The store has around 5,000 sales staff and more than 200 departments. Harrods supplies provisions and household goods to the Queen; china, glass and fancy goods to the Queen Mother; and is the outfitter to the Prince of Wales and the Duke of Edinburgh.

The Food Halls are internationally famed. The wine department stocks 163 brands of whisky; the cheese department, 500 different varieties; the bakery, 130 different types of bread; and the confectionery department sells more than 100 tons of chocolate each year. At Christmas, the store also sells around 100 tons of Christmas puddings and 45,000 mince pies. In the New Year and summer sales wonderful bargains are to be found.

The store can justifiably make its claim 'Harrods serves the

world'. In its distinguished history Harrods has supplied Persian
carpets to Persia, a refrigerator to Finland, an authentic replica
of a 1901 Ford to an Arab sheik, and six *Harrods* bread rolls
costing 30p to New York.

The business began when Henry Charles Harrod took over a
small grocer's shop in the village of Knightsbridge in 1849.
Twelve years later his son Charles Digby Harrod purchased the
shop from him. By the 1880s, in vastly extended premises,
Harrods was employing 100 shop assistants. In 1898 Harrods
installed the first escalator in London. An attendant at the top
dispensed brandy to those overcome by the ride. Between 1901
and 1905 the main part of the present building was erected, and
final rebuilding was completed in 1939.

The east end of Brompton Road meets at a junction with
Knightsbridge and the northern end of Sloane Street. This
northern part of Sloane Street houses a dense area of shops. At
the Knightsbridge end is **Harvey Nichols (16)**, a quality department store specializing mainly in fashion and household goods,
and established here since 1817. On the east side of Sloane
Street are Bendicks, noted for its elaborate hand-made confectionery; Blanchards, for its furniture, and Taylor of London, for
its delicate floral perfumes.

At the east end of Knightsbridge, opposite the beginning of the
Hyde Park Corner underpass, Old Barrack Yard, a narrow lane,
leads south into Belgravia, an area of grand stuccoed terraces.
Originally meadows, Belgravia remained largely undeveloped
until the 1820s, when the estate's owner Lord Grosvenor came
to an agreement with the builder Thomas Cubitt. The area's
social prestige was considerably enhanced by proximity to
Buckingham Palace, especially after Queen Victoria took up
residence there in 1837. Over a period of thirty years Belgravia
developed into a stately area of grand houses and mews built on
soil from the recently excavated St Katharine's Dock. Many of
its larger houses are today occupied by companies and embassies. Its little mews cottages now comprise much of Belgravia's
sought-after residential property.

At the end of Old Barrack Yard in Wilton Row is the
Grenadier Pub (17). Once used as a mess by the Duke of
Wellington's officers, it is said that George IV and the Duke
were customers. Directly outside in Old Barrack Yard is the

remaining stone of what is believed to be the Duke's mounting block. Today this charming pub is full of mementoes to the Duke, as well as military prints and old weapons. Part of the Grenadier's original pewter bar survives and is believed to be the oldest of its kind. During September the pub is reputed to be haunted by the ghost of an officer who was flogged to death after being caught cheating at cards.

The southern end of Wilton Row emerges into the grand and elegant Wilton Crescent. **St Paul's Church (18)** lies to the north in Wilton Place. Built in the Perpendicular style to the designs of Thomas Cundy the Younger, St Paul's was consecrated in 1843, attracting much controversy in its early days for its High Church practices.

To the west of the church is the most delightful collection of streets in Belgravia. **Kinnerton Street (19)** and its tributaries were built around 1825. These tiny courtyards, such as Frederic Mews and Ann's Close, form an attractive 'village' of little shops, pubs and pretty painted houses with carefully nurtured shrubs and window boxes.

Belgrave Square (20) is the focus of Belgravia, 10 acres/4 ha. of lush open space surrounded by grand stuccoed terraces with elegant façades designed in 1827 by George Basevi (1794–1845). Once the homes of aristocrats and statesmen, many are now occupied by wealthy companies and embassies.

At the southern end of Belgrave Place, a walk through **Eaton Square (21)**, with its ample terraces and long strips of trees, is a pleasant route back to Sloane Square ⊖.

Victoria ⊖

Victoria Station, the hub of this area, links London by rail to south-east England and the Continent. The station has a special terminal for Gatwick airport and another is being built at Platform 1 to connect with the proposed new Battersea Power Station leisure complex. Victoria Coach Station is near by. Victoria and Pimlico, to its south, were once low-lying marshlands inhabited by a twilight world of criminals and the poor. But following the opening of Vauxhall Bridge in 1816 and the development of industry around the Grosvenor Canal a decade or so later, housing began to flourish here in the 1840s and 1850s. Although less desirable today than Belgravia, Pimlico has some fine Victorian terraces. Towards the end of the Victorian era the two most noteworthy features of the area came into existence: the Tate Gallery and Westminster Cathedral.

The Tate Gallery opened in 1897 and now houses many of Britain's finest art treasures, including the country's national collection of modern art and one of the most important collections of purely British painting. The British Collection maintains groups of works by most of the country's major artists, including Hogarth, Reynolds, Gainsborough, Constable and, in particular, the Pre-Raphaelites and William Blake. The Clore Gallery is devoted entirely to the works of Turner. The thread of British art beyond 1900 continues in the massive Modern Collection, which begins with Impressionism and stretches through to contemporary European and American art.

Westminster Cathedral, a striking architectural composition of mounting masses in Early Christian Byzantine style, is England's principal Roman Catholic church and seat of the Cardinal Archbishop of Westminster. Its campanile rises high over Victoria Street and the vast proportions of its interior are ablaze with mosaic and ornamented with more than 100 different marbles from around the world.

⊖   ⊖   ⊖

Victoria Station (1) is London's second busiest railway terminal, used by 75 million people every year. Once two separate stations, it now serves commuter traffic from Kent, Surrey and Sussex, as well as airline passengers from Gatwick and cross-

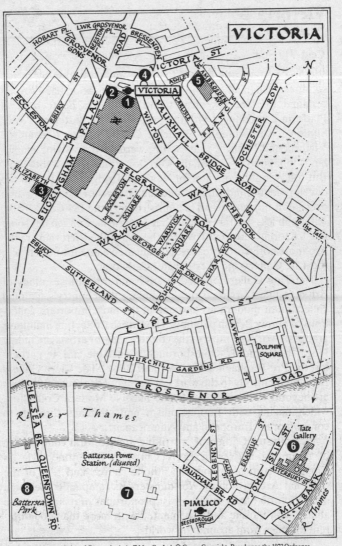

VICTORIA

N

VICTORIA ST

HOBART PL
LWR GROSVENOR PL
GROSVENOR GDNS
GROSVENOR ROAD
BEESTON PL
BRESSENDEN PL

VICTORIA ST

④
VICTORIA
⑤

②
①

ECCLESTON
EBURY ST

ASHLEY

VAUXHALL BRIDGE ROAD

CARLISLE PL

ROCHESTER ROW

FRANCIS ST

AMBROSDEN AVE

PALACE ST

ELIZABETH

③
BUCKINGHAM

BELGRAVE

ECCLESTON ST

ECCLESTON SQUARE

RD

WARWICK

TACHBROOK ST

CHARLWOOD ST

To the Tate

EBURY BR.

SUTHERLAND ST

WARWICK SQUARE

GEORGE'S DRIVE

GLOUCESTER ST

WARWICK SQUARE

ROAD

LUPUS ST

CLAVERTON ST

DOLPHIN SQUARE

CHURCHILL GARDENS RD

G R O S V E N O R   R O A D

R i v e r   T h a m e s

CHELSEA BR.
QUEENSTOWN RD.

Battersea Power Station (disused)

Tate Gallery
⑥

PONSONBY ST

ISLIP ST

ERASMUS ST

ATTERBURY ST

MILLBANK

VAUXHALL BR. RD

REGENCY ST

CAUSTON ST

JOHN ST

R. Thames

⑧
Battersea Park

⑦

PIMLICO

BESSBOROUGH ST

Channel travellers to the Continent. A shopping and eating complex called Victoria Place is upstairs from the main station concourse. The London Tourist Board's **Tourist Information Centre (2)**, open seven days a week, is located in Victoria Station forecourt, and **Victoria Coach Station (3)**, which runs services to the major towns and cities of Britain, is near by in Buckingham Palace Road, south and slightly west of the station.

Little Ben (4), a 30-ft-/9-m-tall miniature replica in the shape of Big Ben (*Westminster* ⊖), stands at the busy traffic junction of Victoria Street and Vauxhall Bridge Road. 'Temporarily' removed in 1964 for street-widening, Little Ben was restored and replaced in 1981 in commemoration of the wedding of the Prince and Princess of Wales. The work was paid for by a French oil company in recognition of the fact that many French people made rendezvous here before setting off for the Channel ports. Victoria Street stretches to the east from Victoria Station past the Department of Trade and Industry, the Army and Navy Stores and the Metropolitan Police Headquarters at New Scotland Yard.

The soaring domed campanile of **Westminster Cathedral (5)**, England's principal Roman Catholic church and seat of the Cardinal Archbishop of Westminster, looks down on Victoria Street from the south. It rises over a mounting composition of masses that make up the distinctive body of the cathedral.

John Francis Bentley (1839–1902) was commissioned by Cardinal Vaughan to design the building. Bentley travelled in Italy for inspiration, returning with this striking design, with its distinctive contrasting banded brickwork made up of no less than 12.5 million hand-made bricks. The fabric of the building was completed by 1903, although for financial reasons its interior decoration was left for future generations – work that still continues today.

A lift immediately within the porch ascends the 273-ft/83-m campanile, which today affords a slightly restricted panorama of London. Dedicated to St Edward the Confessor, its bell, called 'Edward', was donated by the Duchess of Norfolk. Above the tower rises a cross 11 ft/3.4 m high and containing what is thought to be a relic of the true cross on which Christ died.

The interior's vast proportions are impressive. The full splendour of Bentley's design is apparent when viewed from the west

end between the two great columns of red Norwegian granite.
The columns are intended to signify the Precious Blood of Christ
the Redeemer, to which the cathedral is dedicated. The nave,
roofed with three domes, is the widest in England. Flanking
the nave are seven chapels dedicated to various saints and the
Baptistry, each richly decorated with elaborate mosaics. The
Fourteen Stations of the Cross, portraying the passion of Christ
from his condemnation by Pilate to his burial, are depicted on
the main piers of the nave in beautifully crafted bas-reliefs by
Eric Gill. From the main arch of the nave hangs the great Rood
by Christian Symons. It bears painted figures of Christ and the
Mater Dolorosa.

Beyond the nave rises the focal point of the cathedral, the
Sanctuary and High Altar. The Sanctuary is dominated by a
massive *baldacchino*, or canopy, over the High Altar. It stands
on eight columns of yellow marble from Verona, with vaulting
richly inlaid with mosaic. The High Altar is a solid 12-ton block
of granite, undecorated save for five small crosses cut in its upper
surface, symbolizing the five wounds Christ suffered on the
Cross. On the north side of the Sanctuary stands the Metropolitan throne, the *cathedra*, given in memory of Cardinal Vaughan,
the man largely responsible for the inspiration of the cathedral.

Behind the High Altar, the retrochoir houses the Small
Organ. Its partner, the Grand Organ, is situated more than 300
ft/91 m away at the west end. A dual control system, unique
among cathedral organs in Britain, enables the organ to be
played from either end of the cathedral. Westminster Cathedral
is known for its music, particularly for the revival of the works of
the great English pre-Reformation composers such as Tye,
Tallis and Byrd.

The Lady Chapel lies beyond the south aisle of the Sanctuary
and is the most richly decorated of the cathedral's chapels.
Behind its altar a mosaic by Robert Anning Bell depicts Our
Lady with the Holy Child.

South of Victoria ⊖ and bounded by the curving sweep of the
Thames on its eastern and southern sides is the area known as
Pimlico, a low-lying part of London developed by Thomas
Cubitt in the 1830s. Never as desirable as Belgravia (*Sloane
Square* ⊖), Pimlico still has some pleasant terraces of small
early-19th-century houses, such as those in Eccleston Square,
where Sir Winston Churchill once resided. Elsewhere there are

many finely proportioned stuccoed buildings, although their interiors frequently do not live up to the grace and light of the exterior.

Dolphin Square, built in 1937, is one of the largest blocks of flats in Europe, covering some 7.5 acres/3 ha. The complex, a sought-after address, also houses a swimming pool and stylish French restaurant. Near by, in Grosvenor Road, the award-winning Churchill Gardens Estate scheme of flats and maisonettes for 6,500 people was completed in 1962.

Vincent Square, once a bear garden, is now used by West-minster School as a playing field. On the north side of the square stand the premises of the Royal Horticultural Society, which holds regular flower shows in the nearby New Agricultural Hall.

From Victoria ⊖, the Victoria Line travels southward to Pimlico ⊖, from where the Tate Gallery is signposted. Otherwise, it is possible to walk down the busy Vauxhall Bridge Road, turning north, or downstream, along Millbank, which borders the Thames.

Situated on Millbank, with a commanding view of the Thames, is the Tate Gallery, one of the major art galleries of the world. Unlike other notable collections, the Tate's remarkable assembly of works encompasses both classic and modern art and takes an international as well as a national view. Under the same roof are the works of Blake and Bacon, Turner and Kiefer, Constable and Nash.

This fine neo-classical gallery was opened in 1897 on the site of the former Millbank prison, thanks to the funding of sugar magnate Sir Henry Tate (1819–99). Its collection numbers more than 40,000 works and therefore only a small proportion is on view at any one time, and displays are subject to change. Each year the Tate Gallery houses around three major exhibitions with a number of smaller displays. In addition, the gallery has an active educational programme.

A simple chronological sequence provides a skeleton for the layout of the collection, which can be followed backwards or forwards in time from the Tudors to the present, tracing the evolution of British art until Impressionism and then the inter-relationship of British and foreign art through the schools of Paris. Within that chronological sequence individual artists or groups of artists or themes are presented in depth, in rotation because of limitations of space. This layout is further diversified with 'cross-current' displays that trace the persistence of certain themes or ideas through many generations of art. For example, a link could be made between William Blake and Francis Bacon with the knowledge that Bacon painted a study after the life mask of Blake.

As the Tate's aim is to enhance enjoyment and deepen understanding, rather than to encourage visitors to look only at those works with which they are most familiar, it is impossible to guarantee that any individual work of art will be on display. On the other hand, the quality of its collection is so high that masterpieces of the most important genres and periods in British art from the 16th century onwards, and of modern art internationally in the 20th century, will always be on display.

Entering from Millbank, visitors pass through three sculpture galleries before reaching the start of the Tate's chronological sequence of displays. The sculpture galleries serve as the aorta of the Tate layout, and Rodin's *The Kiss* marks the centre spot. South of *The Kiss* is Sir William Reynolds-Stephens's bronze *A Royal Game* (1911), in which Good Queen Bess (Queen Elizabeth I) plays Philip II of Spain at chess. Respective fleets are used as chess-pieces, and it hardly takes a Grandmaster to work out who is about to sweep the board.

The current layout of rooms, most of which will remain in place at any one time, begins with 'Painting in Britain in the 16th and 17th Centuries'. The gallery's earliest picture is John Bettes's portrait of an unknown man in a black cap, painted in 1545 in the style of Henry VIII's great court painter Hans Holbein. The Tate's collection from this period includes work by other court painters: Anthony Van Dyck, William Dobson, Peter Lely and Godfrey Kneller. Next is a room devoted to the age of Hogarth, celebrating this distinguished portraitist, moralist and satirist. Works by Joshua Reynolds, Thomas Gainsborough and George Stubbs are found in the room 'Eighteenth-century painting: the Grand Style', and the next room is devoted to landscape, genre and sporting painting from that century.

Works by the great visionary William Blake include his remarkable pictures *Elohim Creating Adam* and *Beatrice Addressing Dante from the Car* and reflect his highly personal form of Christianity and his belief in a much more significant spiritual world beyond the physical. The Tate is particularly rich in works by John Constable, who based his landscape painting on the direct study of nature rather than on the existing models of the Classical or Dutch style. Next are the rooms 'The 19th-century Academy and the Pre-Raphaelites' and 'Rural Naturalism and Social Realism' (1870–1900).

The room 'Impressionism in France and Britain' includes works by Monet, Pissaro and Degas, as well as Whistler, Sickert, Steer, Sargent, Augustus John and his sister Gwen. 'European Art Around 1900' is represented by works by Gauguin, Vuillard, Modigliani, Picasso, Cézanne and Van Gogh. Next are rooms dedicated to 'The European Avant-Garde 1905–25'; 'Bloomsbury and Vorticism'; 'Stanley Spencer and his Circle'; 'Constructivism and de Stijl'; 'Dada and Surrealism'; 'Figurative Art between the Wars'; 'Paul Nash'; 'Euston Road, Neo-Romanticism and Henry Moore'.

The new American painting that evolved between 1942 and 1952 among a loosely knit group of artists living in or near New York hangs in the rooms 'Towards Abstract Expressionism' and 'Abstract Expressionism', and includes work by Pollock, Rothko and de Kooning. The room 'A New Beginning' reflects Abstract Art in Britain between 1949 and 1956, with works by Hepworth, Nicholson, Pasmore, Lanyon and Hoyland. A room is currently devoted to Anthony Caro, whose welded and painted steel sheets and girders marked a revolutionary change in the degree of abstraction in British sculpture when they appeared in 1960. Other rooms cover Giacometti and the School of Paris 1945–60; British figure painting; Mark Rothko; Minimal Art and recent European and American Art.

In addition to paintings and sculpture, the Tate's Modern Collection also comprises prints and unique works on paper, to be found in the lower galleries. The J. M. W. Turner Bequest, which includes works from every period of Turner's life, can be seen in the Clore Gallery, a recent addition to the orginal Tate building.

Organizers say that **The Battersea (7)**, which will occupy the building and grounds of the old Battersea Power Station, will overtake Disneyland and Disneyworld as the world's premiere leisure and entertainment centre. They hope the complex will attract 5 million visitors a year when it opens.

The old power station building, constructed mainly in 1933, reached new heights in industrial architecture with its tall fluted chimneys and Art Deco interior. It was once the most powerful electricity generating unit in Europe, at its peak contributing one-fifth of London's electricity supply. Built with more than 8 million bricks, at 494 ft/150.5 m long, 525 ft/160 m wide and 170 ft/51.8 m high, it is the largest brick building in the world. Its chimneys top at 337 ft/99.6 m. St Paul's Cathedral would fit comfortably inside. After half a century of service, modern methods of production caused the station to close in 1983.

West of The Battersea is **Battersea Park (8)**, opened in 1853 and lying between Chelsea Bridge and the pretty Albert Bridge. Battersea Park is the venue for London's colourful Easter Parade, as well as various fairground, circus and other performances. In 1985 a shining 110-ft-/33.5-m-high Japanese pagoda was erected overlooking the river.

CENTRAL LINE

Bank ⊖

The square mile of the City of London is the historic and financial heart of London. At its centre is the ancient Guildhall, the home for some ten centuries of the City's civic government and administration. It was here, mainly between 1150 and 1450, that the City wrested its unique privileges from royalty and reluctant central governments based at Westminster. Today the Bank area contains the Bank of England, the country's central bank, the Stock Exchange, Lloyd's insurance market, the London International Financial Futures Exchange based in the Royal Exchange, and many other financial institutions of international importance.

The Guildhall is certainly the finest of England's surviving medieval secular buildings. In its day it was the rival, possibly the superior, of Richard II's Westminster Hall. As a judicial and administrative centre in those days, it housed the weekly Court of Hustings, the courts of the Sheriffs and the Common Council. Today the ancient Court of Hustings has been succeeded by the Court of Common Council, presided over by the Lord Mayor. London's first mayor was installed in 1192, although the title Lord Mayor was adopted later. His splendid official residence, Mansion House, is near by.

The National Westminster Tower, Britain's tallest solid structure, and the new hi-tech Lloyd's building stand in fitting tribute to the power and wealth of the City as a flourishing centre for international commerce. From viewing galleries can be seen the daily business on the market floors of Lloyd's, the Stock Exchange and the London International Financial Futures Exchange. The bustle of the pin-striped population of the City subsides at night, leaving the area largely deserted.

Leadenhall Market, with the delightful Victorian air of its walkways, is noted for its quality food shops. One, Blankley and Son, still devotes itself entirely to the purveyance of champagne and caviar.

St Helen Bishopsgate, a stone church with squat bell tower, has been described as the Westminster Abbey of the City because of its many monuments. These include the tomb chest of Sir Thomas Gresham, founder of the Royal Exchange, and

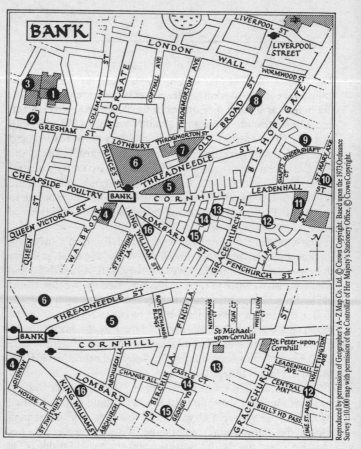

the tomb of Sir Julius Caesar Adelmare, Master of the Rolls and Privy Councillor to James I.

Θ   Θ   Θ

North along Prince's Street and west along Gresham Street is **Guildhall (1)**. Entry to Great Hall from Guildhall Yard is via the modern ambulatory at the west end of Guildhall. Brilliant receptions and banquets as well as the trials of traitors have taken place within these ancient walls. Here, too, the citizens of London demanded reforms to be made by kings and parliaments. In more modern times heads of state have been welcomed and entertained, and the nation's great states-

men, philanthropists and public servants honoured. And each
year Guildhall hosts the sumptuous Lord Mayor's Banquet.

One authority has described the City, with its centre at
Guildhall, as 'the protectress of freedom', adding,

> This principle – the necessity of freedom – was handed down from
> father to son; it became the religion of the citizens; they proclaimed
> it and fought for it; they won it, and lost it; they recovered part of it
> and lost it again. At last they won it altogether and, in winning it,
> they gained a great deal more than they had contemplated or hoped
> for. They won for their descendants, they won for every town
> where the English tongue is spoken, the rights of free men in free
> cities, the rights of the individual, the rights of property.

Such are the free men of the City of London.

After the Norman conquest of 1066, the citizens of London
were already strong enough to make their own terms with
William the Conqueror and receive from him a confirmation of
their ancient liberties. Again, those citizens held the balance
between Stephen and Empress Matilda (1135–54), and assisted
Richard, Cœur de Lion. In 1215 they assisted the barons in
wresting Magna Carta from a reluctant King John, and the
Mayor of the City was one of those specially appointed to see the
terms of the Charter strictly carried out. There was continuous
battling between the citizens and the Plantagenet kings in defence of the City's charters and liberties. In the early 15th
century a glittering array of plenipotentiaries gathered at
Guildhall to discuss the claim of Henry V to the French throne.
The Guildhall has seen celebrations marking the enthronement
of many sovereigns as well as deputations from both Houses of
Parliament, including Cromwell begging for assistance to the
Parliamentary forces and waiting upon the deliberations of its
Common Council. At the trial of King Charles five of its
aldermen and two of its wealthy citizens were named on the
Commission, and two of the aldermen and the two citizens sat in
judgement.

The City of London's civic government has sat here for
probably more than 1,000 years, predating both legal memory
and the first charter given to it by William the Conqueror in
1067. A guildhall has stood on or near this site since the 11th
century, and London's first mayor was installed here in 1192.
Two decades or so later King John granted the citizens of
London the right to hold elections.

Today the local government authority of the City is the

Corporation of the City of London. Its main administrative and executive body, the Court of Common Council, meets here and consists of the Lord Mayor, 24 aldermen and 130 common councilmen. The Lord Mayor is elected from and by the Court of Aldermen, a body that is the only surviving example in England of a municipal second, or upper, chamber. The Lord Mayor's electorate are members of Livery Companies, the ancient craft-guilds of the City (*Mansion House & Cannon Street* ⊖*s*).

The present Guildhall was begun in 1411 and completed nearly thirty years later. The crypt, porch and walls of the medieval Guildhall have survived the Great Fire in 1666 and Second World War bombing. Although three-quarters of the fabric of the building is medieval, its external appearance presents an 18th-century *jeu d'esprit*, its interior the work of the High Victorian Gothic Revival.

Restoration of the Guildhall was completed in 1954 to the designs of Sir George Gilbert Scott. A new roof of oak panelling was provided between stone arches. Light from the new clerestory windows illuminates the roof and the decorative shields of the City's eighty-four livery companies. The frieze below the clerestory level shows the coats of arms of England, the City and the twelve Great Livery Companies. Picked out in gilt Gothic letters in the City's coat-of-arms is its motto, *Domine dirige nos*, 'O Lord guide us'. The cross is that of St George of England, and the sword in the first quarter of the shield represents St Paul, the patron saint of the City. In front hang the banners of the companies.

The windows are decorated with scrolls bearing the names and dates of office of the City's mayors and Lord Mayors. The most recent are at the west end of the south wall. The lower window here, to the right of the Royal Fusiliers monument (1903), is thought to be from the original 15th-century Guildhall.

The Musicians' Gallery occupies the entire west wall. At each end are the splendid carved limewood figures of Gog (north) and Magog (south) by David Evans. Standing over 9 ft/2.7 m high and replacing the ones destroyed in 1940, they depict the mythical characters Gogmagog and Corineus, who represent the ancient conflict between Britons and Trojan invaders that led to the founding of New Troy in 1000 BC. New Troy was the mythical capital city of Albion, or ancient England, and London is said to stand on the same site.

The Guildhall contains monuments honouring national figures including William Pitt (1782), William Pitt the Younger (1813), Lord Mayor William Beckford (1772), Admiral Lord Nelson (1810), the Duke of Wellington (1857) and Sir Winston Churchill (1955).

Permission is required to visit the porch and undercroft. Much of the interior of Guildhall's vaulted Gothic porch is medieval, although the external façade, which can be viewed from Guildhall Yard, was remodelled in 1789 by George Dance the Younger. The 15th-century crypt, entered through its original carved entrance, is the most extensive of its kind in London, and is divided into two parts. The eastern section, itself divided into 12 bays, retains its six original clustered pillars of blue Purbeck marble. Bosses at the intersections of the crypt's complex lierne vaulting display the arms of Queen Elizabeth II, the City of London and many others. The west crypt, once buried beneath roof timbers that collapsed during the Great Fire, was restored to its original state in 1973. It is believed to have been part of an earlier Guildhall, possibly dating as far back as the 13th century. Its vaulted ceiling, resting on four pairs of stone columns, is now regarded as one of the finest in London.

In one of the most exciting archaeological discoveries since the Second World War, the amphitheatre of Roman London was uncovered underneath part of Guildhall. After years of speculation about its location, its remains were unearthed during redevelopment on the site of the former Guildhall Art Gallery, a grand Victorian building erected in 1886 on the east side of Guildhall Yard. That building was bombed in 1944 and within its shell a 'temporary' art gallery was built, which was not demolished until 1987. A long, curved stretch of wall constructed of stone and distinctive pink bonding tiles suggests that internally the amphitheatre was oval-shaped some 164 × 230 ft/50 × 70 m. Its discovery has filled a large gap in the known street-plan of Roman London.

Guildhall's art collection, not currently on view, is destined to occupy the new building that will occupy the site. The west end of the Guildhall site has recently been remodelled as a library and administrative complex.

St Lawrence Jewry-next-Guildhall (2) is the City Corporation's church. A special pew is reserved for the Lord Mayor at the front on the right-hand side of the central aisle. There is a sword rest and cradle for the mace. The Lord Mayor's pew is flanked by those of the Queen's Sheriffs, and there are also special seats for the Court of Aldermen. The Choir Gallery bears the City's coat of arms. Most of the church's furniture was donated by the City livery companies.

The church was founded in 1136 and dedicated to St Lawrence. A late 16th-century painting in the vestibule depicts this 3rd-century saint's martyrdom on a grid-iron in Rome. The original building was situated on the edge of a Jewish trading area, hence 'Jewry', and stood until the Great Fire. It was rebuilt by Sir Christopher Wren in 1677 at a cost of more than £10,000, the most expensive of his City churches.

In 1940 St Lawrence's was almost completely gutted by bombs. At the top of the church's spire flies the original grid-iron weathervane, which now incorporates a replica of the incendiary bomb that caused the destruction. Between 1954 and 1957 Cecil Brown rebuilt the church in the spirit of Wren's original, although his use of stained glass departed from the earlier church. One window in the vestibule commemorates Wren. He is seen flanked by his master mason, Edward Strong, and master carver, Grinling Gibbons. The interior restoration is exceptional, especially the moulded and gilded plasterwork of the ceiling, which is very close to the original. The baptistry contains a font dating from 1620, whose cover incorporates wood from the old Guildhall. Lunch-time recitals take place regularly on Mondays and Tuesdays.

The Guildhall Clock Museum (3) is a monument to the remarkable ingenuity that man has expended in trying to master the measurement of time. Upon the hour, the constant ticking of hundreds of clocks in the museum is interrupted by a tremendous cacophony of chimes. Exhibits represent both considerable technical achievements and exquisite designs. They range in size from tiny watches to large grandfather clocks.

Of particular interest are a curious Italian gas-operated clock; a 19th-century clock whose movement, a ball rather than a pendulum, rolls 2,522 miles/4,059 km a year; a silver skull watch said to have belonged to Mary, Queen of Scots; a wristwatch worn by Sir Edmund Hillary on the ascent of Everest in 1953; the star-shaped watch of 1625 made for King James I and the earliest electric clock.

Much of this important horological collection was bequeathed by the Worshipful Company of Clockmakers, although a number of the exhibits predate the formation of the company in 1631. The oldest surviving clocks date from the 14th century and were made by members of the Blacksmiths' Company. More recently, the collections of the Antiquarian Horological Society and the Osborne Index of Watch and Clockmakers have been added.

Also housed in this building are a collection of playing-cards, lent by the Worshipful Company of Makers of Playing-Cards; the Guildhall Library, an unrivalled collection on the history of London; and the Corporation of London Permanent Collection. The library contains about 150,000 printed volumes, over 30,000 manuscripts, prints, maps and drawings from all periods, and an almost complete set of London directories dating from 1677. The Corporation of London Permanent Collection is a private collection of works of art spanning three centuries.

Mansion House (4) (George Dance the Elder, 1752) situated on the south side of the road junction at Bank, has been the Lord Mayor's residence since 1753. Sadly, this magnificent building in the heart of London's financial district is not open to the public except by written application. Behind its distinctive raised portico of six Corinthian columns and sculptured pediment, Dance created a magnificent suite of State rooms. The most striking is the Lord Mayor's State Banqueting Room, adorned by two large stained-glass windows and whose barrel-vaulted ceiling is supported by sixteen tall Corinthian columns. During the handsome banquets often held here the Lord Mayor occupies the kingly Chair of State (1780). The Saloon contains one of the most prized possessions in Mansion House, a set of 18th-century chairs presented to the Lord Mayor in commemoration of Nelson's victory at the Battle of the Nile (1797). The vaults of Mansion House hold a dazzling wealth of gold and silver plate and insignia as well as the magnificent Pearl Sword, given by Elizabeth I when she opened the first Royal Exchange in 1571. This sword is still presented by the Lord Mayor to the reigning sovereign on his or her entering the City at Temple Bar (*Temple* ⊖).

The Lord Mayor is the head of the City Corporation, its Chief Magistrate and the Chairman of its two governing bodies – the Court of Common Council and the Court of Aldermen. Ancient chronicles record that Henry Fitz Eylwin of Londenstane presided in the Husting during the shrievalty beginning at Michaelmas in 1193, and it is now thought he became the City's first mayor as early as the autumn of 1192. Fitz Eylwin remained mayor for the remaining twenty-five years of his life. Every liveryman of the City Guilds is entitled to vote in Common Hall for Lord Mayor, Sheriffs, Chamberlain, Bridgemasters and a few minor officials.

Since its inception the annual election of the Lord Mayor has taken place on a variety of days, but from 1546 it has been held on Michaelmas Day, 29 September. After the sovereign's approval the new Lord Mayor is sworn in by the Town Clerk at Guildhall on the day before the second Saturday in November in a ceremony known as 'The Silent Change'. The old Lord Mayor transfers the instruments of authority to his successor in complete silence. The following day the new Lord Mayor takes the oath of office before the Judges of the Queen's Bench. During the Lord Mayor's Show, which precedes this ceremony, the new appointee drives in the Lord Mayor's Coach from Guildhall to the Royal Courts of Justice (*Temple* ⊖). His route, lined with onlookers, is a pageant of colourfully decorated floats, each portraying the particular theme chosen that year by the Lord Mayor. On the following Monday the Lord Mayor's Banquet takes place in Guildhall in honour of the outgoing Lord Mayor. One of London's major social events, it is attended by over 700 distinguished guests, including the Prime Minister.

Opposite Mansion House between Cornhill and Threadneedle Street is the impressive **Royal Exchange (5)** building (Sir William Tite, 1844). In front of its monumental Corinthian portico is an equestrian bronze, minus stirrups, of the first Duke of Wellington (1769–1852) by Sir Francis Leggatt Chantrey, as well as a memorial to London troops of both world wars, designed by Sir Aston Webb with figures by Alfred Drury.

An exchange was founded here in 1566 by merchant Sir Thomas Gresham, who recognized the need for a central trading market for merchants. During a visit in 1570 Queen Elizabeth I commanded that it should henceforth be known as the Royal Exchange. The first exchange was destroyed in the Great Fire (1666). The second opened in 1669 and was occupied primarily by the Royal Exchange Assurance Company and Lloyds of London, but it also was destroyed by fire on 10 January 1838. The present Royal Exchange, a classical building designed by Sir William Tite, was opened by Queen Victoria in 1844.

In 1972, after the collapse of the system that loosely pegged
the value of nations' currencies to that of gold, currencies were
floated and allowed to move more freely against each other.
Exchange and interest rates, however, began to fluctuate in a
way potentially destabilizing to international trade and finance.
A market in financial futures, pioneered in Chicago that year,
was opened to lessen such risk.

A financial futures contract is an agreement between two
parties to buy or sell a standardized quantity of a specific
financial instrument (for instance, a foreign currency, gilt-edged
stock or share index) at a future date, but at a price agreed
today.

Viewed from the visitors' gallery it is hard to believe that
millions of pounds are traded each day by the mass of gesticulat-
ing and shouting traders on the floor of the Exchange. Traders,
who generally wear red jackets, conduct business in the octagonal areas in the centre of the floor, known as pits. Pits are
overlooked by observation platforms known as pulpits and
used as vantage points by London International Financial Futures Exchange (LIFFE) staff wearing mid-blue jackets.
Trainee traders, called booth staff or runners, are distinguished
by mustard-yellow jackets. Traders use a particular verbal code
and a recognized system of hand signals. If the palm of the hand
faces away from the body, this indicates a wish to sell contracts;
the hand facing towards the body, a desire to buy. The trader is
required to declare his order by 'open outcry', shouting the deal
loudly enough for everyone else on the floor to hear. Throughout the trading day, blue clearing slips are fed into a computerized matching system to ensure that both parties to the deal have
noted the details correctly.

The Royal Exchange building has been given a facelift: its
stonework has been cleaned, the internal courtyard enlarged,
and two new storeys are to be added to the building.

Britain's central bank, the **Bank of England (6)**, dominates the
north side of Threadneedle Street. For years, all that could be
glimpsed of the internal workings of this famous institution were
the view through the bronze doors of the imposing colonnaded
building and, from its threshold, the Bank Gatekeepers in their
colourful livery of pink tailcoats, scarlet waistcoats and black
trousers. Now, however, the Bank has opened a museum,
entered from Bartholomew Lane, illustrating its history from

the Royal Charter, granted in 1694, to the hi-tech world of modern banking.

The museum's first exhibit is a reconstruction of the former Bank Stock Office, whose impressive counter, ledger rests and subdued top lighting faithfully reproduce an authentic impression of Bank Life in the last century. Originally designed by the distinguished architect Sir John Soane, exhibits at the room's vestibule end illustrate the architectural history of the Bank.

During its first forty years the Bank was located at Mercers' Hall and then at Grocers' Hall before its own building was erected in Threadneedle Street. Although resembling a town house, this building designed by George Sampson and completed in 1734 was probably the first purpose-built bank. Later that century Soane rebuilt much of the Bank, but between the First and Second World Wars his one-storey building was replaced by Sir Herbert Baker's multi-storeyed one, although Soane's impressive windowless curtain wall was retained.

Following the 'Glorious Revolution' of 1688, which brought William and Mary to the throne and saw the establishment of a more stable relationship between the Crown and Parliament, it was a Scottish merchant, William Paterson, who first proposed the founding of a central bank. Revenue was needed to continue the war with France and Paterson suggested founding a bank that could then lend its share capital to the government. Investors were guaranteed an 8 per cent rate of interest. Previously, revenue had been raised by the unpopular method of royal extortion. The book in which Paterson expounded his new theory is displayed, together with the founding Charter and the Book of Subscriptions, which records the £1.2 million raised in eleven days for the war against Louis XIV.

The early years of the Bank saw the introduction of the bank 'note' as a form of receipt. Examples of the forerunners of the modern bank note are on show. The iron chest displayed, the precursor of the modern safe, is the oldest piece of furniture in the Bank, authenticated in a book of 1735.

During the Napoleonic Wars, which called heavily on the public purse, the Bank gained its nickname 'The Old Lady of Threadneedle Street', after it restricted the convertibility of cash payments into gold. This action prompted a contemporary politician to refer to the Bank as 'that elderly lady in the City of great credit and long standing, who had . . . unfortunately fallen into bad company'. Gillray, a quick-witted cartoonist, seized upon the statement and portrayed Prime Minister William Pitt the Younger (the 'bad company') attempting to rob an old lady of her gold in Threadneedle Street.

In 1816 the gold standard was established by statute, fixing a quantity of gold to the pound. An impressive display features a collection of gold coins. Gold bars dating from Roman times, complete with identifying marks, and modern 28-lb/12.7-kg bars (all facsimiles) are housed in the central showcases of the Rotunda and Gold Display.

In the Victorian era the Bank consolidated its position as a central bank and, in a crisis, accepted the responsibility as 'the lender of last resort'. During the First World War the Bank raised £2 billion to fight the war, half in a single issue, the 5 Per Cent War Loan of 1917. After the Second World War, the Bank was nationalized, becoming the banker's bank. Its new charter, granted by George VI, is also on display. Since the end of the last century the Bank of England has not accepted private accounts.

Other features displayed include a Roman mosaic floor, uncovered during excavations for the new building; an interesting collection of silver; and the Bank Note Gallery, the world's finest collection of Bank of England bank notes, showing their development from simple handwritten receipts to the sophisticated notes in use today. An interactive video system explains the work of the Bank today, and a Dealing Desk, similar to those in use in today's money markets, gives live information on gilt-edged stock and securities as well as a flavour of the fast-moving financial world.

More than 9 million people in the United Kingdom are estimated to own shares, without including those indirectly involved through their pension funds or insurance schemes. The **Stock Exchange (7)** is the market place where shares and government bonds are traded. Each year billions of pounds are raised this way by companies and the government.

This modern electronic market-place is open to the public from a viewing gallery at the south end of Old Broad Street. The Stock Exchange was not created overnight, or even brought about by an Act of Parliament, but has a long history of evolution. Britain's first joint stock company was formed in London in 1553. Then, for the first time, the public were allowed to subscribe to ownership in shares of equal denomination. Ownership and day-to-day management were thus separated, with shares tradeable in a market-place. Dealings in shares started in the first Royal Exchange. Brokers moved into the second Royal Exchange after it was rebuilt following the Great Fire. Loan stock made its first appearance in 1694, after the Bank of England was set up to fund the war with France. That decade, brokers were reportedly banned from the Royal Exchange for their rowdiness. However, by that time much business was already being conducted in the fashionable coffee houses in Exchange (now Change) Alley. In the late 1760s, 150 brokers decided to form a subscription club at Jonathan's Coffee House. Later, they opened their own room at New Jonathan's, in Threadneedle Street, after the old one burned down. In 1773 the name was changed to the Stock Exchange. The first Stock Exchange on its present site was built in 1801.

In 1908 the Stock Exchange introduced rules officially separating brokers from jobbers. For many years firms had, by custom, carried on business either as brokers (trading on behalf of their clients) or as jobbers (wholesalers operating on their own account in the market, but dealing only with brokers and not directly with the public). This system continued until 1986, when the largest upheaval in the history of the Stock Exchange took place, the 'Big Bang'. This event was brought about after the abolition of exchange controls in 1979 had made it easier to invest overseas. Member firms in London were thus exposed to competition from overseas brokers, particularly in New York and Tokyo. By comparison, London firms were relatively small and lacked the capital necessary to trade in very large volumes. Further pressure for change came from the government's Office of Fair Trading, which considered that the Stock Exchange's rules were restrictive in three areas: the scales of minimum commissions charged by brokers, the distinction between jobbers and brokers, and the restrictions on outside ownership of member firms.

On 1 March 1986, it was agreed that member firms need not be controlled exclusively by individual members, and that they could be owned by a single outside corporation. Many firms were quickly bought by UK and overseas banks and securities houses. On 27 October 1986, the 'Big Bang' officially took place. The scale of minimum charges was abolished and members were freed to charge on a negotiable basis. The distinction between jobbers and brokers was also scrapped. Either is now able to act as a broker/dealer on behalf of clients, or as a principal. The Stock Exchange, which had moved to a new building in 1970, took advantage of the 'Big Bang' to introduce new electronic dealing systems designed to cope with the increased volume of business. A terminal-based quotation system, called Stock Exchange Automated Quotations (SEAQ), was installed. Today an estimated 95 per cent of business is now transacted on the telephone. Trading on the Stock Exchange floor, around its sixteen distinctive hexagonal 'pitches', has inevitably declined.

Video display units in the visitors' gallery explain how the exchange now operates, and an introductory film is shown at regular intervals.

Outside the Stock Exchange, the view north along Old Broad Street is dominated by the **National Westminster Tower (8)** (R. Seifert and Partners, 1980), Britain's tallest, and Europe's second tallest, solid structure. It rises 600 ft/183 m above the City, far exceeding the dome of St Paul's, whose 365 ft/111 m had dominated the skyline for 250 years. The tower's 52 floors house the 2,500 staff who run the company's international operations, and the building's plan bears a remarkable resemblance to the bank's triangular-shaped logo. The sheer glass windows of the tower unsettled some office staff when they arrived in 1980. To allay their fears a volunteer building worker wearing a hard hat launched himself at a window at full speed to demonstrate the robust glass construction. The building has a central core of reinforced concrete to resist the strongest winds. Laser beams used in the construction work ensured that the top was less than 1 inch/25 mm out of true. Automatic window washers clean the building's 130,000 sq ft/12,077 sq m of bronze-tinted glazing, then recycle the water. The building is open to the general public by prior appointment only.

At the end of Threadneedle Street is the Bishopsgate area. It was once guarded by a City gate of Roman origin, which was rebuilt in the 7th century by Eorconweald, Bishop of London. The approach to **St Helen Bishopsgate (9)** is beneath the north end of the imposing Standard Chartered building, a construction with a marble and glass façade delineated by gleaming chrome. This piece of modern architecture stands in sharp contrast to the squat bell tower rising from the stone body of St Helen's church, framed by shady plane trees. Behind its picturesque double-fronted façade lies an interior rich in history.

St Helen was the mother of Constantine, the first Christian Roman Emperor. It was once thought that Constantine himself built a church here in the 4th century, but no records about St Helen's appear until the mid-12th century. It is known that the church was rebuilt in the 13th century and a nunnery established. The nunnery's church and the parish church were originally separated by an internal wall, with the nunnery occupying the northern half of the building. At the Reformation in 1538 the nunnery was dissolved and the internal wall removed. This has resulted in the present and unusual layout of the church.

Entry is through the west door. To the left is the nuns' church. The four great arches dividing the building date from 1480 and once contained the wooden separating screens. Spanning both sides is a tie-beam roof, many of whose timbers date from 1480. The font in the nuns' church nave dates from 1632. Many monuments transferred here are from St Martin Outwich, a nearby church demolished in 1874. The canopied altar tomb of Alderman Hugh Pemberton (d. 1500) and his wife is one of the finest in the church. The 'Night Staircase' (c. 1500) once led to the nuns' dormitory, giving them direct access to the chapel for night services. In the nuns' chancel is a blocked doorway (c. 1500), once the processional entrance from the sacristy into the choir. In the north wall of the nuns' chancel is the nuns' squint. Through these slots nuns unable to come into church could watch the celebration of Mass. Beside the squint stands the tomb chest of a renowned citizen and mercer of London and the founder of the Royal Exchange, Sir Thomas Gresham (d. 1579). The tomb of Sir Julius Caesar Adelmare (d. 1636), a Master of the Rolls and Privy Counsellor to James I, rests in the centre of the chancel. His monument displays a deed with the seal broken off, symbolizing that he has 'engaged to pay the debt of nature as soon as it may please God'. Beneath the east arch lies the grand marble tomb of Sir William Pickering (d. 1574), ambassador to Spain under Elizabeth I.

The reredos and lower screens in the parish church chancel were part of extensive remodelling in 1893. The richly-carved pulpit (c. 1615) is Jacobean and the wooden sword rest in the chancel is one of the rarest pieces of church furniture in London. It bears the arms of Sir John Lawrence, who was Lord Mayor of London during the Great Plague. The rear choir stalls, of

15th-century origin, came from the nuns' church and have
Grotesque arm-rests.

The south transept houses the organ and two chantry chapels
added in 1354. The Chapel of the Holy Ghost contains a
monument to John de Oteswich and his wife. It is the oldest in
the church, dating from the late 14th or early 15th century. The
piscina, a stone basin used for holy water, and six niches in the
Lady Chapel are from the late 14th century.

Monuments in the nave include those to Alderman Richard
Staper (d. 1608), surmounted by a representation of an
Elizabethan galleon, and the cloth-maker and Lord Mayor Sir
John Spencer (d. 1609), whose large monument, restored to its
original colours, is topped with a winged skull and hour glass.
Between these monuments is the south doorcase (c. 1630)
bearing the royal Stuart arms. Near the west door is a late-18th-
century poor box resting on a 17th-century figure of a bearded
beggar holding out his hat.

On leaving St Helen's turn left along Undershaft, which joins
St Mary Axe.

St Andrew Undershaft (10) is best known as the burial place of
John Stow (1525–1605), historian and topographer of London.
His *Survey of London and Westminster*, published in 1598, has
provided an invaluable insight into London before the Great
Fire. A ruffed figure of Stow, carved in alabaster by Nicholas
Stone (1586–1647), is the subject of an annual ceremony in
April. The Lord Mayor replaces the figure's quill pen, poised in
Stow's hand to 'write something worth reading about'. The old
quill and a copy of Stow's book are presented to the child who
writes the best essay about London.

Built in 1532, St Andrew's is a virtually unscathed survivor of
medieval London, undamaged by either the Great Fire of 1666
or the Blitz. It takes its name from the unusually tall maypole, or
'shaft', once erected annually beside the church. After 'Evil May
Day' in 1517, when a mob of City apprentices rioted in protest at
the dominance of foreign merchants in the City (resulting in the
hanging of one man and the arrest of 300 others), the maypole
was stored in Shaft Alley. In 1549 the maypole was denounced as
a heathen idol, chopped into pieces and burnt.

Interesting interior features include a late Perpendicular nave
arcade of six bays, a Renatus Harris organ dating from 1696 and
an altar rail beautifully crafted in 1704 by the French ironsmith

Jean Tijou, the man also responsible for most of the wonderful wrought-ironwork in St Paul's Cathedral (*St Paul's* ✪).

The west window, with its brilliant and rich colours, dates from 1637 and depicts five prominent Protestant sovereigns: Edward VI, Elizabeth I, James I, Charles I and William III. William III, who was not on the throne when the window was made, has replaced a previous figure, probably Charles II, whose feet remain.

Lloyd's (11) is the world's leading insurance market. Its new hi-tech building (Richard Rogers, 1986), Lloyd's eighth home in nearly 300 years, is perhaps the most important piece of architecture to be built in London since the completion of the Barbican Centre (*Barbican* ✪). Almost anything can be insured here: fleets of ships and aircraft, satellites, factories, oil rigs. A British trans-Arctic expedition team was covered by a £30,000 indemnity policy during their trek to the North Pole. Cutty Sark Whisky offered a £1 million prize to anyone who could catch the Loch Ness monster alive, guarding against loss with a Lloyd's policy. Lloyd's contribution to the United Kingdom economy is enormous, with a premium income capacity exceeding £11 billion annually. It is the country's largest single earner of 'invisible' exports, and underwriters and brokers currently contribute more than £2.5 billion to the UK's balance of payments.

Lloyd's is not a company. It is a society of underwriters, all of whom accept insurance risks for their personal profit or loss, and who are liable to the full extent of their private fortunes to meet their insurance obligations. Lloyd's brokers negotiate the placing of risks with those underwriters by taking them from box to box (derived from the arrangement of benches and tables in 17th-century coffee houses) until they are covered.

Lloyd's Coffee House, once a popular meeting place and reliable source of shipping intelligence, became established in the late 17th century as the recognized place for obtaining marine insurance. Today there are more than 33,000 members of Lloyd's grouped into about 370 syndicates, which vary in size from just a few to more than a thousand individuals. Three-quarters of Lloyd's business originates overseas.

As an object, Richard Rogers's £160 million Lloyd's building possesses the dramatic impact of a vast and unexpected silver structure shoe-horned into a maze of narrow streets. Rogers's brief was 'to maintain Lloyd's as the centre of world insurance and the unity of the [underwriting] Room' – the traditional place where brokers and underwriters conduct business. Rogers's double-height room is filled with the underwriters' stalls, known as boxes, which stand beneath an atrium almost 250 ft/76 m high and crowned with a glazed barrel-vaulted roof. Twin escalators criss-cross the space. Six satellite towers accommodate all the building's services.

The entrance to the public viewing gallery is on the south side, in Leadenhall Place. An external glass observation lift takes visitors to Gallery Four, where an exhibition describes the history of Lloyd's, from its beginnings in Edward Lloyd's Coffee House in the 1680s to the world of the latest electronic communications technology now used by underwriters. A video explains the principles behind Rogers's controversial building, described by one commentator as 'a Rolls-Royce job, but with the engine wrapped around the outside of the coachwork'. The public viewing platform gives a full appreciation of the building's magnificent interior construction, and also a distant view of the Casualty Book and famous Lutine Bell. Recovered from a French frigate that sank loaded with gold in 1799, this bell has now been returned to the original caller's rostrum of 1928, which once stood in almost the same position in a previous Lloyd's building in Leadenhall Street. The practice of striking the bell for an overdue vessel – once for a loss, twice for a safe arrival – still continues.

The walkways of **Leadenhall Market (12)**, with its delightful Victorian air, are lavishly lined with quality food shops selling poultry, meat, fish, fruit, cheese and specializing in game. The marble slabs of Ashdown's are arranged with an abundance of fresh trout, salmon, lobsters and oysters; Butcher and Edmonds provide game in season, and Blankley and Son devotes itself entirely to the purveyance of champagne and caviar.

The area was a market in Roman times, and 30 ft/9 m below ground are to be found the foundations of the basilica of Londinium, once the largest Roman building outside Italy. More than 500 ft/152 m in length, the basilica adjoined the forum, forming an impressive civic centre complex covering some 8 acres/3 ha. The market originated in the 14th century and was named after a manor house noted for its great lead-clad roof. 'Leadenhalle' was destroyed by fire, however, and a poultry market was established on the site. Sir Horace Jones's spacious and airy arcade was erected in 1881.

On the south side of Cornhill are two Wren churches. At the corner with Gracechurch Street is St Peter-upon-Cornhill (1682) and, a little further west, St Michael-upon-Cornhill (1672). The area south of Cornhill is a maze of alleys that still follow their medieval pattern. From the 16th to the 19th centuries this area abounded with well-known coffee houses, which were frequented by gentlemen for business discussions and to learn the news of the day. In the alley leading along the west side of St Michael's is the **Jamaica Wine House (13)**, once also a popular coffee house. The Jamaica Coffee House was the first of its kind, established here in 1652, shortly after the beverage was introduced into Britain. A meeting place for those involved in the Jamaica trade and also an unofficial post office, its principal patrons were captains and merchants. Its successor, the Jamaica Wine House, is essentially the same today as when it opened in 1869. The dimly lit recesses are separated for privacy by its original mahogany screens, and an early copper coffee percolator on display serves as a reminder of the wine bar's earlier trade.

'I say, old boy, where do you hang out?' Mr Pickwick was once asked. 'I am at present suspended at the George and Vulture,' he replied. To this day, the **George and Vulture (14)** is a place of pilgrimage cherished by Dickens lovers. Charles Dickens was a familiar face at this former coaching house and chose to immortalize it in *Pickwick Papers* as the place where Mr Pickwick and his faithful companion, Sam, retired to 'restore' themselves. There has been a hostelry on this site for 700 years. The present building was rebuilt after the Great Fire in 1666. During its time as an inn, coaches pulled up in the adjacent George Yard. Today the George and Vulture is a restaurant. It has always been the practice here to cook steaks on an open grill in the dining room.

At the south end of George Yard, in Lombard Street, is the church of **St Edmund the King (15)**, founded in the 12th century and dedicated to the king of East Anglia. Edmund was tied to a tree and shot with arrows by the Danes for refusing to renounce his religion. After the Great Fire, the church was rebuilt between 1670 and 1679 by Sir Christopher Wren and Robert

Hooke. Its distinctive octagonal lantern and spire were added in 1708.

The church's small oblong interior is remarkable for its woodwork. Much remains from the 17th century, including the wall panelling, organ case, reredos, communion rail and table. Unusually, the altar is sited at the north end. Behind it, on the reredos, are paintings of Moses and Aaron (1833).

Lombard Street is synonymous with City banking. Its name derives from the Lombard merchants of northern Italy who settled here in the 12th century. Barclays, Lloyds, Glyn Mills and Martins banks all once had their head offices here. Walking westward, many banking signs overhang the pavement. Originating in medieval times, but banned as unsafe by Charles II (reigned 1649–85), the signs were hung out once again to celebrate Edward VII's coronation in 1902. On the north side of Lombard Street is the anchor, formerly of William and Glyn's; further along is the grasshopper (1563), formerly Martins and now acquired by the Banque Paribas; and the black horse of Lloyds (1677). To the south is the crown and anchor of National Westminster, and the three crowns of Coutts.

The ground upon which **St Mary Woolnoth (16)** stands has an extraordinary history. Bronze Age men once worshipped here. Romans hallowed the site by building a temple of Concord. A Saxon prince, thought to have been called Wulfnoth, built a timber church and dedicated it to St Mary of the Nativity. There was also a stone Norman church. In 1438 a new building was constructed, but it suffered badly in the Great Fire. Sir Christopher Wren's repairs were also found to be lacking. Wren's brilliant pupil, Nicholas Hawksmoor (1661–1736), erected the present St Mary Woolnoth in 1727.

This wonderful example of the English baroque seems to have been inspired by the Roman Temple of Concord that once stood here. Hawksmoor's four clusters of Corinthian columns, forming a cube within a cube, rise towards a ceiling painted blue and spangled with stars, suggesting a night sky once visible through the open space of a Roman atrium.

Above the west door is the original and beautiful casing from an organ built in 1681 by the celebrated 'Father Smith'. St Mary's has strong links with the Goldsmiths' Company. Goldsmith Sir Martin Bowes (d. 1566) was buried here, leaving provision for the guild to keep his tomb around which his banners were to be hung, in good repair. The tomb perished in

1666, but the banners, which hang on the west wall, are still periodically renewed by his livery company. These banners include the ancient lion's head of England, which is still seen in the hallmark applied by Goldsmiths' Hall; and the coat of arms of Sir Martin Bowes' descendant, Queen Elizabeth the Queen Mother, formerly the Honourable Lady Elizabeth Bowes-Lyon.

A tablet on the south wall commemorates Edward Lloyd (d. 1713) in whose Lombard Street coffee house Lloyd's insurance market began. Opposite, on the north wall, the epitaph of John Newton is engraved on a marble tablet. Newton, a former commander on a slave brig that made the passage to America in the 18th century, was converted to Christianity and eventually became the rector at St Mary's. He made an immense contribution to the abolition of the slave trade through his spiritual influence on William Wilberforce (1759–1833), the politician and philanthropist who eventually secured its end. Newton also wrote the famous hymn *Amazing Grace*.

More recently, St Mary Woolnoth founded a healing ministry for those suffering from stress and tension, an occupational hazard in high-pressure City business life. Office workers doing relaxation exercises in the chancel are a common sight in St Mary's at lunch-time.

Outside, the steps on either side of the tower once led to the crypt. They now provide access to Bank ⊖.

St Paul's ⊖

For more than two centuries after his death the works of architect Sir Christopher Wren (1632–1723) dominated the skyline of the City of London. St Paul's Cathedral was the jewel in the crown of this vista. Challenged now by the invasion of high-rise modern architecture during the latter part of this century, Wren's masterpiece still commands a massive and spectacular presence amidst the rooftops and skyscrapers.

Wren, a child prodigy, inventor, philosopher, Professor of Astronomy at Oxford, founding member and later president of the Royal Society, was responsible in his long lifetime for numerous famous architectural works. He built part of Hampton Court Palace (*Outer London*), Greenwich Palace (*Outer London*) and the Sheldonian Theatre at Oxford, as well as reconstructing nearly all the City churches in the aftermath of the Great Fire of 1666. After the Fire, Wren became one of the three Royal Commissioners for the rebuilding of the city. Appointed Surveyor-General of the King's Works, a position he held for forty-nine years, he produced a grand plan for the rebuilding of the city, a baroque conception with wide radiating boulevards, piazzas and important buildings set in magnificent vistas. His Utopian vision was never realized.

In the early years after the great conflagration Wren busied himself with the reconstruction of the city's churches, eighty-seven of which had been destroyed. Fifty-two were rebuilt, and they reveal Wren's wide-ranging obsession with controlling the forms of geometry in the churches' interior plans, towers and steeples, and with his attempts to create space over and around neighbouring houses and the city's crowded streets. The rebuilding of the city churches provided a training ground for sculptors, carvers, plasterers and masons, many of whom later worked on St Paul's for the rest of their lives.

Drawing on ideas from Donato Bramante (the drums of the dome), Michelangelo (the ribbed section above) and Inigo Jones (the Corinthian portico without pediment from the Old St Paul's Church), Wren used his experience on the city churches to create a number of designs and models for St Paul's. The Great Model of 1673, an impressive oak construction based on the unusual design of a Greek cross, has been preserved. The

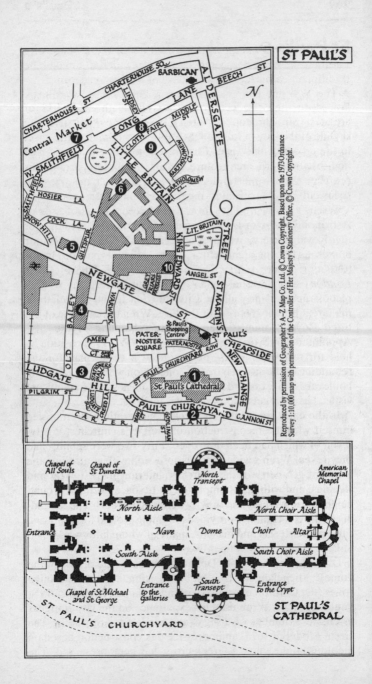

clergy refused to adopt it, displeased about the absence of a Latin cross. Wren was compelled in a new design to combine traditional Gothic layouts with those of Renaissance forms.

The Warrant Design, based on a Latin cross, was finally accepted in 1675, beginning thirty-five years of building work. Although Wren's 1666 axial plan for opening up the City with a splendid processional avenue leading to St Paul's west front was never achieved, it is a testament to his incredible conception that the cathedral has survived until today almost untouched, save a few 19th-century amendments. St Paul's interior has suffered to a certain extent. Heavied in places with unnecessary colours, the Victorians filled its clear glass windows with stained glass and its ceilings with mosaics in an attempt to 'medievalize' the building.

From St Paul's ⊖ it is also possible to visit London's oldest church, St Bartholomew-the-Great, famed for its Norman chancel and mercifully saved from the Great Fire by a shift in wind direction. 'Bart's', London's oldest hospital, is near by. The galleries of the Old Bailey, the most famous criminal court in the nation, if not the world, are open to the public. The Old Bailey's No. 1 court has seen the dispatch of some of the most notorious criminals. The National Postal Museum in King Edward Street houses the most important, and probably the most extensive, collection of postage stamps in the world. On the south side of St Paul's is the City of London Information Centre, which provides a free information service about sights and events inside the square mile of the City.

⊖   ⊖   ⊖

For over thirteen and a half centuries a cathedral has watched over the City of London from the summit of Ludgate Hill, the second highest point in the City. **St Paul's Cathedral (1)**, Sir Christopher Wren's masterpiece, is the fifth great church to occupy this site and is dedicated to London's patron saint.

The first wooden structure, founded in A D 604 by Ethelbert, King of Kent, and two later churches were each destroyed by fire. The Norman cathedral, begun in 1087 and known as Old St Paul's, had become so dilapidated by the mid-17th century that Christopher Wren was entrusted to restore it. However, in September 1666, shortly after Wren presented his plans, Old St Paul's fell victim to the Great Fire, giving Wren his chance to construct a completely new cathedral.

When the site was cleared, Wren requested a workman to

bring him a stone to mark the centre of the new cathedral. A fragment of a tombstone was brought. Inscribed upon it was the word *Resurgam* – 'I shall rise again'. Impressed by this prophetic occurrence, Wren had the word carved beneath a phoenix rising from flames in the pediment above the great south door.

The foundation stone was laid on 21 June 1675, and the last stone, at the apex of the lantern above the cupola, was placed by Wren's son in 1708. To decorate the cathedral, Wren employed the finest craftsmen of the day. Among them were Grinling Gibbons (1648–1720), the master woodcarver, and Jean Tijou from France, who executed the cathedral's exquisite ornamental ironwork.

St Paul's magnificent dome, second only in size to St Peter's in Rome, comprises three separate elements: inner and outer domes and a central cone supporting the lantern and cross. Wren realized the size an outer dome required to give a bold silhouette above the surrounding houses might look cavernous within. The inner dome was built to bring the interior space into proportion. The design also had sufficient strength to enable it to survive the ravages of the Blitz and the dome itself grew to become a symbol of hope in war-torn London.

St Paul's has been the setting of many great occasions, among them the funeral of Sir Winston Churchill (d. 1965) and, more recently, the marriage of Charles, Prince of Wales, to Lady Diana Spencer.

Entry to the cathedral is by the left-hand door of the west front. Its two-tiered portico supports a carved pediment, by Francis Bird, illustrating the conversion of St Paul. On either side rise the baroque-style west towers. The northernmost houses the three old bells that chime every Sunday. In the clock tower is Great Tom, the hour bell weighing five tons, hung in 1716. The Great Paul bell was added in 1882. Weighing 16.75 tons, it is the largest bell in the country and continues the old tradition of ringing each day at 1 p.m. to alert apprentices in the City to the important business of lunch.

Entering the cathedral, to the immediate left is the **Chapel of All Souls**, which is often closed. It commemorates men who died during the First World War, in particular Field Marshal Earl Kitchener (1850–1916), whose face achieved widespread recognition through the recruitment poster 'Your Country Needs You'. Next to the Chapel of All Souls is the **Chapel of St Dunstan**. The mosaics at the east end were the first to be completed by Sir William Richmond (1842–1921), who later decorated the choir and aisles in similar fashion. The screen (1698) is by Jonathan Maine, one of Wren's gifted carvers, who was also responsible for a similar work, exactly opposite, in the south aisle.

From the reception desk at the west end of the nave, guided SuperTours may be booked. These allow access to some parts of the cathedral otherwise closed to the public. Passing eastward along the nave allows an uninterrupted view through the crossing and the choir to the high altar. The nave consists of four bays on either side. Over the bay arches runs the triforium, or gallery, and a clerestory of plain glass.

Above the crossing are Sir James Thornhill's monochrome frescoes, painted on the inner dome in 1719 and depicting scenes from the life of St Paul. Antonio Salviati's (d. 1890) mosaics in the triangular spandrels below the Whispering Gallery depict the four Evangelists – Matthew, Mark, Luke and John – and the prophets Isaiah, Jeremiah, Ezekiel and Daniel. Set into the floor of the crossing is an inscription in Latin, *Si monumentum requiris, circumspice*, 'If you seek his monument, look around you', part of Wren's epitaph written by his son. It was also translated by a witty verger. 'If you seek his monument, Sir-come-spy-see'. A floor tablet located here indicates where Churchill's catafalque rested during his state funeral in 1965.

Straight ahead is the choir, entered only on a guided tour. To the left is the brass eagle lectern made by Jacob Sutton in 1719. To the right is the canopied 17th-century style pulpit shaped like a wine glass which was designed by Lord Mottistone. The dark oak choir stalls beneath crested canopies are the work of Grinling Gibbons and his craftsmen. Each stall forms an individual exposé of the woodcarver's art. Above the west end of the choir is the organ built in 1697 by Bernard Smith, popularly known as 'Father Smith'. Subsequently, the organ was divided in two before being rebuilt in its present position. Gibbons's carving of the organ case provides a beautiful contrast to the gilt organ pipes.

On the left of the south transept east aisle is the first monument (1795) to be placed in Wren's cathedral. Designed by John Bacon the Elder (1740–99), it portrays the 18th-century prison reformer John Howard. Near by is the entrance to the crypt and a wall tablet to Captain Scott, the intrepid and courageous explorer who died returning from the South Pole in 1912. In the eastern corner of the south transept is a monument by Sir Richard Westmacott (1775–1856) commemorating Admiral Lord Collingwood (d. 1810), second-in-command at the Battle of Trafalgar. His superior, Admiral Lord Nelson, who died in the famous battle of 1805, is celebrated in a monument by John Flaxman (1755–1826) in the south transept nave.

In the nave south aisle is a painting from the Pre-Raphaelite school, *The Light of the World* (1900) by William Holman-Hunt (1827–1910). Near the end of the aisle is the Chapel of the Order of St Michael and St George. A door in the south-west corner of St Paul's leads to the Geometrical Staircase (guided tours only). The weight of each of the spiral's ninety-two stone steps, each step embedded only a few inches into the wall at one end, is taken by the one below, down to the ground.

On the other side of the nave, in the central bay of the north aisle, stands St Paul's largest monument, which commemorates the first Duke of Wellington (1769–1852), the 'Iron Duke', victor at Waterloo and Britain's Prime Minister between 1828 and 1830.

Gracing the eastern end of the aisle, on the left, is a statue of Sir Joshua Reynolds (1723–92), painter and first President of the Royal Academy of Arts.

In the north transept west aisle is a plain but beautifully executed terracotta Virgin and Child of recent origin by Josephena de Vasconcellos. Beyond it, in the north transept chapel, is Francis Bird's enormous marble oval font (1727). This chapel is set aside for private prayer.

At the entrance of the ambulatory stands a statue of the great man of letters Dr Samuel Johnson (1709–84), sculpted by John Bacon the Elder in 1795. The gateway into the north choir aisle is the work of the brilliant French ironworker Jean Tijou. Above it, sparkling with colour and gilding, is the mosaic ceiling designed by Sir William Richmond and executed by the stained-glass manufacturers Powells between 1891 and 1907. Similar ceilings adorn the chancel and south choir aisle. Further along, display panels illustrate the wedding of Prince Charles and Lady Diana Spencer in 1981, and on the right the high altar is separated from the north and south choir aisles by Tijou's magnificent wrought-iron gates (*c.* 1695–7). The gilded pilasters, incorporating figures of the prophets and saints, and the crestings surmounting the gates, were added in 1890. Peering through the gates gives a view of the Bishop's Throne, or *cathedra*, at the east end of the south choir stall. The principal church of a diocese contains the *cathedra* and consequently is known as the cathedral church. Opposite, in stark contrast to Tijou's rich ornamentation, are the simple contours and lines of Henry Moore's *Mother and Child*, carved for St Paul's and installed in 1984. At the east end of the north choir aisle, the Chapel of Modern Martyrs commemorates Anglicans who have died for their belief since 1850. Each name is recorded in the book in the marble casket.

The apse houses the American Memorial Chapel, commemorating the 28,000 United States citizens based in Britain who were killed during the Second World War. The tall stained-glass windows, designed by Brian Thomas, represent the service, sacrifice and resurrection of the faithful soldier, and include the coats of arms of each of the American states.

The high altar is a memorial to the people of the Commonwealth who died in the two world wars. The altar is of Sicilian marble beneath a *baldacchino*, or canopy, of English oak. It was designed by E. Dykes Bower and Godfrey Allen at the end of the 19th century, but follows Wren's unused plans.

The south choir aisle is entered at the **Lady Chapel**. The rather plain original altar table here is by Wren. Further along the aisle is an outstanding marble effigy of John Donne (1573–1631), one of the few monuments to survive from Old St Paul's. Although best known for his literary works, Donne was also a Dean of St Paul's.

Beyond the gateway and left, is the entrance to the crypt. The crypt is unusual in extending beneath the entire building (normally the crypt is confined to the area beneath the chancel). Left at the bottom of the stairs leads to the tomb of Admiral Lord Nelson, interred in a black marble sarcophagus originally made for Cardinal Wolsey in 1529. Henry VIII confiscated Wolsey's sarcophagus and it lay neglected until Nelson's state funeral in St Paul's in 1809. Further west is Wren's 'Great Model' of St Paul's. This was his second design for the new cathedral, a plan rejected by the clergy. It lacks the false storey that was added to create a more pleasing balance of dome and cross. The Royal Commission established to improve the plans eventually accepted Wren's third design, known as the 'Warrant Design', after Charles II issued a royal warrant authorizing Wren to make 'variations, rather ornamental than essential'. Although Wren interpreted this dispensation as giving him great latitude over the design, he none the less changed his earlier plan to base the cathedral on a Greek cross to that of a more ecclesiastically acceptable Latin cross.

Off the north side of Nelson's tomb chamber is the Treasury of the Diocese of London. Ecclesiastical plate from around 1500 to the present day, regalia and manuscripts are on display. The most striking vestment is the Jubilee Cape, made for the Queen's Silver Jubilee celebrations in 1977. It is emblazoned with superb embroidery, in gold thread and silk, of the spires of seventy-three London churches, three royal peculiars and St Paul's.

Towards the east end of the crypt, the Duke of Wellington's sarcophagus is surrounded by plaques commemorating Second World War field marshals, including Montgomery of Alamein. Further on is the chapel adopted in 1960 by the Order of the British Empire – men and women are appointed to the order for their distinguished services to the country. In the south-east corner of the crypt, among monuments to many great artists and craftsmen, is the plain marble slab marking the grave of Sir Christopher Wren. Above, his epitaph is inscribed in full.

Returning to the ground floor, in the nave south aisle is the entrance to the galleries. In the unusual acoustics of the **Whispering Gallery** words whispered against the wall will be heard by anyone who presses their ear against any other part of the wall. It also provides a bird's-eye view of the concourse below and an excellent spot from which to view the Thornhill frescoes on the inner dome. Bisecting the windows around the dome are statues of some of the first great teachers at the cathedral. The Stone Gallery encircles the dome on the outside and, about 650 steps from street level, the Golden Gallery gives an impressive panorama of the City.

Situated on the south side of St Paul's Cathedral, the **City of London Information Centre (2)** provides a free tourist information service about places of interest and events in the square mile of the City. It also co-ordinates open-day visits to the City Livery Companies (*Cannon Street & Mansion House ⊖s*).

On Ludgate Hill, west of St Paul's Cathedral, is **St Martin-within-Ludgate (3)**. St Martin's graceful and slender lead spire was designed by Wren to avoid clashing with the cathedral's impressive west front and dome. Indeed, it was built to act as a foil to the vast expanse of green copper. There is a point, far down Fleet Street to the west of Ludgate Hill, from which the spire exactly cuts the middle of the dome.

Ludgate, reputedly first built by King Lud in 66 BC but pulled down in 1760, was once a busy thoroughfare. Wren skilfully provided, behind St Martin's Portland stone front, three solid arches supporting a gallery, to ensure a quiet and rarefied atmosphere. The church's dark interior woodwork is from the 17th century and there is a unique churchwarden's double chair of 1690.

A solitary golden figure, a sword in one hand, a pair of scales in the other, stands 200 ft/61m above the busy junction of Newgate Street and Old Bailey. It is a statue of the Goddess of Justice watching over the **Central Criminal Court**, known as the **Old Bailey (4)**. The Old Bailey is probably the nation's, if not the world's, most famous criminal court. The hammer of justice of its No. 1 Court has dispatched some notorious villains, including the infamous Dr Crippen, who chopped his wife into small pieces (1910). More recently, the Kray Twins, the East End gangland brothers were sentenced here, as well as Peter Sutcliffe, the 'Yorkshire Ripper' (1981).

Justice has been dispensed on this site since the 12th century, initially in the confines of the infamous Newgate Prison. This fearsome gaol, notorious for vice and disease, became dangerous to the judges' health, and so in 1539 the first Old Bailey Sessions House was built. The name 'Old Bailey' derives from the bailey, or *ballium*, a defensive rampart outside the City walls. It is also the name of the wide road on the west side of the courts, which accommodated the busy spectacle of public hangings outside the prison from 1783 to 1868.

Today's Old Bailey, built by E. W. Mountford in 1907, is the third criminal court on this site. Its original four courtrooms have been extended to twenty-three after the East Wing extension was opened in 1972. The Old Bailey's workload is prodigious, taking all the major cases from the City and Greater London and the most important from elsewhere in England and Wales, roughly equivalent to half the more serious crimes brought to trial in the United Kingdom. In an average year the court will hear over 100 murder trials and about the same number of manslaughter cases. Each day the Old Bailey's cells house up to seventy prisoners.

Trials are open to the public when the courts are in session (10.20 a.m.–1 p.m., 2–4.15 p.m.), and there are often large queues for important cases. Entrance is by the East Wing.

St Sepulchre-without-Newgate (5), just outside the north-west gate of the City, corresponds almost exactly in its position in relation to the City with that of the Jerusalem Church built on top of the site of the Sepulchre and Calvary – 'the green hill without a city wall'. The knights of the Crusades, perhaps for that reason, chose this church for their departure to the Holy Lands.

Founded in 1137, it was rebuilt in 1450 and some sections of this church remain despite the Great Fire of 1666. Various alterations in succeeding centuries have resulted in St Sepulchre's late-19th-century exterior embracing a medley of architectural styles within.

The church was once closely associated with Newgate Prison. In 1605 Robert Dowe donated £50 to pay for the tolling of St Sepulchre's 'Great Bell of Bailey' (the 'bells of Old Bailey' from the 'Oranges and Lemons' nursery rhyme) on the morning of executions held outside Newgate Prison. He also instituted the practice whereby at midnight before an execution a bellman would make his way to the prison through an underground passage from the church, tolling a handbell and reciting:

> All you that in the condemned hole do lie,
> Prepare you, for tomorrow you shall die . . .

Considered a charitable act at the time, the final lines of the verse were said through the keyhole of the unfortunates' cell:

> And when St Sepulchre's bell tomorrow tolls,
> The Lord have mercy on your souls!

The execution bell can be seen in a glass case on the column facing the pulpit in the south aisle of the church.

The north chapel, formerly dedicated to St Stephen, became the Musicians' Chapel in 1955. Interred here are the ashes of Sir Henry Wood, a former assistant organist at St Sepulchre's, who later founded the Promenade Concerts at the Royal Albert Hall (*South Kensington* ⊖). His tomb lies beneath the central window of this little chapel, which depicts St Cecilia, patron saint of music, with a young Henry at the organ and Sir Henry conducting one of of his famous Proms. To the right, another window commemorates Dame Nellie Melba, the Australian soprano. The peaches in the corner of the window refer to Peach Melba, the dessert created for her by Escoffier at London's Savoy Hotel. Note the richly embroidered kneelers created in commemoration of musicians.

The church also houses a memorial to Captain John Smith, founder of the American state of Virginia, whose life was saved by the American Indian princess Pocahontas.

North of Holborn Viaduct is **St Bartholomew's Hospital (6)**, or simply 'Bart's', the oldest hospital in London. It was founded by Rahere, a jester and courtier of Henry I, who later took holy orders as an Augustinian. After suffering an attack of malarial fever on a pilgrimage to Rome, he pledged to build a hospital in London on his return. He fulfilled his vow in 1123. Today Bart's is one of the world's greatest teaching hospitals.

The hospital is entered through its striking early 17th-century gatehouse, which has a rare statue of Henry VIII surmounted by two patients couchant. When Henry granted a Royal Charter to St Bartholomew's in 1547, its chapel, situated beyond the archway, became the parish church of **St Bartholomew-the-Less**. The hospital is unique in being the entire parish of the church. The church was originally built of wood as an octagon within a square in 1789 by George Dance the Younger (1741–1825). It was rebuilt in stone in 1825 by Thomas Hardwick (1752–1829) following Dance's plan. The interior reveals monuments to the numerous physicians and surgeons from the hospital. William Harvey, who discovered the circulation of the blood, was chief physician to the hospital in 1609–33. Artist William Hogarth (1697–1764) was appointed a governor in 1734. Cricketer W. G. Grace qualified here in 1879.

Beyond the church, a second archway leads into a square courtyard surrounded by hospital buildings. A staircase in the east end of the north block leads to the Great Hall. Above the staircase hang two vast paintings by Hogarth, *The Good Samaritan* and *The Pool of Bethesda* (1737). On the first floor the Great Hall has an excellent original coffered ceiling and panelling. A stained-glass window (*c.* 1664), installed here in the 18th century, shows Henry VIII presenting a royal charter to the hospital.

Smithfield Market (7) is the oldest, and largest, wholesale meat market in Europe, with an annual turnover of £300 million. Its history began in Saxon times, when a livestock and cattle market was held on 'smooth field'. It was also the scene of tournaments, archery and the great Bartholomew Fair, an event long predating, but immortalized in, Ben Jonson's coarse and vigorous play of the same name. Butchery of a different sort is also known to Smithfield. Scots patriot Sir William Wallace was hanged, disembowelled, beheaded and quartered here in 1305. During the Peasant's Revolt in 1381 Wat Tyler and his rebels confronted Richard II at Smithfield. Tyler was stabbed by the Lord Mayor and retired to Bart's Hospital, but he was discovered and dragged out and beheaded on Smithfield.

The Victorian era witnessed the market's heyday. Sir Horace Jones's fine market building, incorporating an underground level from which meat was brought and dispatched throughout England, opened in 1868. Jones's design, elaborately decorated in characteristic Victorian style, was also highly functional; the open ironwork roof set with louvres provided protection from the sun without denying light and essential ventilation.

Today Smithfield is the last of the great medieval markets on its original site, with Billingsgate fish market now relocated to the docklands and Covent Garden fruit and flower market moved south of the river. Trading occurs mainly between 5 and 9 a.m. By midday it is largely deserted. However, the interior can be seen through the huge cast-iron gates. The sellers', or tenants', stalls, their overhead rails glistening with meat hooks, nestle below the cathedral-like proportions of the roof. A remarkable system of restrictive practices operates at Smithfield. A tenant cannot stock his stall without paying 'pullers-back' and 'pitchers', and in most cases a retailer cannot remove his purchases without paying a 'bummaree'. Meat is taken off the lorries by pullers-back and pitchers carry it into the market. The 200 bummarees, pitchers and pullers-back, who wear traditional blue overalls and caps, are self-employed and paid according to how much they carry. A favourite with the market traders, the Queen Mother has visited the market three times, and on her last visit in 1986 was made an honorary bummaree.

Cloth Fair (8), a quaint street, takes its name from Bartholomew Fair, held here annually from the 12th century until 1855, whose

principal merchandise was originally cloth. Preserved in Cloth
Fair, at No. 41, is a most charming house dating from around
1640, one of the few residences that survived the Great Fire.

St Bartholomew-the-Great (9) is London's oldest church, founded by Rahere in 1123 and famed for its Norman chancel.
Although much of the church did not survive the dissolution of
the monasteries, the oldest and most important part of this
former Augustine priory was saved after local residents objected
to its dismemberment. St Bartholomew's did, however, survive
the Great Fire, due partly to the protection of the old City Wall
and partly to a merciful shift of wind direction, which halted the
flames just 300 yds/274 m away.

From Little Britain, St Bartholomew's is approached beneath
a stone archway surmounted by a Tudor gatehouse built in 1559.
The 13th-century stone arch is all that remains of the west end of
the original nave, which once stretched right to the road. On
entering the church, to the left is the only remaining bay of the
nave (1240). During the dissolution of the monasteries the
transepts and most of the cloisters and nave were removed, but
the chancel and crossing were saved for use as a parish church.
The choir screen, decorated with paintings of the monks' daily
routine, leads into the crossing, which was added in the mid-12th
century. Beyond the crossing is the famous chancel.

Rahere died in 1144, but the decorative tomb to him, standing
to the left of the high altar, was not erected until 1405. At his feet
an angel presents a shield emblazoned with the arms of the
priory. Above the south aisle, to the right of the altar, one of the
triforium arches contains an oriel window, added in 1515. From
here Prior William Bolton is reported to have kept a watchful
eye on Rahere's tomb to ensure that visiting pilgrims placed a
donation in the offertory box. In the 16th century most people
could neither read nor write. Carved below the window is
Bolton's rebus, a pictorial device of recognition, depicting a bolt
from a crossbow and a barrel, or tun; hence Bolt-tun.

In 1331 a Lady Chapel was added behind the altar. From the
Reformation until the middle of the 19th century, many of the
monastic buildings were used for domestic purposes. The Lady
Chapel was, in turn, three times a private house, a printer's
office and a workshop. Benjamin Franklin, later one of
America's great statesman, was employed in the printer's office
here in 1724.

Both the north and south transepts were rebuilt by Sir Aston Webb (1849–1930) in the late 19th century. Near the south transept stands an early-15th-century font, the only medieval example in a City church. Adjacent to the entrance porch is the restored east cloister. Built in 1406, the cloisters once formed a complete square on the south side of the former nave.

The **National Postal Museum (10)** houses the most important and probably the most extensive collection of postage stamps in the world. Established in 1965 on the initiative of a private collector, it contains this benefactor's magnificent and extremely valuable collection of British 19th-century postage stamps, including the famous Penny Black. To this, the Post Office has added its own collection of registration (proof) sheets, dies and artwork, making the most comprehensive research facility for British stamps. The museum's Berne collection of stamps from member-countries of the Universal Postal Union is an almost complete record of every postage stamp or item of postal stationery issued throughout the world since 1878. Around 250,000 stamps are on display. A statue of Sir Rowland Hill, founder of the 'penny post', stands outside. Although the first private penny post was set up in 1680, Sir Rowland can take credit for establishing a uniform public penny post in which letters were charged by weight rather than the number of sheets. Postage was also paid by the sender rather than the recipient. In the same year he was also responsible for the introduction of the world's first adhesive postage stamp, the Penny Black.

Chancery Lane ⊖

Charles Dickens came to London as a small, nervous child. In the city his family led a shiftless existence, moving from borough to borough. His father, a Micawber-like figure, gaily ran up debts and was imprisoned. As a result, the 11-year-old boy was sent to work in Lambert's blacking factory at Hungerford Stairs, off the Strand, where he labelled and tied down blacking pots. The memory of the dirt and decay of the factory never left him and in his youthful imagination London became the oppressive place of blackness and shadows known to David Copperfield. His early walks home from work began a lifetime of perambulations around London, a vigorous shifting city of alleys, courtyards, rookeries, varied little shops and workshops lit only dimly at night by yellow and smokey gas lights; a city populated by criminals, pedlars, vagrants, the poor, drifters and eccentrics for whom life was short and hard.

At the age of 15 Dickens became a lawyers' clerk at Gray's Inn. He soon moved on to undertake a career in journalism and took bachelor lodgings at nearby Furnival's Inn. London, then the largest city in the world and the first to become urbanized, influenced all but one of Dickens's novels. He became the first great novelist of the industrial city and this era of London has become truly his.

Nearly a year after his marriage and on the threshold of fame earned by the successful serialization of *Pickwick Papers*, Dickens, his wife Catherine Hogarth and their first-born son, Charles, moved to No. 48 Doughty Street, now the Dickens Museum. In their brief period at Doughty Street Dickens finished *Pickwick Papers*, wrote *Oliver Twist* and *Nicholas Nickleby*, and began *Barnaby Rudge*.

Of all his novels, however, *Bleak House* is the novel of Chancery Lane. At Lincoln's Inn the memorable and interminable *Jarndyce* v. *Jarndyce* case dragged on to its long-delayed end. In a coffee house in Chancery Lane the despairing old Tom Jarndyce blew out his brains. In the shade of Cook's Court (Took's Court in Cursitor Street) Mr Snagsby, the law stationer in the novel, dealt out his 'blank forms of legal process . . . and other office cutlery!'

None the less, London has its lawyers to thank for conserving

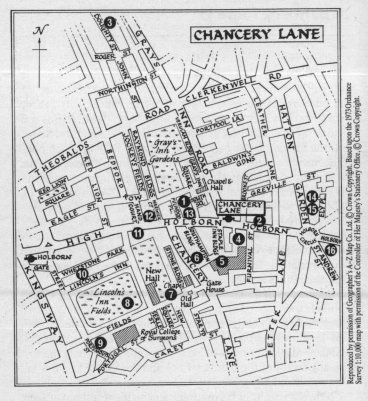

much of the area around Chancery Lane, south through Temple to the Thames. The lawyers' 'inns' were located here, divided into Inns of Court and Inns of Chancery, the former under Crown authority, the latter under the Lord Chancellor. The nine Inns of Chancery, which included Furnival's Inn, could not call students to the Bar and they gradually declined as students enrolled directly to the Inns of Court.

Lincoln's Inn Fields, hidden behind the multi-storey cliffs of High Holborn and Kingsway, is one of the city's under-visited places. On the east side of this leafy square is Lincoln's Inn, one of the four Inns of Court, which dates from 1422. On the square's north side is the Sir John Soane Museum, once the great architect's residence and now the home of his superb collection of antiquities and works of art. Its treasures include paintings by Turner and *The Rake's Progress* by Hogarth. In the square's south-west corner is the Old Curiosity Shop, reputedly the one in Dickens' novel and now a souvenir shop.

Sadly, many of the buildings of Gray's Inn, another Inn of Court, were destroyed during the Second World War. Nevertheless, its Hall still contains one of the most exquisite wooden screens from the Elizabethan period. Next to Chancery Lane ⊖ is Staple Inn, London's only surviving half-timbered Tudor terrace, complete with overhanging oriel bay windows.

The Science Reference Library, nearby in Southampton Buildings, is one of the foremost technical libraries in the world. Its enormous collection of books, serial titles and patents on science, business and commerce is open to any reader. Situated further west along Southampton Buildings are the London Silver Vaults, an underground 'Aladdin's cave'. This seemingly impregnable fortress, with its surveillance cameras, iron bars and portcullises, is open to the public for buying and selling. The professional knowledge of its traders is unrivalled and it is a major market for overseas buyers.

⊖   ⊖   ⊖

North of Holborn is **Gray's Inn (1)**, one of the four great Inns of Court and the place where in 1827 Dickens became a solicitors' clerk for 13s 6d a week at Ellis and Blackmore at No. 1 South Square (1759). 'Gray's Inn, gentlemen. Curious little nooks in a great place like London, these old Inns are,' Dickens wrote in *Pickwick Papers*. He described it less kindly and unfairly in the *Uncommercial Traveller* as 'one of the most depressing institutions in brick and mortar known to the children of men . . .'

The site of Gray's Inn was originally occupied by the London residence of Sir Reginald le Grey, Chief Justice of Chester, who died in 1308. By 1370 his manor house accommodated lawyers. The Inn buildings date from the 16th century, but have undergone renewal since the Second World War. The crest of the Inn is a golden griffin rampant on a black field.

Entry to Gray's Inn is from High Holborn through the gatehouse, a modern reproduction of the 1688 original destroyed in the Second World War. South Square contains the Hall, the Under-Treasurer's Office, Common Room and Library, all of which were also rebuilt after the wartime bombing. Only No. 1 South Square survived. At the centre of the square is a bronze statue of the Inn's most distinguished member, Sir Francis Bacon (Pomeroy, 1912).

Gray's Inn Hall was burnt by enemy bombing in 1941, but its 16th-century style, with stepped gables at either end and Perpendicular tracery, has been reproduced. It contains a notable late-16th-century screen presented to Gray's Inn by Queen Elizabeth I, which is said to have been carved from the timbers of a Spanish galleon captured during the Armada. Shakespeare's *Comedy of Errors* is thought to have been first staged here in 1594. The playwright's patron at that time was the Earl of Southampton, a member of the Inn.

The Chapel has stood on this site since 1315. Rebuilt in 1689, with further restoration in the 19th century, it was also destroyed by bombing in May 1941. Fortunately, its 19th-century windows had been removed and were refitted during post-war rebuilding.

Entry into the gardens and walks is from Field Court through an early-18th-century wrought-iron gateway at the south-east corner of Gray's Inn Square. The gardens were laid out by Sir Francis Bacon in 1606. In their history the gardens have provided a convenient site for duelling as well as a popular meeting place for fashionable society. Samuel Pepys was a frequent visitor. The Raymond Buildings (1825) and the Verulam Buildings (1811) skirt the gardens on the west and east.

East of Chancery Lane ⊖ on the north side of Holborn is the **Prudential Assurance Building (2)**, once the site of Furnival's Inn. Dickens lived here in bachelor quarters at No. 13 while working as a reporter on the *Morning Chronicle* in 1834–7. During his time at Furnival's Inn Dickens began *Pickwick Papers* and also collaborated with the composer John Hullah on their operetta, *The Village Coquettes*. Dickens moved to larger rooms at No. 15 after marrying Catherine Hogarth. 'There is little enough to see in Furnival's Inn,' wrote Dickens in *Martin Chuzzlewit*. 'It is a shady, quiet place, echoing the footsteps of the stragglers who have business there, and rather monotonous and gloomy on summer evenings.' None the less, their rooms were described by Catherine's sister Mary as being most tastefully and elegantly furnished, the drawing room with rosewood and the dining room with mahogany furniture.

Today the huge, vivid red-brick and terracotta building of the Prudential Assurance Company in High Victorian Gothic style looms over the north side of Holborn. Its construction was clearly intended to convince depositors that 'the Pru' would last. The ground floor is decorated with exotic tiles and sumptuous marble. Designed by Alfred Waterhouse in 1879 and extended in 1900, the original west section was rebuilt in 1932. A bust of Dickens 'cowers' in the forecourt.

The **Dickens House Museum (3)** lies north of Gray's Inn in Doughty Street to the west of Gray's Inn Road. During the period between April 1837 and December 1939, when he lived at No. 48, Doughty Street, Dickens rose to fame as a novelist. Doughty Street was a smart middle-class private road, closed off at each end by a gate and attended by porters, or beadles, wearing gold-laced hats and the Doughty arms on the buttons of their mulberry coloured livery.

Dickens' house had twelve rooms on three floors and an attic, was built of pink bricks with a white arched entrance and had a small garden at the back. In the way that Dickens' novels constantly contrast between the well and the sick, between warmth and cold, the light, spacious, glittering and highly coloured interior of No. 48 Doughty Street would in its day have emphasized a comfort, privacy and security not found in the noisy, dark and dangerous streets not far away. The house was saved from demolition in 1923 by the Dickens Fellowship, and has since been painstakingly reconstructed with remarkable attention to detail.

The gilding, mirrors, highly polished furniture and bright colours of the ground floor Dining Room greatly enhanced the atmosphere of the dinner parties Dickens frequently hosted for his growing circle of literary and theatrical friends. Its grandfather clock originally belonged to Moses Pickwick, a coach proprietor from Bath, whose surname Dickens took for his famous character.

The Morning Room contains the family Bible, in which Dickens recorded the births and deaths of his many offspring. Two of those children, Mary and Katie, were born in the house. In the corner is the desk at which Dickens worked as a lawyer's clerk at Gray's Inn. On the wall is the Dickens family tree and there are two examples of the blacking bottles on which Dickens stuck labels as a child.

Fact and fiction merge in the Pantry. Its window comes from the house in Chertsey through which Oliver was pushed by Bill Sikes in the burglary scene in *Oliver Twist*.

At the rear of the first floor is Dickens' Study, complete with the desk he used towards the end of his life when he lived at Gad's Hill Place in Rochester. It has been loaned by Christopher C. Dickens, great-great-grandson of the novelist.

In the cabinet alongside is the curious china monkey that Dickens took with him wherever he lived. The unfinished *Dickens' Dream* by illustrator R. W. Buss hangs above the fireplace, peopled with characters from the author's fertile imagination.

The Drawing Room has been re-created almost exactly as it was in 1839, just after the completion of *Nicholas Nickleby*, down to the lilac-coloured paint used in its decoration. On the second floor the Back Bedroom, or Mary Hogarth's Room, contains mementoes of Dickens's interest in the theatre. The other two rooms on this floor house much material that belonged to the great Dickens collector and former Vice-President of the Dickens Fellowship, Comte Alain de Suzannet (1882–1950). The basement contains an extensive library of Dickens's works and the Still Room, Wash House and Wine Cellar.

On the south side of Holborn, opposite the southern end of Gray's Inn Road, is **Staple Inn (4)**, its much-restored Tudor façade dating from 1589. Originally a wool warehouse used by 'staplers', the name then given to wool traders, Staple Inn became an Inn of Chancery in 1378, training law students. In 1529 Gray's Inn purchased the freehold. During the 17th century the educational role of Staple Inn declined and in 1884 the Inn was sold, part to the Patent Office and the remainder to the Prudential Assurance Company, which is now responsible for its restoration. Through an archway into the Inn's courtyard is the Hall of Staple Inn, which dates from 1580. The hall was almost completely destroyed during the Second World War, but has been rebuilt with some original features. In *The Mystery of Edwin Drood* Dickens describes it as 'one of those nooks, the turning into which out of the clashing street, imparts to the relieved pedestrian the sensation of having put cotton in his ears, and velvet soles on his boots'.

In the south-west corner of Staple Inn, at No. 25 Southampton Buildings, are the **Patent Office and Science Reference Library (5)**. The Patent Office enables individuals or companies to gain patents – legal monopolies for a maximum of twenty years – on hitherto unknown or improved products or manufacturing processes. It was established here in 1855, four years after the Great Exhibition highlighted Britain's growing technological prowess.

The library of the Patent Office was the first in the country to keep all its stock on open access. This tradition has been maintained by its successor, the Science Reference and Information Service (SRIS), now the national reference library for science, business, commerce, patents, trade marks and designs. The library houses more than 50,000 serial titles, nearly 200,000 books and around 25 million world-wide patent specifications.

No prior arrangement is necessary to visit, nor a reader's ticket. A large part of the stock is on open access and readers are free to browse around the collection. Specialist staff can provide assistance. There is a computer search service, and linguists are available, by appointment and free of charge, to help readers decide whether foreign language material is of interest. The reading room at Southampton Buildings offers literature on the physical sciences, engineering, patents and business, and SRIS's branch at No. 9 Kean Street, near Aldwych, covers life and Earth sciences and technologies, medicine, biotechnology, mathematics and astronomy.

The stairwell to the **London Silver Vaults (6)**, a unique underground fortress, is situated off Southampton Buildings. The fifty or so 'fortress-shops' display the finest collection of antique and modern silver to be found anywhere in the world, as well as an unrivalled selection of Sheffield and Victorian plate, jewellery, china, bronzes and *objets d'art*. Wall plaques illustrate the evolution of silver marks. The London Silver Vaults grew out of the original Chancery Lane Safety Deposit Company, which opened near by in 1885.

In the preface to *Bleak House* Dickens pours scorn on the disgraceful and protracted procedures of the Court of Chancery. 'At the present moment,' he wrote in August 1853, 'there is a suit before the Court which was commenced nearly twenty years ago; in which from thirty to forty counsel have been known to appear at one time; in which costs have been incurred to the amount of seventy thousand pounds; which is *a friendly suit*; and which is (I am assured) no nearer to its termination now than when it was begun.' Such cases provided the model for the novel's interminable *Jarndyce* v. *Jarndyce* case.

In Dickens' day London also often suffered so badly from fog that it could turn the city pitch black in the middle of the afternoon. Dickens conjured up such a fog on an implacable November day for his masterful introduction to *Bleak House*: 'Fog everywhere. Fog up the river . . . Fog on the Essex marshes, fog on the Kentish heights . . . Fog in the eyes and throats

of ancient Greenwich pensioners . . . in Lincoln's Inn Hall, at
the heart of the fog, sits the Lord High Chancellor in his High
Court of Chancery.' He warns that the Court 'gives to monied
might, the means abundantly of wearying out the right; which so
exhausts finances, patience, courage, hope; so overthrows the
brain and breaks the heart; that there is not an honourable man
among its practitioners who would not give – who does not often
give – the warning, "Suffer any wrong that can be done you
rather than come here!"'

The **Lincoln's Inn** (7), one of the four Inns of Court, was
founded in the mid-14th century. Its name was probably taken
from Henry de Lacy, third Earl of Lincoln (d. 1311), one of
Edward I's most influential advisers, who owned land close to
the side of the first Inn. His crest appears in the arms of the
Honourable Society of Lincoln's Inn. The Inn moved to its
present site around 1422, taking over a house formerly occupied
by the Bishop of Chichester. Its many distinguished members
have included Prime Ministers Walpole, Pitt the Younger and
Asquith. Oliver Cromwell and his son were both students here,
as were Disraeli and Gladstone. Another of the Inn's great
Benchers was Sir Thomas More.

The present Lincoln's Inn Gatehouse (1958), on Chancery
Lane, is a replica of Sir Thomas Lovell's 16th-century original,
but the oak door dates from that era. Above the arch outside
Lincoln's Inn are the arms of Sir Thomas Lovell, Henry VIII
and the lion rampant purpure [purple] of Henry de Lacy, Earl of
Lincoln. Oliver Cromwell is said to have occupied rooms here as
a young law student. Past the gatehouse to the left are the
16th-century Old Buildings, mainly rebuilt but with original
materials.

Lincoln's Inn Old Hall was originally erected in 1492. After
structural problems were discovered in 1924, a replica Old Hall
was built with the original materials. Still visible on some of the
stones are numbers, which served as positional guides for the
reconstruction. The hall has an open, arch-braced roof with
collar beams, linen-fold panelling and four bay windows. Old
Hall was once the members' dining room and it also served as a
court. Dickens's famous court scene at the beginning of *Bleak
House* was set here. On the interior south wall is an excellent
17th-century carved screen. Opposite is Hogarth's vast painting,
Paul Preaching before Felix (1750). It is often necessary to apply
to the porter's office to enter Old Hall.

Lincoln's Inn Chapel was built between 1619 and 1623 in the late-Perpendicular style, probably to designs by Inigo Jones (1573–1652). John Donne laid the foundation stone and gave the consecration sermon. Here, in 1659, eighty members of Parliament met in secret to take the initial step towards the restoration of the monarchy. The chapel's open undercroft was once intended as a place for students to discuss their studies and for legal practitioners to meet their clients. Many eminent Inn members are buried here. The Honourable Society was known for its charity, and unwanted babies once were often left beside the undercroft. In 1685 Wren renovated and extended the building. James Wyatt added a new roof in 1791; Stephen Salter carried out further work in 1882, and repairs were effected after bomb damage in the First World War. The restored 17th-century stained-glass windows depicting the Apostles are attributed to the Van Linge brothers. The canopied pulpit and communion table are from the early-18th century.

North of George Gilbert Scott's neo-Elizabethan style Old Square are Stone Buildings, a stone-faced three-sided range built in 1780 to the classical-style design of R. Taylor. William Pitt the Younger had chambers here. The buildings are now entirely occupied by lawyers. The elegant New Square was laid out in 1679 by a member of Lincoln's Inn, Henry Serle, and was originally known as Serle's Court. At the north end of the square is an iron screen (1863) with two stone water pumps in front. At its south end is the Carey Street Arch, also known as Wildy's Arch, after the specialist law bookseller's shop that has traded here since 1832. The New Hall and Library building, opened by Queen Victoria in 1845, was built to the neo-Tudor design of Philip Hardwick in 1843–5 and extended by Sir George Gilbert Scott in 1871–3. Lincoln's Inn is said to hold the oldest law library in London, and its collection of some 80,000 legal texts is the most comprehensive in Britain. These buildings are not open to the public.

Lincoln's Inn Fields (8), a tree-filled haven hidden behind High Holborn and Kingsway, is the largest square in central London. It was once common land used for recreation by students at Lincoln's Inn. In the mid-17th century it was developed for housing, albeit only with the reluctant agreement of the lawyers. No. 58 was the original of Mr Tulkinghorn's house in *Bleak House*. In reality No. 58 was also where Dickens' friend and biographer, John Forster, lived. Today, the square's verdant expanse is adorned with London's characteristic plane trees.

Lincoln's Inn Fields boasts many notable former residents, including Charles II's mistress Nell Gwyn; great lawyers such as Sir William Blackstone, author of the *Commentaries on the Laws of England*; and a number of Prime Ministers, including Ramsay MacDonald, who lived here between 1896 and 1911. The south side of the square is now occupied by official buildings of little architectural distinction, except Dance's portico to the Royal College of Surgeons building. The square's oldest house, Nos. 59–60 on the west side, dates from 1640 and was designed in Renaissance style by either Inigo Jones or one of his students.

At the south-west corner of Lincoln's Inn Fields, in Portsmouth Street, is the **Old Curiosity Shop (9)**, a fine example of domestic Tudor architecture and possibly London's oldest shop. In the era of the Stuart monarchs, when cows grazed Lincoln's Inn Fields, the building is known to have been a dairy. Erected in 1567 or thereabouts, the shop is possibly the one immortalized by Dickens in his novel of the same name. It fits the novel's description as 'one of those receptacles for old and curious things, which seem to crouch in odd corners of the town'. Dickens is said to have dealt with a bookbinder named Tessyman, who carried on his business here. The shop now sells souvenirs.

The anguish of Little Nell's death scene in the *Old Curiosity Shop* was derived by Dickens from the trauma of the death of his sister-in-law, Mary Hogarth. Mary, his wife's younger sister, was a permanent guest at Dickens' house in Doughty Street, but only a month after they moved into the house, Mary collapsed after a family visit to the theatre. She died the following day of a heart seizure, aged only 17. Such was the shock that Dickens could not continue writing. His vision of Mary as the incarnation of purity and goodness remained with him for the rest of his life, and until his death thirty-two years later he wore a ring he slipped from the dead girl's hand.

Architect and the Royal Academy's Professor of Architecture Sir John Soane (1753–1837) designed his home in Lincoln's Inn Fields not only to live in, but also as a setting for his extraordinarily varied collection of antiquities and works of art. In later life Sir John obtained an Act of Parliament that stipulated that upon his death his house and its contents should remain unchanged and be opened as a public museum. His wish has been largely fulfilled.

Sir John Soane's Museum (10) is at Nos. 12, 13 and 14 Lincoln's Inn Fields. Soane designed the buildings and, from 1813 until his death, owned all or part of them. Together the three houses form an elegant and balanced composition: the façade of No. 13 (now the museum's entrance) is in his characteristic classical style, decorated with coade stone reproductions of the caryatids at the Erechthion at Athens, and No. 14 matches the plain front of No. 12 which he had designed earlier.

Inside the house the combined dining room and library show how Soane made use of the view into the tiny Monument Yard. Mirrors and an open-plan design combine to create an impression of considerable space within and beyond the room. The panelled ceiling, with scenes from the Greek classics, was painted by Henry Howard. The dining room contains a desk thought to have belonged to Sir Robert Walpole. A portrait of Sir John Soane hangs over the fireplace. Opposite is Sir Joshua Reynolds's painting *Love and Beauty*. The study and dressing room, two small connecting rooms, contain antique Roman marbles, some Renaissance bronzes and small pictures.

Soane designed the picture room to accommodate enough pictures to fill a gallery more than three times its length. It is dominated by Hogarth's humorous composition *The Rake's Progress* (1735), which shows eight phases in the career of Tom Rakewell, and the four stages of *The Election*. There are also paintings by Turner, Watteau and a selection of Soane's own works, including his drawings for the Bank of England.

In the crypt is the Monk's Parlour, a Gothic fantasy intentionally miscellaneous and grotesque, and a parody of the fashionable cult of antiquarianism.

The Sepulchral Chamber contains one of the principal treasures of the museum, the Sarcophagus of Seti I, ruler of Ancient Egypt (1303–1290 B C). When the tomb was discovered in 1817, Soane purchased it after the British Museum declined to pay the £2,000 price.

At the top of the staircase is the Colonnade, which opens into the central area of the museum, called the Dome. This grotto of antiquities contains vases and a bust of Soane by Sir Francis Chantrey (1781–1841).

The New Picture Room was designed in 1889 by James Wild, a curator of the museum. It contains a large *Venetian Scene* by

Canaletto and cartoons by Raphael. Its ante-room displays a watercolour by Turner entitled *The Valley of Aosta*. On the first floor are the North and South Drawing Rooms. On the east wall in the south room is a portrait of Soane and his two sons. In the north room stands the Dance Cabinet, designed by Soane to hold the drawings of his master, George Dance, and Turner's *Admiral Tromp's Barge*.

The **London Weather Centre and Meteorological Office (11)** runs a fascinating little specialist bookshop at No. 284 High Holborn. Forecasts for Europe and the British Isles are provided for up to five days ahead. An assessment can also be given by its friendly staff to those wishing to know how the climate is performing 'back home', wherever that may be. Further along High Holborn, at No. 49, is **HMSO Books (12)**. Her Majesty's Stationery Office (HMSO) is the United Kingdom government publisher and, with an estimated 40,000 titles in print and 8,000 new items each year, it is among the largest publishers in the world. HMSO is primarily involved with providing Parliament with printed material necessary for its work, such as *Hansard*, acts, bills and White Papers, but it also publishes on behalf of government departments. Any purchaser of *The Highway Code* is an HMSO customer.

The ground floor bar of the famous **Cittie of York Pub (13)** is one of the longest in Britain. Voluminous vats, housed in an overhead gallery, once filled bottles for consumption below. Tucked away beneath the cathedral-like proportions of a high trussed roof are intimate mahogany cubicles along one side of the bar. The restored coal stove of 1815 came from the hall of Gray's Inn.

A little further to the east along the north side of High Holborn is Leather Lane, which holds a busy lunch-time general market. East again along Holborn from Leather Lane is Holborn Circus. At its centre is an equestrian bronze of Queen Victoria's consort, Prince Albert, waving his hat to the City of London (Charles Bacon, 1874). Leading off Holborn Circus to the north is Hatton Garden, the home of London's diamond and jewellery trade. On the north-east side of Holborn Circus, at the bottom of Charterhouse Street, is Ely Place. This delightful little thoroughfare of 18th-century houses occupies the former site of Ely House, the late-13th-century London residence of the rich and powerful Bishops of Ely. In 1772 the property reverted to

the Crown and to this day Ely Place is still officially a private
road supervised by its own top-hatted gatekeepers.

In 1874 **St Etheldreda's (14)** was the first pre-Reformation shrine
restored to Catholic hands in England. It is also the sole survivor
of the magnificent complex of domestic buildings once built by
William de Luda, Bishop of Ely, at the end of the 13th century.
Except for part of Westminster Abbey, it is London's only
surviving work from the reign of Edward I (1272–1307).

St Etheldreda was a Saxon queen, who became a nun and
founded Ely Abbey. Etheldreda died from a tumour of the
throat in 679, and every year on 3 February, St Blaise's Day (St
Blaise saved a boy from choking to death on a fish bone), the
ceremony of the Blessing of the Throats is given here. Two unlit
candles are held in the form of a cross near those suffering from
throat diseases. A feretory in the upper church contains part of
St Etheldreda's hand.

The church is entered along a cloister in which, by tradition,
Henry VIII first met Thomas Cranmer, whom he later
appointed the first Protestant Archbishop of Canterbury. At the
end of the cloister, on the right, is the crypt. The crypt may well
have been used as a chapel by local residents when the upper
church was the bishop's private chapel. Its heavy, blackened
13th-century timbers and massive 8-ft-/2.4-m-thick walls of rug-
ged masonry reinforce the church's deep roots in the past.

St Etheldreda's is a fine example of Gothic architecture. It has
features of the Decorated Style (1290–1360), indicated by some
of the most delicate tracery of walls and windows in existence.
The tracery work in the east window has undergone considerable restoration since the Second World War. The stained-glass
depicting Christ flanked by the four evangelists is post-war.

One of the statues in the church commemorates St John
Houghton, the Prior of the London Charterhouse, then a
Carthusian monastery (*Farringdon* ⊖). Houghton's dealing with
Henry VIII had a less favourable outcome than those of
Cranmer. Houghton refused to acknowledge the ecclesiastical
supremacy of Henry VIII and was hanged, drawn and quar-
tered at Tyburn in 1535.

St Etheldreda's holds a Strawberrie Fayre each June in Ely
Place. The finest strawberries in London were once grown here
and Shakespeare extols their reputation in *Richard III*, when
the Duke of Gloucester requests of the Bishop of Ely:

> '. . . When I was last in Holborn
> I saw good strawberries in your garden there.
> I do beseech you send for some of them.'

Ye Old Mitre Pub (15), tucked away in Ely Court, was built in 1546 by Bishop Goodrich for his palace servants. An inscribed mitre on the side of the tavern records this fact. Elizabeth I is said to have danced around the cherry tree whose preserved trunk is inside the tavern.

The first record of **St Andrew, Holborn (16)** (Wren, 1690) is contained in a charter of Westminster Abbey, which mentions a wooden Saxon church built here in 951, with the dedication *Sancte Andreas*. In the 12th century it was replaced by a Norman stone church. In 1348 John Thavie left houses and shops 'to maintain forever the fabric of St Andrew's church'. It escaped the Great Fire, but was rebuilt between 1684 and 1690, and is the largest of Wren's parish churches.

On a winter's night in 1827 a Dr William Marsden found a young girl dying of exposure in St Andrew's churchyard. Unable to gain admission for her at any hospital, the young surgeon founded the Royal Free Hospital for the poor in Gray's Inn Road, since removed to Hampstead.

The church's 18th-century pulpit, font and organ came from the Foundling Hospital at Berkhampsted. The organ had been a gift from the composer Handel. The original Foundling Hospital was in Lamb's Conduit Fields, now Coram's Fields (*King's Cross/St Pancras* ⊖), and the tomb of its founder, Thomas Coram, is placed at the west end of the church.

Beside St Andrew's is the City Temple, one of the oldest Free Churches in London.

Holborn ⊖ & Covent Garden ⊖

Covent Garden is one of London's foremost attractions. Its focal point, the Covent Garden Market piazza, was for centuries the site of a fruit, vegetable and flower market. This beautiful square has been carefully preserved, although it now houses an array of shops dealing in arts, crafts, antiques, books, prints, fashion, food and gifts, as well as restaurants, cafés, pubs and wine bars, and hosts a variety of street entertainment.

Covent Garden took its name from an ancient convent garden, but after Henry VIII dissolved the monasteries, the land was given to the Bedford family for their services to the Crown. In the 1630s the fourth Earl of Bedford commissioned Inigo Jones to prepare an architectural scheme for the area. Jones designed the first and finest of London's residential squares, which became known as the Piazza. The focus of his piazza was St Paul's Church, the only part of Jones's scheme to survive. Church and piazza were essentially Italian in style, with some Antique references taken from the combination of a temple and forum. 'London the ring, Covent Garden the jewel of that ring,' the Earl of Bedford was pleased to observe.

Jones's piazza has always been a meeting place. It was soon adopted as a market place, receiving a royal licence in 1670. Throughout the 18th century this market continued to grow, becoming overcrowded by the 1820s. In 1830 a classical style market building was erected, later roofed over with a great iron and glass structure. By the 1960s the market was again overcrowded, and it moved south of the Thames, to Nine Elms, Battersea, in 1974. The pretty market building was preserved, refurbished and converted to its present use.

Other adjacent buildings have also been renovated, including the old flower market, which now houses the London Transport Museum and the Theatre Museum. The London Transport Museum contains a collection of road and rail vehicles used in the metropolis over the last 150 years.

The theatre is Covent Garden's other great historical tradition. The Theatre Museum, Britain's richest holding of theatrical material, is appropriately sited within earshot of both the Royal Opera House, Covent Garden, and the Theatre Royal, Drury Lane. The Royal Opera House, Covent Garden, is one of

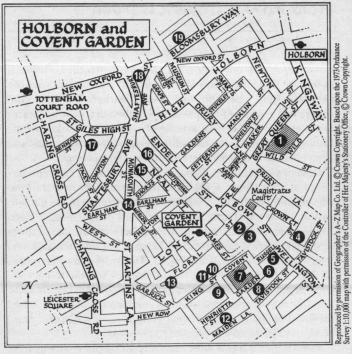

HOLBORN and COVENT GARDEN

the world's principal centres of opera and ballet, and home of both the Royal Opera and the Royal Ballet. A theatre has stood on its site for more than 250 years.

The Theatre Royal, Drury Lane, probably London's best known venue for musicals, was first established in 1663 under royal charter from Charles II. It revived theatre from virtual extinction under Cromwell and the Puritans, and allowed stage drama to flourish in a way not seen since Elizabethan days.

Covent Garden ⊖, on the Piccadilly Line, is the best station from which to see Covent Garden. From here take Long Acre east, turning south into Bow Street. The Royal Opera House, Covent Garden, is on the west side of Bow Street.

Otherwise, leave Holborn ⊖ by the Kingsway exit and walk south along Kingsway. The second turning on the west side is Great Queen Street, which leads into the heart of Covent Garden.

The huge **Freemasons' Hall (1)** in Great Queen Street, head-quarters of the Masonic Order in England, houses the Museum of the United Grand Lodge of England, the world's major collection of symbols, regalia, medals and items about this secretive organization.

Freemasonry is variously claimed to date back to the days of Noah, to Osiris and Isis, to Solomon and his temple, to the Crusades, to Cabbalism and to the Rosicrucians, but it appears that the first Grand Lodge started in London in 1717 among a group of men tired of sectarianism and devoted to deism and the natural sciences. It then spread abroad. Now, there are more than 600,000 initiates in 8,000 lodges in England and Wales, some 1,500 lodges in London alone. Hundreds are in the City, and Freemasonry is said to underpin all the great and influential institutions of the Square Mile. Membership is thought to flourish among such assorted groups as military officers, the police, medical consultants and, generally, the liberal professions. There are no women Freemasons. All members are reportedly sworn on pain of death and ghastly mutilation not to reveal masonic secrets to outsiders. Lodges carry out their secret business in their Masonic temples. The brotherhood's stated aims are morality, fraternity and charity.

Exhibits in the museum of the United Grand Lodge include documents, fine engraved glassware, decorated porcelain, plate and pottery. Artefacts particular to Freemasonry include medals, known to Masons as 'jewels'; some hand-painted and embroidered aprons and sashes from the 18th century; a family tree of royal Freemasons from 1660 to the present day; and an illustrated list of famous Freemasons, whose number includes Dr Barnardo, Rudyard Kipling, W. S. Gilbert and Arthur Sullivan, and Winston Churchill.

The first Freemasons' Hall was erected in 1776 and the present three-storey building is the third to stand on this site. Tours of the museum include the library and Grand Temple. The library holds nearly 40,000 books on the subject of Freemasonry and can be consulted by arrangement.

At the west end of Great Queen Street cross Drury Lane into Long Acre. Bow Street leads off to the south from Long Acre. The **Royal Opera House (2)**, on the west side of Bow Street, has seen memorable performances by many of the world's great opera and ballet stars in its nearly 150 years as an opera house.

Adelina Patti made her debut here in 1861 in *Don Giovanni*. She was the first London Aida, the first Juliette, and unrivalled for the beauty and clarity of her tone. Patti was succeeded by the Australian soprano Nellie Melba, who became Covent Garden's prima donna for a quarter of century. She was introduced by Augustus Harris, whose regime at Covent Garden turned it into one of the Europe's foremost operatic institutions. In 1911 Covent Garden's ballet traditions were laid after Nijinsky and Pavlova delighted audiences during a visit by Diaghilev's Russian Ballet company. After the First World War the young Irish ballerina Ninette de Valois made her Covent Garden début. Since the end of the Second World War memorable nights have included the Margot Fonteyn–Rudolf Nureyev performances; the Maria Callas–Tito Gobbi *Tosca*; the Peter Hall–George Solti *Moses and Aaron*; *Pelléas et Mélisande* conducted by Boulez; Klemperer's production of *Fidelio*; ballets by Kenneth MacMillan and Frederick Ashton, and performances by Joan Sutherland, Janet Baker, Anthony Dowell and Lynn Seymour.

A theatre has occupied this site since about 1732, although it became an opera house only in 1847. The first Covent Garden theatre was built by John Rich, the producer and actor, who possessed letters patent (which enabled him to erect the theatre) originally granted to the famous actor and playright Sir William Davenant by Charles II. For more than a century it was mainly a theatre, except for a short operatic interlude at the beginning when works by Handel were performed. In 1808 the first theatre was burned down and a second was designed by Richard Smirke, architect of the British Museum. In 1847 Covent Garden became the Royal Italian Opera Company, but in 1856 the theatre again burned down during a large fancy-dress ball.

Edward Barry, son of the designer of the Houses of Parliament, was appointed architect and rebuilt the theatre together with Floral Hall, a giant Crystal Palace-type structure used for concerts. His much admired creation was built in Roman classical style and contained a grand Corinthian portico with five columns of Portland stone. The frieze behind is by Flaxman (1809) and was recovered from the previous theatre. The auditorium of the Opera House is decorated in white and gold with warm contrasting deep crimson and rose hangings, and a pale blue dome. The plaster relief over the proscenium, with its musical motif, is by Raffaelle Monti.

The opera house was closed during the First World War, and

between 1924 and 1931 opera performances were confined to merely eight or ten weeks in the summer. For the rest of the time the building was used as a dance hall. After the end of the Second World War the Covent Garden Opera Trust under Lord Keynes transformed the house into the national and permanent home for British opera and ballet companies. A ballet company of acknowledged standard, Ninette de Valois' Sadler's Wells Ballet, which was already in existence, transferred to and re-opened the Royal Opera House that February with a performance of *The Sleeping Beauty*, with Margot Fonteyn dancing the role of Princess Aurora. In 1956 the company was granted a charter and became the Royal Ballet.

Meanwhile, Austrian refugee Karl Rankl was appointed musical director and built up the infant opera company, which gave its first performance, Purcell's *The Fairy Queen*, in December 1946. Sir George Solti, the company's musical director between 1961 and 1971, brought glamour and excitement to the house and in 1968 the official title Royal Opera was conferred on the company. His successor, Sir Colin Davis, widened Covent Garden's appeal. The company's productions are generally sung in the original language.

The opera house is to undergo a facelift and its facilities are to be extended. **Floral Hall (3)**, which adjoins the Royal Opera House to the south, will largely be redesigned, although its attractive Bow Street frontage is to be preserved. Designed by Barry, Floral Hall was intended as a flower market and a venue for promenade concerts. Floral Hall was London's first ornamental iron and glass building, and one of the finest examples from the mid-19th century. During a period of financial trouble at the theatre the hall was leased as an annexe to the fruit and vegetable market, and, sadly, in 1956 its magnificent vaulted glass roof and dome were destroyed by fire. Traders continued to use the building until the 1970s, when the fresh produce market moved to Nine Elms, Battersea. Since then, Floral Hall has been used as a set and scene store for the Royal Opera House, and this use will continue after the planned redevelopment.

Opposite the Royal Opera House is Bow Street Magistrates' Court and Police Station, famed as the birthplace of the British police. The first crime-fighters, a group of volunteer 'thief-takers', became established in Bow Street in the 18th century. At that time London was noted for its moral decadence, a city infamous for bestial sports, gambling, corrupt politics and gin shops. The underworld characters of Covent Garden, a lawless area riddled with dark back alleys of crime, corruption and robbery, were epitomized in John Gay's play *The Beggar's Opera*. The novelist Henry Fielding became the area's magistrate in 1747. An enlightened figure, Fielding realized the link between social deprivation and crime, and ran an honest and compassionate court. Before the era of 'Mr Fielding's people' citizens were selected and enlisted temporarily as constables, but their law enforcement duties were customarily delegated to ineffective old 'Charlies'. By the turn of the century Fielding's thief-takers had become known as the 'Bow Street Runners'. The Metropolitan Police Force came into being after an Act of Parliament in 1829.

Bow Street Police Station houses the Metropolitan Police Historical Museum, a private collection of police equipment and clothing since 1829 that can be viewed by appointment.

South along Bow Street, east into Russell Street and immediately south into Catherine Street lies the **Theatre Royal, Drury Lane (4)**, Covent Garden's other great theatre, which played a vital role in the revival of this art form after its virtual extinction during the Puritan era. Playwright, Poet Laureate and actor Sir William Davenant had gained letters patent from Charles I to erect a theatre shortly before Cromwell came to power in 1642. Davenant joined Charles II's court in exile, where he met a kindred spirit, Thomas Killigrew. After the Restoration, the two were given more or less complete control over London theatre.

Killigrew's company, the King's Company of Players, opened at the Theatre Royal in 1663 with the full approval of the monarch. It was here that Nell Gwyn, one of the theatre's orange sellers, caught Charles II's eye. She went on to become a fine actress, particularly in comic roles, and the King's mistress. Unfortunately, Killigrew's theatre was struck by fire nine years later, but a second was designed and built by Sir Christopher Wren. This stood for more than a century. It was rivalled by a number of local theatres, particularly the Covent Garden Theatre, which opened in 1732.

During the early years of the 18th century Charles Macklin managed the Theatre Royal and transformed the highly mannered acting of the period by encouraging actors to plumb the full human depth of drama. David Garrick, who became co-manager of the Theatre Royal in 1747, continued this progress towards theatrical naturalism. When Garrick retired in 1776, Richard Sheridan took over and put on the highly successful *The School for Scandal*. During Sheridan's time the theatre was found unsafe, demolished and rebuilt. Again it was burned.

The present theatre was designed by Benjamin Wyatt, although it retains some of the Wren structure, and was opened in 1812. Its portico and colonnade were added later. In the 19th century actors Edmund Kean and his son Charles appeared on the Theatre Royal's stage, as did the most famous of all clowns, Joseph Grimaldi. From 1879 the theatre's greatest manager, Augustus Harris, who also managed the Covent Garden Opera House, presented an incredibly varied repertoire of performances, including splendid Christmas pantomimes. Ellen Terry and Sir Henry Irving also appeared in Shakespeare seasons.

This century, fittingly, the musical *My Fair Lady* broke previous box office records here with an incredible run of 2,281 performances. Other musicals have included *Oklahoma*, *South Pacific*, *The King and I*, *Hello Dolly* and *Mame*. Recent successes have been *A Chorus Line*, *The Pirates of Penzance* and the New York hit *42nd Street*.

The Theatre Royal Drury Lane is the only London theatre to retain its original internal Georgian features. The auditorium was rebuilt in 1922, but the elegant Georgian domed entrance hall, rotunda, staircases and first-floor Grand Saloon have been preserved. Guided tours are available.

From Russell Street, facing west across Bow Street, is the Covent Garden market building, with its Tuscan columns, triangular pediment, arcades and glass roof. The entrance to the **Theatre Museum (5)** is on the south side of Russell Street. Britain's richest holding of theatrical material is held in this branch of the Victoria and Albert Museum (*South Kensington* ⊖), which opened in 1987 on 23 April, Shakespeare's birthday. An enormous golden angel, the Spirit of Gaiety, which once stood on top of the Gaiety Theatre in Aldwych, greets visitors at the door. Admission tickets are purchased from an historic box office from the old Duke of York's Theatre in Drury Lane.

All the performing arts are represented here – theatre, ballet, opera, music hall, variety, circus, mime, puppetry and pop. The collection covers the British stage from the end of the 17th century, and contains programmes, playbills, newspaper cuttings, texts, correspondence, the libretti and music of operas and

ballets, portraits of performers, miniature set models, engravings, toy theatre sheets, prompt books, drawings and designs,
and an array of photographs. There is the complete set of *Swan
Lake* costumes used by the Russian Imperial Theatre and then
by Diaghilev's Ballets Russes. Also on display is a 19th-century
harlequin's outfit, rare 18th-century Italian stage costumes,
Dame Alicia Markova's ballet costumes, a Mick Jagger jump-
suit, John Lennon's grey velvet collared suit, one of Pete
Townshend's broken guitars, Beatles' clothes and one of Elton
John's outrageous costumes.

The Lower Foyer and Theatre, which are used for meetings
and events, have been built in the Edwardian style. They also
house the museum's collection of paintings. Every day, except
Sunday, the museum's café-cum-wine bar remains open until
8 p.m. for pre-theatre refreshment.

Beneath the lofty Victorian canopy of Covent Garden's old
Flower Market, in the eastern corner of the piazza, is the
London Transport Museum (6), an excellent repository of information about the origins and evolution of London's transport
system. It consists mainly of the road and rail vehicles that have
been used in the metropolis over the last 150 years.

London Regional Transport is obliged under Transport Acts
to conserve its heritage, and today its collection includes buses,
trams, trolleybuses, trains and much other fascinating paraphernalia associated with keeping the capital's population on the
move. The museum originated in the collection of early buses
formed by London General Omnibus Company in the 1920s and
1930s.

The earliest exhibit is a replica of the Shillibeer Horse Omnibus (1829), named after George Shillibeer (1797–1866), inventor of the hearse and promoter of the omnibus. Another
favourite, from the early days of the London Underground,
is the L23 steam locomotive (*c.* 1866), which once pulled
coaches on what is now the Circle Line. Buses include a
Knifeboard Horse Bus (*c.* 1850–1900), a Garden Seat Horse
Bus (*c.* 1885–1914) and the classic Type B motor bus
(1910–27).

The museum's working exhibits are particularly popular.
Children can 'drive' a tube train, tram or modern bus; operate
the points laid out in a full-size section of underground tunnel
segments; or try the 'dead man's handle'. Informative displays,

maps, photographs and audio-visual presentations, explaining 200 years of public transport in London, place the exhibits in their social contexts and show the profound effect of easy and rapid mobility on the growth of London and its people. London Transport's posters are famed for their artistic quality, and a large selection are on sale.

Covent Garden Market (7) is one of London's newest and liveliest shopping areas. Throngs of theatre-goers, actors, artists, dancers, musicians, tourists and business people congregate in this attractive and exciting *quartier* of London. Although the departure of the old fruit, vegetable and flower market was a sad occasion for many, the restored market building has now been revitalized with wine bars, pubs, restaurants and dozens of shops selling an astonishing array of speciality products. Buskers and street entertainers provide some of the best free entertainment in the capital.

Originally laid out as a square in the 17th century, the focus of the square today is Charles Fowler's market building, built in 1830 in the Graeco-Roman manner. It has been described as 'a structure at once perfectly fitted for its various uses; of great architectural beauty and elegance; and so expressive of its purposes for which it is erected'. Such a commendation could equally be applied to its new function as a shopping and entertainment complex.

Five parallel thoroughfares divide the building: North Row, North Avenue, Central Avenue, South Avenue and South Row. Together, its individual units form a balance of high-quality shopping. A market is held in North Avenue, for antiques and bric-a-brac on Mondays, and for general crafts during the rest of the week. The first floor terrace of the Punch and Judy Pub gives a good view of the piazza and its constant stream of buskers. Outside the Cabaret Mechanical Theatre a mechanical 'doctor' will write a prescription for a small fee. Pollock's Toy Theatres supply charming reprints of children's cardboard theatres from yesteryear. Light Fantastic in South Row exhibits a marvellous collection of holograms.

The redeveloped Jubilee Hall, once part of the vegetable market on the south side of the piazza, was opened by the Queen on 12 August 1987. Jubilee Hall, originally intended to commemorate the fiftieth year of Queen Victoria's reign in 1887, proved a late arrival on completion in 1903. It now contains flats, offices, a sports hall and the **Jubilee Market (8)**, an open general market and perhaps the only surviving continuity of tradition with the old fruit, vegetable and flower market.

At the west end of the piazza the portico of **St Paul's Covent Garden (9)** has become the stage for a myriad of street entertainments. The entrance to the churchyard of St Paul's is through a small court called Inigo Place in Bedford Street. The Bedford coat of arms, with lion and scallop shells, is situated above the gates leading into Inigo Place.

St Paul's was the focal point of Inigo Jones's grand design for Covent Garden. It was also the first new Anglican church built in London since the Reformation. St Paul's simple design, a double square ground plan, reflects the changed nature of religion after that religious upheaval. Before the church was built the Earl of Bedford insisted that St Paul's should be 'not much better than a barn'. Instead, Jones constructed 'the handsomest barn in England'. St Paul's Italianate style, with its shallow angled roof, blends simplicity with beautiful proportions and great dignity. Although the original church was burned down, a more or less exact replica was built by Thomas Hardwick (1752–1829) in 1793.

St Paul's is known as the actors' church. Inigo Jones himself was an accomplished theatrical designer. There are memorials to Ivor Novello, Boris Karloff, Margaret Rutherford, Vivien Leigh, Hattie Jacques, Dame Ellen Terry, Sir Noel Coward, Sir Charles Chaplin, Kenneth More and Edith Evans, as well as a gruesome monument to the Theatre Royal actor-manager Charles Macklin (d. 1797), who killed a fellow actor in a quarrel over a wig at Drury Lane. The monument depicts Macklin's stick piercing the eye of his unfortunate tormentor.

A carved limewood wreath on the screen at the west end is by Grinling Gibbons (1648–1720), the prolific master woodcarver. Gibbons is buried here, as is Thomas Arne (d. 1778). A monument to Arne on the north wall includes the first line of his setting of 'Rule Britannia'.

It was under St Paul's magnificent Tuscan portico that Professor Higgins first met flowerseller Eliza Doolittle in George Bernard Shaw's play *Pygmalion*, on which the musical *My Fair Lady* was based. Inigo Jones's portico was constructed at the east end of the church as a grand entrance on to the square. His plan, however, would have resulted in the siting of the altar at the west end of the church. The then Bishop of London, William

Laud, objected to such a departure from ecclesiastical tradition and the entrance was never used.

A plaque records that Punch's famous puppet show was first performed in England here in a sophisticated miniature theatre, and witnessed by Samuel Pepys in 1662. The event is now celebrated each year with a puppeteers' service and May Fayre. Today the historic tradition of street entertainment under Jones's fine portico is continued by a flourishing collection of jugglers, fire-eaters, mime actors, musicians, singers and acting troupes.

To the north of the piazza, at No. 43 King Street, is **Thomas Archer House (10)**, probably the finest example of an early-18th-century town house in London. It was designed by Thomas Archer in 1716 for Admiral Edward Russell, Earl of Orford, one of the most powerful men of his time. Despite alterations (*c.* 1870), its façade is still characteristic of Archer's baroque style. The flat front is distinguished with two fluted Corinthian pilasters decorated with elaborate capitals, and tall segment-topped windows. The house is open to the public by prior appointment only.

Further west, at No. 38, is the **Africa Centre (11)**, a cultural centre, educational institute and meeting place. It contains a bookshop, African restaurant and visual arts gallery hosting frequent exhibitions.

South of Covent Garden, in Maiden Lane, **Rule's Restaurant (12)** is reputedly London's oldest. Established in 1798 by Thomas Rule, the restaurant's drawings, paintings, cartoons and playbills form a living museum to its illustrious patrons, who have included Dickens, H. G. Wells, Laurence Olivier, Charlie Chaplin and Buster Keaton. Its most distinguished guest was Edward VII, who, as the Prince of Wales, made rendezvous here with his mistress, the beautiful Lily Langtry. Today it is possible to sit at their 'table for two' by the lattice window on the first floor. Their signed portraits remain, as does the secret door that allowed the Prince to enter and leave unseen.

Tucked into a quiet corner of the Covent Garden area, the **Lamb and Flag (13)** in Rose Street retains the atmosphere of a country pub. Built in 1623, it is one of the few wooden-framed buildings to survive in central London. Its sparse decor, sawdust-strewn floors, walls hung with ageing prints, and traditional food reflect few concessions to change. The pub became known as the Bucket of Blood after its association with prize-fighters. A wooden beam over the bar bears a Latin inscription in praise of drink. It translates:

> To die in a pub is my definite plan,
> With my mouth to the tap, just as close as I can.
> Then the angels would say, when their singing began,
> 'O Lord, please show mercy to this boozey man.'

The area to the north of the piazza is a maze of criss-crossing streets, which boast some of the most unusual and interesting shopping in London. Running east from Rose Street is **Floral Street**, noted for its fashionable clothes shops, particularly Paul Smith, at No. 43, which caters for the sartorial needs of the younger English gentleman. Pilot, at No. 34, is a popular specialist shop selling the original *Tin-Tin* books in French, as well as other paraphernalia connected with Hergé's boy hero. Little Women at No. 4 Langley Court, on the north side of Floral Street, specializes in clothes for petite women, those up to 5 ft 2 in/1.6 m in height.

The retail outlet of Patricia Roberts, designer of luxurious knitwear, is at No. 31 **James Street**. Next door, at No. 30, are to be found the beautifully packaged toiletries, biscuits and preserves made by Crabtree and Evelyn.

The west section of **Long Acre**, which crosses the north end of James Street, contains Edward Stanford Ltd, at Nos. 12–14, one of the largest map and chart retailers in the world. The Arts Council Bookshop, at No. 8, sells national and international exhibition catalogues as well as books, postcards, posters, artist's materials and music whose recording has been sponsored by the Council.

Stringfellows, the fashionable night club, is in **Upper St Martin's Lane**. At No. 57 **Monmouth Street**, is 'showbiz' shop Dress Circle, which sells records, posters and a general array of items associated with the latest West End musicals.

Mercer, Monmouth and Earlham Streets, and Shorts Gardens meet at the **Seven Dials (14)**, a junction once the reputed haunt of mobsters, and referred to in numerous books, including Agatha Christie's *Seven Dials Mystery* and Dickens's *Sketches by Boz*. At its centre once stood a six-faced Roman Doric pillar, designed by Edward Pierce (1630–95). The seventh dial is thought to have been the pillar itself, acting as a sundial. Pillar sundials were popular in 17th-century London, but the 40-ft-/ 12-m-high monument was said to have been demolished in 1773 by a mob after a rumour circulated that a bag of gold lay buried beneath it. However, recent research has disclosed that it was deliberately demolished that year because it was used as a rallying point for undesirables. Public subscription enabled a replica to be erected in 1989.

In the passage joining Shorts Gardens and Monmouth Street is a delightful courtyard called **Neal's Yard (15)**, occupied by a 'village' of health-food shops and an apothecary. The Neal's Yard Wholefood Warehouse is popular for bulk-buying cereals. The Farm Shop provides fresh organically grown food. Numerous types of flour, all ground on the premises, are sold at the Flour Mill. The Bakery produces whole-wheat, organic and other interesting breads. The Apothecary is crammed full with tiny bottles containing many natural remedies. The Therapy Rooms practise acupuncture, aromatherapy, massage and other healing skills.

In the northern half of Monmouth Street, at the Monmouth Coffee House (No. 27), a wide variety of blends of coffee can be sampled and purchased. Mysteries, at No. 11, the psychic supermarket, stocks everything from packets of incense sticks to crystal balls.

The village atmosphere of Covent Garden continues into **Neal Street (16)**. From the north end, its fascinating shops include The Kite Store (No. 69), selling every imaginable type of engineless flying contraption, from a traditional Chinese kite to a boomerang; Comic Showcase (No. 79), stocking new and old American comics, Asterix books and related materials; Argon (No. 72), popular for pop graphics and postcards, quirky designer watches, neon illuminations and a general selection of weird and wonderful ornaments; Ray Man (No. 64), retailing traditional Eastern and African musical instruments, and some vividly coloured dragon heads like those used in Chinese parades; Astrohome (No. 47), for high-tech furniture and ornaments; One Off (No. 56), a gallery of highly individual furniture made in limited editions; The Bead Shop (No. 43), offering thousands of clay, shell, wooden, glass, plastic, metal and fabric beads; Contemporary Applied Arts (entrance at No. 43 Earlham Street), a retail outlet for some of the best rising and established craftsmen in Britain today; the London Ecology Centre (entrance at No 45 Shelton Street), containing an exhibition gallery, restaurant and bookshop; the Natural Shoe Store (No. 21 Neal Street), with its wholesome-looking shoes for men and women; Artemide (No. 19), specializing in Italian high-tech designer furniture and lighting; The Tea House (No. 15a), selling everything imaginable related to tea; and Neal Street East (No. 5), a treasure trove of orientalia – kimonos, fans, silks, antique jewellery and beautiful Japanese *yukatas*.

Walk south along Neal Street to return to Covent Garden ⊖ or, from the north end of Neal Street, take Shaftesbury Avenue north a short distance and turn west into St Giles High Street. **St Giles-in-the-Fields Church (17)** lies to the south.

The church was established by Matilda, Henry I's queen, in 1101 as the chapel of a monastic leper hospital. She dedicated it to St Giles, the patron saint of lepers and outcasts. The church's tradition of concern for outcasts continued for many centuries through the practice of extending a 'cup of charity' to prisoners on their way from Newgate Prison to Tyburn gallows.

In 1623 a new church was built, but Henry VIII shut the monastery during the Dissolution. In 1644 the Great Plague first broke out among Flemish weavers in the parish of St Giles. The following year, 3,211 deaths were recorded in the parish, 1,361 in the month of July alone.

Another church was erected after architect Henry Flitcroft won a competition held under the Fifty New Churches Act of 1711. Flitcroft's church, the one standing today, has a plain classical exterior. Rising above its west pediment is a square tower that changes, above the clock faces, into an octagon surmounted by a short steeple. The interior is a pleasing example of the Palladian style with a pale blue barrel-vaulted ceiling, Ionic columns in Tuscan red and much gilded moulding set off by French grey.

The church contains a monument to George Chapman (d. 1634), who first translated Homer into English. Architect Sir John Soane was buried in the churchyard in 1823.

Returning east along St Giles High Street, turn north into Shaftesbury Avenue. On the south-east corner of the junction between Shaftesbury Avenue and New Oxford Street is **James Smith and Son (18)**, suppliers of umbrellas.

The umbrella originated in the Orient as a symbol of rank, a token of civilization that once shaded noble heads in ancient China, Persia and the Roman Empire. In the 18th century it was introduced to Britain to shelter gentlemen from the rain.

The family firm of James Smith and Son has been supplying canes, sticks, whips and umbrellas since 1830, and from its present premises since 1867. Swagger sticks have been purchased here by officers; canes by schoolmasters; swordsticks by dandies; and stout walking sticks of ash and chestnut by country squires; and even ceremonial wands by African chieftains. On display in the shop is a collection of ceremonial maces made for African native commissioners, each about 5 ft/1.5 m high with a silver elephant on top. Prime Ministers Gladstone and Bonar Law bought their brollies here, as did Lord Curzon, one-time Viceroy of India and Foreign Secretary.

Sticks and umbrellas are made in the firm's basement workshop from a variety of materials including hazel, ash, cherry, chestnut, crab apple, birch, oak, blackthorn, furze, bamboo, maple, hickory, ebony and malacca. Disregarding superstition, customers are encouraged to open umbrellas under the shop's high ceilings. To James and Son, umbrellas are not just utilitarian items; rows of floor-to-ceiling mirrors ensure that umbrellas can also be appraised as fashionable purchases by the discerning customer. Prices start at around £10; £50 for those sporting a gnarled wooden handle, and £200-plus for silver-handled ones.

East along New Oxford Street, Bloomsbury Way leads off to the north-east. **St George's, Bloomsbury (19)** (Nicholas Hawksmoor, 1731) lies immediately on the north side of Bloomsbury Way. St George's extraordinary steeple, a stepped pyramid, was inspired by Pliny's description of the tomb of Mausolos (d. 353 BC) at Halicarnassus. Until 1871 the pyramid's angles were adorned with two 10-ft-/3-m-long lions, crawling down, and two unicorns, ascending, designed to represent the royal arms. The pyramid now is surmounted by a statue of George I as St George. Reproductions of this original spire appear on two lamp standards flanking the church's steps.

Like all of Hawksmoor's six London churches, St George's was built under the Fifty New Churches Act of 1711. Its plan, a square within a square, echoes his design for St Mary Woolnoth (*Bank* ⊖), on which he was working at the same time. St George's was built after the repectable parishioners inhabiting the northern part of St Giles's parish objected to passing through the notorious district known as the Rookery, scene of Hogarth's *Gin Lane*, on their way to church.

New Oxford Street joins High Holborn in the east. A short distance east along High Holborn, at its junction with Kingsway and Southampton Row, is Holborn ⊖.

Tottenham Court Road ⊖ & Leicester Square ⊖

The British Museum is one of the world's great museums. Under 7 acres/12.8 ha. of roof the creative high points of many ancient civilizations are set out among the museum's astonishing collection of several million items, including the celebrated Elgin Marbles from the Parthenon in Greece; the Rosetta Stone, a slab of black basalt discovered in 1799, which finally unlocked the secret of ancient Egyptian hieroglyphics; crude stone tools almost 2 million years old from the Olduvai Gorge, Tanzania; jewellery and other artefacts from the 6th-century Anglo-Saxon royal burial ship found at Sutton Hoo, Suffolk; the most comprehensive collection in the West of articles from the Indian sub-continent covering the period from the third millennium BC to the last century; as well as the finest collection of Chinese porcelain in Europe.

Under the same roof, in the British Library Galleries, are some of the world's greatest literary treasures. Kept here are two of the four surviving copies of Magna Carta, King John's charter of 1215 enshrining the agreement with his barons; the 7th-century Lindisfarne Gospels, the most outstanding masterpiece of English book illumination richly designed with Anglo-Saxon ornamentation and created at the island monastery of Lindisfarne; the Codex Sinaiticus, from the mid-4th century, and the Codex Alexandrinus, from the first half of the 5th century, two of the three earliest and most important manuscripts of the Bible; the Diamond Sutra of 868, the first dated example of printing found in a cave in northern China; and the Gutenberg Bible (1455), the first book printed from movable metal type.

Not far from the British Museum is Bedford Square, the only complete Georgian square left in Bloomsbury and traditionally the headquarters of many of Britain's leading publishing houses.

South from Tottenham Court Road ⊖ is Charing Cross Road, a thoroughfare lined with bookshops. Until the 1970s, No. 84 housed the premises of Marks and Co, second-hand booksellers made famous by the American writer Helen Hanff. Hanff based her book *84 Charing Cross Road* on her correspondence with the

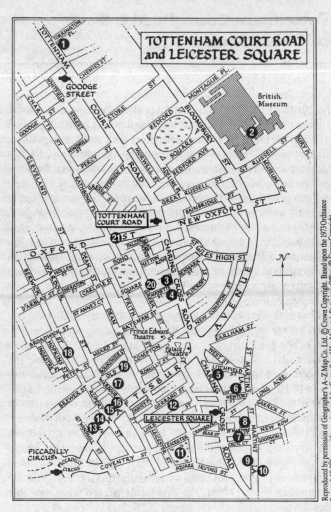

TOTTENHAM COURT ROAD
and LEICESTER SQUARE

shop's members of staff after the Second World War. Such old-fashioned quality and traditional specialist service is still to be found in many bookshops lining the road and surrounding streets. Zwemmer is best known for its art books. Antiquarian and second-hand bookshops huddle together in Cecil Court, off Charing Cross Road. Foyle's, reputedly the world's largest bookshop, is certainly the largest in London, its shelves stocking at any one time around 6 million titles.

West of Charing Cross Road is Leicester Square, once noted for its theatres and variety halls, and now the heart of London's movieland. To its north are Chinatown and Shaftesbury Avenue. The best Cantonese cuisine outside South-east Asia is to be found in Chinatown, and the theatres of Shaftesbury Avenue form the heart of London's theatreland.

North of Shaftesbury Avenue is Soho, an area that has long been infamous as the 'red-light' district of central London. Today its red-light reputation is less well deserved, although the area still retains a colourful cosmopolitan and bohemian atmosphere. Some peep shows survive, but the area is becoming better known for its gastronomic reputation.

Tottenham Court Road stretches north from the Underground station and is lined with hi-fi and electronics shops. In the northern part of Tottenham Court Road on the east side is Heal's, the furniture retailers now owned by Sir Terence Conran's Storehouse Group. Earlier this century it was Heal's who pioneered room set displays found today is nearly every furniture store. Not only do Conran's successful Habitat Store and Heal's now occupy the same building, but they also share the same broad retailing philosophy, bringing modern design to the masses at reasonable prices.

⊖   ⊖   ⊖

From Tottenham Court Road ⊖'s northern exit Tottenham Court Road stretches to the north. The premises of **Heal's Habitat (1)** are at No. 196. Furnishing retailers Habitat shot to fame with a style based on simplicity, functionalism and taste. The chain-store's founder, Sir Terence Conran, opened his first Habitat store in the 1960s. Its success was meteoric and the shops continue to sell thousands of different items, from the humble tin opener to stylish sofas, for making a home. Each is distinguished by a combination of bright colours, clean lines, modern materials and reasonable prices.

In 1983 Habitat acquired Heal's, an old, established furnishing business founded in 1910 by John Harris Heal in nearby Rathbone Place. Heal's passed through six generations of the Heal family before being taken over by Conran.

Great Russell Street leads off to the east from Tottenham Court Road past the Central London YMCA. It crosses Bloomsbury Street and, a short distance beyond on the north side of Great

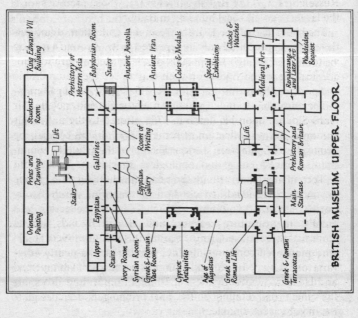

BRITISH MUSEUM UPPER FLOOR

King Edward VII Building

Students' Room

Prints and Drawings

Oriental Painting

Lift

Upper Egyptian

Stairs

Ivory Room

Syrian Room

Greek & Roman Vase Rooms

Galleries

Prehistory of Western Asia

Babylonian Room

Stairs

Ancient Anatolia

Ancient Iran

Coins & Medals

Special Exhibitions

Room of Writing

Egyptian Gallery

Clocks & Watches

Medieval Art

Renaissance and Later Art

Waddesdon Bequest

Lift

Prehistory and Roman Britain

Cypriot Antiquities

Age of Augustus

Greek and Roman Life

Main Staircase

Greek & Roman Terracottas

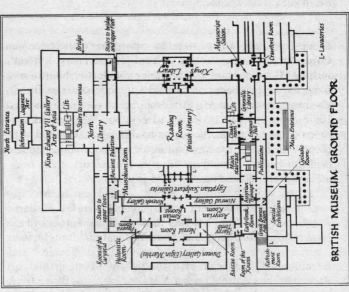

BRITISH MUSEUM GROUND FLOOR

North Entrance

Information

Japanese Art

King Edward VII Gallery Arts of Asia

Lift

Stairs to entrance

North Library

Bridge

Stairs to bridge and upper floor

Ancient Palestine

Mausoleum Room

Reading Room (British Library)

Kings Library

Manuscript Saloon

Crawford Room

Grenville Library

Lift

Stairs to upper floor

Nireah Gallery

Assyrian Rooms

Nimrud Gallery

Egyptian Sculpture Galleries

Engaved Hall

Main staircase

Cloak-room

Cloak-room

Publications

L — Lavatories

Room of the Caryatid

Hellenistic Room

Bassae Room

Phrats Rooms

Assyrian Room

Room of the Kouts

Duveen Gallery (Elgin Marbles)

Nereid Room

Harpy Tomb

Early Greek Room

Greek Bronze Age Room

Nimrud Room

Assyrian Transept

Special Exhibitions

Cycladic Room

Main Entrance

Refresh-ment Room

Russell Street, is the **British Museum (2)**, whose premises form the largest neo-classical building in Britain.

The sheer size of the British Museum's collection of antiquities can be appreciated only by repeated visits. Around 4 million visitors pass through the portals of the museum's grand neo-classical façade each year on their way to see the innumerable and priceless treasures that adorn its 2.5 miles/4 km of galleries.

The museum's founder, physician, naturalist and traveller Sir Hans Sloane, upon his death in 1753 offered to the nation his immense private collection of some 82,000 objects comprising plants, fossils, minerals, antiquities, curiosities, books, manuscripts, prints, coins and zoological specimens. Parliament passed an Act that year authorizing the holding of a public lottery to raise funds to establish a museum, which finally opened at Montagu House in 1759. Sloane's collection was rapidly augmented by purchases and gifts of all kinds, and its premises began to creak at the seams. In 1823, after George IV presented his father's magnificent library to the museum, Parliament voted funds for appropriate new premises. Over a period of thirty years, under architect Robert Smirke and, after his retirement, his younger brother Sydney, the museum arose as it is today. Montagu House was demolished.

In the early 1880s the museum's natural history collection moved to South Kensington to what is now the Natural History Museum (*Sloane Square* ⊖). Its newspaper collection was moved in 1905 to a new library built at Colindale, north London, and in 1970 the museum's ethnographical collection found a new home at the Museum of Mankind (*Bond St* ⊖). The British Museum's holdings at Great Russell Street now comprise the following collections: Greek and Roman; Western Asiatic; Egyptian; Prehistoric and Romano-British; Medieval and Later; Oriental; Coins and Medals; Prints and Drawings; and the British Library Galleries.

The **Greek and Roman Galleries** (ground floor rooms 1–15, 22, 23, upper floor 68–73, basement 77–85) contain artefacts from the distinctive culture that flourished in the Cycladic Islands between 3200 BC and 2000 BC, notably enigmatic Bronze Age marble figures; Bronze Age material from Minoan Crete, including gold jewellery from the Aegina Treasure and the mysterious gold figure of the 'Master of the Animals'; Mycenaean antiquities and weapons; Archaic period Greek sculpture; the room of the *kouroi*; the harpy tomb; the marble high-relief frieze from the Temple of Apollo at Bassae; the Nereid Room, containing the reconstructed façade of the Nereid Monument from Xanthos; the Caryatid, one of six columns that once supported the porch of the Athenian temple known as the Erechtheion; selections of Greek vases from the museum's extensive collection, one of the largest and most comprehensive in the world; Etruscan sculpture; galleries of Latin and Greek inscriptions and sculptures; a colossal marble horse, once part of the tomb of Mausolus at Halicarnassus, one of the seven wonders of the ancient world; Roman portraits; Roman mosaics, chiefly from Asia Minor and North Africa; a room devoted to aspects of daily life in ancient Greece and Rome; and the Portland Vase, a Roman jar of blue and white glass (27 BC–AD 37) illustrated with scenes from the story of Peleus and his immortal sea-goddess bride Thetis. In 1988 the Portland Vase, the earliest known example of Roman cameo glass and one of the earliest specimens of glass blowing, was deliberately broken. In 1845 a drunk smashed the vase to pieces. It took six months to repair but a century later the glue started to give out. The vase was taken apart and put together with an early form of epoxy resin. By 1988 the vase was again brittle, weak and near collapse. The restoration was carried out to comply with the conservators' rule that the repaired object should look as perfect as possible to the public from a distance of 6ft/1.8m while the repairs should be obvious to an expert who studies it from 6in/152mm.

The most famous treasures in the Greek and Roman Galleries are the Elgin Marbles. These sculptures from the mid-5th century BC, which once formed a great frieze inside the colonnade of the Parthenon, were rescued by Lord Elgin at the beginning of the 19th century and are now displayed in the Duveen Gallery. The frieze shows a procession of horses with flaring nostrils, chariots, sacrificial cattle, musicians, maidens and elderly human attendants approaching a gathering of great gods and goddesses. Sculptures from the outside of the Parthenon are exhibited in the transepts at either end of the gallery.

The **Western Asiatic Galleries** (ground floor rooms 16–21, 24, 26, upper floor 51–59, basement 88–90) contain antiquities from the Sumerian, Babylonian and Assyrian civilizations, ancient Persian cultures, from the Parthians, Sassanians, Urartians, Hittites, Phoenicians, as well as ancient Palestine and the states of the Arabian peninsula. They cover the period from the earliest agricultural settlements *c*. 7000 B C, until the advent of Islam in the 7th century A D. The collections derive mainly from archaeological expeditions sponsored by the museum.

Treasures include the Black Obelisk (*c*. 825 B C), with inscriptions showing Shalmaneser, King of Assyria, receiving tribute from various foreign rulers; a massive human-headed winged lion and bull from the palace of Assyrian King Ashurnasirpal II (883–859 B C), as well as a stone statue of the King wearing ritual dress and sets of bronze gates and sculptures, all from Nimrud (north Iraq); a colossal human-headed winged bull (*c*. 710 B C) from a gate at Assyrian King Sargon II's city Khorsabad (north Iraq); stone panels and sculptures that once decorated the state apartments in the palace of Ashurbanipal, the last great Assyrian king at Nineveh (north Iraq); a room about the early history of writing, including the 'flood tablet', written in the cuneiform script and whose narrative has strong parallels with the biblical story of Noah's ark; bronzes and sculptures from South and North Yemen; ivories from Nimrud; antiquities from Syria; and an Archaemenian golden armlet dating from the 5th century B C.

The **Egyptian Galleries** (ground floor room 25, upper floor 61–6) cover all periods in the development of the ancient Egyptian civilization to the Christian era, with extensive collections of papyri and burial objects. The galleries house the finest collection of Egyptian sculpture outside Egypt. The Egyptian sculpture room is entered past a pair of red granite reclining lions of Amenophis III. Its stunning collection is chronologically ordered and includes the upper part of a colossus of Rameses II made of two differently coloured granites (*c*. 1250). At the southern end of the gallery is the Rosetta Stone, a slab of black basalt discovered in 1799 and inscribed with a decree dated to the ninth year of Ptolemy V (196 BC), written in ancient Greek and in two forms of ancient Egyptian script: hieroglyphs, or sacred writing; and demotic, or the people's writing. Through its Greek section the stone provided the clue to deciphering hieroglyphics, a script unread for 1,400 years.

There are rooms of mummies, brightly-painted mummy cases, masks, embalming equipment, and the sand-dried body of 'Ginger' (so called on account of the colour of his hair) – a man of the Predynastic period who died over 5,000 years ago. In the Third Egyptian room there are many exquisite wall-paintings from burial tombs, as well as papyri of various editions of the Book of the Dead – collections of spells to enable the deceased to travel safely through the Underworld to Heaven. The Abusir temple accounts form the earliest surviving body of written papyri. Other rooms contain household artefacts, pottery, scarabs, jewellery and glassware from Predynastic Egypt. The Coptic Corridor has portraits from the Roman period.

The **Prehistoric and Romano-British Galleries** (upper floor rooms 35–40) contain artefacts from the Paleolithic and Mesolithic periods gathered throughout the world, as well as objects from the Neolithic, Bronze Age and Iron Age in Europe and from Roman Britain. The Man before Metals display contains crude stone tools almost 2 million years old from the Olduvai Gorge, Tanzania, a re-creation of a Neolithic burial site in Britain and some fascinating Stone Age art. Other treasures include a small carving of a mammoth (*c*. 10,500 BC); the Rillaton gold cup found in Cornwall, which dates from 1600–1500 BC; the Electrum torc, or neck-ring, from the 1st century BC, found in Norfolk; and the Witham Shield (c. 200–100 BC) discovered in Lincolnshire and one of the finest examples of early Celtic metalwork in Britain. The exhibits in the Roman Britain room include a mosaic of Bacchus on a tiger, found in Leadenhall Street, London; the Lullingstone wall-plaster (4th century AD); the Mildenhall platters from a hoard of 4th-century Roman silver, one of the finest sets of tableware found anywhere in the Roman Empire; and the Vindolanda tablets, the earliest group of written records discovered in Britain.

The **Galleries of Medieval and Later Antiquities** (upper floor rooms 41–7) deal with the art and archaeology of Europe and other Christian and Jewish cultures, from the early Christian period to the 20th century. Early medieval treasures include the Lycurgus Cup, a late Roman cage cup from the 4th century AD, carved from a single block of glass; items of Viking and Celtic metalwork; and jewellery and other artefacts from the Anglo-Saxon royal burial ship (*c*. AD 625) found at Sutton Hoo, Suffolk. From the era spanning the 9th to the 15th centuries there are antiquities from the Byzantine, Carolingian, Romanesque and Gothic periods, including the Lewis chessmen, 12th-century walrus ivory chessmen discovered on the Isle of Lewis in 1831. The royal gittern (*c*. 1290–1330), the only surviving major English musical instrument of the Middle Ages, with intricately carved beasts, hunters and foliage, is displayed in a standing case. Also displayed is the Royal Gold Cup of the kings of England and France, one of the museum's outstanding possessions. The gallery of clocks and watches illustrates the development of timekeeping from the medieval period to the beginning of the 20th century. The Renaissance Corridor contains objects from the Renaissance to the 18th century.

The **Oriental Galleries** (ground floor room 34, upper floor 74, 75) contain perhaps the most comprehensive collection in the West of articles from the Indian sub-continent covering the period from the third millennium B C to the last century, as well as the finest collection of Chinese porcelain in Europe. The series of Buddhist sculptures from Gandhara (1st–6th centuries A D) includes the Gandharan Reliquary, one of the most celebrated objects from the Buddhist world. Important works from South-east Asia include the life-size gilt-bronze figure of Tara (9th–10th centuries A D), the seated bronze Buddha from Burma (12th century A D) and a collection of Javanese bronzes (8th–14th centuries A D). There are artefacts from the world of Islam, Central Asia, China, Korea and Japan. The Chinese exhibits are arranged chronologically from the Neolithic period, and include a bronze ritual vessel from the 11th or 12th century B C, chariot fittings, an early lacquer box of the Han dynasty (206 B C–A D 200) and fine porcelain.

The **Coins and Medals Collection** (upper floor room 50) comprises coins of all places and periods from the 7th century B C to the present day, as well as medals, decorations, tokens, coin weights and paper money.

The **Prints and Drawings Room** (upper floor room 67) contains a changing selection from the British Museum's holdings as well as occasional loan exhibitions. Its holdings form one of the great collections of European prints and drawings, and include groups of works by Michelangelo, Raphael, Dürer, Rubens, Rembrandt, Lorrain and Watteau. It contains the only known large-scale cartoon by Michelangelo, the *Virgin and Child*. The series of woodcuts, etchings and engravings is one of the most comprehensive in existence, and includes works by Schongauer, Dürer, Lucas van Leyden and Rembrandt.

The **British Library** is dispersed over more than ten locations in London. By law, it must receive one copy of every book, periodical and newspaper published in the United Kingdom. In 1986 its collection totalled 16 million books held on 360 miles/ 579 km of shelving. Each year 2 miles/3.2 km of new shelving is needed to house this expanding archive. The British Library's Reference Division forms one of the world's greatest libraries. Two of the division's departments, the Department of Printed Books and the Department of Manuscripts, are still based in the British Museum building, although the British Library was placed under a separate authority in 1973. Many of its treasures are on display and there are special exhibitions.

The entrance to the **British Library Galleries** (ground floor rooms 29–33) lies on the east side of the museum's entrance hall. The galleries occupy most of the ground floor and mezzanine of the British Museum's east wing. Entered first is the **Grenville Library**, named after Thomas Grenville MP (d. 1846), whose collection it houses. On display are Western illuminated manuscripts – on one side, those of British origin, on the other, manuscripts from the Continent. The earliest English item is the 8th-century Vespasian Psalter, written and illuminated at Canterbury. There is also the 10th-century Benedictional of St Ethelwold and the 14th-century Luttrell Psalter, whose decoration is one of the richest sources of illustrations of everyday life in the Middle Ages. Secular items include what is thought to be the world's most beautiful copy of the popular Middle Ages work, *Roman de la Rose*.

The **Manuscript Saloon**, devoted primarily to manuscripts of historical and literary interest, houses the outstanding masterpiece of English book illumination, the Lindisfarne Gospels (*c.* 698), created at the island monastery of Lindisfarne and richly designed with Anglo-Saxon ornamentation. There are also two of the four surviving copies of the Magna Carta, King John's charter issued in 1215 to enshrine his agreement with his barons, as well as an almost contemporary copy of the Venerable Bede's *Ecclesiastical History*. The Codex Sinaiticus, from the mid-4th century, and the Codex Alexandrinus, from the first half of the 5th century, are two of the three earliest and most important manuscripts of the Bible. Other works include the autographs of many major literary figures, royal monograms, an early English manuscript of *Beowulf* and Nelson's last letter to Lady Hamilton. The **Crawford Room** is used for special exhibitions.

The **King's Library**, the first part of the present museum buildings, was completed in 1827 in order to house George III's library. On display at the south end of the gallery are fine examples of books, manuscripts and scrolls from the Orient, Africa and Europe. The history of writing and its associated materials, both Eastern and Western, is comprehensively documented. Examples of bookbinding from the 16th century to the present day adorn the centre of the gallery. A case of documents relating to Shakespeare shows a document bearing his signature as well as a copy of *First Folio*, the first collected edition of his plays printed in 1623.

The north part of the gallery concentrates on the history of the book and its importance in the spread of knowledge. Treasures include the Diamond Sutra of 868, the first dated example of printing found in a cave in northern China, and the Gutenberg Bible (1455), the first book printed from movable metal type. Early printing in England is represented by the work of William Caxton and Wynkyn de Worde. There are also musical works and children's books, which range from classic editions of Hans Christian Andersen's tales to the *Beano* comic. Also on view is a large selection from the library's extensive philatelic collection, including a Penny Black of 1840 and the very rare 1847 Post Office issues of Mauritius.

A changing selection of themed exhibits from the Map Library, one of the world's most important cartographic collections, is displayed in the **Map Gallery**.

The British Library's famous high domed **Reading Room**, which contains more than a million books, can be visited without a reader's pass. Attendants conduct groups, on the hour from Monday to Saturday between 11 a.m. and 4 p.m., from an assembly point at the door on the north side of the hall. However, a reader's pass, or prior application, is required to use the Music Library, whose magnificent collection of more than 11 million pieces of printed music spans the 16th century to today; the Official Publications Library, the principal reading room for holdings of British and foreign official publications; the Department of Manuscripts; and the Philatelic Collection, which holds more than 6 million items.

The British Library gives regular gallery talks and slide lectures, and also publishes a wide range of illustrated books and catalogues relating to its collections. Work has begun on a new library building near St Pancras Station, which is due to open in the early 1990s.

Return to Tottenham Court Road ⊖. Charing Cross Road, which stretches south from the junction with Oxford Street, New Oxford Street and Tottenham Court Road, is lined with dozens of bookshops. **Collets International Bookshop (3)** at Nos. 129–31, contains excellent general and children's sections on its ground floor, a specialist Russian and Slavonic section upstairs, and titles concerning politics and social sciences in the basement. Further to the south, at No. 64, is the Colletts Penguin Bookshop. Opposite the international bookshop is Denmark Street, or 'Tin Pan Alley', which houses shops selling musical instruments and the offices of several music publishers, as well as science fiction bookshop Forbidden Planet.

Foyle's (4), at Nos. 113–19 Charing Cross Road, claims to stock around 6 million titles on its shelves. The shop's labyrinthine, and somewhat haphazard, layout over five floors can make locating a particular book a little trying for the customer. The cookery department is exceptional. Foyle's began in 1904 when William and Gilbert Foyle, after failing the Civil Service entrance examinations, decided to advertise their unwanted textbooks for sale. Initially, they traded from home, acquiring premises in Charing Cross Road two years later. The business has remained in the family.

South along Charing Cross Road is Cambridge Circus, dominated by the Palace Theatre, which opened as Richard D'Oyly Carte's Royal English Opera House in 1891. In modern times it has staged highly successful musicals, notably *The Sound of Music* (1961–7) and *Jesus Christ Superstar*, Britain's longest-running musical. Andrew Lloyd Webber, composer of *Jesus Christ Superstar*, bought the theatre in 1983 to ensure its future as a venue for major musicals, a 'palace of music', and has had its red-brick and terracotta façade restored.

Zwemmer (5) has three bookshops in the section of Charing Cross Road south of Cambridge Circus. This family firm is best known for art books. No. 80 specializes in photography, cinema and graphic design. Zwemmer's impressive art and architecture sections have expanded across the road into No. 24 Litchfield Street, and the firm's Oxford University Press Bookshop, which stocks leading publications of academic and educational interest, is further south at No. 72 Charing Cross Road.

At Nos. 5 and 8 Great Newport Street, leading off the east side of Charing Cross Road, is the **Photographers' Gallery (6)**, a non-profit-making organization providing a permanent showcase for a wide variety of works by professional photographers from Britain and abroad. The gallery's Tom Hopkinson and Bill Brandt Rooms display internationally known or specifically commissioned exhibitions. The Portfolio Room is reserved for exhibitions selected from the portfolios of young or unknown photographers. The gallery's specialist shop has new, out-of-print and rare books on both the technical and artistic aspects of photography. Its reference library contains around 1,500 books and thousands of slides covering the full range of the photographic medium.

Running parallel and to the east of the southern part of Charing Cross Road is St Martin's Lane. Connecting the two thoroughfares are St Martin's Court and Cecil Court. Among the small shops, gas lamps and stage doors of St Martin's Court is **Sheekey's (7)**, perhaps London's oldest fish restaurant. Behind its long mirrored oyster bar and Art Deco tiles, oysters have been opened and prepared since 1896. Motor Books, at Nos. 33 and 36 St Martin's Court, stocks car workshop manuals, military, naval and aviation books; and railway titles.

Cecil Court is lined with antiquarian and second-hand bookshops. Stage Door Prints, at No. 1, specializes in prints on ballet, opera and the theatre; Dance Books, at No. 9, covers human movement and anatomy from ballet to ballroom; music books are the expertise of Travis and Emery, at No. 17; the Victorian ephemera of Pleasure of Past Times, at No. 11, include many works on entertainment; for 'seekers' there is Watkins Books, at Nos. 19–21, dealing in the mystical, the occult and oriental religions; Robert Chris, at No. 8, specializes in alternative medicine and health; and Alan Brett, at No. 24, holds works on topography and cartography.

The **Albery Theatre (8)** in St Martin's Lane was the venue for Noel Coward's first play. At the **Duke of York's (9)** Puccini saw a one-act play called *Madame Butterfly*, which he later transformed into his famous opera. The **London Coliseum (10)**, home of the English National Opera, is on the east side of St Martin's Lane. All operas here are sung in English. New Row is dotted with interesting shops, including Arthur Middleton Ltd – Antique Scientific Instruments, its windows a glinting miscellany of brass apparatus. Goodwin's Court is a charming alley of bow-windowed Regency houses.

Leicester Square (11) today is the heart of movieland London. Its cavernous cinemas have superseded the music halls of yesteryear, but have kept alive the square's tradition of entertainment on a grand scale. Many movie blockbusters are given their British première on the huge screens of the Empire, the Odeon and the Leicester Square Theatre. Pedestrianization has acted as a magnet for visitors.

In the 18th century the square was a fashionable residence. In its central garden stands a monument to Shakespeare as well as busts of some illustrious former local residents. Painters Hogarth and Reynolds, surgeon John Hunter, scientist Sir Isaac Newton all once lived in or nearby the square, and are now commemorated in sculpture. In 1981 a bronze statue of Charlie Chaplin, portrayed in his characteristic costume with bowler hat and walking stick, was unveiled in the south-west corner of the square.

The Swiss Centre was erected in the north-west corner of the square in 1963. It houses many Swiss companies, Swiss restaurants and a coffee shop as well as the Swiss Fair shops. Opposite, outside the north-west corner of the central garden, the distances from London to other Commonwealth cities are set into the pavement.

On the west side of the square the Society of West End Theatres operates a half-price ticket booth. Tickets are available only on the day of performance, after 12.30 p.m. for matinees, and after 2.30 p.m. for evening performances. On the north side of the square, in Leicester Place, the French church Notre-Dame de France, which was burned in 1940, has been nearly completely rebuilt. Its interior contains a mural by Jean Cocteau and over the altar is an Aubusson tapestry, also designed by Cocteau.

To the north of Leicester Square, centred around Lisle Street, Gerrard Street and part of Wardour Street, is London's **China-town (12)**. Chinese-style gateways at the entrances to the Gerrard Street pedestrian scheme are decorated with traditional ethnic lattice patterns of the 18th and 19th centuries and incorporate, in elegant ironwork, the Chinese characters for welcome or greeting. The colour scheme is predominantly red, a happy colour for the Chinese.

The emphasis in Chinatown is on food and eating. Gerrard Street is populated by Chinese supermarkets as well as some of the best Cantonese restaurants outside South-east Asia. At lunch, *dim sum*, a plethora of small delicious dishes steamed and served in bamboo baskets, is offered at New Loon Fung restaurant in Gerrard Street. Mr Kong, at No. 21 Lisle Street, is considered by many to be the best Cantonese restaurant in Chinatown. Head-chef Mr Kong's steamed scallops are renowned as an appetizer. Chinatown's restaurants also offer Peking, Shanghai and Szechuan dishes and there are Chinese cake shops selling a variety of baked delicacies, whose fillings range from bean paste to lotus seeds. There are also shops supplying martial arts equipment, acupuncturists and herbalists and, in the Chinese Community Healthcare Centre at the Gerrard Street clinic, there is also an expert on geomancy, or *foongsui*, a form of Chinese fortune telling.

The lavish festivities of the Chinese New Year take place in late January or early February. The highlight of these carnival-style street celebrations is the dragon dance (the dragons are, in fact, lions). Bright red packets of 'good luck' money, or *hung pao*, dangling outside restaurants and shops are snatched by the dragons as they twist and turn their way through the crowded streets.

Shaftesbury Avenue, the heart of theatreland, runs to the north of Chinatown and celebrated its centenary in the 1980s. At its southern end are four of London's top theatres. The avenue's oldest survivor is the **Lyric (13)**, which dates from 1888. The **Apollo (14)**, named after the Greek god of music, was originally intended to stage musicals. The **Globe (15)** is noted for its quality comedies; in 1927 a sensation was created here when an actor first appeared on stage in pyjamas. In the 1930s John Gielgud played his renowned Hamlet at the **Queen's (16)**.

Soho mainly to the north of Shaftesbury Avenue, is infamous as the red-light district of central London. In the late 17th century, however, the area had many aristocratic residents, but by the 1770s it fell from favour as the nobility moved west to fashionable Mayfair. There followed an influx of Huguenot refugees skilled in lace-making, optics and jewellery. They were followed by Italian musical instrument makers, Jewish tailors and, finally, Chinese immigrants. Today its red-light reputation is less well deserved, and it is one of the best areas in London to go shopping for food. Salamis hang like stalactites in its delicatessens, and small shops, pubs and continental restaurants nestle between the offices of the advertising, film and ancillary industries.

St Anne's Church, Soho, (17) lies at the southern end of

Wardour Street. The original church, dedicated in honour of Queen Anne, was built towards the end of the 17th century to the designs of either Sir Christopher Wren or his pupil William Talman. All that remains today of this earlier construction is the replacement tower and steeple built by Samuel Pepys Cockerell in 1803 and now inhabited by the Soho Society. The rest of the church was destroyed by bombing in 1940. The steeple terminates in two intersecting barrels, which have a clock face on either side. A plaque commemorates author Dorothy L. Sayers, whose ashes are buried beneath the tower.

Parallel to Wardour Street on the west side is Berwick Street, home of the daily **Berwick Street Market (18)**. Barrow boys and stall-holders shout their wares, mainly fruit and vegetable, particularly exotic varieties. Kopelvitch's famous lace shop is at No. 84.

A kerbstone slightly larger than its neighbours and formed of red granite in adjacent Broadwick Street marks the site that triggered one of Britain's most important medical discoveries. During 1845 a chlorea epidemic swept through the Parish of St James in Soho. By the careful mapping of its victims, local doctor John Snow observed that a local pump that supplied clean 'sweet' water was the epidemic's source. Sweeping aside contemporary medical wisdom that cholera was carried in a miasma – an invisible cloud floating in the air – Snow persuaded the parish elders to immobilize the pump by removing its handle. This was done and the epidemic subsided. The red granite kerbstone marks the spot where the pump once stood. Snow's methodology, by looking at the disease's pattern of occurrence not just its symptoms, gave birth to a new form of medical research, now called epidemiology. The pub nearby is named the John Snow.

Old Compton Street (19) runs east from Wardour Street. In the 1950s it was fashionably bohemian and appealed to the likes of Francis Bacon, Augustus John, Brendan Behan and Colin MacInnes. During the skiffle era, its 2Is coffee bar developed a loyal hip following, including Cliff Richard and Tommy Steele, and has now entered British rocklore. Today Old Compton Street's inhabitants include Moroni's, at No. 68, stocking newspapers and magazines from all round the world; Patisserie Valerie, at No. 44, known for its pastries; the chic Soho Brasserie at Nos. 23–5; and near by, at Nos. 19–21, is a Wheeler's fish restaurant, which opened in 1856.

In Frith Street, on the north side of Old Compton Street, is
Ronnie Scott's famous jazz club. On the corner of Greek Street
is the Prince Edward Theatre, where the hit musical *Evita*
opened in 1978. L'Escargot restaurant, at No. 48 Greek Street,
was opened by Georges Gaudin at the beginning of the century,
and his motto 'Slow but sure' can be seen outside the premises
beneath a representation of him riding a snail. In Dean Street,
Gaston Berlemont, Soho's longest-serving landlord, has kept
the French pub unchanged for forty years, and the neighbouring
Groucho Club caters for the media and books business. It took
its name from Groucho Marx's one-liner that he wouldn't want
to join any club that would have him as a member.

The **House of St Barnabas-in-Soho (20)** (Joseph Pearce, 1746),
a fine Georgian mansion standing on the corner of Soho Square
at No. 1 Greek Street, was once the home of wealthy MP and
City Alderman Richard Beckford. It is the last remaining house
preserving the decorations of 18th-century Soho Square. Since
1862 it has been a charitable institution for distressed women in
London. Its interior is rich in woodcarving and decorative
plasterwork, particularly around the principal staircase and in
the Council Chamber ceiling, which, with its many cherubs, is
one of the finest examples of the English rococo style of the
1750s. Another interesting feature is the 'crinoline' staircase,
built with bowed wrought-iron banister rails designed especially to accommodate the breadth of ladies' fashionable
hooped petticoats popular during the period.

Across Soho Square to the north, Soho Street emerges on
to the eastern end of **Oxford Street (21)** (for Oxford Street
west, see *Marble Arch* ⊖). Tottenham Court Road ⊖ is at the
easternmost point of Oxford Street.

Oxford Circus ⊖ & Piccadilly Circus ⊖

London's two most famous shopping streets, Oxford Street and Regent Street, cross each other at Oxford Circus. The circus is one of two built along John Nash's grand triumphal way, a route that was to allow the Prince Regent, later George IV, to drive north from his Carlton House mansion in Pall Mall past Piccadilly Circus, Nash's second circus, to Portland Place and finally to the newly created Regent's Park. Nash's New Street, now Regent Street, was to be the first of a series of urban improvements enabling London to lose its provincial image and rival other European capitals. Circuses were built to ease the intersections with Oxford Street and Piccadilly, providing the street with a visual continuity.

This desire for visual continuity also gave rise to one of London's most distinctive churches. All Souls in Langham Place, Nash's only surviving church, was designed with the unusual combination of a curved portico and sharp pointed spire. Nash adopted this design after local residents forced a detour in his grand throughfare. His solution to the problem enabled All Souls to look the same whatever the angle viewed, thereby gently drawing the eye through the curve and into Portland Place to the north. The sweeping curve of Regent Street between the circuses, known as the Quadrant, was designed to house many small shops behind a colonnade. Such was its commercial success, however, that nearly all Nash's façades have since been demolished to accommodate larger premises. Nevertheless, the street retains a calm and dignified air.

Today the landmark of Regent Street is undoubtedly Liberty and Co., famed for its fine fabrics, carpets, antiques and fashion. Women from all over the world come here to purchase the store's distinctive Liberty-print scarves. The street houses many other fashionable shops, including Laura Ashley, a name that has become synonymous with the most English of English design; Garrard's, the Crown jewellers; Aquascutum, whose trenchcoats are now a classic interpretation of the English gentleman look; and Hamleys, the largest toyshop in the world.

Nash's wide thoroughfare was also designed to divide aristocratic Mayfair, on its west, from the poorer quarters of Soho to the east. The divide is epitomized today by two streets that run

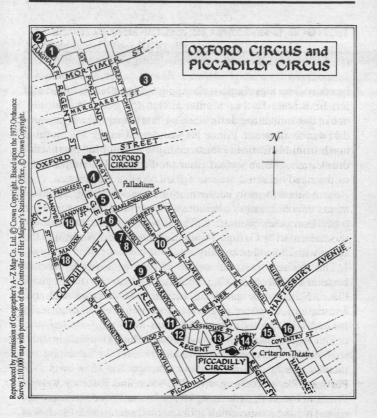

parallel on either side of Regent Street. On the Soho side, the heart of the swinging and psychedelic Sixties was located in Carnaby Street, whose shops once overflowed with outrageous floral fashions. By contrast, on the Mayfair side, Savile Row has housed the finest and most conservative gentlemen's bespoke tailoring in London, since the middle of the 19th century.

At the southern end of Regent Street is Piccadilly Circus, now a vortex of traffic, illuminated at night by large neon lights. Here Nash's scheme has been entirely swept away. The famous figure of Eros, London's first sculpture in aluminium, stands at its centre. On the east side of the circus is the Trocadero, a new development containing the Guinness World of Records, the London Experience and the Light Fantastic audio-visual experiences.

⊖   ⊖   ⊖

The view northward from Oxford Circus along Regent Street is dominated by the tall fluted steeple of **All Souls, Langham Place (1)**. Its unique silhouette, a circular portico of tall Ionic pillars surmounted by a spire set on a ring of columns, combines a typically Greek peristyle with a spire. The latter feature could not have been further removed from the classical tradition. When it was built the design caused outrage and questions were asked in Parliament. All Souls was described as 'a deplorable and horrible object and a disgrace to the metropolis', 'a great flat candlestick with an extinguisher on it'. Nash was subjected to ridicule and was caricatured impaled on his sharp spire.

All Souls is the only surviving church by John Nash, architect of so many of London's buildings. Faced in Bath stone, it has a traditional galleried interior. The altarpiece by Richard Westall was presented by George I V. During the Second World War the church was damaged by bombing, but has since been restored. In the 1970s it was modernized to provide a new undercroft containing a meeting hall, refectory and studio broadcast facilities. Building work revealed Nash's unusual inverted brick arch foundations. The Morning Service on B B C Radio 4 is normally broadcast live each day from All Souls.

The B B C acquired the site of **Broadcasting House (2)** in order to build new, enlarged headquarters after broadcasting expanded rapidly during the 1920s. Designed in 1931 by G. Val Mayer to be in keeping with the Adam and Regency style of Portland Place, Broadcasting House has continued to house the offices of the corporation's Director-General and the board room of its Governors. Although the building's gleaming oblong exterior of white Portland stone was camouflaged with grey paint during the Second World War, it still suffered bomb damage, but, despite an explosion in the heart of the building one night in 1940, the corporation continued to broadcast the news. Above the main entrance of Broadcasting House is Eric Gill's sculpture of Prospero sending Ariel out into the world, symbolizing broadcasting.

Returning towards Oxford Circus, a short detour along Margaret Street leads to **All Saints, Margaret Street (3)**. William Butterfield's design (1859) is the epitome of High Victorian Gothic and an outspoken example of the revival with its dense use of colour, ornamentation and contrasting textures. The church's uniquely 19th-century style employed red and black brickwork in an unprecedented fashion. The exterior is a fore-taste of its highly animated interior, in which every surface clamours with a multitude of hues of granite, marble, alabaster and a kaleidoscope of tiles.

At the east end of Margaret Street, Wells Street leads south to Oxford Street. Located to the west, between Oxford Street and Oxford Circus, are many of London's popular chain stores, particularly those selling shoes and clothes. Slightly to the east of Oxford Circus, Argyll Street leads to the south and is the home of the **London Palladium**, a popular venue for shows and musicals, including the Royal Variety Performance. The Palladium is the largest theatre in London apart from the Coliseum in St Martin's Lane. In the theatrical profession it is said that you're not really a star until you've played the Palladium.

Regent Street is known throughout the world as one of London's premier shopping streets. Although its shops once rivalled – even eclipsed – those of Bond Street in exclusivity, today the position has changed. The stores lining this broad thoroughfare sell goods whose quality and price exceed that of Oxford Street, but they do not now match those of Bond Street or Jermyn Street.

Most of Nash's buildings have gone, their downfall probably brought about by the street's commercial success in the 19th century. Towards the end of that century Regent Street's clientele began to change, the wealthy Victorian middle classes taking over from the aristocracy as its main customers. To maintain the same returns, the volume of business had to increase, necessitating larger premises. Nash's colonnades restricted such expansion and so, at the beginning of this century, many of his buildings were demolished. Their replacements have more functional frontages, but have retained the street's calm dignity.

Laura Ashley (4) has two shops in Regent Street. Laura Ashley's fashion and furnishing fabrics have captured a traditional, timeless quality and been one of the retailing success stories of the post-war era. Its premises at No. 256–8, Regent Street specialize in interior design and further south, at No. 208, is the store's outlet for fashion.

Mr Dickins began business in Oxford Street in 1790, moving to Regent Street in 1835. In the 1890s the business was joined by Mr Jones. The **Dickins and Jones (5)** department store, which has stood on its present site at No. 224 Regent Street since 1919, comprises around twenty-five fashion shops, each representing established and emerging designer names. It caters for both sexes in everything from high fashion to formal evening wear.

Liberty and Co. (6) is undoubtedly the shopping landmark of Regent Street. The store's scarves are famed for their unique prints, and worn by women all over the world. Each year Liberty produces a new collection of around fifty designs in silks, cotton and wool.

Arthur Lasenby Liberty, the store's founder, told his artist and designer friends that he would transform fashions in dress and interior decoration. Such was his impact that Liberty became a virtual impresario of the decorative arts not long after the store was established in 1875 at No. 218A Regent Street. His 'Liberty colours', delicate pastel tints of blue, green, yellow, gold and coral, became an influential element in the Aesthetic Movement. The fabrics, delicate Indian silks, which he imported from the East, were favoured by the Pre-Raphaelite painters for the way they would drape on models. His customers included Rossetti, Burne-Jones and Whistler, and by 1888 Liberty himself was participating in their Arts and Crafts Society. Later, Liberty popularized Art Nouveau in England to such a degree that the Italians named it '*Stile* Liberty'. The store remains at the forefront of design, known not just for its flower prints, but also for avant-garde geometrics and abstracts.

At the International Exhibition held in Kensington in 1862 Liberty became fascinated with the East, notably Japan. Initially, his store sold ornaments and *objets d'art* from the East, but Liberty soon expanded it to incorporate fabrics, oriental carpets and china. Today, Liberty's buyers continue to visit the Orient to purchase jewellery, ornaments and carpets, and the store is full of unusual and exotic Eastern merchandise. Liberty's Oriental Department sells fine hand-worked pieces, silks, saris, old china and antique ornaments and a wide selection of caftans and djellabahs. Baskets, cane-work, lacquer trays, toys and fans are to be found in the Eastern Bazaar.

Liberty moved to its present site during the 1920s. Its concave, columned Regent Street frontage is surmounted by a 115-ft/ 35-m frieze portraying Liberty's links with the Orient. Treasures from far-off lands, borne by camel, elephant and ship, are seen sailing towards a statue of Britannia. The store's northern façade, in Great Marlborough Street, was built in Tudor style with wood from the timber of two men-of-war, HMS *Impregnable* and HMS *Hindustan*, and is adorned with a clock depicting St George and the Dragon. On the hour the two characters emerge to continue battle.

The **Jaeger (7)** shop at No. 204 Regent Street sells an established line of elegant and well-made clothing. Although Jaeger's clothes may be more sober than many of their more fashion conscious counterparts, their classic and exclusive designs are aimed to ensure a look that lasts.

According to the *Guinness Book of Records*, **Hamleys (8)**, at Nos. 188–196 Regent Street, is the biggest toy shop in the world, with ten floors of toys, games, sports, crafts, books, magic and everything else to delight the young at heart. William Hamley's first toy shop was opened in 1760 in High Holborn. Hamleys today resembles a giant playroom, alive with demonstrations of computer games, radio-controlled vehicles, robots, wind-up toys and video-screens advertising the latest crazes. Traditional dolls and teddy bears are, of course, still supplied.

Mappin and Webb (9), at No. 170 Regent Street, are known for silver plate as well as their reproductions of classic designs and their own more modern designs. Jonathan Mappin began his business as a silversmith in Sheffield in the second half of the 18th century and quickly made a name for himself. His heirs expanded to London during the 19th century. John Newton Mappin was joined by George Webb to form a partnership that has now become a household name in jewellery and fine silverware.

The psychedelic paving stones of **Carnaby Street (10)** were once walked by trendsetting mini-skirted girls with beehive hairdos, the embodiment of the Swinging Sixties. Such was its reputation for the outrageous and brash clothing found in its boutiques that the street gained an entry in the *Oxford English Dictionary*: 'Carnaby Street *n* (usu. *attrib.*) fashionable clothing for young people'. Carnaby Street also gave the word 'boutique' its popular currency. Some 'way out' trends can still be found here, but today this pedestrianized street has a more sophisticated cosmopolitan impact. One of its long-standing businesses is Inderwick's, the tobacconist. Founded in Wardour Street in 1797, John Inderwick started the fashion for Meerschaum pipes. Its near neighbour is Mary Quant, the epitome of the Swinging Sixties, with her Colour Shop.

Garrard (11), at No. 112 Regent Street, are Crown jewellers and suppliers of fine quality silverware. Not surprisingly, prices are high but any item purchased here will undoubtedly last generations. Annually, in February, Garrard is employed to clean the Crown Jewels in the Tower of London.

Like Burberry, the name **Aquascutum (12)** has become synonymous with fine quality raincoats, its name formed from two Latin words meaning 'water' and 'shield'. Since the middle of the 19th century officers and gentlemen have been protected from the rigours of the British and other climates by Aquascutum. Even royalty, in the form of King Edward VII, helped popularize the company's rainwear, but the best advertisement for Aquascutum took place in 1953, when Sir Edmund Hillary and Sherpa Tensing, wearing jackets and trousers made of its special wool fabric, hoisted the British flag at the summit of Mount Everest. Acquascutum's trenchcoats are now a classic interpretation of the English gentleman look.

Daniel Nicols, a bankrupt French wine merchant, fled Paris and opened the Café Restaurant Nicols in Glasshouse Street in 1865. Two years later he expanded his restaurant into No. 68, Regent Street, where it remains today. The 1890s made the **Café Royal (13)** famous. Artists and writers flocked here to enjoy the benefits of one of the finest wine cellars in Europe. The artist Whistler signed his bills with a butterfly mark. Oscar Wilde was a leader of Café Royal society. Epstein, Sickert, Shaw, Augustus John, Beardsley and Max Beerbohm were regularly seen here, and so, too, in the early days of the 20th century, were two future kings, Edward VIII and George VI.

During the 1920s this section of Regent Street, known as the Quadrant, was entirely rebuilt. 'They might as well have told us that the British Empire is to be pulled down and redecorated,' wrote the dismayed poet Crosland. J. B. Priestley, T. S. Eliot and Compton Mackenzie continued the Café Royal's Bohemian reputation into the 1930s. After the Second World War, a decline ensued, but the Café Royal has flourished again under the direction of Sir Charles Forte, of the Trust House Forte empire. Today the famous Le Relais Restaurant is a brasserie, called Nicols, after the Café Royal's founder. The refurbished Grill Room preserves some of the elegant Edwardian atmosphere of its predecessor. The gilt caryatids and mirror were retained from the original restaurant, a room Cecil Beaton was once moved to describe as 'the most beautiful room in London'.

Piccadilly Circus (14) is one of London's major focal points and was once thought of as the 'hub of the Empire'. Nash laid out Regent's Circus South, as it was then called, in 1819, but the arrival of Shaftesbury Avenue during the 1880s reduced the circus to an ill-shaped vortex of converging streets. By 1923, with the arrival of gigantic illuminated advertisements, Nash's elegant circus had become a gaudy mixture of disparate elements. Although the question of the redevelopment of Piccadilly Circus has been something of a national hobby for over 100 years, it has only been resolved recently. The façades of its existing buildings are being preserved, and an underground warren of subways excavated. A paved piazza has been built surrounding the statue of Eros, a redeeming feature of the circus. Albert Gilbert's now refurbished statue, the capital's first to be cast in aluminium, was intended to represent the angel of Christian charity, not the Greek god of love. On the west side of Piccadilly Circus, behind the façade of Sir Reginald Blomfield's French-baroque style building of the 1920s, once the famous Swan and Edgar department store, is the Centre at the Circus, a shopping precinct and record superstore. The south side of Piccadilly Circus is distinguished by the French Renaissance style façade of the Criterion Theatre. Its exotic neo-Byzantine Marble Hall, built in 1874, has been restored to something of its original glory as the Criterion Brasserie, complete with marble walls inlaid with mosaics of semi-precious stones and a gold mosaic ceiling. Opposite the Criterion is the London Pavilion.

During the 1920s the **London Pavilion (15)** – 'the good old Pav' – became famous for staging reviews by Noel Coward and C. B. Cochran. Converted to a cinema in 1934, it remained in business continuously until 1981, closing for only one month during the Blitz. It re-opened in 1988 as the capital's latest retail and leisure complex. Behind its elegant façade, retained from the Pavilion of 1886, the developers have constructed three levels of shops, an American diner restaurant and Rock Circus – a new Madame Tussaud's venture with fifty wax figures depicting rock and pop music since Bill Haley and the Comets 'Rocked around the Clock' in 1955. Here, aided by audio animatronic techniques, the latest lighting and a unique personal stereo sound system, the Beatles are brought together to 'perform' again.

The Trocadero (16), a shopping, restaurant and entertainment centre that opened in 1984, houses the Guinness World of

Records, the London Experience and Light Fantastic. In the Guinness World of Records models, videos and electronic displays bring to life the more dramatic records found in the *Guinness Book of Records*. The display is divided into six 'worlds' – human, animal, sports, entertainment, our planet Earth, and structures and machines. In the human world, visitors can compare their weight with that of one of the world's heaviest men and watch the world's population increasing on a digital display at the remarkable rate of 161.6 people per minute.

The London Experience, a 30-minute multi-screen audio-visual show, features the history, sights and sounds of London from Roman times to the present day. It invites the visitor to share in the horror of the Plague and the Great Fire, as well as the hunt for Jack the Ripper and the devastation of war-torn London.

Light Fantastic is described as the world centre of holography. Its 8,000 sq ft/743 sq m contain some of the world's finest holograms, plus displays about their applications in industry, medicine and science.

The Trocadero began its history in the 1740s as a tennis court. In succeeding years it became a circus, a theatre, a music hall and a venue for exhibitions and entertainments, although it was probably best known as the most luxurious of the Lyons Corner Houses. Today's Trocadero is built around an 80-ft/24-m atrium, enhanced with trees, shrubs and a waterfall. Its three floors are linked by marble walkways and escalators. The ground floor contains thirty shop units, including the Piccadilly General Store, a traditional market recreated with original costermonger barrows, street lamps and period advertising posters. The lower floor accommodates Food Street, a re-creation of a Far Eastern market place with restaurants serving Singaporean, Japanese, Thai and Malaysian cuisine.

Piccadilly stretches west from Piccadilly Circus for nearly 1 mile/1.6 km to Hyde Park Corner. Despite its fame, Piccadilly retains few buildings of historical merit, with the exception of Wren's St James's Church (*St James's Park* ⊖); Burlington House, the home of the Royal Academy of Arts (*Bond Street* ⊖); and, at some distance west past Fortnum and Mason (*St James's Park* ⊖), the luxurious Ritz Hotel. Most frontages are now taken over by airline offices and travel bureaux.

Returning across Piccadilly Circus and along Regent Street, opposite Aquascutum and Garrard, Vigo Street leads west towards **Savile Row (17)**. Since the middle of the 19th century Savile Row has housed the finest gentlemen's bespoke tailors in London. A made-to-measure suit purchased in Savile Row may cost more than £500, but it will last a lifetime. The street's best-known tailors are Gieves and Hawkes at No. 1. Originally the company was two separate firms founded, respectively, in 1785 and 1771. They came together in the 1970s, combining a wealth of outfitting experience under the roof of their beautiful 18th-century premises.

Gieves began business in Portsmouth as a naval outfitter. Admiral Lord Nelson was an early customer. The Duke of Wellington and other distinguished customers had their clothes made by Hawkes. After the Crimean War Gieves expanded its business, supplying officers with all their needs wherever they were, thereby ensuring that customers when cadets would remain customers when admirals. Gieves began providing sea chests, life-saving waistcoats, as well as the booklet *Customs and Etiquette of the Royal Navy*, now in its sixth edition. During the Second World War the 'man who never was' wore a shirt made by Gieves. The fictitious Major Martin of the Royal Marines, whose body was washed up in Spain carrying Allied invasion 'secrets', wore the garment as just one small detail making up this grand deception. However, the man who devised the plan, Ewen Montagu, considered the acquisition 'the only real brick we dropped': a bill for the transaction had been left in the pocket. It was 'unthinkable' for a gentleman to pay cash at Gieves.

Henry Poole, at No. 15 Savile Row, feels like a London club, with its leather library chairs and quiet gentlemanly atmosphere. The original Henry Poole, one of the largest and finest tailors of his day, was immortalized by Disraeli in his novel *Endymion*.

The customer at H Huntsman and Son, No. 11, is measured first by the coat fitter for the coat, then by the trouser fitter before the respective patterns are cut.

Tommy Nutter, at Nos. 18–19, is the most stylish of Savile Row's bespoke tailors. The shop has a waistcoat gallery displaying as art the fine materials from which waistcoats can be made.

At lunch-time on 30 January 1969, the Beatles gave their final public performance from the rooftop of No. 3 Savile Row, then the headquarters of their record company, Apple. Occupants of the street, unaccustomed to such goings-on, called the police to stop the 'noise'.

St George, Hanover Square (18), located near Hanover Square at the corner of St George Street and Maddox Street, was the first church in London to have a portico. John James's handsome Corinthian portico proved popular and was followed quickly by St Martin-in-the-Fields (*Embankment* ⊖) and St George's, Bloomsbury (*Tottenham Court Road* ⊖), all built under the Fifty New Churches Act of 1711. St George's most famous parishioner was composer George Frideric Handel, who lived in nearby Brook Street. During the 19th century St George's became a fashionable church for weddings. Shelley was married here in 1814, Disraeli in 1839, George Eliot (Mary Evans Lewis) in 1880, Asquith in 1894 and John Buchan in 1907. Theodore Roosevelt, a president of the United States, was also married here in 1886.

The **London Diamond Centre (19)**, with its large collection of precious and semi-precious stones, houses an exhibition that shows the transformation of diamonds from the mine, through cutting, sawing and shaping to final faceting and polishing. The centre's resident goldsmith can also be seen mounting and setting gems in rings. For a small charge, experts will value stones, and there is much jewellery for sale.

Bond Street ⊖

For 250 years Mayfair has been London's most exclusive area, and for the wealthiest and most fashionable people, Bond Street, Mayfair's principal street, remains first and foremost a shopping place for beautiful, rare and expensive things. Its international fame for providing all the accessories of gracious living – elegant fashions, gold, precious jewels, antiques, works of art – was established in the 18th and 19th centuries. Many of its shops continue to enjoy royal patronage.

Mayfair is bounded on the north by Oxford Street, on the east by Regent Street, on the south by Piccadilly and on the west by Park Lane. The area derived its name from the notorious May fair held in the 17th and early 18th centuries in what is now Shepherd Market. The development of Mayfair began in the 1660s in the south-east corner near Piccadilly Circus, spreading west, then north. By the mid-18th century Mayfair was covered with the houses of the aristocracy, who had moved westwards from previously fashionable Covent Garden and Soho. Its numerous mews streets, once inhabited by domestic servants, artisans and small fashionable shops, are a legacy of the aristocracy's need to have services close at hand.

Bond Street was a favourite haunt of the fashionable man-about-town during the Georgian and Regency eras. The likes of George (Beau) Brummell and other Regency dandies kept tailors and hatters busy with their refined sartorial requirements for garments such as hand-made embroidered coats and waistcoats, narrow trousers and accessories.

In the Victorian era Bond Street began to lose its residential status, but maintained a leading position in the world of fashion. Its shops displayed an ever-increasing range of exotic merchandise drawn from Britain's expanding colonial possessions. During Victoria's reign Bond Street also rose to prominence in the art world. Sotheby's, the world's most famous and largest auctioneers, is still based here.

Today many new international arrivals, such as Tiffany's of New York, Giorgio Armani and Emanuel Ungaro, have joined older established firms such as Asprey's and Tessiers.

The Mayfair area has retained much of its well-bred Georgian air and social cachet, although it now houses the headquarters of

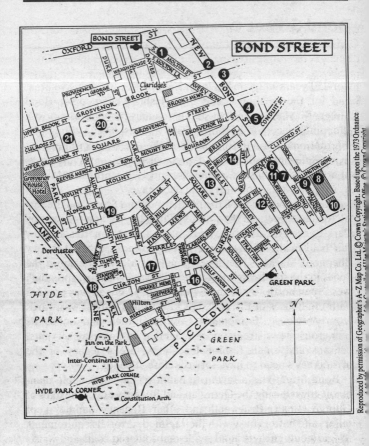

banks, advertising agencies, exclusive shops and international hotels. The Museum of Mankind, whose superb collection forms one of the world's greatest assemblies of the art and artefacts of tribal societies, is based in Mayfair, as is the Royal Academy of Art, which holds its world-famous Summer Exhibition of paintings each year.

❖ ❖ ❖

On the south side of Oxford Street, South Molton Street lies immediately to the east adjoining the northern end of Davies Street. The beau monde of Mayfair is immediately apparent on entering the **South Molton Street (1)** pedestrian precinct. Its chic fashion and jewellery shops and continental-style pavement cafés contrast sharply with Oxford Street's giant chain stores. One of its best-known fashion shops is Brown's, at Nos. 23–7, a designer emporium stocking international designer names, with prices to match. Ebony, at No. 45, sells imaginative and flamboyant garments. Opposite the south end of South Molton Street is No. 25 Brook Street, the home of George Frideric Handel for thirty-four years until his death in 1759. It is one of only two properties surviving from the original early 18th-century Brook Street development. Claridge's, one of London's most famous hotels-de-luxe, is also in Brook Street. At its east end, Brook Street leads into New Bond Street.

Bond Street's (2) fame as the 'high street of Mayfair' has evolved over the last three centuries. It was fashionable for members of Georgian society to be seen promenading its length, exhibiting their finery and enjoying the window displays. The street was built in two stages. The southern part, Old Bond Street, was developed in the 1680s by Sir Thomas Bond, and the longer northerly extension, New Bond Street, was laid out in the 1720s. Bond Street has never been noted particularly for architectural merit, but it quickly became famous for luxury shopping. Its residents have included novelist and famous Bow Street magistrate Henry Fielding, historian Edward Gibbon, writers Jonathan Swift and Laurence Sterne, as well as Admiral Lord Nelson. Today traditional firms and more recent arrivals seek to preserve the street's distinctive atmosphere: its sense of taste, quality, beauty and courteous service accompanied by the highest prices.

Fenwicks (3), at the junction with Brook Street, is a small department store specializing in women's clothes. Next door is Smythson's, stationers to the Queen. Further south, at Nos. 34–5 is **Sotheby's (4)**. This firm of fine-art auctioneers and valuers was established in 1744 and for many years concentrated on the book trade, handling the great libraries of Talleyrand and Napoleon. In 1917, when Sotheby's moved to Bond Street, it began to seriously challenge Christie's (*St James's Park* ⊖) in the art business. Behind its modest façade, Sotheby's is now the most powerful fine-art auction house in the world, with an annual international sales turnover running to more than £1,000 million. Bond Street's oldest feature, and Sotheby's mascot, is an Egyptian statue of the god Sekhmet (*c.* 1320 BC) situated above its entrance.

For people selling possessions, Sotheby's provides expert appraisal and an estimate of the likely value at auction free of charge and without obligation to sell. After the valuation a reserve price is fixed, the price below which it is agreed that the lot will not be sold. A sale catalogue is drawn up and sent to private collectors, dealers, museums and galleries all over the world to attract the keenest bidders. Sotheby's is open for previews and auctions on weekdays between 9.30 a.m. and 4.30 p.m. With very few exceptions, sales are open to the public free of charge. A clear signal is the only action that constitutes a bid at auction. It is a myth that an involuntary scratch of the nose could be construed as an offer to purchase. At major auctions a computerized currency display board instantly converts bids into other major currencies.

After the sale, the proceeds and a settlement statement follow in thirty days. Sotheby's commission rates are generally 10 per cent for lots at £10,000 and over, and 15 per cent for those below. Sotheby's offer two valuable forms of five-year guarantee for works of art in their sales. Any lot proving to be a forgery may be returned by the buyer within five years of the auction and the money will be refunded. For modern paintings – Impressionist, contemporary and modern British – there is also a guarantee of attribution; if the consensus of scholarly opinion about authorship should change over the five-year period, money will be refunded.

Opposite Sotheby's, on the west side of New Bond Street, are top fashion shops, including Yves Saint Laurent at No. 113, and Polo: Ralph Lauren at No. 143. The beautiful 19th-century shop-front of No. 143 once belonged to Savory and Moore, the famous chemists. The finest shop front in New Bond Street, however, is on the east side at No. 26, **Tessiers (5)**, jewellers and silversmiths established here since 1856. On the corner of Bruton Street and New Bond Street is the Time and Life building (No.157). Designed by Michael Rosenauer in 1952, its balustrade includes a carved stone screen by sculptor Henry Moore. Further south along New Bond Street is a mass of fine jewellery shops.

The **House of Asprey (6)**, at Nos. 165–9, is London's principal shop for buying gifts designed to impress. The extravagant luxury, traditional dignity and exquisite craftsmanship of its silver, gold, leather and other wares is unrivalled. Asprey's extensive range of goods, designed to cater for those born with a silver spoon in the mouth, ranges from gold swizzle sticks and cigar cutters, leather desk sets, silver candlesticks, hand-made dinner services and magnificent antique clocks, to million-pound necklaces. For the less well-heeled, an Asprey's 'bargain basement' displays such items as silver-plated lemon squeezers and expanding champagne stoppers.

William Asprey, descendant of a long line of Huguenot craftsmen, founded Asprey's in 1781. The company moved its shop and design workrooms to Bond Street in 1848. The business has passed unfailingly from father to son, maintaining a family relationship with its distinguished clientele. Asprey's high standards have been continually recognized by the honour of 'royal appointment' to every reigning sovereign since Queen Victoria granted a warrant in 1861. Almost every crowned head in the world has also purchased from the company. Asprey's staff are a rare breed, saturated in traditions of loyalty, service and dedication. Prices are not usually displayed – the customer who has to ask, cannot afford. Also outstanding for luxury gifts is **Cartier (7)** at Nos. 175–6, a name synonymous with exclusivity in the jewellery trade. Everything made at Cartier is instantly recognizable by its fine and delicate workmanship, and the company keeps meticulous records of every piece it has ever made. A service they offer is to redesign and make up any piece of jewellery to a customer's requirements.

Many fine art dealers are established in Old Bond Street, notably Arthur Ackermann at No. 3 and Agnew's at No. 43. Six generations of Agnews, father to son, have successfully managed the firm, which pioneered the modern style of large-scale dealing. In 1876 Agnew's constructed the first purpose-built, top-lit and well-proportioned dealers' galleries, still used by the firm today. Agnew's has recently been able to reinstate the galleries to their original design and decoration, working only from a watercolour of the building, painted just after it was completed, and a scrap of original plum, gaufraged, mohair wall-covering.

In 1873 Mr Benson and Mr Hedges opened their tobacconist's shop at No. 13. Sac Frères, at No. 45, is the only shop in the world to specialize in amber. Chocolate manufacturers Charbonnel et Walker are on the west side of the street at No. 28. Chocolates here are hand-made in traditional Victorian moulds and, at a price, it is possible to have personal moulds made up. Charbonnel et Walker offer the Drawing Room selection of bittermints; After Dinner Edwardian mints; Boxes at the Theatre, wrapped in floral paper; silk covered Hatboxes; House Party, Shooting Party and Nursery selections; as well as Charles Heidsieck champagne-flavoured truffles in an edible chocolate champagne bottle. Luxury leather and shoe specialists, Gucci, are nearby at No. 27.

East along Burlington Gardens on its south side is the Burlington Arcade. A few paces further is the **Museum of Mankind (8)**, which houses the Ethnographic Department of the British Museum, which possesses one of the world's greatest collections of the art and artefacts of tribal societies. The museum gives imaginatively staged and regularly changing exhibitions about non-Western societies and cultures. There are works, ancient and modern, from the indigenous peoples of Africa, Australia and the Pacific Islands, North and South America, and from certain parts of Asia and Europe. Displays are often elaborate reconstructions of natural settings. Once the museum brought a four-man family team of craftsmen from the Torajan island mountains of Indonesia, together with the appropriate amount of uru wood (similar to cedar), bamboo and rattan, to build and paint a rice barn. They were each paid with a buffalo. Exhibitions are changed approximately once a year.

Artefacts that belonged to Sir Hans Sloane, founder of the British Museum, form the core of the collection. Works gathered during the great voyages of exploration were added later, notably from Captain Cook's trip to the South Seas. Cook's donations include a Tahitian mourner's dress and a wood kava bowl. Both are often displayed in the museum's permanent room of treasures. The museum still meticulously gathers material from societies whose life-style is fast being modernized.

The museum is housed in a beautiful Italianate building designed in the 1860s by Sir James Pennethorne. It has a large reference library, publishes informative handbooks and guides, and shows many free films.

Burlington Arcade (9), with its tiny bow-windowed shops, protected by the Crown as a masterpiece of Regency architecture, is the aristocrat of shopping thoroughfares and known for its antiques, jewellery and knitwear. Courtesy is graciously enforced by its own corps of top-hatted constables, known as

Beadles. The arcade was designed by Samuel Ware for Lord George Cavendish in 1819 to discourage litterbugs throwing oyster shells – the Regency equivalent of fish and chips – into the garden of his home, Burlington House, now the premises of the Royal Academy of Arts. It was Cavendish's enthusiasm for 'correct' behaviour that brought about the arcade's code of conduct – no singing, whistling, open umbrellas, large parcels or running.

Since 1868 **Burlington House (10)** has been the home of the **Royal Academy of Arts**, the oldest society in the country devoted solely to fine arts. The Academy, which was founded in 1768 and whose first president was Sir Joshua Reynolds, is today the major loan exhibition organization in the country, giving shows throughout the year. Its Summer Exhibition, held every year since 1769, has become a national institution, with sales now exceeding £1 million. During the Summer Exhibition the Academy's gallery walls are crowded top to bottom with more than 1,300 selected contemporary works, a forum for material by any artist regardless of qualification. The main selection process takes place over four days. Around 15,000 works are considered by the Hanging Committee, which now consists of seventeen full and associate Royal Academicians, presided over by the Academy's president and the Senior Hanger. The committee then sub-divides into twos and threes for the week-long hanging process, which is also the final winnowing.

Members of the Academy, or academicians, are entitled to put 'RA' after their name. Upon election to the society every artist is required to donate an example of his or her work. The academy has thus accumulated a fine collection of major British artists spanning more than 200 years. Other works acquired as gifts include paintings by Turner, Constable, Gainsborough and Reynolds, as well as the only Michelangelo sculpture in Britain, a Carrara marble tondo entitled, *Madonna and Child with the Infant St John*.

Burlington House, the only survivor of half a dozen great noblemen's mansions built on the north side of Piccadilly in the 1660s, is also the home of many learned societies, including the Society of Antiquaries.

A short distance to the east of Burlington House sixty-nine 'sets' of chambers form Albany Courtyard, Piccadilly. The Albany has remained almost unchanged since 1804. Lord Byron

and former premier Edward Heath are among the many illustrious people to have dwelled here.

Returning to Old Bond Street, next to Charbonnel et Walker,
the Royal Arcade leads through to Albemarle Street, lined by
yet more art galleries.

The **Faraday Museum (11)** lies behind the Royal Institution's
impressive façade of fourteen Corinthian columns by Lewis
Vulliamy. Here, Michael Faraday (1791–1867) made many of
his important discoveries about electricity and magnetism. In
1972 his Magnetic Laboratory was restored to its original
appearance. This basement laboratory is next to a newly created
museum housing a unique collection of his original apparatus. It
is arranged to illustrate the more important aspects of Faraday's
immense contribution to the advancement of science in his fifty
years of work here. Personal possessions and public honours are
displayed as well as cases devoted to Faraday's discoveries about
alloy steels, light, magnetism, optical glass and benzene. The
Great Cylinder Machine, used by Faraday and his teacher, Sir
Humphrey Davy (1778–1829), in their observations of electrical
discharge, is also on show. In addition, there are individual cases
about Davy, the inventor of the miners' safety lamp, and
Thomas Young (1773–1829), who deciphered the British
Museum's Rosetta Stone and propounded the wave theory of
light.

Ely House (12), at No. 37 Dover Street, is an almost perfect
example of 18th-century Palladian architecture. Built by Sir
Robert Taylor (1714–88) in 1776 as the new London residence
of the Bishops of Ely, its Portland stone arched windows are
surrounded by vermiculated decoration suggestive of roughly
prepared Roman stonework. The three first floor windows have
Corinthian columns with pediments and stone balustrades. A
bishop's mitre is above the central first floor window. The
overall impression of the building is one of harmony, balance
and proportion, which displays the refined and delicate taste
that distinguished Georgian Palladianism. The building is not
open to the general public.

From the west side of Dover Street, Hay Hill emerges just south
of **Berkeley Square (13)**. The popular song 'A Nightingale Sang
in Berkeley Square' immortalizes the nostalgia of the pre-war

years. The bird was first introduced to the square, however, in a novel, *When the Nightingale Sang in Berkeley Square*, written by Michael Arden in the 1920s. Berkeley Square was laid out in the 1730s, taking its name from the first Lord Berkeley, a local landowner and a Royalist commander in the Civil War. Most of its original houses no longer exist, although on the west side Nos. 42–6 and Nos. 49–52 form an excellent group of mid-18th-century houses. The famous architectural historian Nikolaus Pevsner has described No. 44 as 'the finest terrace house of London'. Built by William Kent in 1744, it is now the home of the Clermont Club. The square's garden is shaded by some fine plane trees planted in 1789. At its centre is an early-19th-century pump house with a Chinese-style roof. London's exclusive private nightclub Annabel's is on the west side of Berkeley Square.

Adjoining the east side of Berkeley Square, **Bruton Street (14)** was once part of land acquired by the first Lord Berkeley of Stratton, who also owned estates near Bruton in Somerset. At No. 26 are the business premises of the internationally known couture firm established by the late Norman Hartnell. Hartnell was London's first fashion designer to take a show to Paris. Hartnell's most eminent customer, Elizabeth II, was born in Bruton Street on 21 April 1926. The Lefèvre Gallery at No. 30 specializes in contemporary and impressionist paintings. Culpeper, the herbalist, at No. 21, sells a wide variety of health and beauty products based on herbs.

Bruton Place, at the east end of Bruton Street, is a quiet mews that once contained stables and coachhouses of the great houses in Berkeley Square. **The Guinea**, with its picturesque façade, is one of London's best pub restaurants and famed for its steak pies and charcoal grills. A tavern is thought to have existed here since the 15th century. Bruton Place leads back to Berkeley Square. Diagonally opposite, across the square in its south-west corner, Fitzmaurice Place joins the square to Curzon Street.

George F. Trumper (15), man's perfumer and court hairdresser, was established here in 1875. By royal appointment, the firm are barbers to Prince Andrew and Prince Edward. Trumper, in his time, could boast to have cut the hair of every male member of the royal family. Methods have changed little since then. A brisk rub of the scalp is deemed more beneficial than a blast with a modern hairdryer.

The alleyway on the opposite side of Curzon Street leads into
Shepherd Market (16), situated in the heart of Mayfair. Its
village atmosphere, with its narrow streets, small shops, old
public houses and pavement cafés, makes it a popular lunch-
time spot. The area hosted a May fair – hence Mayfair – from
1688 until the mid-18th century, although the fair may actually
date from as early as Edward I's time, when he gave the inmates
of the nearby St James's lepers' hospital the privilege of a fair 'to
be kept on the eve of St James's, the day, and the morrow, and
the four days following'.

Shepherd Market derives its name from Edward Shepherd,
who established an open-air food market here in 1735. Only his
name lives on. The charming **Shepherd's Tavern** was built in
1708 and has distinctive Georgian bow windows. Inside is an
18th-century sedan chair once owned by the Duke of Cumberland, more recently used as a telephone kiosk.

Along Curzon Street, a little further west past Chesterfield
Street, is **Crewe House (17)**, a charming Georgian mansion set in
its own grounds. Framed by trees and an expanse of grass, its
grounds are highly distinctive for Mayfair, an area facing enormous development pressure. Crewe House was built by Edward
Shepherd in the 1730s and acquired its present name after the
Earl of Crewe purchased the property in 1899.

Continuing west, Curzon Street emerges into **Park Lane (18)**.
For many centuries Park Lane was a narrow road bounded on its
west side by a brick wall enclosing Hyde Park. In the mid-18th
century a number of substantial houses were erected on its east
side. Today Park Lane, which stretches from Marble Arch to
Hyde Park Corner, is a busy dual carriageway and the mansion
houses have made way for some of London's more expensive
hotels – the Dorchester, the Grosvenor, the Hilton, the Inn on
the Park and the Intercontinental. A taste of the 'high life', in
both senses of the word, is gained from the Hilton's twenty-
eighth-floor Roof Bar, which serves up some of the best
cocktails, and views, in London.

Deanery Street runs past the Dorchester into South Audley
Street. At its junction with South Street is **Thomas Goode (19)**.
For more than 150 years Thomas Goode's family have been
selling an exquisite selection of the world's finest china, glass and
crystal. Goode became a royal warrant holder to Queen Victoria

and, in the early years of this century, also royal supplier to the kings of Italy, Spain and Portugal. Through the shop's unique mechanical doors, opened by a system of weights and a fine example of Victorian inventiveness, the opulent fabric of the showrooms has remained virtually unchanged since 1845. Royal Worcester, Crown Derby, Crown Staffordshire, Minton and Coalport are on sale, and there are several rooms displaying tea, breakfast, coffee and dinner services, as well as an excellent glassware department stocking Waterford, Stuart, Tudor, Baccarat, Webb, Edinburgh and St Louis crystal.

At the northern end of South Audley Street is **Grosvenor Square (20)**, which was built approximately between 1725 and 1731 as the centre-piece of the Grosvenor Estate acquired by Sir Thomas Grosvenor in 1677. It immediately provided a suitably grand setting for the houses of the titled and well-to-do. One of the square's former residents was John Adams, first American ambassador to the United Kingdom and later his country's second president. Adams lived here in 1785–8 at No. 9, in the square's north-east corner. His house is one of the two remaining houses from the original development.

For many years Grosvenor Square has been known as London's 'Little America'. During the Second World War, when many United States military services were administered from the square, it became known as 'Eisenhower Platz'. The famous general's European Headquarters were situated at No. 20, in the north-west corner, now commemorated by a plaque. Franklin D. Roosevelt, America's war-time president, is commemorated in a bronze statue by Sir William Reid Dick on the north side of the square's garden. British subscribers paid for it in just one day with 200,000 donations, each not exceeding five shillings. Mrs Roosevelt unveiled it in 1948.

Dominating the west side of the square is the **United States Embassy (21)**, completed in 1961. It is surmounted by an enormous eagle, whose wing span measures a full 35 ft/10.6 m.

From the north-east corner of Grosvenor Square, Brook Street leads east, then Davies Street north, back to Bond Street ⊖.

Marble Arch ⊖

Marble Arch once stood in front of Buckingham Palace as its triumphal entrance. However, the arch now stands at the western end of Oxford Street, London's busiest shopping thoroughfare. Near the Arch, at the north-east corner of Hyde Park, is Speakers' Corner, London's famous Sunday forum for free speech, dissent and eccentricity. Anybody can stand on a soap-box here and say anything, provided it is not treasonable, obscene, racist or likely to cause a breach of the peace.

Oxford Street began to develop in 1739, but it was not until the late-19th century that it began to flourish as a major shopping area. The drapers, furniture and shoe-makers' shops lining the street then began to give way to the first department stores. Today the western portion of Oxford Street contains Selfridge's, Britain's second largest department store after Harrods; the largest of the Marks and Spencer stores, and John Lewis.

The Wallace Collection, housed in Hertford House, Manchester Square, is one of the outstanding private collections in the world. Included among its treasures is a remarkable collection of 18th-century French paintings that rivals those held in the Louvre. There are works by Watteau, Boucher and Fragonard. The Wallace Collection also possesses Frans Hals's world famous picture *The Laughing Cavalier*.

⊖   ⊖   ⊖

Leave Marble Arch ⊖ by the Hyde Park exit. The steps at exit 3 lead to the Marble Arch traffic island. **Marble Arch (1)** was designed by John Nash (1752–1835) after the Arch of Constantine in Rome. It was erected in 1827 as a triumphal entrance to Buckingham Palace (*St James's Park* ⊖), but was much criticized. The arch was removed in 1847, and four years later re-sited at its present location at the north-east entrance to Hyde Park. A statue of George IV was intended to surmount the Arch, but the King died before its completion. The statue is now to be found in Trafalgar Square (*Embankment* ⊖). In 1908 the Arch became isolated as a traffic island to ease road congestion at this busy junction. Only the royal family and the Royal Horse Artillery are officially allowed to pass beneath the Arch.

Anybody who wants to get on to a soapbox and say anything,

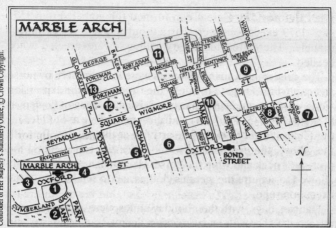

provided it is not treasonable, obscene, racist or likely to cause a breach of the peace, can do so from **Speakers' Corner (2)** (via exit 4 of the subway) on Sunday afternoons. Public speaking began here in 1872 after Parliament granted the right of public assembly. Keir Hardie, George Bernard Shaw, Nye Bevan and Lord Soper are among a wealth of notable figures who have at some time aired their views here. Speakers' Corner, close to the former site of Tyburn gallows, owes its origin to the earlier custom of allowing condemned prisoners to make a last speech to the crowd. Today the political upheavals of all parts of the world are reflected in the rhetoric to be heard at Speakers' Corner. Eccentrics, as ever, are popular with the crowd. Amplification is forbidden, and money may not be demanded.

Return to Marble Arch ⊖ via the subway and leave the station by the Oxford Street northside exit. A little to the west along Oxford Street at the junction of Edgware Road is **Tyburn Memorial (3)**. The north-east corner of Hyde Park lies at the point where two Roman roads crossed. Watling Street passed from north to south, and is now known as Edgware Road and Park Lane. The Via Trinobantina, now known as Oxford Street and Bayswater Road, crossed from east to west. As an important junction, it was, to the medieval mind, just the place to site the largest gallows in London. An inscribed circular slab set into the traffic island at the bottom of Edgware Road commemorates Tyburn Tree, as it was then known. It was the city's principal place of execution from the 12th century until

1783. Before 1571 a great elm formed the gibbet. From 1571 until 1579 executions were carried out under a raised timber triangle. Thereafter temporary gallows were erected when needed.

The condemned, many of whom were brought here by horse and cart from Newgate Prison in the City (hence the expression 'gone west'), would customarily receive a nosegay of flowers at St Sepulchre's (*St Paul's* ⊖) and a last mug of ale at St Giles-in-the-Fields (*Holborn* ⊖) before arriving at the gallows. Beneath the gibbet, the executioner would place the rope around the prisoner's neck and whip the horse. Hangmen were customarily allowed to acquire the victim's clothes and to sell lengths of the execution rope.

Hanging days, with their holiday atmosphere and side shows, attracted vast crowds and were often deemed public holidays. In 1714, at the execution of highwayman Jack Sheppard, more than 20,000 spectators were crammed into specially erected stands. Sheppard had made himself famous by his daring escapes from prison, even escaping once from the condemned cell at Newgate, where he had been especially manacled. At the gallows his confederates planned to cut him down before he was properly dead and to resuscitate him. However, their plans were foiled after members of the crowd, thinking Sheppard's body was being taken for anatomical dissection, fought with his rescuers. After 1783, public hangings were moved to a site outside Newgate Prison.

Oxford Street (4) is perhaps London's busiest and longest shopping thoroughfare. Its western section stretches from Marble Arch to Oxford Circus (*Oxford Circus* ⊖). Many major department and chain stores, including the world famous Selfridge's, are located along its length. Oxford Street was originally named Tyburn Road after Tyburn Stream, which it crossed. It took its present name in the 18th century from Edward Harley, second Earl of Oxford, who acquired land on the north side of the street in 1713. Oxford Street is highly accessible to public transport: only taxis and buses are allowed along most of it and four tube stations have entrances situated on it (*Marble Arch* ⊖, *Bond Street* ⊖, *Oxford Circus* ⊖, *and Tottenham Court Road* ⊖).

The tills of **Marks and Spencer's (5)** large Oxford Street branch are said to take more money per square foot of shop floor than any other retailer in the world. The Marks and Spencer chain, now something of a British institution and patronized by royalty, sells an estimated one-tenth of all clothes worn in Britain and its St Michael trade-mark is now known throughout the world.

This remarkable business, nicknamed 'Marks and Sparks', was established in 1884 when a Jewish refugee from Poland, Michael Marks, established his Penny Bazaar on a stall in a Leeds market. He was later joined by Yorkshireman Tom Spencer. Today the company's turnover runs to hundreds of millions of pounds. Its merchandise, acclaimed for quality and good value, is particularly popular with tourists. The Oxford Street branch employs interpreters, who, between them, speak more than twenty languages.

Selfridge's (6) is the busiest and best-stocked department store in Britain after Harrods (*Sloane Square* ⊖). The Selfridge's building is a spectacular neo-classic hybrid in the *beaux-arts* manner, resplendent with Ionic columns, which dominate a whole block on the north side of Oxford Street. Following a precedent set by the flamboyant and extravagant Mr Selfridge, everything in the store is on a grand scale. Its perfumery department is reportedly the largest of its kind in Europe. There is a wonderful food hall stocked with high-quality provisions, and the store maintains its own Miss Selfridge collection of women's clothes.

Harry Gordon Selfridge, an American, arrived in London in 1906 determined to build the finest store ever seen in Britain. Despite rumours of impending bankruptcy, he opened Selfridge's three years later. It revolutionized British shopping, with its exciting window displays, a bargain basement, annual sales, credit system, roof garden and handsome and spacious departments with all goods in full view. In 1928 the world's first television department sold the Baird televisor, the first television set, for £6 10s 1d.

The London Tourist Board maintains an information office at Selfridge's. Assistants speak several languages.

Continuing eastward is **John Lewis (7)**. This is the flagship store of one of the largest retailing businesses in Britain, the John Lewis Partnership, known for its household equipment and fabrics. John Lewis's slogan is 'never knowingly undersold'. Prices are reasonable, and if purchasers find the price for the same item lower elsewhere, John Lewis will refund the difference.

Tucked away on a quiet corner of Henrietta Place and Vere Street, north of busy Oxford Street, stands **St Peter's Church (8)**, occupied by the London Institute of Contemporary Christianity. Its baroque interior is adorned with an ornamental plasterwork ceiling in the nave, although, with a certain lack of architectural sympathy, the church's aisles have been partitioned for offices. Three of its four stained-glass windows, added in the late-19th century, were designed by the Pre-Raphaelite painter Sir Edward Burne-Jones and executed by his contemporary William Morris.

The second Earl of Oxford, Edward Harley, who acquired a large estate in this area in the early 18th century and was responsible for developing a great deal of Oxford Street, also had a hand in the design of St Peter's. On completion in 1724, architect James Gibbs received considerable public acclaim for his work. The church foreshadowed the pinnacle of Gibbs's work, St Martin-in-the-Fields (*Embankment* ⊖), which was completed two years later by many of the same craftsmen. Both churches have similarities in style, if not scale. This is most apparent in St Peter's west façade. The two churches are rectangular in plan, with a portico at the west end straddled by a tower and steeple. St Peter's steeple takes the form of a double cupola. Beneath, the clock faces have an unusual irregularity – the front face has two hands, the other two only one hand each.

On the north side of St Peter's, Wimpole Street leads north towards the exclusive area for private medicine centred around Harley Street. The British Dental Association Museum, at No. 64 Wimpole Street, holds an interesting collection of dental artefacts. Wimpole Street crosses Wigmore Street.

Wigmore Hall (9), situated on the north side of Wigmore Street, was originally known as Bechstein Hall when it opened in 1901. Over the decades it has achieved a fine reputation for its classical music concerts. Its intimate atmosphere and excellent acoustics have made it a focal point for chamber music and recitals. Soprano Elisabeth Schwarzkopf and pianist Daniel Barenboim made their London débuts here.

The houses in **St Christopher's Place (10)**, a Victorian by-way on the south side of Wigmore Street, have been remodelled and the roadway pedestrianized. It has the special attraction of a 'secret' place, with its fashionable clothes shops, bistros and cafés.

Further west along Wigmore Street is Duke Street. At its northern end is Manchester Square, where Hertford House, the home of the **Wallace Collection (11)**, is located. The Wallace Collection is famed for its 18th-century French paintings and furniture, and is one of the outstanding private collections of the world. It also has an extensive collection of armour.

Hertford House, which houses the collection, was built in the late 1770s for the fourth Duke of Manchester and was then known as Manchester House. Sir Richard Wallace, the illegitimate son of the fourth Marquess of Hertford, gathered much of the collection and renamed the house in 1872. His widow bequeathed the collection to the nation, and it was opened to the public in 1900.

The collection is displayed in twenty-five rooms on the ground and first floors. The highlight of the collection is the first floor gallery, over 100 ft/30m long, which contains a host of magnificent paintings. These include Titian's *Perseus and Andromeda* (1554), one of seven canvases illustrating the works of Ovid; *Dance to the Music of Time* (*c*. 1638) by Poussin; *Rainbow Landscape* by Rubens; and the world-famous *The Laughing Cavalier* (1624) by Frans Hals.

Galleries 13 and 14 contain characteristic work by Canaletto and his pupil Guardi depicting Venice. Gallery 14 also contains fine furniture, Sèvres porcelain and the remarkable Régulateur Clock, with its elaborate astronomical movements. Galleries 15 to 18 contain Dutch and Flemish painting of the 17th century, notably works by Rembrandt and Rubens. Gallery 21 houses perhaps the finest collection of French 18th-century painting and furniture to be seen in a single room. There are pictures by Watteau (*La Toilette*), Boucher (*La Modiste*), Fragonard (*The Swing*) and Greuze. On the ground floor the arms and armour collection is displayed in Galleries 5 to 8.

The Grand Staircase leading up to the first floor is flanked by a magnificent balustrade (1733–41) of forged iron and bronze, chased and gilt. Its walls are hung with outstanding paintings by the 18th-French artist François Boucher.

Fitzhardinge Street joins the east side of Manchester Square to **Portman Square (12)**. The north-west corner of Portman Square contains two fine Adam houses, No. 20 by Robert Adam and No. 21 by James Adam, both built around 1776. No. 20, known as Home House, was built for Elizabeth, Countess of Home. Its interior decoration is some of the finest in London, and the building's entrance hall and staircase can be viewed at most times.

Around the corner, but still numbered as No. 21, is the **Heinz Gallery (13)**, which contains the Royal Institute of British Architects' collection of drawings. Exhibitions are periodically given on various themes chosen by the Institute. At other times the gallery is closed to the public. The Institute has a collection of around 200,000 drawings, the largest of its kind in the world. It covers the work of Inigo Jones, Wren, Soane, Barry, the Adamses, Gilbert Scott, Lutyens, Frank Lloyd Wright and Le Corbusier.

From the south-west corner of Portman Square, Portman Street leads south to Oxford Street. Marble Arch ⊖ is 150yds/ 137m to the west.

Lancaster Gate ⊖ &
Hyde Park Corner ⊖

The pleasant airy surroundings of Hyde Park, the largest of London's parks, extend over 340 acres/138 ha. of grass, trees and a lake. Its many amenities include boating on the Serpentine lake, swimming from the Lido, fishing by permit, football pitches, tennis courts, cycling tracks, bowling and putting greens and a playground. From the Bathurst Riding Stables, north of Lancaster Gate ⊖ in Bathurst Mews, rides around the park can be booked.

In the south-east corner of the park is Apsley House, once the home of the first Duke of Wellington, the 'Iron Duke', who defeated Napoleon at Waterloo. Wellington was also the Ranger of Hyde Park and his house, with its spectacular Waterloo Gallery and marvellous collection of paintings, is now open as a museum.

The Saxon manor of Eia, or island, was once defined by the twin courses of the slow and winding Westbourne stream and the Tyburn. Around the time of Domesday the manor was subdivided and one part was named Hyde, hence the name of the park. Henry VIII appropriated the land from the abbot of Westminster Abbey in 1536, and enclosed it with a high fence, or paling, as his private hunting ground. Later, Charles I opened it to the public, but Charles II took it back into royal possession. Nearly a century afterwards deer were hunted by royalty for the last time in Hyde Park. Also in the 18th century 250 acres/101 ha. of land at the west end of the park were developed to form what is now Kensington Gardens (*Queensway* ⊖).

The park is entered through **Marlborough Gate (1)** opposite Lancaster Gate ⊖. Strictly speaking, this section of the park, on the east side of the Long Water, is part of Kensington Gardens rather than Hyde Park. Ahead, the Italian gardens and fountains and the former Pumping House are said to have been designed by Queen Victoria's consort, Prince Albert. Sir Christopher Wren designed **Queen Anne's Alcove (2)**, where this queen was fond of taking afternoon tea.

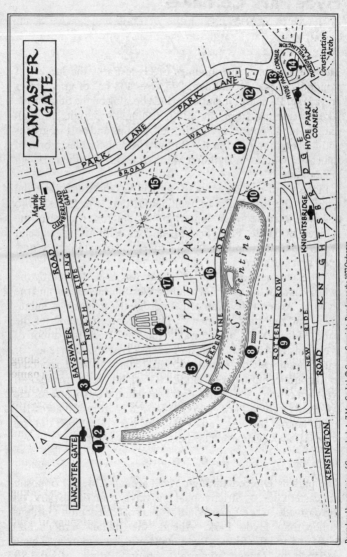

LANCASTER GATE

HYDE PARK

The Serpentine

By the side of the lodge at **Victoria Gate (3)** is the **Pets' Cemetery**, a graveyard of miniature tombstones. The Duke of Cambridge, Ranger of Kensington Gardens, opened the cemetery in 1880 to console his wife after the death of her favourite dog. By the end of the First World War more than 300 dogs and cats, even a few birds, had been interred here.

Beside the **Hudson Bird Sanctuary (4)** is sculptor Jacob Epstein's controversial memorial to author and naturalist William Henry Hudson. At its unveiling the extreme symbolism of its daring depiction of Rima, the spirit of Nature from Hudson's book *Green Mansions*, caused considerable consternation and it has been disfigured on more than one occasion. The **Magazine (5)**, or Powder House, was built in 1805 as an armoury and weapon store.

The elegant **Serpentine Bridge (6)** affords a fine lakeside view to the east along the Serpentine. The bridge was constructed in 1826 by George Rennie, son of John Rennie, who built the former London, Southwark and Waterloo Bridges in the early 19th century. In 1730 Queen Caroline, wife of George II, created the Serpentine by damming the River Westbourne. To the south of the Serpentine Bridge are the Serpentine and Pergola restaurants, popular spots in the summer months. Exhibitions of modern art are held in the **Serpentine Gallery (7)**. The **Lido (8)**, an enclosed area with deck-chairs and changing rooms for swimming and sunbathing, lies on the south bank of the Serpentine and is open from dawn until dusk.

Fashionable society once rode on horse and by carriage along the broad, tree-shaded avenue known as **Rotten Row (9)**, a name thought to derive from *route du roi*, 'the king's way'. Rotten Row, the first continuously lamp-lit road in the kingdom, was built in the winter of 1689–90 by William III's surveyor of roads as part of a royal carriage drive between Westminster and Kensington Palaces. Later, Queen Victoria frequently rode there and George V was the last sovereign to use the thoroughfare regularly. Today carriages are no more, but Rotten Row is still a favourite exercise route for the horses of the local riding stables. Rotten Row's cast-iron railings were scrapped during wartime and to mark the thoroughfare's tercentenary in 1990 new ones are to be erected.

This section of Hyde Park once housed the Great Exhibition of 1851. Six million people flocked here from all over the world to see some 14,000 trade exhibits, housed in the Crystal Palace,

Joseph Paxton's vast structure of iron and glass. Queen Victoria
and Prince Albert took great interest in the international extravaganza, and the exhibition's £165,000 profit was used to establish the first museum in South Kensington. The Crystal Palace
was re-erected in 1852 at Sydenham in South London, but later
burned down.

By tradition, the 'standing stone' in **The Dell (10)** was brought
from Stonehenge by order of Charles I. This seven-ton lump of
Cornish stone was, in fact, once part of a drinking fountain
erected here in 1861. When the fountain was dismantled,
however, it proved too heavy to move and so has remained. The
Bandstand (11) to the east of The Dell hosts concerts on Sunday
afternoons during the summer. Further east, adjacent to Park
Lane, is the **Achilles Statue (12)** by Richard Westmacott (1775–
1856). One of the first nude statues to stand in public in
England, it much dismayed the group of women who commissioned it to commemorate the first Duke of Wellington. The
monument takes its form from the *Horse Tamer* on the Monte
Cavallo in Rome, and was cast from twelve 24-pound French
guns captured by the Duke's men. The torso of Westmacott's
sculpture was of Homeric proportions; its head loosely re-
sembled that of Wellington, but lower down it was obviously
underendowed.

For thirty-five years until his death in 1852, the Duke of Wellington occupied **Apsley House (13)** at the south-eastern corner of
the park. In his fine 18th-century house, now a museum, he
gathered an excellent collection of paintings and other *objets
d'art*. Little has changed since the Duke resided here.

Waterloo banquets, held annually in the Waterloo Gallery in
celebration of the Duke's victory, were once a high point of
London society and military life. In this room today, below
Wyatt's splendid white and gold Versailles style ceiling, are
hung some of the Duke's most prized paintings. Many came
from the Spanish royal collection, stolen by Napoleon's brother
Joseph Bonaparte, but captured by Wellington after the Battle
of Vittoria in 1813. Wellington, a gentleman and diplomat,
offered to return them, but the grateful King of Spain declined
and his ambassador in London wrote: 'His Majesty, touched by
your delicacy, does not wish to deprive you of that which has
come into your possession by means as just as they are honourable.' The pictures include *The Water Seller of Seville* by

Velázquez, and a huge equestrian self-portrait by Goya. A representation of the Waterloo Banquet of 1836 shows the room's layout on one of these great occasions.

Other rooms house many gifts made to the Duke, which include furniture, silver plate, beautiful porcelain services, swords and medals. At the foot of the imposing spiral staircase stands a colossal nude statue of Napoleon. Carved in 1810 by Antonio Canova, the French commander thought its great proportions to be ridiculous compared to his somewhat diminutive stature. Napoleon ordered its removal from the Louvre, and in 1816 it was bought by the British government. The statue was presented to Wellington by the Prince Regent, later George IV.

Apsley House was constructed to the designs of Robert Adam (1728–92) during the 1770s for the second Earl Bathurst, also Baron Apsley. In 1817 the Duke of Wellington acquired the house and commissioned Benjamin Dean Wyatt (1775–1850) to redesign the building. It was refaced in Bath stone and a Corinthian portico and a new west extension were added. For many years Apsley House was known as 'Number One, London', although the reason for such an address remains unknown.

A toll gate stood at **Hyde Park Corner (14)**, the western entrance to London, until the early 19th century. Today Hyde Park Corner is probably the city's busiest road junction. At its centre, on a large traffic island, is the enormous Constitution Arch, designed by Decimus Burton and erected in the 1820s. The Apsley Screen to the north is also by Burton and was envisaged as a grand ceremonial entrance to Hyde Park from Buckingham Palace. Near Constitution Arch is a bronze statue of the Duke of Wellington mounted on his favourite horse, Copenhagen.

The **Ceremonial Parade Ground (15)** in Hyde Park is the scene of gun salutes on royal occasions, such as the birthdays of the Queen and Queen Mother. The **Royal Humane Society's Boathouse (16)**, situated on the north side of the Serpentine, was built following several drowning accidents in the Serpentine. This society was founded in 1774 by Dr William Hawes to encourage knowledge about life-saving. To the north of the boathouse is the **Hyde Park Police Station (17)** and the Ranger's Lodge.

Queensway ⊖

Kensington Gardens has an intimacy not found in its large neighbour, Hyde Park. The gardens have the true privacy of a royal park and, unlike Hyde Park to the east, are undisturbed by traffic. Here nannies once promenaded their charges along the gardens' tree-lined Broad Walk, and this tradition continues today in the children's playground, whose fairy-tale precincts are entered past Elfin Oak, carved with the figures of fairies, elves and small animals. This playground owes its existence to J. M. Barrie, author of *Peter Pan*, and a statue of his ever-youthful boy is to be found elsewhere in the gardens. Round Pond is a focus for model boat enthusiasts, and kite-flying is permitted from open land near by.

In 1689 William III bought what was then called Nottingham House, a Jacobean mansion built in 1605, and instructed Sir Christopher Wren to rebuild it. From then until 1760 this rather modest red-brick house became the main royal residence. Queen Mary took a great interest in its garden, laying it out in formal Dutch patterns. Queen Anne, however, disliked the style and had it uprooted. Queen Caroline, wife of George II, extended the gardens to 275 acres/111 ha. by annexing a large tract of Hyde Park. William IV opened the park to the public all the year round and in 1843 a Flower Walk was created. Kensington Palace was virtually abandoned in 1760. Later, the palace was restored, then opened to the public in 1899. Further renovated in 1975, the magnificent State Apartments re-create the Stuart and Hanoverian periods.

About 200 years ago it became the practice for ladies and gentlemen to be presented at court and on these occasions earnest attention was paid to dress. The palace now houses the wonderful Court Dress Collection, which shows the evolution of such finery from the costume of the mid-17th century to the tulle dresses of the 1950s.

Kensington Palace was chosen by the Prince and Princess of Wales as their London residence. Their home is in the ten-roomed three-storey wing on the west side behind the State Rooms. Their neighbours include Prince Michael of Kent, the Duke of Gloucester and Princess Margaret.

Queensway, once Black Lion Lane, received its name soon

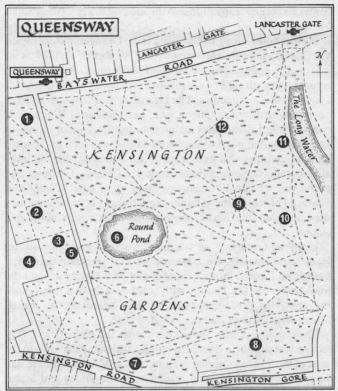

QUEENSWAY

LANCASTER GATE

LANCASTER GATE ROAD

QUEENSWAY

BAYSWATER

KENSINGTON

Round Pond

GARDENS

KENSINGTON ROAD

KENSINGTON GORE

The Long Water

after Queen Victoria's accession. As a young princess she rode along it from the palace.

⊖   ⊖   ⊖

Black Lion Gate, opposite Queensway ⊖, forms the north-west entrance to Kensington Gardens. From here Broad Walk, lined with limes and maples, connects Queensway with Kensington. The **Children's Playground (1)** is located on the west side of Broad Walk. This pretty playground owes its existence to J. M. Barrie, author of *Peter Pan*, who generously provided the first swings and slides. The **Elfin Oak**, a magnificent tree stump standing at the playground's entrance, was carved with the delicate figures of fairies, elves and other small animals by Ivor

Innes. Its recent renovation was inspired by the comedian Spike
Milligan.

Further south along Broad Walk is the **Orangery (2)**, designed
for Queen Anne by Hawksmoor and Vanbrugh in 1704 as an
informal supper room for summer gatherings. Restored and
refurnished with tubs of camellias, it is a jewel of the country's
Queen Anne architecture. The Orangery's historic statues have
been provided by the Queen from her gardens at Windsor. It
contains four rustic deities sculpted during the reign of Elizabeth
I by Francavilla, pupil of Giovanni da Bologna, one of the most
famous sculptors after the death of Michelangelo. The building
also contains fine examples of carving by Grinling Gibbons, and
a fine pair of late-17th-century vases by Gabriel Cibber and
Edward Pearce. In the summer the Orangery is sometimes now
used for chamber music concerts, for which it is admirably
suited.

From the Orangery, an avenue of bay trees and holly bushes
leads south towards the arboured walk of pleached limes that
have been formed into a beautiful arched walkway around the
Sunken Garden (3). Planted with swathes of flowers throughout
the year, this garden, opened in 1909, re-creates the formal
Dutch-style gardens that once existed here.

The entrance to the State Apartments and Court Dress Collection is at the north-east corner of **Kensington Palace (4)**, to the
west of the Sunken Garden. The rambling Whitehall Palace had
been the principal London residence of the Tudor and Stuart
monarchs, but the smoke and oppressive air at Whitehall was
unsuited to William's chronic asthma and his wife, Mary, felt
shut in there. In 1689 William III acquired what was then
Nottingham House and instructed Sir Christopher Wren to
reconstruct the building. Nicholas Hawksmoor was appointed
clerk of the works. When compared with its contemporary,
Versailles, William's palace has more the informal atmosphere
of a country house than the imposing grandeur of a royal palace.
Its interior took on a more palatial character after alterations by
Colen Campbell and William Kent during the reign of George I.
Kensington House became the principal royal residence until
the death of George II in 1760, although it was not until the 19th
century that the house became known as Kensington Palace.
Queen Victoria was born here in 1819, and the palace is now the
London home of the Prince and Princess of Wales.

The State Apartments, whose rooms date from the reigns of

William III, George II and Victoria, have been open to the public at various times since 1899.

At the top of the oak Queen's Staircase on the first floor, the Queen's Apartments are essentially as they were in Wren's day. Queen Mary's Gallery has fine oak panelling, with an elaborately carved cornice and door-heads by William Emmett. Two gilt mirrors serving as overmantels with sumptuous carved and gilt surrounds are the work of Grinling Gibbons. The Queen's Dining Room retains its 17th-century panelling and the Queen's Drawing Room displays an ornate cornice of acanthus leaves with the crowned monogram of William and Mary. On the south wall a late-17th-century inlaid cabinet, attributed to Gerrit Jensen, contains 17th- and 18th-century Oriental porcelain. Adjoining the Drawing Room is Queen Mary's Bedchamber, beautifully decorated in a deep blue and with a bed that originally belonged to James II. Particularly striking is the large and elaborate writing cabinet, intricately decorated with boule and marquetry inlay and semi-precious stones.

Beyond the Drawing Room is the Privy Chamber, with an impressive painted ceiling by William Kent. Its three Mortlake tapestries, woven for Charles I when he was Prince of Wales, are part of a set representing the seasons of the year. William Kent's brightly painted ceiling in the Presence Chamber is the earliest example in England of the distinctive Pompeiian style of decorative painting.

Wren's King's Grand Staircase has wrought-iron work by Jean Tijou. The striking *trompe l'œil* murals are by Kent. The King's Gallery was designed to house the finest pictures in the royal collection. Its paintings are exclusively from the 17th century. To the right of the fireplace is Rubens' *Jupiter and Antiope*, and there is also the excellent Van Dyck picture *Cupid and Psyche*, thought to have been painted for Charles I. Above the fireplace is a wind dial made for William III, who frequently sailed to Holland and liked to ensure favourable winds.

Most of the furnishings and fittings in the Duchess of Kent's Dressing Room belonged to Queen Victoria. The young Victoria's beautifully preserved toys are displayed in the Ante Room. In Queen Victoria's Bedroom is the cot used by each of her nine children. Another of Kent's ceiling paintings adorns the King's Drawing Room. The magnificently carved ivory throne and footstool in the Council Chamber were presented to Queen Victoria by the Maharajah of Travancore for the Great

Exhibition of 1851. Returning through the King's Drawing Room, on the right is the principal state room of the palace, the Cupola Room. Its lavish decoration was intended to evoke Roman-style grandeur, comprising giant fluted Ionic pilasters, massive marble doorways supported by Ionic columns and niches containing gilded statues of Roman gods.

Returning to the ground floor, through the Queen's side of the palace and down the Queen's Staircase, is the Court Dress Collection. The collection is a beautiful display showing the evolution of court dress and uniform from the mid-18th century to the 1950s. The collection contains a nucleus of some 400 uniforms, the earliest, a court dress of 1750. The style of the dresses after about 1820 followed the fashionable line of formal costume, although certain additions – feather and veil head-dresses, gloves, a bouquet or a fan and a train – were demanded by court regulations. However, uniforms did not develop with male fashion. Many remained unaltered in style for decades, with white silk stockings, buckled shoes and swords worn on most formal occasions. The costume is shown in appropriate room settings. The route of this excellent exhibition passes through the Red Saloon, now restored to its original Victorian grandeur, and the North Drawing Room decorated as it was in 1820. The display concludes with the wedding dress worn by HRH the Princess of Wales in 1981.

Leaving Kensington Palace to the east, past the Sunken Garden, is a statue of **Queen Victoria (5)**, sculpted in 1893 by her daughter Princess Louise. The **Round Pond (6)**, created by Queen Caroline, is opposite. It covers 7 acres/2.8 ha. and has been a focus for model sailing boat enthusiasts since Victorian times.

At the southern end of the Broad Walk, branching off to the east, lies the picturesque **Flower Walk (7)** with its tame squirrels, the prettiest part of the gardens. A combination of ornamental trees and flower beds are carefully planned to make the most of each season. The grandiose **Albert Memorial (8)** (*South Kensington* ⊖) designed by Sir Giles Gilbert Scott, commemorates the depth of Queen Victoria's grief at the death of her husband, Prince Albert. It was completed in 1872 and faces the Royal Albert Hall from the south of the Gardens.

At the centre of the gardens is the bronze equestrian figure of **Physical Energy (9)** by G. F. Watts (1904). **Queen Caroline's Temple (10)** is a charming little classical-style piece of garden architecture designed in 1726 by Kent and recently restored.

On the west side of The Long Water is Sir George Frampton's bronze of **Peter Pan (11)**, donated by J. M. Barrie and a great favourite with children. Its pedestal is adorned with figures of squirrels, rabbits and mice. The giant granite obelisk, **Speke's Monument (12)**, is a memorial to that great explorer of Africa who discovered the source of the Nile. This walk can be continued into Hyde Park; see *Lancaster Gate* ⊖.

OUTER LONDON

South-east

Dulwich Picture Gallery, England's oldest purpose-built gallery, houses perhaps the largest private art collection in the country. The collection dates from 1626, when a friend of William Shakespeare, actor Edward Alleyn, bought Dulwich Manor and founded Dulwich College. Its historical nucleus is formed by Alleyn's picture collection, supplemented in 1686 by the inclusion of theatrical paintings belonging to William Cartwright, an actor who turned bookseller after the Puritans closed the theatres.

The gallery was opened early in the 19th century. French writer Noel Desenfans (1745–1807) settled in England and, with his English wife's dowry, set himself up professionally as an art dealer. In 1790 he was asked by the King of Poland to assemble a collection of paintings, but as the Kingdom of Poland ceased to exist five years later, Desenfans was left with the bulk of this collection. In 1814 a specially-built gallery was opened to display the collection. Sir John Soane (*Chancery Lane* ⊖) designed the building, which also contained a circular temple-like mausoleum for the sarcophagi of Desenfans, his wife and the gallery's other benefactor, Francis Bourgeois.

The gallery's treasures have since been supplemented by a number of bequests and its works now include: Rembrandt's *Girl Leaning on a Window Sill*; *Lady Venetia Digby on her Death-bed* by Van Dyck; *Jacob with Laban and his Daughters* by Lorrain; *Hagar in the Desert* by Rubens; Poussin's *The Nurture of Jupiter*; *The Linley Sisters* by Gainsborough, and the charming portrait *Queen Victoria, aged four* by Denning. Hogarth added the word 'Anglus' to his signature on the half-length portrait *Unknown Man*, registering his dissatisfaction with the virtual monopoly of English portraiture by Continental artists at the time.

Near the museum are the green spaces and Georgian façades of Dulwich Village. Dulwich College, designed in the North Italian Romanesque style, is perhaps London's most ornate school building. Opposite the college is a millpond with picturesque 18th-century cottages. Further south along College Road is the last remaining toll gate in London.

*Directions: West Dulwich BR from Victoria BR. Take the South
Circular Road east. Gallery Road leads off to the north. The gallery
is at its northern end.*

A manor has existed on the site of **Eltham Palace** since Saxon
times. Odo, Bishop of Bayeux, was given the manor after the
Norman Conquest. Henry III and his court visited the manor
over Christmas in 1270. In 1297 it passed to Anthony Bek,
Bishop of Durham, who rebuilt it. Bek constructed the moat and
the walls within the moat, which are still in evidence today.
After Bek's death in 1311, Eltham became one of the principal
royal residences for the next 200 years. Isabella, wife of Edward
II, lived here for twenty years. Her son, later Edward III, spent
his early childhood at Eltham and as sovereign held a number of
Parliaments here. Edward instituted the Order of the Garter
during a grand tournament here to celebrate his victory at the
Battle of Crecy. Richard II replaced the wooden bridge over the
moat with a stone one, the predecessor of the 15th-century
bridge seen today. His many improvements were supervised by
Geoffrey Chaucer, clerk of the works.

Eltham Palace reached its peak during the reigns of Edward
IV and Henry VII, as both monarchs normally kept residence.
The Great Hall was erected during Henry VII's reign. Brick-
built, faced with stone along its length and decorated with
grotesque heads, this 100-ft-/30-m-long building is one of the
best preserved medieval halls in the country. Its spectacular
hammer-beam roof of four centred arches comprises massive yet
intricately moulded timbers. The hall also has a canopy, screen
and minstrels' gallery. The royal apartments once ran at right
angles to the main hall. The apartments' foundations remain,
together with a number of underground passages and chambers.
The two existing lawns on either side of the building were
once courtyards surrounded by various domestic and military
buildings.

During the reign of Henry VIII, Wolsey was installed as Lord
Chancellor in the chapel at Eltham. The timbered Chancellor's
Lodging survives from this period. Surrounding the palace is the
Great Park, where the King once hunted. Henry VIII, however, began to lose interest in Eltham and decamped to Greenwich Palace. During the Civil War the building was ransacked
and became uninhabitable. In 1931 Sir Stephen Courtauld obtained the lease and restored the Great Hall. Excavations have

revealed the plan of the medieval and Tudor buildings. Courtauld built a new house and redesigned the gardens. The property is currently occupied by the Institute of Army Education.

> *Directions: Mottingham Station B R from Charing Cross B R. Take Court Road north. The palace is in Tilt Yard Approach, which leads off to the west.*

GREENWICH

Greenwich, the 'green village' in Anglo-Saxon, has an ancient history, but it reached the peak of royal favour in the Tudor era. Henry VIII was born at Greenwich Palace in 1491, Mary I in 1515, and Elizabeth I in 1533. The palace fell into decline and was demolished, but its site then became Wren's Greenwich Hospital, now the Royal Naval College. To its south lies the magnificent Queen's House, England's first Palladian villa, now the National Maritime Museum, the world's largest naval museum. Still further south, at the summit of Greenwich Hill, is Wren's Old Royal Observatory. The Greenwich Meridian, the line of zero longitude, where eastern hemisphere meets western, runs through the observatory.

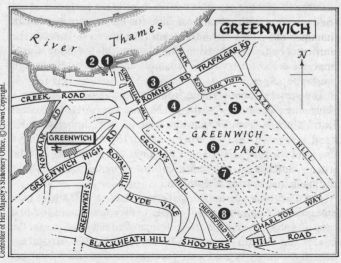

The *Cutty Sark*, the last and most famous great sailing clipper, and *Gipsy Moth IV,* the yacht in which Sir Francis Chichester sailed single-handed around the world, have now both been placed in dry dock in Greenwich as museums. In a round domed building beside the river are the lift and steps down to the tunnel beneath the Thames to the Isle of Dogs. Canaletto's fine view of Greenwich painted from there in 1750 is now displayed in the National Maritime Museum. From the southern tip of the Isle of Dogs the Docklands Light Railway runs north, then west, through Docklands (p. 408) back to the City.

> *Directions: Greenwich BR via Charing Cross BR. Take Greenwich High Road north. It leads into Greenwich Church Street. The* Cutty Sark *is at its northern end.*

The **Cutty Sark (1)** is the last of the clippers, the great sailing ships that once plied the tea trade from China. She now lies in dry dock, her intricate standing rigging set and taut, sails stowed below, as if docked between tea-runs.

The *Cutty Sark* was launched on 22 November 1869 at Dumbarton in Scotland. Her owner, retired Captain John Willis, known as 'Old White Hat' after his distinctive tall white hat, built the *Cutty Sark* to wrest from the *Thermopylae* the Blue Riband of the Ocean, the annual race from China to England with the first of the season's tea. In the 1860s a premium of ten shillings a ton with a bonus of £100 for the captain was worth having. Sadly, the *Cutty Sark* never beat her rival. Indeed, she was launched a week after the opening of the Suez Canal provided a shorter route for steamers and signalled the end of the clipper era.

The vessel's name is taken from the 'cutty sark' – in Scots, a short linen chemise – worn by Nannie the witch in Robert Burns's poem 'Tam O'Shanter'. Nannie, the clipper's figurehead, is seen with her left arm extended. Her fingers would have once clenched the tail of Tam O'Shanter's horse as they fled the witch's clutches. A cutty sark cut out of metal was the ship's distinguishing masthead emblem.

The *Cutty Sark* carried her last cargo of tea in 1877 and in 1883 entered the Australian wool trade. Unlike tea, where the first crop was at a premium, wool-run ships were held back to get the last of the clip for London's January wool sales. Under the superb captaincy of Richard Woodget the *Cutty Sark* beat her rival *Thermopylae*. After her stint on the wool trade, the *Cutty Sark* was sold to the Portuguese, but twenty-seven years later she returned to Britain. Driven into Falmouth Harbour by a gale, she was seen by Captain Wilfred Dowman, a master mariner and fine seaman. As an apprentice on the *Hawksdale*, Dowman had once spotted the *Cutty Sark* slicing through the ocean and had fallen in love with her. He acquired the clipper for £3,750 and re-rigged and restored her.

In 1957 the *Cutty Sark* was opened as a museum. On display are mock-ups of holds of tea and wool; exhibits about the days of sail; perhaps the finest clipper ship model ever made; Captain Woodget's original logs; and an exhibition of figureheads from the Long John Silver Collection, the largest and finest collection of merchant ship's figureheads in the world, together with a selection of paintings.

At the age of 66, Francis Chichester sailed single-handed round the world in **Gipsy Moth IV (2)**. Before embarking on his epic 226-day, 29,630-mile/47,675-km voyage in this 54-ft-/16.75-m-ketch, he had attended signalling classes on the *Cutty Sark*. On his return to Britain in 1967 he was knighted by the Queen at Greenwich. The Queen used the sword with which Elizabeth I had knighted Sir Francis Drake here. *Gipsy Moth IV* is placed in dry dock next to the *Cutty Sark* for public viewing.

The **Royal Naval College (3)** was built on the site of the former Greenwich Palace, which had been vandalized and had fallen into disrepair during the Civil War. Following the naval victory over the French at La Hogue in 1692, Queen Mary commanded Sir Christopher Wren to build a naval hospital for elderly and wounded seamen. Pensioners were accommodated here until 1869. In 1873 the building was occupied, as it is today, by the Royal Naval College, formerly in Portsmouth.

The building consists of four blocks: King Charles's building, built to the designs of Inigo Jones's pupil John Webb as a proposed palace for Charles II; Queen Anne's building, completed in 1728 by Vanbrugh to Wren's original plans; King William's building, with a west façade by Vanbrugh; and Queen Mary's building, a replica of the King Charles block completed in 1751. Only the Painted Hall in the King William block and the Chapel in the Queen Mary building may be visited. The interior of the Painted Hall is by Hawksmoor and the decoration of its ceilings and walls was begun in 1708 by James Thornhill. The

Hall consists of three levels, the Great Hall, the Upper Hall and the vestibule with cupola. The magnificent allegorical ceiling of the Great Hall depicts William and Mary providing Europe with freedom and peace. The chapel was completed in 1742 to Wren's designs and, after a fire in 1779, was redecorated by James 'Athenian' Stuart and William Newton as a rococo interior in Wedgwood pastels. The painting above the altar is by Benjamin West.

Queen's House (4) was the first Palladian house to be built in Britain. This 17th-century architectural masterpiece built by Inigo Jones is joined by colonnades to two 19th-century wings, and houses the largest naval museum in the world. The **National Maritime Museum** holds 2½ million artefacts, including 1 million ships' plans, the earliest dating from the late 17th century; 4,000 ship models; 4,000 oil paintings; 70,000 watercolours, prints and etchings; 500,000 historic photographs; and 60,000 books, the earliest being the *Ptolemy Atlas* of 1475. The museum traces its origins back to the Royal Naval Museum in Somerset House in the 18th century, to the picture collection of Charles I and the institution of the Royal Observatory by Charles II in 1675.

The Queen's House was originally begun in 1616 as a summer residence for Anne of Denmark, wife of James I, but she died before her 'House of Delights' was finished. Work ceased, and it was not until 1636 that John Webb completed the villa for Queen Henrietta Maria, wife of Charles I. Its interior reputedly matched the splendours of Venice. The house was left empty during the Civil War, but following the Restoration, Queen Henrietta Maria occupied it once again. After the Glorious Revolution in 1688, the Queen's House was scarcely used by the royal family. By the early 19th century it had become a school for the children of naval ratings, which it remained until the museum was established in 1937.

The entrance hall to the Queen's House is a perfect 40-ft-/ 12.19-m-cube, a staggering innovation for people still used to Elizabethan panelled halls. It was designed to hold masques and other social events. The design of its marble floor echoes the pattern of the painted ceiling above. A graceful spiral white marble staircase, the first unsupported staircase in England, leads up to the first floor gallery, the Queen's Bedroom and Drawing Room. It is known as the Tulip Staircase because of its graceful wrought-iron balustrading. The flowers are, in fact, the French fleur-de-lis. The Queen's Bedroom has a fine view of the river, and was designed by Inigo Jones with a ceiling by Thornhill. This ceiling has an allegorical painting at its centre, surrounded by mottoes and fleurs-de-lis, within the outer cove of 'grotesques'.

The view north from the Queen's House was preserved at Queen Mary's insistence, now between the twin buildings of the 18th-century Seamen's Hospital, latterly the Royal Naval College. The East Bridge Room was added during the house's enlargement by Webb in 1662 and intended as the King's Privy Chamber. Charles and Henrietta Maria spent their last night together at Queen's House before she fled to France. The Orangery and Loggia above it look out on the park and the Old Royal Observatory.

Queen's House contains the museum's Tudor and Stuart collections. These include fine ship models as well as a number of paintings depicting British sea power, notably sea pieces by the Van de Veldes, father and son, who had a studio here in the 1670s. There are also 17th-century wall maps of the world, portraits of Drake and Hawkins, *Inigo Jones* by Hogarth, Mortlake tapestries, early navigational instruments and engraved glassware.

The east wing is devoted to the maritime world of the 19th and 20th centuries, when sail gradually gave way to steam and the great transatlantic routes became established. On the upper floors are galleries with displays about the navy, from the Napoleonic Wars through to the Second World War.

Displays in the west wing include the gallery on Captain James Cook, whose voyages almost doubled the size of the known world; the Archaeology of the Boat Gallery, with its replicas of ancient craft; the Yachting Gallery; the Medal and Seal Rooms; the Royal and Merchant Navies of the 18th Century; the Nelson Galleries, which contain the uniform the great admiral was wearing when he was shot at the Battle of Trafalgar in 1805; the Library and Reading Room; and the museum's bookshop and information desk.

The adjoining New Neptune Hall is dominated by the 1907 paddle tug *Reliant*, whose engines and boiler room can be walked through. Also housed here are displays about lighthouses, lightships and cargo handling among many others. The Barge House next door contains the gilded royal barge of 1732 built for Frederick, Prince of Wales, son of George II, and last used by Prince Albert in 1849.

Burial mounds in **Greenwich Park (5)** suggest that Bronze Age tribes once lived here. A Roman road and villa have also been found. In 1427 Henry V's brother, the Duke of Gloucester, built a house on the river and enclosed a stretch of land to Greenwich Hill, foreshadowing Greenwich Palace. Henry VI turned the house into a royal palace, and during the reign of Henry VIII Greenwich reached the peak of royal favour. In the Victorian era Greenwich Park became a popular recreational area. Its view over London is justly famous.

Charles II founded the **Old Royal Observatory (6)** in 1675 to aid mariners in navigation, instructing Sir Christopher Wren to build a small observatory on a high point in the royal park. The Astronomer Royal, John Flamsteed, who had previously used the White Tower in the Tower of London for his observations, laid the foundation stone and cast the observatory's horoscope. Wren designed a house for Flamsteed of red brick and stone dressings, with an upper balustrade and miniature canted cupolas. In the adjacent summer house, built in 1676 and used by Flamsteed as his Solar Observatory, is the tombstone of his successor Edmond Halley.

Wren designed the beautifully proportioned Octagon Room with a high ceiling so that Thomas Tompion's pendulum clocks, used by Flamsteed, could be accommodated. Early telescopes are displayed here. Elsewhere in the house there are displays about the history of the measurement of time, which include nocturnal time-keeping instruments, hour-glasses, sundials, mechanical instruments and the Harrison Chronometer. Outside, the red time ball on the roof was erected in 1833 as a visual time signal for navigation on the Thames, and for clockmakers in Clerkenwell. The ball rises to the top of the mast and falls at precisely 1 p.m. GMT.

The Meridian Building is a mid-18th-century addition built to house the observatory's growing collection of astronomical instruments. Through it passes the Greenwich, or Prime, Meridian, indicated by a brass strip in the courtyard's floor. Until the late 18th century each country used its capital as the zero line of longitude. The *British Nautical Almanack*, published in 1767, proved both indispensable for navigators and popular with map-makers, and in 1884 it was internationally agreed that the Greenwich Meridian would form the zero meridian – the point at which the Eastern and Western Hemispheres meet. The world's time zones were thus established. The Meridian Building houses Airy's Transit Circle, from which more than 750,000 observations were made until the last one in 1954. Instruments on display include Halley's 8-ft/2.4-m iron quadrant and 5-ft/ 1.5 m transit, and Bradley's Zenith sector and 8-ft/2.4-m transit.

In 1857 the Great Equatorial Building was added, designed to house the observatory's first large telescope. In 1936 the observatory began the control of the Speaking Clock. After the Second World War, because of the smoke and street lights of metropolitan London, the observatory has moved out of London and its former buildings were gradually opened as a museum.

The Caird **Planetarium (7)** was opened near the Old Royal Observatory in 1965. It once housed large telescopes now at Herstmonceux. A wide variety of programmes on the moon and stars is given in the building at various times.

Ranger's House (8), a red-brick villa on Blackheath, with its fine panelled rooms, dates from 1700 and is now the home of the Suffolk Collection of British Portraits and Old Master Paintings. In 1974, the house was opened to the public, and its chief attractions are a magnificent series of full-length Jacobean portraits by William Larkin, a group of royal portraits by Lely and others, and the remaining paintings from a collection of Old Masters that once contained Leonardo's *Virgin on the Rocks*, now in the National Gallery. The house's Chintz Room is a fine example of an early-18th-century bedroom.

The Dolmetsch Collection of early musical instruments is housed on the first floor. Arnold Dolmetsch (1858–1940) devoted his life to the revival of interest in the music of the past, breaking with the Victorian view that 'real' music started with Beethoven or possibly Mozart and that anything earlier was an imperfect attempt to reach this 19th-century ideal. Dolmetsch, a part-time teacher at Dulwich College with an interest in both old instruments and old music, rejected the view that J. S. Bach was a 'musician's musician', that the viol was a failed ancestor of the violin, and questioned why Purcell's music was known only to scholars. His collection, a small part of which is also housed in the Horniman Museum (p. 380), consists of three groups of instruments: old instruments for use as examples and for performance; original instruments, which he restored, repaired or adapted; and modern instruments, which he designed and constructed in accordance with earlier principles. In Room 1 are his early instruments, which reflect the evolution of music and its instruments from before 1600, when music was conceived as a series of interlocking melodies of equal importance formed into a balanced whole, into the 17th and 18th centuries, when music became less intimate and more public, and where one principal melodic line was supported by a strong bass and supporting harmonies. The instruments here include an early-17th-century Italian archlute, an 18th-century English guitar, recorders and a transverse flute.

In the Dressing Room is a display of engravings of musical instruments and portraits of influential composers and performers.

The Period Room is laid out to give an impression of amateur music-making in the 18th century. In Room 4 are instruments restored by Dolmetsch and others he designed himself. On the ground floor is the Green Harpsichord of 1896, Dolmetsch's first harpsichord, made at the suggestion of William Morris.

> *Directions: From Ranger's House take the Chesterfield Walk north to Croom's Hill. Croom's Hill is one of London's oldest known roads, 'crom' being the Celtic word for crooked. The road leads down into Stockwell Street, which meets Greenwich High Road. Greenwich B R is 250 yds/228 m to the south-west.*

Tea magnate Frederick Horniman, whose firm was the first to sell tea in packets, travelled the world collecting an almost unbelievable range of extraordinary objects. He brought to his home in Forest Hill Navajo Indian art; Benin bronzes from the west coast of Africa dating from the 16th century; a Spanish torture chair from the time of the Inquisition; shadow puppets from Java; a life-size model walrus; 2,000 active bees; masks and a marvellous miscellany of other objects. His collection grew so large that it outgrew the house and in 1898 he decided on a purpose-built museum. Four years later he presented the museum to the people of London. Designed in Art Nouveau style, the **Horniman Museum** has a large decorative mosaic on its main façade showing an allegory on the course of human life.

The museum has three sections: ethnography, natural history and musical instruments. Horniman was particularly interested in the Red Indian peoples and the museum is particularly rich in their artefacts. The museum's Navajo sand painting was made in 1966 out of sand and charcoal by a hereditary medicine man of this Red Indian people to a traditional design known as the 'whirling log'. The Egyptian section houses mummies and a grave dating from 3000 BC, reassembled as it was found. There are, in addition, works covering Eskimo, Islamic, Eastern, Pacific, Australian and African cultures.

The Horniman's collection of musical instruments is of international standing. It spans over 2,000 years and covers both European and non-European cultures. The museum's natural history section includes a number of live exhibits in the aquarium and vivarium. The Horniman gives a number of changing special exhibitions, free lectures and concerts.

Directions: Forest Hill BR from Charing Cross BR. Take London Road west. The Horniman Museum lies on its north side.

The **Thames Barrier** is the world's largest movable flood barrier. Completed in 1982, it is part of a flood defence scheme for London that includes a system of raised banks downstream on the Thames estuary and flood gates on smaller rivers and creeks. Banks have also been raised upstream as far as Teddington.

The barrier was sited at Woolwich Reach because of the good chalk foundations for its giant piers. It was also the best approach for shipping. The barrier spans 656 yds/600 m across the river and consists of ten separate movable steel gates that pivot. They are supported between concrete piers, which house the hydraulic machinery. The foundations for each of the main central piers equal those of a power station. Together the piers and sills contain half a million tonnes of concrete, enough to build almost 10 miles/16 km of motorway. When raised, the four main gates each stand as high as a five-storey building, as wide as the opening of Tower Bridge. They weigh over 3,700 tonnes. heavier than a navy destroyer. During the 1980s the gates normally closed due to high water on only two or three occasions each year. In the next century, as the relative level of land and sea changes, the number of closures is expected to increase to perhaps ten a year. The visitors' centre houses an exhibition hall, working models and an audio-visual show. Short round-the-barrier cruises leave from a nearby pier.

> *Directions: Woolwich BR from Charing Cross BR. Take Charlton Church Street north to the junction with Woolwich Road. Turn west on to Woolwich Road. Unity Way lies to its north.*

South-west

CHISWICK

Until the mid-19th century Chiswick was a country village, located in a loop of the Thames. Attractive Georgian houses with bow windows and balconies still line streets running down to the river, notably in Chiswick Mall.

Hogarth's House, where William Hogarth (1697–1764), satirical painter and critic of art and society, lived from 1749 until his death, is a charming Georgian mansion, which he called his 'box by the Thames'. Hogarth was born in the capital and apprenticed at the age of 15 to a silversmith, engraving what he later called the 'monsters of heraldry', armorial bearings, on gold and silver work. While making a living as an engraver, Hogarth taught himself painting, evolving a pragmatic, intuitive, expressive art. Although he enjoyed the companionship at London's coffee houses and taverns of many members of the country's intellectual élite, Hogarth's sympathies lay with the critical, enlightened middle classes. His friends included David Garrick, the actor-manager at the Theatre Royal, Drury Lane, and writer-magistrate Sir Henry Fielding. Hogarth joined the free drawing school and later married the daughter of Sir James Thornhill, the serjeant painter to the King and the first knighted English-born artist. In allying himself with Thornhill, the adaptor of the late baroque style, Hogarth opposed the aristocratic and intellectual clique sponsoring the neo-classical revival lead by the Earl of Burlington, the influential art lover and patron. For his vociferous antipathy to their snobbish and exclusive admiration for the old masters and their prejudice in favour of the works of foreign artists regardless of merit or state of preservation, the 'lovers of dark pictures' ensured that Hogarth's early works were totally excluded from royal interest. Although Hogarth's small, informal group portraits, or 'conversation pieces', were initially popular commissions with the aristocracy, his moral tales, such as *The Harlot's Progress* and *Marriage à la Mode*, which satirized 18th-century society, were too honest for Hogarth to become an appendage to upper-class life. In an amusing swipe against the connoisseurs Hogarth installed over the front door at his house in Leicester Fields, now

Leicester Square, a gilded head of the fashionable 17th-century society portrait painter Sir Anthony van Dyck.

In 1735 Hogarth was elected as a governor of St Bartholomew's Hospital (*St Paul's* ⊖) and produced for its main staircase the historical paintings *Pool of Bethesda* and *The Good Samaritan*. Hogarth's considerable philanthropic works included a full length, highly realistic and sympathetic portrait of Captain Thomas Coram, founder of the Foundling Hospital for orphan children (*King's Cross/St Pancras* ⊖). There, with other contemporary artists, Hogarth produced the first public exhibition of contemporary art in England, foreshadowing the formation of the Royal Academy in 1768. Later, in a pioneering move to ensure wide distribution, Hogarth cut on wood blocks *Beer Street*, *Gin Lane* and *Four Stages of Cruelty*, biting scenes critical of the depravity of contemporary life.

The latter part of Hogarth's life was characterized by bitterness and an inability to resolve the tension between pure painting, which raises no ethical problems or questions of meaning, and art, which records the commitment to moral standpoints. The contemporary rococo movement's delight in the decorative use of paint is manifest in his pictures, but Hogarth had no desire to withhold promoting his own moral values. His attempts at a synthesis of comedy, comment and satire within dignified historical painting or portraiture were judged as lacking the poise required for favourable critical opinion. As a result Hogarth's legacy fell more to literature than painting. Only on the Continent were his painting skills fully appreciated.

Hogarth's house in Chiswick was opened as a museum in 1909. It contains many of his famous engravings, including the series *The Harlot's Progress*, *Industry and Idleness*, *London Scenes*, *The Election* and *Marriage à la Mode*, as well as his engraving toolbox.

> *Directions: Turnham Green ⊖ (District Line). Turnham Green leads south to Chiswick High Road. A short distance east, Chiswick Lane leads south to the Great West Road. Hogarth Lane is to the west and reached by the subway.*

Lord Burlington (1694–1753), connoisseur, patron of the arts and leader of the intellectual clique that sponsored the 18th-century neo-classical revival, inspired the creation of **Chiswick House**, a magnificent country villa modelled on Palladio's Villa

Rotonda near Vicenza. Burlington, one of the first English noblemen to round off their education with a grand tour of the Continent, was converted to the simplicity and serenity of Palladianism by the young Scottish architect Colen Campbell. Completed around 1729 largely to his own designs, Burlington's house at Chiswick was built not as a home, but as a temple to display his works of art and as a venue for cultured *conversazioni* for the entertainment and edification of such friends as Pope, Swift, Handel and the philosopher Bishop Berkeley.

William Kent, a follower of Inigo Jones (who a century earlier had modelled buildings on Palladio), was responsible for much of the house's interior decoration and for its splendid park. The house is approached along an avenue of classical busts carved on decorative shafts. An octagonal dome rises above the portico and is lined on either side by large obelisks. The interior of the house has been carefully restored to its appearance during Burlington's time. Although largely unfurnished, some selected paintings and mirrors have been hung. The lower floor displays drawings and sketches concerning the house and its restoration. At the foot of the elaborate double staircase are two statues: Palladio, on the left, and Jones, on the right, both carved around 1730 by Rysbrack. The small symmetrical rooms on the upper, principal floor, are interconnected around the central octagon. The walls of the Red, Blue and Green Velvet Rooms have been lined with flock wallpaper matching their original appearance, and the house contains some spectacular gilded ceilings by Kent as well as a fireplace inspired by Inigo Jones. Chimney flues lead out to the obelisks on the roof.

The gardens were the first to break with the contemporary and formal Dutch style. Many buildings and follies have fallen down or been demolished during the history of the house, but there remains a picturesque landscape of serpentine paths, a Doric column, an Ionic temple, a number of statues and obelisks, a cascade, a deer house and a variety of other interesting constructions. The Inigo Jones Gateway was erected in 1621 outside Beaufort House in Chelsea, but presented to Burlington by Sir Hans Sloane in 1736.

> *Directions: From Hogarth House, return to the Great West Road flyover/subway complex and take Burlington Lane, which leads to the south-west. Chiswick House and Park lie to the north of Burlington Lane.*

Built on the banks of the Thames, **Ham House** has been called the sleeping beauty among country houses. Thanks to the Earls of Dysart, who lived at Ham for nearly 300 years, this red-brick house has survived largely unaltered since the 17th century, a monument to the taste of the Restoration era. No expense was spared on its sumptuous interior, with rooms 'furnished like a great prince's'. Inventories of the house survive from which it is clear that the walls were once hung with tapestries, damask and velvet, beds covered with satins; and furniture upholstered in brilliant matching colours. The house has been restored to its 1678 arrangement, a time when it was at its zenith under Elizabeth Dysart, Duchess of Lauderdale. In 1948 the Dysart family presented the house with most of the original furnishings to the National Trust. A few appropriate pieces have since been added by the Victoria and Albert Museum. The magnificent oak staircase has been completely regilded, and has a beautiful balustrade of carved arms. On the first floor are works by Hilliard, Oliver and Cooper, the finest collection of miniature portraits in the country outside the Victoria and Albert Museum. Ham House's remarkable 17th-century formal style garden has also survived and has been restored and replanted by the National Trust. There is a beautiful Cherry Garden.

Directions: Richmond ⊖ (District Line). Bus 71 (except Sundays) or 65 to the Fox and Duck Inn at Petersham. By foot via the towpath along the Thames from Richmond Bridge, or along Petersham Road south from Richmond ⊖. During the summer Hammerton's Ferry runs between Ham and the towpath below Marble Hill House (p. 394).

On the banks of the Thames, 15 miles/24 km south-west of London, is the magnificent **Hampton Court Palace**. It combines some of the best Tudor architecture in England with splendid designs by Wren. Hampton Court was a favourite country home, hunting lodge and pleasure palace for successive generations of English monarchs in the 16th and 17th centuries. It owes its existence to four builder-patrons: Cardinal Wolsey, Henry VIII, and William and Mary.

The palace's western section was commissioned by Thomas Wolsey as a manor house in 1514, when he was Archbishop of York. The following year Wolsey became Cardinal and Lord Chancellor and, in 1518, Papal Legate. The proportions of his mansion grew to include 280 guest rooms, a staff of nearly 500, set in an estate extending over 1,800 acres/728 ha. As Henry VIII's richest and most powerful subject, Wolsey lived in a house more splendid than perhaps any palace in the country. His home was also a model of hygiene. Every part of the house was drained by great brick sewers into the Thames. Mindful of royal power, however, Wolsey assigned his great house to the king in 1525, but was allowed to remain in residence. But, after failing to secure papal approval of Henry's divorce from Catherine of Aragon, the Cardinal fell from favour and was stripped of his titles. He retired to York in 1530 and after his arrest for high treason, died on his way to trial.

Henry VIII moved into Hampton Court and turned it into one of the most sumptuous palaces that England had ever known. He constructed the Great Hall, the Great Watching Chamber and annexes around the Kitchen Court, including the Haunted Gallery, a library and a guardroom. Five of Henry's six wives lived here. Jane Seymour died in the palace in 1537 after giving birth to Henry's only son, later Edward VI.

Elizabeth I conducted both state and private business from Hampton Court. During her reign the fate of Mary Queen of Scots was decided here. During the Commonwealth Oliver Cromwell used the palace personally and it remained unscathed, unlike many other royal buildings.

Further rebuilding commenced following William and Mary's accession in 1689. Sir Christopher Wren was commissioned to design 'a new Versailles'. Initially, Wren intended to demolish the whole palace, but Mary's premature death in 1694 and a shortage of money forced William to abandon the plan. Only Henry VIII's state apartments were pulled down. During Wren's time four buildings in French Renaissance style were built around the new Fountain Court. Antonio Verrio, Grinling Gibbons, Jean Tijou and Louis Laguerre were among the many notable master craftsmen who contributed to the palace.

Queen Anne had Wren design and Gibbons decorate a small Banqueting House and began the furnishing and decoration of the State Apartments, only finally completed under George II, the last monarch to reside at the palace. In the 18th century many rooms were converted to grace-and-favour accommodation. In 1838 Queen Victoria opened the State Apartments, gardens and nearby Bushy Park to the public.

The exterior of the palace is noted for its moat and bridge,

built by Henry VIII and guarded by the 'King's Beasts'; the
Great Gatehouse, with its Tudor oriel windows and arms of
Henry VIII; the **Base Court**, the largest surviving Tudor court;
and **Anne Boleyn's Gateway**, which leads into **Clock Court**.
There, on the inner side of the gateway, is the face of a great
astronomical clock made by Nicholas Oursian in 1540, which
displays the hour, day, month, phase of the moon and the time
of high water at London Bridge. At the centre of the clock the
sun is depicted revolving around the Earth, the Ptolemaic view
prevailing in 16th century England.

Fountain Court, the core of Wren's design for William and
Mary's new palace in 1694, contrasts with the Tudor
architecture. It is built in brick and enhanced with Portland
stone. The **State Apartments** and **Queen's Private Apartments**
are on the first floor, with accommodation for staff, courtiers
and guests both above and below. The entrance to the State
Rooms is in the south-east corner of the Clock Court.

The most noteworthy features of the palace's interior include
the spectacular ceiling paintings of the **King's Bedroom** and the
King's Staircase by the celebrated Italian artist Antonio Verrio.
In the bedroom is a composition depicting the hunter Endymion
lying in the arms of Morpheus, the god of sleep, and above the
staircase are the gods, goddesses and heroes of ancient Rome.
The balustrade is by Tijou. The state bed, chairs and stools are
original, and the tapestries are from the 16th-century Abraham
series. The cornice by Gibbons is judged to be some of his finest
work. More than 3,000 pieces of armour are displayed in the
King's Guard Chamber, all as arranged in the 17th century.

The **Queen's Gallery** houses tapestries from the Flemish
Alexander series of the 18th century, and the outstanding
marble fireplace was carved by John Nost in the 17th century.
The **Queen's Drawing Room** was decorated for Queen Anne by
Verrio in 1705, and from its window there is a splendid view
of the Great Fountain Garden. The three-roomed **Prince of
Wales's Suite** was decorated by Vanbrugh for Queen Anne,
and its bedroom contains a bed with a painted dome and delicate
late-18th-century embroidery. The **Cartoon Gallery** contains
historical paintings of Henry VIII's reign.

In the **Communication Gallery**, which links the King's and
Queen's State Apartments, are 17th-century portraits by Lely of
the ladies of Charles II's court, originally hung at Windsor
Castle and still known as 'the Windsor Beauties'. At the end of

the gallery, a door leads to some Tudor rooms, including **Wolsey's Closet**, with its early-16th-century wall paintings and ornate gilt gesso ceiling adorned with Tudor roses and the feathers of the Prince of Wales.

The **Queen's Staircase** has a Tijou balustrade, and wall and ceiling paintings by Kent and Honthorst. The **Haunted Gallery** linked the Chapel Royal with Wolsey's state apartments, and is reputedly haunted by Catherine Howard, Henry VIII's fifth wife, executed for adultery. The **Chapel Royal** was built for Wolsey, but little survives internally from this period. Its fan-vaulted ceiling was added by Henry VIII in 1536, and the stars are Pugin's 19th-century redecoration. The wooden reredos is by Gibbons, and the painting above it by Thornhill.

The **Great Watching Chamber** was built in 1536 as a guard-room for Henry and is all that remains of his state apartments. The panelled ceiling incorporates coloured bosses displaying his coat of arms and that of his third wife, Jane Seymour.

The **Great Hall** of 1554 was Henry's most important addition to Hampton Court, and he was so impatient to have it finished that craftsmen were ordered to work by candlelight. Leading members of his household once feasted at a high table set on a raised dais here. Others ate at common tables set along the side walls. The hammer-beam roof contains the monograms and badges of Anne Boleyn and Jane Seymour. Its walls are hung with 16th-century Flemish tapestries. At the far end of the hall is the minstrels' gallery. The **Great Kitchens** are the most extensive examples of Tudor kitchens, and continued in use until the 18th century. The **Renaissance Picture Gallery** displays paintings on wood from the royal collection.

Hampton Court's grounds include the **Fountain Garden** in front of the east façade of Wren's building. Its yew trees were laid out for William III by London and Wise as a *patte d'oie*, or goose-foot pattern. The **East Grounds** were laid out for Charles II by Mollet. Jean Tijou executed some of his finest work for the Hampton Court gardens, namely a spectacular wrought-iron screen of twelve panels. In the **Lower Orangery** are Mantegna's nine *Cartoons of the Triumph of Caesar* from the 15th century, purchased by Charles I and thought to be the oldest paintings on canvas. The grounds also contain the **Knot Garden**; the colourful **Pond Garden**, laid out around 1700 and remodelled earlier this century; the **Banqueting House**, built in 1700 by Wren to house William's summer banquets; the **Vinery**, with its great vine of the Black Hamburgh variety planted in the reign of George III; the **Old Close Tennis Court**; and the **'Tudor' Tennis Court** where real tennis, the forerunner of lawn tennis, is still played. Finally, there is Hampton Court's famous **Maze**, laid out in its triangular shape in 1714.

> *Directions: Hampton Court BR via Waterloo BR. Take Hampton Court Bridge over the Thames. The palace lies to the east.*

KEW

The **Royal Botanic Gardens** at Kew (1) are the most famous botanical gardens in the world. Kew's remarkable 'living collections' of plants grown by scientists for study are open to the public, the product of two centuries of careful, and often hazardous, plant hunting. Expeditions have scoured the wild places of the world for new plant material, sending back seeds and cuttings of bizarre life-forms that now flourish placidly by the Thames. The gardens cover an area of nearly 300 acres/120 ha. In the 18th century they were the private grounds of three royal residences: Kew Palace (the Dutch House), Kew House (the White House) to the north, and Ormond Lodge (later Richmond House) to the south. In 1802 the grounds were joined, although the Old Deer Park remains separate.

A beautiful garden existed here as early as the 17th century. In 1759 Augusta, Dowager Princess of Wales, created a botanic garden of some 9 acres/3.6 ha. During the reign of George III, Capability Brown landscaped much of the gardens and by 1789 5,500 different species were known to be present. Following the tradition of one of the garden's directors, the distinguished botanist and traveller Sir Joseph Banks, various 'plant hunting' expeditions greatly supplemented the garden's collection of delicate and exotic species. Queen Victoria presented Kew Gardens to the nation in 1841, following the recommendations of a Royal Commission.

The gardens are popular as a family day-out, especially in the spring and early summer. But Kew has sections for every season and type of plant. Commonplace ones are juxtaposed with rare and priceless foreign species, and trees stand singly or in selected groups. The garden has some excellent views and is now home to some 50,000 species from all parts of the world. Visitors can dip their noses into *Dehepainia smaragdina* and instantly recoil from the nasty odour of the aptly named Smelly Socks Plant; see the

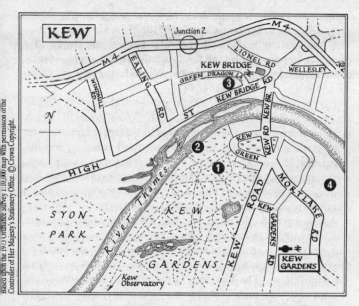

Based upon the 1975 Ordnance Survey 1:10,000 map with permission of the Controller of Her Majesty's Stationery Office. ©Crown Copyright.

embossed bumps of *Preissia quadrata*, said to have been the inspiration behind Braille; smell the aromas of the chamomile lawn, and inspect the carnivorous pitcher plant. The giant water lily, *Victoria amazonica*, starts about the size of a pea. Sown in a pot in January, by the end of July it occupies a pool half the size of a tennis court. Its magnificent flowers open at 2 p.m., close at 10 p.m., dying slowly the following day before finally sinking into the water. First cultivated at Kew in 1849, it is now one of the garden's great attractions. It is said that only after its name had been registered was it realized the tactlessness of linking the name 'Amazon' to the Queen's name. Her Majesty was kept in ignorance of the plant's full name until her dying day.

The undersurface of the giant water lily was the inspiration for the Crystal Palace of 1851, and the great glasshouses that followed. One of those soaring creations of glass and cast iron, erected before Crystal Palace, is Kew's Palm House, built by Decimus Burton, and judged by some to be superior to his Crystal Palace. The revolutionary nature of the commission – to design a house for trees – precluded the normal forest of load-bearing columns inside the building. Spiral steps now take the visitor up towards the roof of this gossamer balloon to marvel at the palm tops. Decimus Burton also designed the

Temperate House, an angular, fussy and magisterial building quite different to the cool elegance of the Palm House.

A rose garden lies outside the Palm House, and the nearby pond is watched over by the ten Queen's Beasts, stone replicas of those designed to stand outside Westminster Abbey at the coronation of Queen Elizabeth II.

The gardens' other specialist houses include the Alpine House, a rock landscape built beneath a glass pyramid, which includes a refrigerated bed; the Tropical Waterlily House, open only in the summer; the Aroid House; the Ferneries; and the Australian House. The Orangery houses temporary exhibitions, a bookshop and tea-room. The Marianne North Gallery has more than 800 works on botanical and entomological subjects donated by painter and traveller Marianne North.

At the western end of the gardens are the Queen's Cottage, the Japanese Gateway and Kew's Pagoda. The cottage was a summer house built for Queen Charlotte and contains prints by Hogarth. The Japanese Gateway is a near actual size copy of *Chokushi Mon*, 'The Gateway of the Imperial Messenger', in Kyoto. Sir William Chambers's 163-ft/49.7-m, ten-storey pagoda, built in 1761, stands at the end of a long vista and is one of many follies adorning the gardens. It was then an expression of fashionable chinoiserie reflecting respect, among other things, for the invention of the botanical garden by the early Chinese.

Kew's outstanding scientific establishment is world-renowned for research and conservation work. Its private herbarium and library contain more than 5 million dried plants, a sizeable proportion of the 30 million plant species that may exist in the world, as well as over 120,000 books and around 160,000 prints and drawings.

Although one of the worst storms ever to hit Britain decimated Kew Gardens in October 1987 – 500 of the 11,000 trees were felled by the storm and another 500 damaged – much new building and restoration has taken place in recent years. The cast-iron frame of the Palm House was found to be in a very bad state and was completely recast and rebuilt. In 1987 the Princess of Wales opened a new conservatory named after her, the most technologically-advanced plant house in the world, a structure housing ten different landscaped environments, all with computer-controlled heating and ventilation. The main area of the conservatory is given over to the tropics, with running water and tree ferns creating a wonderful luxuriance close to lily pools and swamps. There are forest regions, cloud and tropical, and masses of succulents from the new world, plus a splendid display of orchids, which can be viewed from virtually any level. There are also areas for desert and insectivorous plants.

Kew Palace (2) a small Jacobean mansion, originally known as the Dutch House, is the only survivor of a small group of royal residences at Kew Green. The dark-red brick house with Dutch attic gables was built in 1631 by Samuel Fortrey, a London merchant of Dutch parentage. It became the smallest royal residence when it was acquired in 1728. George III and Queen Charlotte adopted the house as a summer residence in 1802. It remained unoccupied from 1818. The house's panelled interior is mainly from the 18th century, with 19th-century furnishings. The Queen's Gardens, opened by Queen Elizabeth II in 1969, are laid out in formal 17th-century style with characteristic herbal plants of the period.

A number of original engines are always to be found in steam at **Kew Bridge Steam Museum (3)** which is devoted to the development of the steam engine. Its working engines include the Boulton and Watt (1820), the 90-inch (1846), the Easton and Amos (1863) and the Hawthorn Davey Triple (1910). The Cornish beam engines, used for pumping out the county's mines, were also used to pump London's water.

In addition, the museum contains traction engines; steam lorries; smaller stationary steam engines; water supply relics, including a main made from hollowed-out tree trunks; steamboats, including the *Consuta*, a high-speed launch built in 1898; a forge; a steam railway on 2-ft/0.6-m gauge; and the tall standpipe tower outside.

The massive archives at **Kew Public Record Office (4)** are estimated to have sufficient capacity to house every confidential state document until the year 2000. These range from top secret Cabinet minutes to the most humble agricultural report. In 1838 the Public Record Office Act established a national archive for the records of central government and the central courts of England and Wales. The Kew archives, opened in 1977, are among the most up-to-date document storage buildings in the world. The contents are housed in a controlled air-conditioned environment and items are requisitioned via computer terminals. The records at Kew are predominantly from modern 19th- and 20th-century departments of state, but they also include such items as William Morris's and other registered pattern designs from the last century. Admiralty and Treasury records stretch back further. Many documents remain secret from public scrutiny. Records that can be inspected here include the entire Cabinet minutes from Lloyd George's premiership to that of Clement Attlee; dispatches from the Crimea; Palmerston's diplomatic correspondence; and the archives of both world wars. The Public Record Office in Chancery Lane (*Temple* ⊖) contains the PRO museum.

> *Directions: Kew Gardens* ⊖ *(District Line). Take Kew Gardens Road north, where it meets Kew Road. Turn north along Kew Road. The main entrance to Kew Gardens is to the west.* Syon Park and House *(p. 396) are near by, north of the Thames, and some distance upstream.*

Marble Hill House, a fine example of the 18th-century Palladian tradition in English country houses, is situated in a beautiful location by the Thames. The Palladian style, named after Italian Andrea Palladio (1508–80), strove to imitate the architecture of ancient Rome and was first introduced to England by Inigo Jones in the early 17th century. One hundred years later Lord Burlington, influenced by the young Scottish architect Colen Campbell, was inspired to lead the neo-classical revival in Britain. Campbell's Marble Hill House (1729) emerged as a result. Henrietta Howard, mistress of George II and later Countess of Suffolk, commissioned the house as a summer retreat from court life where she entertained poets and the dilettanti of the age.

The villa has survived almost unchanged, although in 1902 it nearly became a building site. In 1966 Marble Hill House was re-opened as a historic house museum and is now home of a collection of paintings from the early 18th century, including *Le Lecteur* by Gravelot and Wilson's charming view of *The Thames at Marble Hill*.

The climax of a visit to Marble Hill House is the Great Room. Resplendent in white and gold beneath a deeply coved ceiling and a wealth of carving, the room is contained within a cube of

24 ft/7.3 m, proportions ultimately derived from Palladio via Inigo Jones's Single Cube room at Wilton House. One of its elaborately carved Great Tables has been recently returned after discovery in Australia. The table now constitutes the only piece of furniture dating from Lady Suffolk's occupancy. Two original overdoors and an overmantel from a set of five Roman landscapes by Giovanni Paolo Panini in 1738 have also been restored to their former positions. The direction of light and perspective in Panini's overmantel painting *Statues in a Ruined Arcade*, when viewed from the doorway to Lady Suffolk's bedchamber, suggest that it was specially commissioned for the room. The house contains much early Georgian walnut and mahogany furniture.

The Northey Suite has some fine original needlework, and eight rare and beautiful Chinese mirror paintings have been put on display here. The grounds are the result of a collaboration between the poet Alexander Pope and Charles Bridgeman, landscape gardener to George I and George II. Seasons of 'picnic promenades' take place in the summer on Sunday evenings on the lawns stretching from the villa to the Thames. Near by is the long and beautiful Montpelier Row, one of London's finest early Georgian terraces.

Directions: Richmond ⊖ (District Line). Then Buses 90B, 202, 270, 290. Alternatively, by foot via the towpath along the Thames from Richmond Bridge to Ham House, where, in the summer, a ferry links Marble Hill House to its neighbour (p. 386).

Architect Robert Adam transformed the Elizabethan mansion at **Osterley** into an elegant neo-classical villa. Today **Osterley Park House** stands as perhaps the finest surviving example of his work. Room after room remains as he designed it, in the most meticulous detail, between 1763 and 1782 for Robert Child, a grandson of the wealthy banker Francis Child, who purchased the house in 1711. Its Georgian room displays, adorned by many of Osterley's original pieces of English furniture, combine to form a dazzling exhibition of the finest designs and furnishings of the third quarter of the 18th century.

The Library ceiling is a masterpiece of Adam plasterwork. Every item in the Hall, except the statues, is by Adam. Only the Gallery, the ceilings in the Drawing Room and Eating Room are from Sir William Chambers's earlier redecoration in the 1750s; the rest is Adam's work. Sunflowers and ostrich feathers form the theme of the Drawing Room. In the Tapestry Room the French Gobelins' tapestries create the effect of a leafy bower in which are suspended *trompe l'œil* paintings by Boucher. The domed and gilded four-poster bed in the Osterley State Bedchamber was once compared by Horace Walpole to 'a modern head-dress'. Adam designed it as a Temple of Venus, with velvet and silk hangings and garlands of silk flowers. The house stands in a landscaped park with lakes, garden temples and an Elizabethan stable block.

> *Directions: Osterley ⊖ (Piccadilly Line). Take Great West Road east. Turn north into Thornbury Road. Osterley Park is straight ahead.*

Capability Brown assisted in the design of **Syon Park Gardens**, while Robert Adam worked on **Syon House**. In 1837 these gardens, with their many rare species of plants, were opened to the public. Also in the grounds today are the Great Conservatory, the Butterfly House, the Heritage Collection Motor Museum and a large rose garden to the south of the house. The conservatory, which contains cacti, an aviary and an aquarium, was constructed in 1827 by Charles Fowler, the same year he constructed the market at Covent Garden. The Butterfly Collection is one of the world's largest collections of live butterflies. In this tropical greenhouse it is possible to see the butterfly at various stages of development, as well as various spiders, locusts, ants and scorpions.

The Heritage Motor Museum owns around 300 historic vehicles, from a three-wheeled Wolseley of 1895 to early Jaguars and various prototypes that never reached production. More familiar are the Austin Seven and Lord Nuffield's own Bullnose Morris. Many marques represented in this British collection have disappeared as the country's motor industry has gradually amalgamated. Only a third of the collection is on display at any one time, but there are usually models by Alvis, Austin (the millionth Austin), Daimler, Jaguar (D-type of 1953), Lanchester, Leyland (Leyland Straight 8 of 1927), Rover, M G (Old No. 1 of 1925), Standard and Triumph.

Syon, named after Mount Zion, has been the London home of the Percys, the Dukes of Northumberland, since 1594. The estate had earlier been given to Lord Protector Somerset following the dissolution of the monasteries. He built his Tudor mansion, Syon House, on the site in 1550, but was executed soon after. When James I came to the throne, the house passed to the Percys. In 1761 Adam was asked to design some of the house's interiors.

Adam's formal Great Hall has a black-and-white marble pavement reflected in the ceiling. There are statues of the *Apollo Belvedere* and *The Dying Gladiator*. The Ante-room is in Roman style with Ionic columns, green marble and scagliola pillars, a patterned scagliola floor and gilded statues. The columns in the State Dining Room are Corinthian, and there are deep purple niches with more copies of antique statues. Red silk made in the 18th century at Spitalfields covers the walls of the Red Drawing Room, and the ceiling is by Cipriani. There are paintings by Van Dyck and Lely, and the carpet was designed by Adam. The Long Gallery was planned as the ladies' retiring room. The Print Room contains some fine walnut marquetry inlaid cabinets of the late 17th century.

From the colonnaded east front of Syon House it is possible to see Kew Gardens across the Thames. The Northumberland Lion, with its outstretched tail, crowns the building.

> *Directions: Syon Lane B R via Waterloo B R. Take Spur Road south and turn east along London Road. The entrance to Syon Park lies to the south of London Road.*

The Wimbledon Lawn Tennis Championships, tennis's oldest and most important event, take place over 'Wimbledon fortnight', commencing in the last week in June. The All England Lawn Tennis and Croquet Club was founded at Worple Road in Wimbledon in 1868, and the first men's championship was held just over a decade later. The club moved to its present site in 1922.

The **Wimbledon Lawn Tennis Museum** was opened in 1977 to mark the centenary of the first championship. Its displays cover the game's history from Real, or Royal, Tennis to the most recent championships; from a polite pastime to a highly competitive professional spectator sport. Its collection of tennis costumes illustrates the spread of the sport from the leisured classes in the 19th century to its mass popularity today. The history of the racket is told with historic and modern equipment, and the bouncing rubber ball, without which the game could not have developed, is given its proper place in the museum. There are details of every major player, including some life-size models, and all the Wimbledon Championships, since the advent of open tennis in 1968. The famous Centre Court can be viewed, there is a tennis quiz, and the museum's Kenneth Ritchie Wimbledon Library houses the country's foremost tennis archive.

> *Directions: Southfields* ⊖ *(District Line). Take Wimbledon Park Road south, which leads into Church Road. The museum is on the west side.*

The **Cricket Memorial Gallery** is located at Lord's Cricket Ground, home of the Marylebone Cricket Club, the MCC, whose history is to a striking degree the history of cricket. The club dates its birth from the day in June 1787 on which 'nine gentlemen of the County of Essex, with two given men' played 'eight gentlemen of the County of Middlesex, with two gentlemen of Berkshire and one of Kent'. The match took place in Dorset Square for a purse of 100 guineas and the Middlesex side won by 93 runs. Dorset Square was one of three grounds promoted by the former farm labourer Thomas Lord. The MCC moved to its present ground, Lord's, in 1814. Cricket remained a gentrified, if not aristocratic, pastime even though W. G. Grace helped begin to transform the game into a mass spectator sport in his forty-year career, which began at Lord's in 1865. That year the MCC first advertised in the national press for cricket memorabilia for a museum at Lord's.

Just over twenty years later the élite of Victorian society gathered for a majestic meal held to celebrate the club's first centenary. By this time the MCC had virtually annexed world-wide control of cricket, running everything, making laws, selecting sides and arranging tours and tests. The company at the dinner was so illustrious that W. G. Grace only just squeezed in, given a seat farthest but one from the top table. In this era the professional player customarily touched his cap to his amateur captain and changed in a different dressing room. At the centenary meal the wine list offered no less than six varieties of champagne and there were seventeen speeches. Kent captain Lord Harris declared that 'cricket is now a great medium for instilling healthy and manly ideas into the minds of the hard-worked lower classes.' But he drew attention to his deep concern at the trend, so far confined to smaller cricket clubs, of giving cups as prizes to winning teams. In a passionate appeal to the press he encouraged the true cricketer to discourage 'such meretricious inducements' and to keep cricket 'the one example of a contest with no reward but that of honour'. The Provost of Eton expounded on how cricket had improved moral standards throughout the country, and the club's president pointed out that 'the mowing machine has revolutionized the game'.

In 1953 the MCC's collection was opened as a public museum to commemorate the cricketers of all lands who gave their lives in the two world wars. Kept here always are the famous Ashes, since 1883 the victor's prize in test matches between England and Australia. The Ashes are, in fact, the remains of a burned cricket bail in a small urn, presented by two Melbourne ladies to the victorious England side that year.

The museum possesses the bat with which W. G. Grace made his hundredth century, as well as his snuff-box and *Punch* cartoons. Portraits include Ruskin Spear's *Freddie Trueman*, R. Hannaford's *Sir Donald Bradman*, as well as a small bronze of Alec Bedser by David Hynne, and many photographs and cigarette cards. A display charts the development of the game since its beginnings 300 years ago, when sheep-farmers played with a ball of wool. There are guided tours of the grounds and the club's Long Room.

Directions: St John's Wood ⊖ (Jubilee Line). Take Wellington Road south. Lord's Cricket Ground is on its east side.

Sigmund Freud, the father of psychoanalysis, escaped from the Nazi menace in June 1938. After living in Vienna for more than seventy-five years, he arrived in London at the age of 82 and settled in Hampstead, where he died the following year. In the house now designated **The Freud Museum** he completed his last work *Moses and Monotheism* and began writing *An Outline of Psychoanalysis*, published posthumously. He had managed to persuade the Nazis to allow him to take his extensive library, correspondence, carpets, furniture and large collection of Greek, Roman, Egyptian and Oriental antiques, but not before being forced to pay a 'fugitive tax'. The house was lived in by his family until the death of his daughter, Anna, in 1982. Then it was dusted down, packing cases prised open and experts began piecing together the jigsaw of Freud's career.

The house's six rooms are preserved as they were in 1939. The museum is complete with Freud's analysis couch, draped with an oriental rug, his desk and correspondence to family and friends. It also includes his library of 2,000 books and a collection of more than 3,000 Greek, Roman, Oriental and Egyptian antiquities. The museum houses temporary exhibitions on various aspects of psychology and psychoanalysis.

*Directions: Finchley Road ⊖ (Jubilee and Metropolitan Lines).
Cross to the eastern side of Finchley Road. Take Netherhall Gardens
north. First right is Nortley Terrace, which intersects Maresfield
Gardens.*

Highgate Cemetery contains what is probably the finest necro-
polis in the country. This Victorian Valhalla, built on the
southern slopes of Highgate Hill, is a maze of rising terraces,
winding paths, tombs and catacombs, and contains some of the
most celebrated, and often the most eccentric, funerary
architecture to be found anywhere. It was once the most
favoured place to be buried. In its east and west sections, which
cover 37 acres/14 ha., approximately 166,000 bodies are buried
in 51,000 tombs.

Architect Stephen Geary founded the London Cemetery
Company in the 1830s at just the right moment. London's
population was growing enormously. At the beginning of the
century it was around 1 million, but by the close it was nearer 5
million. Church graveyards were literally bursting at the seams.
Geary and landscape gardener David Ramscy set about making
their cemetery more beautiful and unusual than any rival,
thereby hoping to persuade affluent Victorians that, as in life,
they would want something expensive in death.

The cemetery was consecrated in 1839 and such was its success
that in 1857 an extension was opened on the east side of Swain's
Lane. A hydraulic system was installed that lowered coffins from
the chapel in the west cemetery into a basement. From there
they travelled by tunnel under Swain's Lane to the new
cemetery. After the Second World War the graveyard fell into
neglect until 1975 when the newly-formed Friends of Highgate
Cemetery began restoration work.

The Egyptian Avenue leads towards a self-contained community of the dead entered through an iron gateway under a
massive pharaonic arch flanked by obelisks. On either side of
this route, which leads to a Valley of the Kings, are heavy metal
doors, each leading into an individual vault. Next is the Circle of
Lebanon, with vaults built round and into a circular island of
land surmounted by a large cedar tree. Above this is the
cemetery's third great feature, the Terrace Catacombs, an
underground gallery beneath the terrace. Scientists Michael
Faraday and Jacob Bronowski, and poet Christina Rossetti are
buried in the west cemetery. In the east cemetery are the tombs

of Karl Marx, writer George Eliot, philosopher Herbert Spencer and actor Sir Ralph Richardson.

> *Directions: Archway ⊖ (Northern Line). Take Highgate Hill north-west, which joins Highgate High Street. Bisham Gardens leads off to the south-west into Swain's Lane.*

ISLINGTON

The Borough of Islington stretches north from the outskirts of the City of London for over 3 miles/5 km. Many of its interesting features are to be found around the area known as the Angel. Shops, markets, pubs and theatres contribute to Islington's lively community atmosphere, centred around Islington High Street and Upper Street, near the Angel. The borough also has some fine Georgian squares and streets, including Canonbury Square, Milner Square and Cloudesley Square.

Sir Walter Ralegh once lived in Islington. So, too, did Thomas Paine, whose book *The Rights of Man* did much to inspire the French Revolution. Charlie Chaplin once performed at Islington's Collins Music Hall, and Joseph (Joey) Grimaldi, a local theatre manager, is now customarily referred to as the 'father of clowns'.

Camden Passage (1) is a narrow old by-way whose myriad stalls and tiny shops rival Portobello Road (*Notting Hill Gate ⊖*) as London's best-known antique street market. Unlike Porto-bello Road, however, the outdoor pitches have not engulfed the shops. The covered part has up-market ceramics and silver. The market is good for high-grade bric-à-brac and curios and is almost tat-free. A market of a different kind, **Chapel Market (2)**, takes place off the west side of Upper Street. This is a traditional London street market selling fresh fruit and vegetables.

A little further to the north stands 'the Aggie', the Royal Agricultural Hall, built in 1862, under whose vast glass roof was once held the annual Smithfield livestock show and early motor shows and Cruft's dog shows. It has been converted into the **Business Design Centre (3)** for conferences and exhibitions.

For some years its small theatre pubs have gained Islington a reputation as a focus for alternative culture. Productions at both the **King's Head** in Upper Street, and the **Old Red Lion Inn** in St John's Street have transferred to the West End in the wake of critical acclaim. The **Almeida Theatre (4)**, in Almeida Street, is

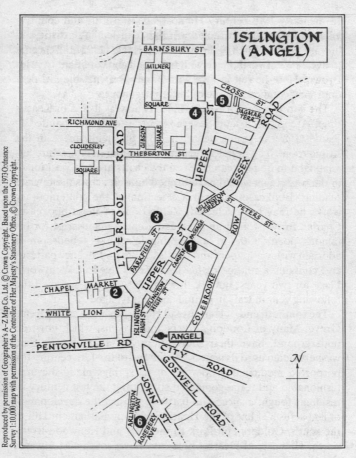

known for its productions of avant-garde music and drama. On Saturday and Sunday afternoons there are shows at the **Little Angel Marionette Theatre (5)**, in Dagmar Passage.

South of Angel ⊖, in Rosebery Avenue, **Sadler's Wells Theatre (6)** has been delighting audiences since the latter part of the 17th century, when it was a side attraction at a popular medicinal well. The Royal Ballet and English National Opera started here. Today it is the home of the New Sadler's Wells Opera. Leading opera, ballet and dance companies are also regularly featured.

Directions: Angel ⊖ (Northern Line).

In the early 19th century Hampstead's fresh air and country-village atmosphere attracted a number of leading artistic and literary figures. In 1818 the poet John Keats (1795–1821) came to live at Wentworth Place with his friend and confidant Charles Brown. Here he fell in love with Fanny Brawne, the girl next door, and composed some of his greatest poetry.

The sitting room of **Keats House** is now as it was in Keats's time. A copy of Joseph Severn's portrait of Keats, painted in Rome after the poet's death, is over the mantelpiece in the sitting room. The detailed layout of the room in the picture has enabled it to be re-created. Even the chairs are now positioned in the way Keats would have draped himself across them while reading. Bookcases contain a selection of the contemporary works he may have selected. Behind one of these bookcases Charles Brown found and rescued Keats's manuscript for his famous poem 'Ode to a Nightingale'. Keats's bedroom is adorned with wallpapers and textiles based on Regency patterns and contains a replica of his bed. Keats lived at Wentworth Place for two years, but fell ill with consumption and died the following year in Italy in virtual anonymity, aged 25.

The southern end of Hampstead Heath lies at the end of Keats Grove. Many of London's rivers and streams, which now run underground, have their source here. In Henry VIII's time washerwomen used its waters. At the end of the 17th century the purported medicinal properties of its springs made the area fashionable and it has remained so. During the last century its residents fought a successful battle to protect the development of 800 acres/324 ha. of the Heath, including Parliament Hill to the south, Golders Hill Park to the west and Kenwood to the north. Hampstead Heath offers fine views south-east towards the City. An ancient barrow left by prehistoric tribes lies on Parliament Hill.

> *Directions: Hampstead ⊖ (Northern Line). Take Hampstead High Street south, which leads into Rosslyn Hill. Turn west into Downshire Hill. Keats Grove leads off to the south. Otherwise, walk across Hampstead Heath to the north to Kenwood House.*

Kenwood House, a magnificent neo-classical villa adjacent to Hampstead Heath, houses the Iveagh Bequest of Old Masters and British paintings. Architect Robert Adam remodelled the house after 1764 for the first Earl of Mansfield, William Murray,

the famous 18th-century Lord Chief Justice. Adam also designed much of the interior decoration and furnishings, including the library, one of his best interiors. Edward Guinness, first
Earl of Iveagh, saved the house from demolition in 1925 and
bequeathed his art collection two years later.

Kenwood's paintings include Rembrandt's late *Self Portrait*,
and *The Guitar Player* by Vermeer, as well as works by Hals,
Van Dyck, Cuyp and Turner. Its marvellous series of British
portraits includes works by Reynolds, Romney and Gainsborough. The house's growing collection of 18th-century furniture has received key Adam pieces returned from America,
including some original Kenwood furniture, and there are also
collections of 18th-century shoe buckles and jewellery.

Special exhibitions are held every year in the upper rooms,
usually illustrating some aspect of 18th-century painting. The
beautiful grounds, with woods and a lake, flowers and sloping
lawns, provide an idyllic setting for lakeside concerts in the
summer. In the spring and autumn music recitals and poetry
readings are held in the 18th-century Orangery.

> *Directions: Archway* ⊖ *(Northern Line) or Golders Green* ⊖
> *(Northern Line), then Bus 210.*

The **Royal Air Force Museum**, the **Battle of Britain Museum**, and
the **Bomber Command Museum** occupy the site of the historic
former Hendon airport, where Grahame-White established his
pre-First World War flying school.

In its exhibition hall, in two hangars dating from the First
World War, the RAF Museum displays around forty aircraft
ranging from the 1909 Blériot XI and Sopwith Camel, to the
supersonic Lightning Mach 2. Surrounding the hall are galleries
dealing with different periods of aviation from the Royal
Engineers' balloon experiments in the 1870s, through Royal
Flying Corps Workshops of the First World War to the present
day. Audio-visual displays re-create various aspects of the work
of the RAF. Between the two main hangars is the Camm
Collection, commemorating Sir Sidney Camm, designer of the
Hawker Hart, Hurricane, and the P1127 'jump jet', the forerunner of the Harrier. The museum also has a collection of paint-
ings, drawings, design drawings and sculptures as well as the
Department of Aviation Records, which includes the Brabazon
Papers covering the history of powered flight up to 1964. Other

exhibits include von Richthofen's flying helmet and an ejector
seat.

The Battle of Britain Museum is devoted to 'the few' who did
so much to preserve the country from a German invasion in
1940. A Spitfire Mk I and a Hurricane are shown under
camouflage alongside each other. German planes are represented by an ME109, JU 87, JU 88, Heinkel III and a Stuka
dive-bomber.

The Bomber Command Museum possesses the only surviving
Wellington bomber, as well as a Lancaster, Halifax, and B17
Flying Fortress. There is a replica of Sir Barnes Wallis's 'Bouncing Bomb', and a re-creation of the office of this engineering
genius. From the First World War there are a DH9A aircraft
and a Sopwith Tabloid. Two 'V' bombers, the Vulcan and the
Valiant, represent post-war aircraft.

*Directions: Colindale ⊖ (Northern Line). Take Colindale Avenue
north. The aerodrome is straight ahead.*

Doris and Charles Saatchi began acquiring the works of Minimal
artists in the mid-1960s, forming their own collection in 1970.
The **Saatchi Collection** gave an inaugural exhibition in 1985, in
the premises of a former paint warehouse north of St John's
Wood.

The collection has hundreds of works, including massive
sculptures and oversize canvases by many of the world's foremost modern artists, from Richard Artschwager to Andy
Warhol. The Saatchis' policy has been to buy works in large
quantities. Over a short period the collection bought 19 paintings by George Baselitz, 23 by Anselm Kiefer, 24 by Francesco
Clemente and 27 by Julian Schnabel. The Collection tries to
exhibit works in separate spaces so that individual artists can be
shown in some depth, no more than three or four artists at one
time, and therefore less than 10 per cent of the collection is ever
on display at one time. There are also works by Donald Judd, Cy
Twombly, Sol LeWitt, Frank Stella, Robert Ryman, Carl Andre
and John Chamberlain, as well as Dan Flavin's *Diagonal of May
25, 1963*, the first use of the fluorescent tube in his work.

*Directions: St John's Wood ⊖ (Jubilee Line). Finchley Road runs
north. Take Boundary Road leading to the west.*

The thunderous roar of 100,000 supporters' voices is replayed to
visitors as they pass down the players' tunnel towards the
hallowed turf of **Wembley Stadium**. At the Royal Box 'the Cup'
can be raised aloft, the moment of ultimate glory for football fan
and player. The daily behind-the-scenes tours of Wembley also
include the players' changing rooms and the Trophy Cabinet,
which houses fifty years of cups and medals.

Wembley's career as the mecca of English football began on
28 April 1923, when Bolton Wanderers and West Ham United
met in the FA Cup Final. It was the first, and last, 'pay at the
gate' Cup Final. Stands were packed to over-capacity, spilling
supporters on to the pitch. Incredibly, by modern standards, it
took just one mounted policeman to restore order.

Nearly every great name in soccer history has since played
here, but Wembley's links with the grassroots of football are also
maintained. During the FA Cup knockout competition the
lowliest of amateur sides, in theory at least, could succeed
against all odds and emerge from the players' tunnel on Cup
Final day.

In 1948 the Olympic Games were staged at Wembley. It was
here that England clinched the World Cup in 1966. The Pope
conducted a sermon from its turf in 1982 and during Live Aid, in
1985, 72,000 spectators packed into the stadium and millions
world-wide watched a pop music charity extravaganza in aid of
Africa's starving peoples.

*Directions: Wembley Park ⊖ (Metropolitan and Jubilee Lines) or
Wembley Central ⊖ (Bakerloo Line).*

East

DOCKLANDS

London's Docklands, dubbed the 'Metropolitan Water City of the 21st Century', are currently being transformed by one of the greatest commercial booms ever seen in the capital. In an unprecedented wave of new investment in buildings and communications, more than 8 sq miles/20 sq km of dereliction and decay are being regenerated into a visionary business and residential environment set by the banks of the Thames. At its heart on Canary Wharf, amidst a sea of cranes and armies of construction workers, the single largest commercial development in Europe is to rise, a controversial multimillion-pound financial centre aimed at rivalling the City of London.

Docklands is divided into four main areas. **Wapping** and **Limehouse** occupy a narrow strip of land on the north bank of the Thames stretching east from St Katharine's Dock to the edge of the Isle of Dogs. The **Isle of Dogs**, actually a peninsula, is surrounded on three sides by a great loop of the Thames. Further east again are the massive **Royal Docks**. The **Surrey Docks** stretch east from London Bridge first in a narrow tail, then filling a broad peninsula on the south side of the Thames.

The Thames has served London as a major artery of trade and transportation since Roman times. During the Middle Ages wealthy City merchants gained control of the Port of London and by the 16th century their companies had taken advantage of the new trade with the Orient and the New World. River congestion and excessive smuggling resulted in the introduction of a series of supervised 'legal quays' between London Bridge and the Tower in the late 16th century. None the less, by the latter part of the 18th century congestion on and beside the river became so severe that traders moved downstream to deeper water and more spacious riverbank locations east of the City.

The Industrial Revolution and Britain's rapidly expanding empire heralded the docks' greatest era. Great sailing ships like the *Cutty Sark* raced other clippers laden with exotic cargoes to the bustling Port of London. In order to satisfy the country's booming trade a vast system of enclosed docks was constructed east from the Tower of London to Gallions Reach 10 miles/16 km away. Development began when the West India Dock

Company opened London's first large enclosed docks in 1802 on the Isle of Dogs. Serviced by substantial warehouses, protected from tides by locks, and from pilfering by 20-ft-/6-m-high walls, the West India Docks proved an immediate success. Other companies soon followed suit. The London Docks and the East India Docks appeared in 1805, the Surrey Docks on the south bank in 1807, St Katharine's in 1828 and Millwall in 1868. The Royal Docks, the largest group, comprise the Royal Victoria Dock, which opened in 1855; the Royal Albert, which opened in 1880; joined finally in 1921 by the King George V Dock. The formation of the Port of London Authority in 1909 ensured the survival of the docks into much of the 20th century, but by the 1960s London's docks began to fall into disuse. By the late 1970s containerization and commercial pressure for the quick turn-round of ships had resulted in a desolate waterscape environment.

The heritage of the docklands has been preserved in an exhibition centre housed in 'W' Warehouse beside Royal Victoria Dock. It can be visited only on a guided tour organized by the Museum in Docklands office, and its exhibits include traditional dockers' tools, early diving equipment and the workshops of such dockside trades as rope rigging, cooperage and tobacco processing. Ultimately, this collection of artefacts will form a permanent museum in Docklands.

In 1981 the London Docklands Development Corporation (LDDC) was formed as the enabling body to oversee the docklands' regeneration programme, securing a budget for public investment in an infrastructure of roads, drainage, street lighting, communications and transport.

The **Docklands Light Railway (DLR)** passes through and above Docklands to the tip of the Isle of Dogs. This 15-minute ride on the DLR's computer-controlled, driverless trains begins at DLR Tower Gateway, near the Tower of London (*Tower Hill* ⊖), and terminates at DLR Island Gardens, where a pedestrian tunnel leads under the river to Greenwich (p. 373). The DLR also runs a service into the heart of East London to DLR Stratford. The DLR's distinctive red, white and blue liveried trains are tended by a Train Captain, who checks tickets and operates the doors.

The DLR's trains accelerate eastwards from DLR Tower Gateway through southern Whitechapel past the old Royal Mint immediately on the right. Coins were first struck here in 1810.

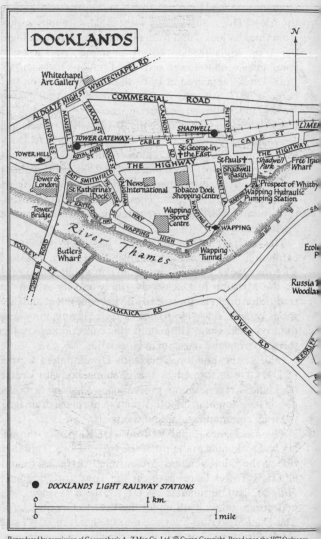

DOCKLANDS

N

Whitechapel Art Gallery

WHITECHAPEL RD

ALDGATE HIGH ST

COMMERCIAL ROAD

MANSELL ST

LEMAN ST

CANNON ST

SUTTON ST

LIMEN

MINORIES

TOWER GATEWAY

CABLE ST

SHADWELL

CABLE ST

THE HIGHWAY

TOWER HILL

ROYAL MINT ST

DOCK ST

St George-in-the East

St Pauls†

Shadwell Park

Shadwell Wharf

Free Trad Wharf

EAST SMITHFIELD

THE HIGHWAY

Shadwell Basin

GARNETT LA

Prospect of Whitby

Tower of London

VAUGHAN ST

News International

Tobacco Dock Shopping Centre

Wapping Hydraulic Pumping Station

St Katharine's Dock

ST KATHARINE'S WY

MILK ST

WAPPING LA

WAPPING

Tower Bridge

WAY

Wapping Sports Centre

WAPPING HIGH ST

WAPPING

TOOLEY ST

TOWER BR. ROAD

Butler's Wharf

River Thames

Wapping Tunnel

SA

Ecol P

Russia Woodla

JAMAICA RD

LOWER RD

REDLIF

● DOCKLANDS LIGHT RAILWAY STATIONS

0   1 km

0   1 mile

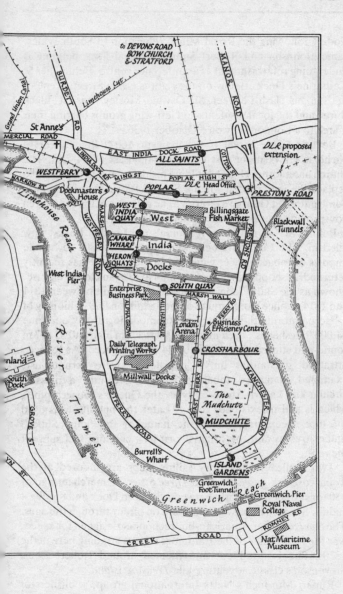

Today, following the Royal Mint's relocation to South Wales, James Johnson and Robert Smirke's Royal Mint building is undergoing refurbishment as a conference centre. Behind lies St Katharine's Dock. Below on the right is **Cable Street**, scene of the famous clash between Sir Oswald Mosley's fascist 'black shirts' and the local residents and left-wing groups barring their march to a London rally on 5 October 1936.

Beyond Cable Street is the majestic 160-ft/48-m tower of Nicholas Hawksmoor's **St George-in-the-East** (1714–26). The church has another church building inside it, built in the 1960s to replace the void caused when a Second World War incendiary bomb gutted St George's interior. The galleries of the old church now provide four flats, one of them the rectory.

Behind St George's are Wapping's old **London Docks**, now filled in. The London Docks were opened in 1805 to handle imports of tobacco, rice, wine and brandy. Trade has recently returned. A shopping village is now located in an old warehouse, known as the Skin Floor, at **Tobacco Dock**. Built between 1811 and 1814, it once stored much of the 18 million lb/8 million kg of tobacco entering the country, accommodating at any one time 24,000 'hogsheads', each measuring 4 ft/1.2 m high and 23 ft/7 m round and stuffed with 1,200 lb/544 kg of tobacco. As tobacco attracted substantial duty, 'hogsheads' were scrupulously examined, damaged tobacco being tossed into a massive circular kiln known irreverently as 'the Queen's tobacco pipe', which is still in existence today. Later the building was used to store sheepskins, hence the name of the floor. Superb timber trusses and the original cast-iron columns still support the roof.

Two replica 18th-century sailing ships are moored at the Tobacco Dock quayside. The *Three Sisters*, a merchantman of 330 tons, traded regularly between Tobacco Dock and the West Indies. She is to house an exhibition on piracy through the ages. The *Sea Hawk*, an American-built schooner designed for speed, was the forerunner of the Baltimore clippers trading here in the 1820s. She is fitted out and themed around Robert Louis Stevenson's classic adventure tale *Treasure Island*.

Rupert Murdoch's News International group, publishers of *The Times*, the *Sunday Times*, the *Sun* and the *News of the World* newspapers, constructed its highly fortified 'Fortress Wapping' building near by. Its victory in the acrimonious industrial dispute with the printing unions in 1986 over the use of new typesetting technology changed the face of Fleet Street for ever.

From DLR Shadwell, Shadwell Basin is on the right behind John Walters's St Paul's church (1819–20), one of the 'Waterloo' churches built in thanksgiving for the defeat of Napoleon. **The Prospect of Whitby**, reputedly the oldest surviving riverside pub in London, is near by. Built in 1520 and a haunt of smugglers and thieves, it was originally known as The Devil's Tavern. In 1777 its name was changed after the *Prospect*, registered at Whitby, moored off the tavern and became a local landmark. Painters Turner and Whistler and authors Dickens and Pepys have imbibed here.

Opposite the *Prospect* sits the **London Hydraulic Company Pumping Station**, erected in 1889–92 and, until its closure in 1977, the world's last working hydraulic pumping station on a public system. It once transmitted Thames river water under a pressure of 800 lb/sq in (2341 kg/sq cm) through a system of 850 miles/1,368 km of pipes powering lifts, lock gates and dock machinery all over London. The building is the new home of the Academy of St Martin-in-the-Fields, the most recorded orchestra in the world, for use as a rehearsal and recording studio.

On the right leaving DLR Limehouse is Limehouse Basin. Regent's Canal enters the Thames here, allowing an excellent view across the river to Rotherhithe and Surrey Docks. To the left is Hawksmoor's **St Anne, Limehouse** (1714–24), which boasts the highest public clock in London after the Palace of Westminster. Its dials were once illuminated to aid river navigation at night. A 9-ft-/2.7-m-high stone pyramid sits amidst the tombstones of its leafy churchyard, some faint carving on its surface suggestive of the symbolism of Freemasonry.

The train enters the Isle of Dogs after DLR Westferry. Henry VIII once housed and exercised his dogs here. On the right is the old Dockmaster's House. Dockers used to wait at 7.45 each morning in front of the massive posts of No. 1 Gate, once the main entrance to the West India Docks, to be 'called-on' in the competitive scramble for casual labour at the docks.

DLR West India Quay is situated at the junction with the Poplar-to-Stratford arm of the DLR network. To the left is the new **Billingsgate Fish Market**, which moved here in 1982 from its historic City location. To the right are the North Quay warehouses and cranes. Built in 1802, the warehouses were used to store vast quantities of sugar imported from the West Indies. Three cranes have been preserved from the dozens that once pierced the Docklands' skyline.

West India Docks to the south are made up of the Import Dock, Export Dock and South Dock. The central quay, known as **Canary Wharf**, is destined to become the centre-piece of Europe's largest commercial development, a rival financial centre to the City, already nicknamed London's 'Wall Street-on-Thames'. The plans for Canary Wharf include Britain's tallest building at over 800 ft/244 m, one of three massive towers reaching up into the Docklands' sky that together will provide 12 million sq ft/1.1 million sq m of office space. A mini-city will be formed by vast squares, water courts, exhibition and conference facilities, and hotels. Some 250 shops and restaurants centred on a sky-lit arcade will be attached to DLR Canary Wharf. The great satellite dish of Mercury Communications' earth station looms above the east side of West India Docks, relaying messages between London's business community and the rest of the world.

Beyond DLR Heron Quays is the South Dock, originally constructed as a short-cut for ships to avoid the long journey around the sweep of the Isle of Dogs. The Maritime Trust's Historic Ships can sometimes be seen moored here. The *Res Nova*, a Dutch clipper barge, has been converted into a restaurant. To the right, painted a distinct bright red, are the first new buildings piled over the water. DLR South Quay is surrounded by a conglomeration of dazzling new office developments attracted by the Isle of Dogs' Enterprise Zone. The gleaming, blue-tinted South Quay Plaza accommodates the editorial staff of the *Daily Telegraph*. The Business Efficiency Centre, on the left before DLR Crossharbour, houses the **Docklands Visitor Centre**, with its exhibitions and a regularly updated audio-visual presentation explaining the area's redevelopment. The **London Arena**, on the right, has been transformed from a banana shed into an enormous indoor sports centre that can seat 12,000 spectators.

The journey from DLR Crossharbour to DLR Mudchute is bounded on the right by **Millwall Docks**, opened in 1868 to handle grain and timber imports, and on the left by parkland known as **The Mudchute**. The Mudchute was formed from silt extracted from the docks and 'shot' across the road. 'Mudchuting' ceased in 1900. Today 'The Muddie', Docklands' largest open green space, housing an urban farm, is jealously guarded from development by local residents.

A viaduct built in 1872 for the Millwall Extension Railway now carries the light railway from DLR Mudchute over Millwall Park to its southern terminus, DLR Island Gardens. The DLR information centre is situated beneath the station. **Island Gardens** occupy the tip of the Isle of Dogs peninsula. A breathtaking view stretches across the Thames to Greenwich, the heart of London's maritime heritage. The gardens were opened in 1895 to mark the spot where the great architect Sir Christopher Wren viewed his masterful naval hospital building. Some years later this same vista inspired Canaletto to record on canvas his celebrated view of the Thames, *Greenwich Palace*, now on show at the National Maritime Museum. Wren's building is now occupied by the Royal Naval College. It remains beautifully framed by the slope of Greenwich Park, which has poised at its summit the Old Royal Observatory building. The Old Royal Observatory, reached by the Greenwich Foot Tunnel at the west end of Island Gardens, gives an outstanding panoramic view of Docklands stretching from Tower Bridge in the west through three heavy curves in the river to the Royal Docks and the **Thames Barrier** (p. 381) in the east. The tunnel emerges opposite the *Cutty Sark*, near Greenwich Pier.

To complete a round trip of the Docklands, boats leave Greenwich Pier for Tower Pier every thirty minutes. The journey along the capital's oldest thoroughfare can be extended further upstream for a full spectacle of riverside London. Thames Line, the waterborne equivalent of the DLR, has launched a regular service. Its sleek modern catamarans travel downstream to West India Pier on the north bank of the river and to Greenwich on the south.

On deck, the eye can behold the architectural miscellany of old and new Docklands, its tiny wharves and rambling warehouses punctuated with steel and glass constructions.

Leaving Greenwich Reach behind, the Thames curves northwest around the Isle of Dogs. **Burrell's Wharf**, to starboard, was the scene of the disastrous launch of Brunel's ill-fated steamship *Great Eastern* in 1857. The ship was so large that the launch had to be carried out sideways, but the operation went seriously wrong, leaving the ship grounded on the mud for months. Following her unsuccessful career as a passenger ship, she was eventually scrapped in 1888. Overlooking Millwall Outer Dock is the *Daily Telegraph* print works. To port is the quiet residential haven of **Greenland Dock**, named after a former association with the whaling trade. Some gardens to starboard commemorate Sir John McDougall, the inventor of self-raising flour. His granary once towered over Millwall Dock. Further upstream stands the gaping warehouse of Seacon's steel terminal. The luxury **Cascades** apartments flow down to West India Pier. The river sweeps west around the Surrey Docks peninsula after Limehouse Reach. **Free Trade Wharf**, a business, residential and leisure development, incorporates a pair of the East India Company's original saltpetre warehouses and the wharf entrance of 1795. A major development in Bermondsey, to port approaching Tower Bridge, is **Butler's Wharf**, where the Conran Foundation has opened the Design Museum (*Tower Hill* ⊖). Tower Hill ⊖ is a short walk north from Tower Pier.

The Shoreditch area, in the heart of the East End, was once the centre of furniture- and cabinet-making in London. The interesting, small **Geffrye Museum** is devoted to domestic craftsmanship, celebrating the everyday rather than the grand or opulent. It is housed in the old Geffrye, or ironmongers, Almshouses (1715), a group of a dozen or so dwellings arranged round a courtyard. The museum is named after Sir Robert Geffrye, Lord Mayor of London in 1685 and Master of the Ironmongers' Company. The museum is laid out as a series of room settings displaying the style and furniture to be found in London homes from Elizabethan times to the 1930s.

Off the museum's re-created Georgian street, with its 18th-century shop-fronts, are a woodworker's workshop, complete with primitive pole lathe, and a traditional open-hearth kitchen. The Elizabethan Room of around 1600 has a rush-strewn floor and oak panelling. The Stuart Room has a doorway and panelling from the Master's Parlour of the Pewterers' Company Hall, and its ceiling is a replica of the parlour.

The William and Mary Room, with its English writing table in black-and-gold lacquer work, leads into the John Evelyn's 'Closet of Curiosities', named after the diarist and antiquary, whose mosaic-inlaid ebony cabinet is on display. All the room's items relate to objects listed in his inventory of 1702 and have been assembled to give the idea of the kind of miniature museum that was popular in the 17th century.

The chapel, with its box pews and unusual four-tiered pulpit, is much as it would have been when the building was an almshouse. A spinet and Chippendale style furniture is to be found in the Early Georgian Room. The museum has further rooms arranged in Late Georgian, mid-Victorian and 1930s styles.

Directions: Bethnal Green ⊖ (Central Line). Take Cambridge Heath Road north, turn west into Hackney Road. Cremer Street leads off to the north to a junction with Kingsland Road. Turn north. The museum is on the east side of the road.

William Morris (1834–96), designer, painter, architect, poet and social reformer, spent his boyhood days in the house now called the **William Morris Gallery**, later going to Oxford. At the university he was influenced by the art critic and theoretician John Ruskin. Morris came to share Ruskin's belief that art could flourish only if it was once again joined by craftsmanship. Ruskin held that during the Renaissance the artist had been elevated to the status of 'genius' and that the craftsman's role had been neglected. Morris came to define art as 'man's expression of his joy in labour'. His antipathy towards the effects of industrialization on society – he saw the factory system depriving the artisan of the creative satisfaction of responsibility for the complete production of an article – gave rise to a nostalgia for the Middle Ages, in his perception an idyllic pre-industrial age. It also echoed the Gothic Revival, which had become the dominant architectural style.

In 1861 he founded the manufacturing and decorating firm of Morris, Marshall, Faulkner and Co., in which painters Rossetti, Burne-Jones, Madox Brown and architect Philip Webb were also partners. Rossetti recalled how the firm had come about: 'One evening a lot of us were together, and we got talking about the way in which artists did all kinds of things in olden times, designed every kind of decoration, and someone suggested – as more of a joke than anything else – that we should each put down five pounds and found a company.' The company was incredibly successful and through it Morris exercised a profound influence on English industrial design and interior decoration during the latter part of the century. It brought about a revolution in public taste. His rich foliage wallpaper patterns have become famous, but Morris's influence extended to furniture, tapestry, stained glass, carpets and much more.

In 1890 Morris founded the Kelmscott Press to improve the standards of printing and book design, himself designing ornamental letters and borders as well as type fonts of black-letter face revived from the medieval period he favoured. In 1877 he founded the Society for the Preservation of Ancient Buildings and in 1884 organized the Socialist League. He was a prime mover in the Arts and Crafts Movement of the period.

The house was opened to the public shortly after the end of the Second World War and is a monument to every facet of Victorian art and design, holding fine collections of 19th- and early-20th-century painting, notably work by the Pre-Raphaelites and sculpture by Rodin. There are exhibits about the work of William Morris and Co., which include displays of wallpapers, textiles, embroidery, tapestry, book designs, stained glass, ceramics and furniture. In some cases working drawings and finished artefacts are displayed together to demonstrate the processes of designing and making. The museum's treasures include: the 'medieval' helmet and sword designed in the 1850s as props for the Oxford Union murals; the Beauty and the Beast tile panel designed by Burne-Jones in 1863; the Woodpecker Tapestry; ceramics by William de Morgan and the Martin Brothers; the Kelmscott Chaucer, Morris's masterpiece in fine printing; and furniture by Ernest Gimson and Sidney Barnsley. Morris's techniques and philosophy are explained, and the museum houses a library of material about this remarkable man and his circle.

Directions: Walthamstow Central ⊖ *(Victoria Line). Take Hoe Street north. This meets Forest Road. Lloyd Park is to the west.*

Useful Information

AIRPORTS

Gatwick	0923 28822/31299
Heathrow	081 759 4321
London City	071 474 5555
Luton	0582 405100
Stansted	0279 502380

HOSPITALS WITH CASUALTY DEPARTMENTS

Charing Cross, Fulham Palace Road, W6	081 748 2040
Guy's, St Thomas Street, SE1	071 407 7600
Hammersmith, 150 Du Cane Road, W12	081 743 2030
Royal Free, Pond Street, NW3	071 794 0500
St Bartholomew's, West Smithfield, EC1	071 600 9000
St Mary's, Praed Street, W2	071 262 1280
University College Hospital, Gower Street, WC1	071 387 9300

COMMONWEALTH HIGH COMMISSIONS

Australia, Australia House, Strand, WC2	071 379 4334
Canada, 1 Grosvenor Square, W1	071 629 9492
India, India House, Aldwych, WC2	071 836 8484
Kenya, 45 Portland Place, W1	071 636 2371
New Zealand, New Zealand House, Haymarket, SW1	071 930 8422
Nigeria, 9 Northumberland Avenue, WC2	071 839 1244
Singapore, Chancery, 2 Wilton Crescent, SW1	071 235 8315

EMBASSIES AND CONSULATES

Austria, 18 Belgrave Mews West, SW1	071 235 3731
Belgium, 103 Eaton Square, SW1	071 235 5422
Brazil, 32 Green Street, W1	071 499 0877
Denmark, 55 Sloane Street, SW1	071 235 1255
Egypt, 75 South Audley Street, W1	071 493 6030
Finland, 38 Chesham Place, SW1	071 235 9531
France, 58 Knightsbridge, SW1	071 235 8080
Greece, 1a Holland Park, W11	071 727 8040
Hungary, 35 Eaton Place, SW1	071 235 4048
Iceland, 1 Eaton Terrace, SW1	071 730 5131
Israel, 2 Palace Garden, W8	071 937 8050
Italy, 14 Three Kings Yard, Davies Street, W1	071 629 8200

Japan, 46 Grosvenor Street, W1	071 493 6030
Jordan, 6 Upper Phillimore Gardens, W8	071 937 3685
Korea, 4 Palace Gate, W8	071 581 0247
Luxembourg, 27 Wilton Crescent, SW1	071 235 6961
Netherlands, 38 Hyde Park Gate, SW7	071 584 5040
Norway, 20 Pall Mall, SW1	071 235 7151
Portugal, 11 Belgrave Square, SW1	071 235 5331
Romania, 4 Palace Green, W8	
Saudi Arabia, 30 Belgrave Square, SW1	071 245 9779
South Africa, South Africa House, Trafalgar Square, WC2	071 930 4488
Spain, 24 Belgrave Square, SW1	071 235 5555
Sweden, 11 Montagu Place, W1	071 724 2101
Switzerland, 16 Montagu Place, W1	071 723 0701
Turkey, 43 Belgrave Square, SW1	071 235 5252
USSR (Soviet Embassy), 18 Kensington Palace Gardens, W8	071 229 6412

OTHER USEFUL NUMBERS

Air Travel Advisory Bureau, 320 Regent Street, W1	071 636 5000
British Travel Centre, 4–12 Lower Regent Street, SW1	071 839 2470
City of London Information Centre, St Paul's Churchyard, EC4	071 606 3030
Legal Advice Bureau, Victoria Park Square, E2	081 980 4205
London Country Buses and Green Line Coaches	07372 42411
London Regional Transport, 55 The Broadway, SW1	071 222 1234
(for 24-hour information on bus and underground services)	
London Tourist Board & Convention Bureau, Tourist Information Centre, Victoria Station (BR), SW1	071 730 3488
River Boat Information Service	071 730 4812
Victoria Coach Station (National Express), 164 Buckingham Palace Road, SW1	071 730 0202
Weather Forecast (24-hour recorded information service)	071 246 8091

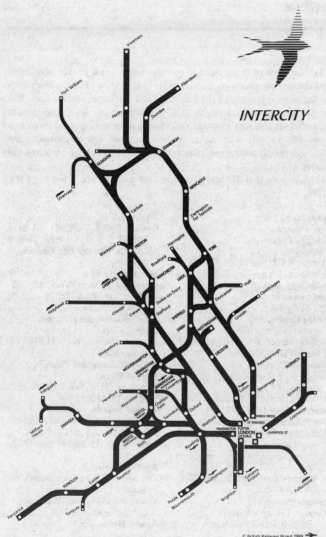

INTERCITY

© British Railways Board 1989

Index

This section is both an index to the text and a quick source of essential sightseeing information. Each entry is followed by the page number(s) of the main reference in the text and relevant Tube, British Rail (BR) or Docklands Light Railway (DLR) stations, in alphabetical order, with the nearest one in *italics*; additional information includes, where relevant, the full address, telephone number, opening hours (appt indicates an appointment is necessary), and notice of an admission charge (£).

Please note that 071 and 081 telephone prefixes are in use as of May 1990.

FOR THE BEST IN PAPERBACKS, LOOK FOR THE 🐧

In every corner of the world, on every subject under the sun, Penguin represents quality and variety – the very best in publishing today.

For complete information about books available from Penguin – including Puffins, Penguin Classics and Arkana – and how to order them, write to us at the appropriate address below. Please note that for copyright reasons the selection of books varies from country to country.

In the United Kingdom: Please write to *Dept E.P., Penguin Books Ltd, Harmondsworth, Middlesex, UB7 0DA.*

If you have any difficulty in obtaining a title, please send your order with the correct money, plus ten per cent for postage and packaging, to *PO Box No 11, West Drayton, Middlesex*

In the United States: Please write to *Dept BA, Penguin, 299 Murray Hill Parkway, East Rutherford, New Jersey 07073*

In Canada: Please write to *Penguin Books Canada Ltd, 2801 John Street, Markham, Ontario L3R 1B4*

In Australia: Please write to the *Marketing Department, Penguin Books Australia Ltd, P.O. Box 257, Ringwood, Victoria 3134*

In New Zealand: Please write to the *Marketing Department, Penguin Books (NZ) Ltd, Private Bag, Takapuna, Auckland 9*

In India: Please write to *Penguin Overseas Ltd, 706 Eros Apartments, 56 Nehru Place, New Delhi, 110019*

In the Netherlands: Please write to *Penguin Books Netherlands B.V., Postbus 195, NL–1380AD Weesp*

In West Germany: Please write to *Penguin Books Ltd, Friedrichstrasse 10–12, D–6000 Frankfurt Main 1*

In Spain: Please write to *Longman Penguin España, Calle San Nicolas 15, E–28013 Madrid*

In Italy: Please write to *Penguin Italia s.r.l., Via Como 4, I-20096 Pioltello (Milano)*

In France: Please write to *Penguin Books Ltd, 39 Rue de Montmorency, F-75003 Paris*

In Japan: Please write to *Longman Penguin Japan Co Ltd, Yamaguchi Building, 2–12–9 Kanda Jimbocho, Chiyoda-Ku, Tokyo 101*

A CHOICE OF PENGUINS

The Russian Album   Michael Ignatieff

Michael Ignatieff movingly comes to terms with the meaning of his own family's memories and histories, in a book that is both an extraordinary account of the search for roots and a dramatic and poignant chronicle of four generations of a Russian family.

Beyond the Blue Horizon   Alexander Frater

The romance and excitement of the legendary Imperial Airways East-bound Empire service – the world's longest and most adventurous scheduled air route – relived fifty years later in one of the most original travel books of the decade. 'The find of the year' – *Today*

Getting to Know the General   Graham Greene

'In August 1981 my bag was packed for my fifth visit to Panama when the news came to me over the telephone of the death of General Omar Torrijos Herrera, my friend and host...' 'Vigorous, deeply felt, at times funny, and for Greene surprisingly frank' – *Sunday Times*

The Search for the Virus   Steve Connor and Sharon Kingman

In this gripping book, two leading *New Scientist* journalists tell the remarkable story of how researchers discovered the AIDS virus and examine the links between AIDS and lifestyles. They also look at the progress being made in isolating the virus and finding a cure.

Arabian Sands   Wilfred Thesiger

'In the tradition of Burton, Doughty, Lawrence, Philby and Thomas, it is, very likely, the book about Arabia to end all books about Arabia' – *Daily Telegraph*

Adieux: A Farewell to Sartre   Simone de Beauvoir

A devastatingly frank account of the last years of Sartre's life, and his death, by the woman who for more than half a century shared that life. 'A true labour of love, there is about it a touching sadness, a mingling of the personal with the impersonal and timeless which Sartre himself would surely have liked and understood' – *Listener*

FOR THE BEST IN PAPERBACKS, LOOK FOR THE

A CHOICE OF PENGUINS

Riding the Iron Rooster   Paul Theroux

An eye-opening and entertaining account of travels in old and new China, from the author of *The Great Railway Bazaar*. 'Mr Theroux cannot write badly ... in the course of a year there was almost no train in the vast Chinese rail network on which he did not travel' – Ludovic Kennedy

The Markets of London   Alex Forshaw and Theo Bergstrom

From Camden Lock and Columbia Road to Petticoat Lane and Portobello Road, from the world-famous to the well-kept secrets, here is the ultimate guide to London's markets: as old, as entertaining and as diverse as the capital itself.

The Chinese   David Bonavia

'I can think of no other work which so urbanely and entertainingly succeeds in introducing the general Western reader to China' – *Sunday Telegraph*. 'Strongly recommended' – *The Times Literary Supplement*

The Diary of Virginia Woolf
Five volumes edited by Quentin Bell and Anne Olivier Bell

'As an account of intellectual and cultural life of our century, Virginia Woolf's diaries are invaluable; as the record of one bruised and unquiet mind, they are unique' – Peter Ackroyd in the *Sunday Times*

Voices of the Old Sea   Norman Lewis

'I will wager that *Voices of the Old Sea* will be a classic in the literature about Spain' – *Mail on Sunday*. 'Limpidly and lovingly, Norman Lewis has caught the helpless, unwitting, often foolish, but always hopeful village in its dying summers, and saved the tragedy with sublime comedy' – *Observer*

Ninety-Two Days   Evelyn Waugh

With characteristic honesty, Evelyn Waugh here debunks the romantic notions attached to rough travelling. His journey in Guiana and Brazil is difficult, dangerous and extremely uncomfortable, and his account of it is witty and unquestionably compelling.